SPSS FOR WINDOWS
MADE SIMPLE

RELEASE 10

Paul R. Kinnear

Colin D. Gray

Department of Psychology,

University of Aberdeen

PSYCHOLOGY PRESS
ALERE FLAMMAM
Taylor & Francis Group

Psychology Press Ltd, Publishers
27 Church Road
Hove
East Sussex
BN3 2FA
UK

www.psypress.co.uk

Reprinted with annotated dialog boxes and output 2001

British Library Cataloguing-in-Publication Data

A catalogue record for this book is available from the British Library

ISBN: 1-84169-118-6

Cover design by Jim Wilkie

Printed and bound in the UK by TJ International, Padstow, from camera-ready copy provided by
the authors

CONTENTS

Contents

Contents

Contents

Contents

PREFACE

This book is intended for the reader with little or no experience of SPSS. Most readers, however, are likely to be computer users, and those who are familiar with the Windows operating system may wish to omit all of Chapter 2 (Windows Operations for SPSS) except the final section, which describes the opening and closing of SPSS in Windows. Throughout the book, the text refers to operations in Windows NT, but other versions of Windows provide very similar environments.

SPSS for Windows Made Simple (SPSS Release 10) is similar in scope and intended readership to our earlier books. In recent years, SPSS has produced a rapid succession of releases, only some of which have introduced significant changes. For example, SPSS 8 (described in the 3rd Edition of this book) is similar to SPSS 7 (the version described along with SPSS 6 in the 2nd Edition), but SPSS 8 had more powerful facilities for editing the output listings and graphics. When the 3rd Edition went to press, SPSS 9 was imminent, but apart from further improvements in the graphics and interfacing with a wider variety of external data bases, that version turned out to be very similar to SPSS 8. Hard on the heels of SPSS9 has come SPSS10, which incorporates a radical change in the manner in which data are entered. The Data Editor now offers two displays: one for naming and specifying variables, the other for the data. In our view, this is a great improvement, because it obviates the series of dialog boxes previously required to create variables, to give them meaningful names, to assign value labels, to specify the manner in which the data are displayed in the Data Editor, and so on. A table of the principal differences among the SPSS Releases is appended to this Preface.

The gratifyingly positive reception that our books have received from researchers, students and tutors has strongly confirmed the need for an introductory text with illustrative examples and exercises for private or course study. Like its predecessors, this new book is the product of many years of experience in teaching the use of SPSS. The illustrative material includes annotated selections of SPSS output, screen images of windows and dialog boxes. The accompanying comments, together with worked examples and further exercises, clarify the points that, over the years, have arisen most frequently during our SPSS practical classes at the University of Aberdeen. As the title indicates, the emphasis is upon simplicity and clarity, rather than comprehensiveness. However, the range of problems and techniques included is wider than the selections available in several other introductions to SPSS, and there is advice on many problematic aspects of SPSS.

Readers familiar with our previous books will notice some changes. There is a new introductory chapter (Choosing a Statistical Test), complete with flow diagrams that identify some of the most common research situations and suggest statistical tests. This chapter replaces Chapter 5 in previous books. The new Chapter 5 contains material on Graphs and Charts that has now outgrown Chapter 4. There are also new sections and exercises on One-Sample Tests and Logistic Regression, which is becoming a preferred alternative to Discriminant Analysis. The Exercises following most chapters contain chapter-specific material, but six new Revision Exercises have been added at the end of the book. These questions require the reader to analyse a data set without the cueing that a chapter context would provide.

In outline, the chapter contents are as follows.

Chapter 1 explains some research terms and offers guidelines for choosing a statistical test. Five common situations are identified, and the choices of appropriate statistical tests are shown in flow charts. At various points, however, the reader is warned that it is never safe to proceed automatically to make formal statistical tests without preliminary exploration of the data. Chapter 2 reviews some of the Windows operations that are most useful for running SPSS. Chapter 3 describes, in detail, the inputting and editing of data. Chapter 4 focuses on exploratory data analysis (EDA) with SPSS. In Chapter 5, there is more EDA, with the emphasis upon graphs and charts. The remaining chapters describe the use of a variety of statistical methods: t-tests, their nonparametric equivalents and other one-sample tests; the analysis of variance; correlation and regression; the loglinear analysis of data in multiway contingency tables; prediction of category membership using discriminant analysis and logistic regression; the use of factor analysis to identify latent variables.

Throughout the preparation of this book, we have been most fortunate in having the advice, encouragement and SPSS expertise of John Lemon, Senior Computing Adviser at Aberdeen University's Directorate of Information Systems and Services. We are also very grateful to Caroline Green, Teaching Fellow, for her many helpful suggestions, especially for the Exercises. Our Departmental Computing Officers have given us their unfailing support. Some of our readers, including Professor Leslie Walker, School of Medicine at the University of Hull, kindly suggested new topics for the present edition. Finally, we would like to express our gratitude to all those who, though too numerous to mention individually, have contributed advice or comments, or helped in some other way.

Paul Kinnear and Colin Gray.
April, 2001.

Principal Differences among recent SPSS for Windows Releases

Release	SPSS 7	SPSS 8	SPSS 9	SPSS 10
Data Editor	Data Editor with dialog boxes	Data Editor with dialog boxes	Data Editor with dialog boxes	New Data Editor comprising Variable View and Data View spreadsheets
Menu for tests	Statistics	Statistics	Analyze	Analyze
Summarize	Items in Summarize submenu	Items in Summarize submenu	Items divided into Reports and Descriptive Statistics submenus	Items divided into Reports and Descriptive Statistics submenus
Case Summaries	In Statistics menu	In Statistics menu	In Reports menu	In Reports menu
Value Labels	In Utilities menu	In Utilities menu	In View menu	In View menu
Output	Introduction of tabulated output in the SPSS Output Navigator	Introduction of dynamic interactive charts and graphs in the SPSS Viewer	SPSS Viewer	SPSS Viewer
Factorial ANOVA	General Linear Model/ Simple Factorial...	General Linear Model/ GLM - General Factorial...	General Linear Model/ Univariate...	General Linear Model/ Univariate...
Within Subjects ANOVA	General Linear Model/ GLM - Repeated Measures...	General Linear Model/ GLM - Repeated Measures...	General Linear Model/ Repeated Measures...	General Linear Model/ Repeated Measures...

CHAPTER 1

CHOOSING A STATISTICAL TEST

1.1	**SOME RESEARCH TERMS**
1.2	**CHOOSING A STATISTICAL TEST: SOME GUIDELINES**
1.3	**SIGNIFICANCE OF DIFFERENCES**
1.4	**ANALYSIS OF VARIANCE DESIGNS**
1.5	**MEASURING STRENGTH OF ASSOCIATION BETWEEN VARIABLES**
1.6	**PREDICTING SCORES OR CATEGORY MEMBERSHIP**
1.7	**ONE-SAMPLE TESTS**
1.8	**FINDING LATENT VARIABLES: FACTOR ANALYSIS**
1.9	**A FINAL COMMENT**

1.1 SOME RESEARCH TERMS

This book is intended for those working in disciplines in which the units of study (people, plants, coelocanths) vary with respect to what is being studied. Therein lies a problem. It is difficult to generalise about all people, all animals, all trees, all coelocanths) on the basis of knowledge about only some of them. This is why researchers in such disciplines must make use of the methods of statistics.

An important concept here is that of a **sample**. A sample is a selection of observations (often assumed to be random) from a reference set, or **population**, of possible observations that might be made. By analogy with a lottery, it may be helpful to think of a population as the numbers being churned around in the barrel, and the sample as those actually drawn. Sampling implies **sampling variability**: samples from the same population can vary markedly in their characteristics. It follows that a random sample is not necessarily **representative**: it may have very different characteristics (e.g. mean, and standard deviation) from those of the population from which it has been drawn.

When we carry out an experiment on reaction speed with 100 participants, we invariably do so because we want to make inferences about the reaction speeds of people in general, in the same circumstances. It is the population that is of interest, not the sample. But to make such an inductive inference about all people on the basis of data from just some people is to risk a false conclusion.

Measures of characteristics of a sample (the mean, the standard deviation, and so on) are known as **statistics**. The corresponding characteristics in the population are known as **parameters**. Our research question is invariably about the characteristics of the population (parameters), not those of a sample (statistics). **Statistical inference** is a set of methods for making qualified inductive inferences about parameters on the basis of the statistics of samples.

We turn to the discipline of statistics when
  (1) we want to describe and summarise the data as a whole;
  (2) we want to confirm that other researchers repeating our study would obtain a similar result.

It is in connection with (2) that the need for formal **statistical tests** arises. The researcher may see theoretically important patterns in a set of data. But are these merely sampling variability or real patterns that would emerge were the project to be repeated?

Statistical inference, being inductive, is subject to error. One aspect of statistical inference is the calculation of **estimates** of population parameters (e.g. the population mean) from the statistics of samples (the sample mean). The value of the sample mean is a **point estimate** of the population mean. But the sample mean may be wide of the mark as a point estimate. From the statistics of a sample, however, it is also possible to specify a range of values, known as a **confidence interval**, within which one can say, with a specified level of certainty, that the true population mean lies. A confidence interval is an example of an **interval estimate**.

Variables

A **variable** is a characteristic or property of a person, an object or a situation, comprising a set of different values or categories. Height is a variable, as are weight, blood type and gender. **Quantitative variables**, such as height, weight or age, are possessed in **degree** and so can be <u>measured</u>. Measurements reflect the degree to which a characteristic is possessed by expressing the amount as so-many units on an independent scale – inches, pounds, kilograms, and so on. In contrast, **qualitative** variables, such as sex, blood group or nationality, are possessed only in **kind**: they cannot be expressed in units. With qualitative variables, only counts of cases falling into the various categories can be made, as when, for example, we note that among an audience, there are 60 men and 40 women.

Types of data: Measurements, ordinal and nominal

The result of a research project is a set of **data**, that is, a body of information about the variables possessed by the humans, animals, trees, or whatever else is being studied. A set of data might contain information about people's heights, weights, attitudes, blood groups, ages, genders, and so on.

There are three main kinds of data:
- (1) **Measurements** (often known as **interval data)** are numbers expressing quantity as so-many units on an independent scale. Heights and weights are obvious examples. However, in the same category, it is usual to include performance scores, such as the number of times a participant hits a target, as well as IQs, responses to questionnaires and other psychometric data.
- (2) **Ordinal** data consist of ranks, assignments to ordered categories, or of sequencing information. For example, if two judges give the same set of ten paintings ranks from 1 (for the best) to 10 (for the worst), the data set will consist of 10 pairs of ranks, one pair for each painting. To take another example, if 100 participants are asked to rate objects by placing them in one of five ordered categories, where 1 is very bad and 5 is very good, the result will resemble 100 sets of ranks with **ties**, that is, with several objects sharing the same rank.
- (3) **Nominal** data relate to qualitative variables or attributes, such as gender or blood group, and are records of category membership. Nominal data are merely <u>labels</u>: they may take the form of numbers, but such numbers are merely arbitrary code numbers representing, say, the different blood groups. Any other numbers would have served the purpose just as well.

While both measurements and ordinal data relate to quantitative variables, only in the former does each datum give quantitative information independently of the other data. Ranks mean nothing individually: they merely enable the reader to say that one individual has more or less of some variable than another individual with a different rank.

Sometimes the term **categorical data** is used to denote either purely nominal assignments or assignments to ordered categories. This term straddles our distinction between types (2) and (3) above.

Hypotheses

Data are not gathered just for the sake of it. Research is driven by the desire to test a provisional supposition about nature known as a **hypothesis**. Often, a hypothesis states that there is a causal relationship between two variables: it is an assertion that the value of one variable, the **independent variable (IV)**, at least partially determines that of another, the **dependent variable (DV)**. For example, it might be hypothesised that ingestion of a certain drug improves skilled performance, in which case the IV is presence/absence of the drug, and the DV is task performance.

Univariate, bivariate and multivariate data sets

It is sometimes useful to classify data sets according to the number of dependent variables (**DVs**) observed during the course of the investigation. If a data set consists of observations on only one variable (as when it contains people's heights), it is a **univariate** data set. If there are two variables (height and weight), it is a **bivariate** data set. If there are three or more variables (height, weight, reaction time, number of errors), it is a **multivariate** data set.

Experiments and quasi-experiments

An **experiment** is a planned procedure that gathers comparative data under controlled conditions. In a true experiment, the IV is <u>manipulated</u> by the investigator. For example, the above drug hypothesis could be tested by comparing the performance of a sample of people who have taken the drug with that of a comparison, or **control**, group who have not. (It is usual to improve the comparability of the two groups by presenting the controls with a **placebo**, that is, a neutral medium closely resembling that in which the drug was presented to the **experimental** group.)

The IV is controlled by the investigator, and its values are determined <u>before the experiment is carried out</u>. This is achieved either by **random assignment** of the participants to the pre-set conditions or by deciding to test each participant under all conditions, assuming that is feasible. The DV, on the other hand, is *<u>measured during the course of the investigation.</u>*

In the foregoing example, the IV, unlike, say, gender, blood group, or nationality, is not an intrinsic property of the participants: the participants were assigned at random to the experimental or the control group. In other circumstances, however, the hypothesis might be that some aspect of a person's gender, nationality, religion or age group affects, say, their views on some issue. For example, do men and women have different views about violence on television? Such a hypothesis could only be tested by interviewing some men and women and comparing their views. Here, the IV is gender, and the DV is attitude to violence. In this case, however, the participants have not been assigned to the categories making up the IV: the latter is an intrinsic property of the participant. Such **quasi-experiments** often produce results that are difficult to interpret unequivocally. The problem with quasi-experimental research is that the IV, being a **participant** (or **subject**) **variable**, is itself a whole package of variables, some of which may not be under the control of the investigator. Some of the difficulties with quasi-experimental research can be overcome by following an appropriate sampling strategy. For example, in the gender-and-attitudes experiment, the men and woman would be sampled from comparable social strata and similar age bands. But there is always the possibility that the effects of gender will be entangled, or **confounded**, with those of uncontrolled, **extraneous** variables.

Experimental versus correlational research

In true experiments and quasi-experiments, the IV is manipulated by the researcher, either directly, as in the former, or by sampling, as in the latter. In **correlational research**, the variables studied as they occur in the participants. For example, it might be hypothesised that cheerfulness (the DV) is promoted by exercise (the IV). One might test this hypothesis by asking participants in a study to rate themselves on cheerfulness and to say how often they take exercise. Here the problems of interpretation are multiplied. It may well turn out that the cheeriest people take the most exercise and the gloomiest the least, and that moderately cheerful people take moderate amounts. But the putative IV may not be the real cause of the correlation, which may be socioeconomic status, personality, physical type or a myriad other possible variables.

Implications for data analysis

Typically, the data from experiments and quasi-experiments are processed using statistical methods that are rather different from those used with data from correlational research. In the next section, we offer the reader some advice on choosing statistical tests.

1.2 CHOOSING A STATISTICAL TEST: SOME GUIDELINES

It is common for authors of statistical texts to offer advice on choosing statistical tests in the form of a flow chart, decision tree or similar diagram. The numerous schemes that have been proposed vary considerably, and sometimes contradict one another. The reason for the inconsistency is partly that most classifications tend to break down in certain circumstances. Moreover, in some situations, the correct choice has been hotly disputed.

On one matter at least, however, there is general agreement. **There is no such thing as a decision tree that will automatically lead the investigator to the correct choice of a statistical test in all circumstances.** Some of the later chapters contain examples of the dangers that arise from taking such an automatic approach to the selection of a statistical test. At best, a decision tree can serve only as a rough guideline. **Ultimately, a safe decision requires careful reflection upon one's own research aims and a thorough exploration of one's own data before making any formal statistical test.**

Considerations in choosing a formal statistical test

The choice of a statistical test depends upon:
- the **research question**
- the **plan**, or **design**, of the research
- the **type of data** that you wish to analyse

This list is by no means comprehensive; nor do we intend to imply that any fixed ordering of these three aspects is appropriate in all situations. Moreover, the three questions are not necessarily independent: a decision about one often has implications for the others.

The research question

We shall identify five basic research questions that can be answered by making formal statistical tests (Figure 1). For each situation, the appropriate techniques will be discussed in the sections indicated in the figure.

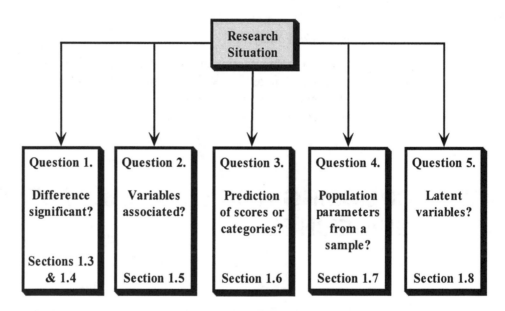

Figure 1. Five types of research situation

The questions are as follows:
1. Is a difference (between averages) significant? For example, is resting heart rate the same before and after a fitness course? (Sections 1.3 and 1.4)
2. How strongly are variables associated? For example, do tall parents tend to have tall children? (Section 1.5)
3. Can scores on a target variable (or category membership, if the variable is qualitative) be predicted from data on other variables? For example, can university performance be predicted by aptitude tests? (Section 1.6)
4. From a single sample of data, what can be said about the population? For example, is a coin as likely to turn up heads as it is tails? (Section 1.7)
5. The user has a multivariate data set, perhaps people's scores on a battery of ability tests. Can these scores be accounted for (or

classified) in terms of a smaller number of latent variables? For example, can performance in a variety of intellectual pursuits be accounted for in terms of general intelligence? (Section 1.8)

1.3   SIGNIFICANCE OF DIFFERENCES

The question of whether two means are significantly different is one that arises naturally in the context of experimental or quasi-experimental research, where the performance of the participants under different conditions is being compared. The question of the nature of the data seldom arises in such circumstances, because in true experiments, the data usually take the form of measurements in the sense defined above. Occasionally, however, the researcher must resort to tests that have been designed for use with ordinal or nominal data.

Suppose that in a simple drug experiment, performance under two different conditions (experimental and control) has been measured. The means may have markedly different values. But would a similar difference be found if the experiment were to be repeated? Here the researcher wishes to test the statistical significance of the difference between the mean scores achieved under the experimental and control conditions.

1.3.1   The design of the experiment: Independent versus related samples

Of crucial importance in the choice of an appropriate statistical test is the question of whether the experiment would have resulted in **independent samples** or **related samples** of scores.

Independent samples

Suppose we select, say, 100 participants for an experiment and randomly assign half of them to an experimental condition and the rest to a control condition. In this type of experiment, the assignment of an individual to a particular group has no effect upon the group to which another participant is assigned. The two **independent samples** of participants thus selected will produce two independent samples of scores. A useful criterion for independent samples of data is that there must be <u>no basis for pairing the scores in one sample with those in the other</u>. An experiment in which an independent sample of participants is tested under each condition is known as a **between subjects experiment**.

Related samples

Often, there is a basis for pairing the scores in two (or more) samples. Suppose that each of fifty people shoots at a triangular target and at a square target of the same area, producing two samples of scores. Each score in either sample can be paired with the same participant's score under the other condition. The experiment thus produces two **related samples** of scores, or a set of **paired data**. The scores in two related samples are likely to be substantially correlated, because the more able participants will tend to score better on both tasks than the less able participants. An experiment in which each participant is tested under all conditions is known as a **within subjects experiment.** Within subjects experiments are also said to have **repeated measures** on the independent variable.

Having repeated measures is not the only way of generating related samples of data. Suppose, for example, that the participants in a two-group study were pairs of identical twins, fraternal twins, or even pairs of siblings from the same family, with one member of each pair being tested under only one condition. The outcome of such an experiment would also be two related samples of data, because the choice of an individual for one sample constrains assignment to the other.

Different statistical tests are appropriate for use with independent and related samples of data.

1.3.2 Flow-chart for selecting a suitable test for differences between averages

Figure 2 outlines the considerations leading to a choice of a statistical test of the significance of differences between means (or frequencies, if one has nominal data). If there are more than two conditions, an analysis of variance (ANOVA) may be applicable (see Section 1.4). In this section, we shall consider only the comparison between two conditions, such as male versus female, or experimental group versus control group.

To use this chart, begin at the START box and consider how many conditions there are in the experiment. If there are two conditions, then proceed down the chart to the next stage. The next questions are whether the samples are independent or related and whether the data are measurements, as opposed to nominal assignments. The appropriate test is then shown in the bottom box. If there are more than two conditions, an ANOVA should be considered and the flow-chart in Figure 3 (see page 15) can be used to ascertain which ANOVA test might be appropriate.

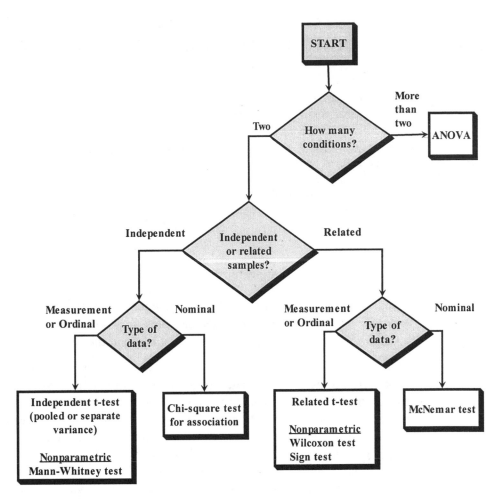

Figure 2. Flow-chart showing the selection of a suitable test
for differences between averages

1.3.3   Two conditions: The t-tests

To compare the levels, or averages, of two *independent samples* of data in the form of measurements, the **independent-samples t-test** is often appropriate (see Figure 2).   In its original form, the independent-samples t test uses an average, **pooled** estimate of the supposedly constant population variance. For this reason, it is sometimes known as the **pooled t-test**.

Sometimes, however, the data may not conform to the requirements of the independent-samples t-test.   If the sample variances and/or sample sizes are markedly different, the **separate-variance t-test** is a safer choice.

When one wishes to compare the means of two *related samples* of data, as when each participant in an experiment has been tested under both an experimental and a control condition, the **related samples t-test** should be considered.

1.3.4 Two conditions: Nonparametric tests

The t-test is an example of a **parametric test**: that is, it is assumed that the data are samples from a population with a specified (in this case normal) distribution. Other tests, known as **nonparametric tests**, do not make specific assumptions about population distributions and are therefore also referred to as **distribution-free tests**.

There are circumstances in which a t-test can give misleading results. This is especially likely to occur when the data set is small and there are some highly deviant scores, or **outliers**, which can inflate the values of the denominators of the t statistics.

Figure 2 identifies the nonparametric equivalents of the independent and related samples t-tests. With two independent samples of measurements, a nonparametric alternative to the independent-samples t-test is the **Mann-Whitney U test**. With two related samples, two nonparametric equivalents of the related-samples t-test are the **Wilcoxon test** and the **Sign test**.

There has been much controversy about the use of nonparametric tests instead of t-tests with some kinds of data. While some authors (e.g. Siegel & Castellan, 1988) strongly recommend the use of nonparametric tests, others, such as Howell (1997) emphasise the robustness of the parametric t-tests to violations of their assumptions and the loss of power incurred by the use of the equivalent nonparametric tests. We suggest that, provided the data show no obvious contraindications, such as the presence of outliers, marked skewness or great disparity of variances (especially if the last is coupled with a large difference in sample size), a t-test should be used. There are also circumstances in which the removal of outliers from the data set followed by another t-test is a defensible procedure. Otherwise, a nonparametric equivalent should be considered. Ratings are a grey area, and there has been considerable debate over whether they should be analysed with parametric or nonparametric tests. If, however, the data are measurements at the ordinal level in the first place, as with sets of ranks, or nominal data, a nonparametric test is the only possibility.

In a planned experiment, the data usually take the form of measurements. Occasionally, however, one might have the situation in which each participant attempts a task and either a pass or a fail is recorded. If so, a two-group experiment will yield two independent samples of **nominal data**. Here the research question is still one of the significance of differences, albeit of differences between frequencies, rather than differences between means. With independent samples, a **chi-square test of association** will answer the question of whether the success rates in the two groups are significantly different.

Two correlated samples of dichotomous nominal data: The McNemar test

Suppose that ten people are asked whether they are for or against a proposal before and after hearing a debate on the issue. This is essentially a **within subjects experiment**, in which each participant is observed under two conditions: **before** (an event) and **after**. On both occasions of testing, each person's response is coded either as 0 (against) or 1 (for).

See Chap. 6

Since the same person produces two responses, we have a paired nominal data set; for which the **McNemar test** is appropriate if one wishes to claim that the debate has resulted in a change of opinion.

1.4 ANALYSIS OF VARIANCE DESIGNS

The **analysis of variance (ANOVA)** is actually a whole set of techniques, each based upon a model of how the data were generated and culminating in tests that are appropriate for that particular model only. It is therefore important to identify ANOVA designs correctly, in order to choose the right tests. In this section, only some of the most common ANOVA designs will be described. There are many others, which can be found in standard statistics textbooks such as Winer, Brown & Michels (1991).

In the ANOVA, a **factor** is a set of related conditions or categories. The conditions or categories making up a factor are known as its **levels**, even though, as in the qualitative factors of gender or blood group, there is no sense in which one category can be said to be 'higher' or 'lower' than the other. The terms **factor** and **level** are the equivalents, in the context of ANOVA, of the terms **independent variable** and **value**, respectively. A factor can be either a true independent variable or a participant characteristic, such as gender, that we 'manipulate' *statistically*, by sampling people from each of some set of categories. In ANOVA, participant variables are treated in exactly the same way as IVs that are directly manipulated by the experimenter.

1.4.1 Between subjects and within subjects factors

Some factors are **between subjects**: that is, the participant is tested under only one condition (i.e. at one level) of the factor. Gender is an obvious example. Other factors are **within subjects**, that is, the participant is tested under all the different conditions (levels) making up the factor. A design with a within subjects factor is also said to have **repeated measures** on the factor.

Returning to the simplest two-group drug experiment, in which the performance of an experimental (drug) group is compared with that of a control (placebo) group, we have **one treatment factor (Drug)**, comprising two conditions or **levels**: Drug Present and Drug Absent. Since different samples of participants perform under the different conditions, this is a **between subjects experiment**. Should the investigator wish to study the effectiveness of more than one drug, the performance of two or more groups of participants on different drugs could be compared with that of the controls. In that case, there would still be one treatment factor, but with three or more levels.

Now suppose that another investigator wishes to test the hypothesis that words presented in the right visual hemifield are recognised more quickly than those presented in the left hemifield. Fifty participants are each presented with twenty words in the left and right hemifields and their median response times are recorded. In this experiment (as in the drug experiment), there is **one treatment factor** (Hemifield of Presentation) comprising two levels (conditions): Left Field; Right Field. But this time, *the same participants perform under both conditions*. This experiment is said to be of **within subjects** design, or to have **repeated measures** on the Hemifield factor.

In the general case of a one-factor, within subjects experiment, the factor would comprise three or more treatment conditions, or levels, and each participant would perform under all conditions. For example, to test the hypothesis that the accuracy with which a participant shoots at a target depends upon the shape of the target's perimeter, each participant might be tested with circular, square, triangular and diamond-shaped targets. Here the treatment factor (Shape of Target) would have four levels: Circle, Square, Triangle and Diamond.

In Table 1, the designs of the between subjects and within subjects one-factor experiments are shown schematically.

Table 1. Between subjects and within subjects experiments with one treatment factor			
(a) The one-factor between subjects experiment			
	Levels of the Drug factor		
	Control	**Drug A**	**Drug B**	**Drug C**
Participants	Group 1	Group 2	Group 3	Group 4
(b) The one-factor within-subjects experiment			
	Levels of the Shape factor		
	Circle	**Square**	**Triangle**	**Diamond**
Participants	The same participants perform with all four shapes			

1.4.2 Factorial designs: Between subjects and within subjects experiments

In addition to the effects of different drugs upon fresh participants, a researcher might also wish to investigate their effects upon those who have voluntarily gone without sleep for twenty-four hours. Accordingly, an experiment is planned as shown in Table 2, which shows a design with two factors: State (Fresh, Tired); Drug (Drug A, Drug B). An experimental design with two or more factors is known as a **factorial** design.

Table 2. A two-factor factorial between subjects experiment		
Levels of the State factor	**Levels of the Drug factor**	
	Drug A	**Drug B**
Fresh	Group 1	Group 2
Tired	Group 3	Group 4

Between subjects factorial experiments

Notice that, in Table 2, a different sample of participants performs at each of the four combinations of the two treatment factors. Since each participant is tested only once, this type of experiment is said to be of **between subjects factorial** design. It can also be described as having **two factors with no repeated measures**. Factorial designs are discussed in Chapter 8.

Within subjects factorial experiments

Table 3 shows another kind of factorial experiment.

Table 3. A two-factor factorial within subjects experiment				
Levels of the Shape factor:	**Triangle**		**Square**	
Levels of the Colour factor:	**Blue**	**Green**	**Blue**	**Green**
Participants	The same participants perform under all four combinations of shape and colour			

As before, there are two factors, which in this case are:
(1)   Shape of Target (Triangle, Square);
(2)   Colour of Target (Blue, Green).

This time, however, every participant is tested at both levels of both factors. This type of factorial design is known as a **within subjects factorial** experiment. Alternatively, the experiment in Table 3 can be said to have **repeated measures on both factors.** Within subjects designs are discussed in Chapter 9.

1.4.3 Mixed or split-plot factorial experiments

Suppose that, in addition to the effects of target colour, the experimenter wishes to test the hypothesis that men and women produce their best performances with targets of different colours. Table 4 shows the experimental design. Once again, there are two factors, which in this example are:
  (1)   Gender (Male, Female);
  (2)   Colour of Target (Red, Blue).

The first factor is between subjects; but the second factor is *within* subjects, because each participant shoots at both the red and the blue target. Factorial experiments with a mixture of between subjects and within subjects factors are known as **mixed** (or **split-plot**) factorial experiments. These are discussed in Chapter 10.

See
Chap.
10

Table 4. A two-factor mixed factorial experiment with one between subjects factor (Gender) and one within subjects factor (Colour of Target)

	Levels of the Colour of Target factor	
Levels of the Gender factor	**Red**	**Blue**
Male	Each participant is tested with red and blue targets	
Female	Each participant is tested with red and blue targets	

1.4.4 Flow-chart for ANOVA

The between subjects, within subjects and mixed (or split-plot) factorial ANOVA are based upon different models of the data, and require different tests. The presence of a within subjects (or repeated measures) factor in an experiment results in the gathering of related (rather than independent) samples of data, which has important implications for the computation of the F ratios. Figure 3 offers some guidelines for the choice of the appropriate ANOVA or its nonparametric equivalent (if there is one).

To use this chart (Figure 3), begin at the START box and consider how many factors there are in the experiment. If there are two or more factors, work down the right-hand side of the chart. If there is just one factor, work down the left-hand side.

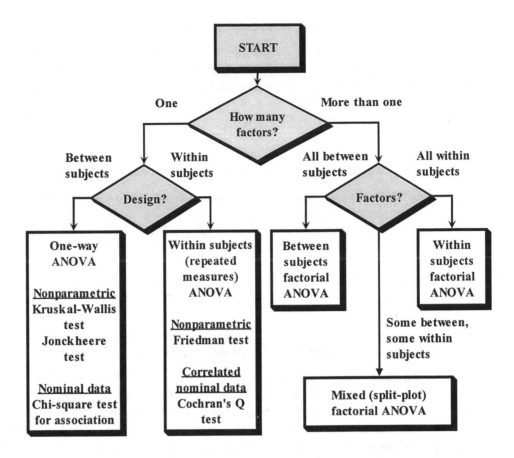

Figure 3. Flow-chart for ANOVA designs

1.4.5 Analysing the results of one-factor experiments

See
Chaps.
7 & 9

Figure 3 outlines the decisions leading to the correct choice of ANOVA model for an experiment with one factor. The **one-factor between subjects ANOVA** is often called the **one-way ANOVA** and is more fully described in Chapter 7. The **one-factor within subjects ANOVA** (sometimes called the **subjects by treatments** or **randomised blocks** ANOVA) is described in Chapter 9.

The case of two conditions only: Equivalence of t-tests and ANOVA

The reader will have noticed that at the beginning of the section on ANOVA, the one-factor ANOVA was illustrated with the same simple two-condition experiments that were used to illustrate the use of the t-tests. A natural question, therefore, is whether, in this special case, the independent and related t-tests would lead to the same decision about the null hypothesis as would the one-way and within subjects ANOVA, respectively. In fact, they do.

An alternative to one-way ANOVA: The Kruskal-Wallis k-sample test

So far, we have been considering the use of nonparametric alternatives to t-tests. For data sets comprising more than two sets of measurements, however, there are also equivalent nonparametric tests. The **Kruskal-Wallis k-sample test** is equivalent to the one-way ANOVA: it is appropriate for <u>independent samples</u> of scores. The Kruskal-Wallis test is described in Chapter 7.

Independent samples of dichotomous nominal data

Suppose that a sample of participants is divided randomly into three equally-sized groups: two experimental groups (Group A and Group B) and a Control group. Each participant is tested with a criterion problem, a 1 being recorded if they pass, and a 0 if they fail. With the resulting nominal data set, a **chi-square test** for association can be used to test the null hypothesis that, in the population, there is no tendency for the problem to be solved more often in some conditions than in others (see Chapter 11).

Correlated ordinal data: The Friedman test

Suppose that twenty people rank ten paintings in order of preference, each person assigning the ranks of 1 and 10 to their most preferred and least preferred painting, respectively. This operation will yield ten related samples of data, each sample comprising the ranks assigned to one painting by the twenty raters. Is there a tendency for some paintings to receive higher ranks than others? An appropriate test for use with this type of data is the **Friedman test**, which is considered more fully in Chapter 9.

Three or more sets of correlated dichotomous nominal data: Cochran's Q test

Suppose that each person in an experiment is tested under all conditions, and that a 1 is recorded for a successful performance under a given condition and a 0 otherwise. This is a one-factor, within subjects experiment, which has produced related samples of nominal data. Figure 3 suggests that an appropriate test of the null hypothesis of no difference in performance among the conditions is **Cochran's Q test**, which is described in Chapter 9.

1.4.6   Analysing the results of factorial experiments

Figure 3 shows that for each of the three types of factorial design described here, there is a special ANOVA, which is appropriate for that kind of design only. The between subjects, within subjects and mixed ANOVA are described in Chapters 8, 9 and 10, respectively.

1.5 MEASURING STRENGTH OF ASSOCIATION BETWEEN VARIABLES

Do tall fathers tend to have tall sons, short fathers to have short sons and fathers of medium height to have sons in the medium range of height? This question is one of a **statistical association** between the two variables Father's Height and Son's Height. To answer the question, you would need a data set comprising the heights of a substantial sample of fathers and those of their (first) sons.

1.5.1 Flow-chart for selecting a suitable test for association

Figure 4 outlines the questions one needs to answer in order to make a decision about an appropriate measure of association.

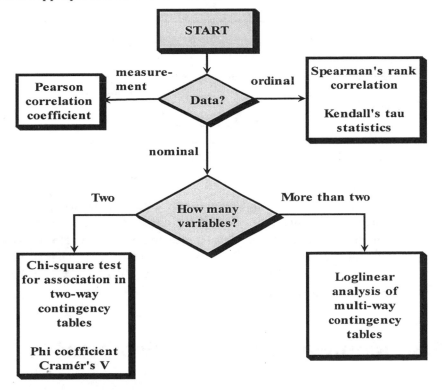

Figure 4. Flow-chart showing measures of association

See Chap. 11

Begin at the START box and consider whether the data are measurements or ordinal. If the two variables are in the form of measurements, a **Pearson correlation** should be considered. However, as we shall see in Chapter 11, there are circumstances in which the Pearson correlation can be highly misleading. **It is essential to examine the data first before proceeding to obtain the correlation coefficient.**

Measuring association in ordinal data

Now suppose we ask two judges to rank twenty paintings in order of preference. We shall have a data set consisting of twenty pairs of ranks. Do the judges agree? Again, our question is one of a statistical association. However, since the data are ordinal, a **rank correlation** is an appropriate. There are two kinds of rank correlation: (1) **Spearman's rank correlation**; (2) the **Kendall tau** statistics. Both types are considered more fully in Chapter 11.

See
Chap.
11

1.5.2 Measuring association in nominal data: Contingency tables

Suppose that Fred claims to possess telepathic powers. Accordingly, in an experiment designed to test his claim, an experimenter tosses a coin 100 times, and Fred, seated behind a screen, states, on each occasion, whether the coin turned up heads or tails. Table 5 presents the results of the experiment in what is known as a **contingency table**, an array designed to display the association (if any) between qualitative variables.

Table 5. A contingency table		
Fred's Guess	**Experimenter's toss**	
	Head (H)	**Tail (T)**
H	45	9
T	8	38

See
Chap.
11

The presence of an association can be confirmed by using a **chi-square test** (see Chapter 11). Since the value of the chi-square statistic depends partly upon the sample size, it is unsuitable as a measure of the strength of association between two qualitative variables. Figure 4 names two statistics that measure strength of association between qualitative variables: **Cramér's V** and the **phi coefficient**. Both measures are discussed in Chapter 11.

1.5.3 Multiway contingency tables

See
Chap.
13

In the past three decades, there have been dramatic developments in the analysis of nominal data in the form of multiway contingency tables. Previously, tables with three or more attributes were often 'collapsed' to produce two-way tables. The usual chi-square test could then be applied. Such 'collapsing', however, is fraught with risk, and the tests may give highly misleading results. The advent of modern **loglinear analysis** has made it possible to tease out the relationships among the attributes in a way that was not possible before (see Chapter 13).

1.6 PREDICTING SCORES OR CATEGORY MEMBERSHIP

If there is an association between variables, it is natural to ask whether this can be exploited to predict scores on one variable from knowledge of those on another. Such prediction is indeed possible, and the methods by which this is achieved will be briefly reviewed in this section.

There are also circumstances in which one would wish to predict not scores on a target, or criterion variable, but membership of a category of a qualitative variable. For example, it is of medical and actuarial interest to be able to predict membership of an 'at risk' category on the basis of a patient's (or client's) smoking and drinking habits. Statistical techniques have been specially devised for this purpose also.

The purpose of the methods reviewed here is to predict a target, or **criterion** variable (the term **dependent variable** is also used in this context) from scores on other variables, known variously as **regressors, predictors**, and **independent variables**. The predictors need not always be quantitative variables: qualitative variables, such as gender and blood group, are often included among the predictor variables in research of this kind.

1.6.1 Flow-chart for selecting the appropriate procedure for predicting a score or a category

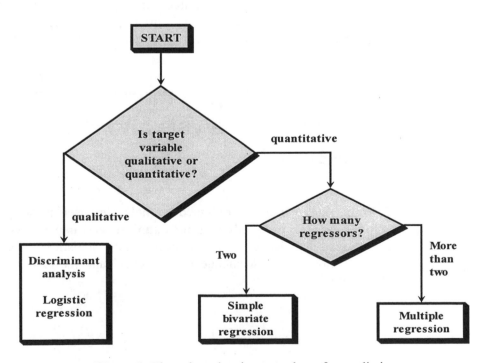

Figure 5. Flow-chart showing procedures for prediction

19

To use the flow-chart (Figure 5) for selecting the appropriate prediction procedure, begin at the START box and consider the question whether the target variable is qualitative (e.g. with categories such as pass and fail) or quantitative (e.g. examination scores).

If the target variable is quantitative, a **regression method** should be considered. In **simple regression**, there is one predictor; in **multiple regression**, there are two or more. Regression is the subject of Chapter 12. If the criterion variable is qualitative, the techniques of **discriminant analysis** and **logistic regression** should be considered. They are discussed in Chapter 14.

1.6.2 Simple regression

In some US universities, the authorities are interested in predicting students' grade point averages after a year of study from the scores they achieved on aptitude and intelligence tests when they matriculated.

Suppose that, given a student's verbal aptitude score at matriculation, we want to predict the same student's grade point average a year later. This is a problem in **simple regression**, and its solution is described in Chapter 12.

1.6.3 Multiple regression

A student's grade point average is associated not only with verbal aptitude, but also with numerical ability. Can grade point average be predicted even more accurately when both verbal ability and numerical ability are taken into account? This is a problem in **multiple regression**. If grade point average is correlated with both verbal and numerical aptitude, multiple regression would produce a more accurate prediction of a student's grade point average than will a simple regression upon either of the two regressors considered separately.

1.6.4 Predicting category membership: Discriminant analysis and logistic regression

Two statistical techniques designed to help the user make predictions of category membership are **discriminant analysis** and **logistic regression** (both are discussed in Chapter 14). In recent years, logistic regression, being a somewhat more robust technique than discriminant analysis, has become the preferred method.

1.7   ONE-SAMPLE TESTS

Much psychological research involves the collection of two or more samples of data.   This is by no means always true, however: sometimes the researcher draws a *single* sample of observations in order to study just <u>one</u> population.

The situations in which one might use a one-sample test are of two main kinds:
  (1) One may wish to compare a sample distribution with a hypothetical distribution, such as the normal.   This is a question of **goodness-of-fit**.
  (2) One may wish to make inferences about the parameters of a single population from the statistics of a sample, either for the purpose of ascertaining whether the sample is from a known population or estimating the parameters of an unknown population.

1.7.1   Flow-chart for selecting the appropriate one-sample test

Figure 6 summarises the circumstances in which a researcher might make various kinds of one-sample tests.   The tests reviewed in this section are more fully considered in Chapter 6.

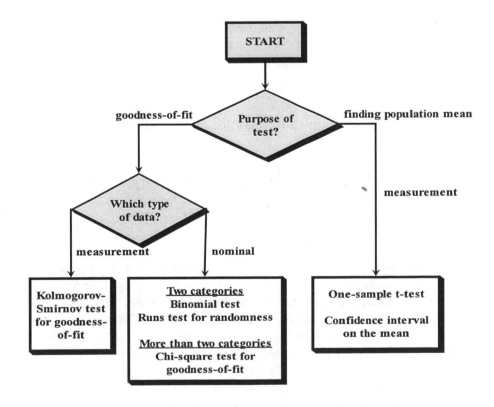

Figure 6. Flow-chart of one-sample tests

21

Begin at the START box and consider the purpose of the test. If it is to test for goodness-of-fit, move down the left-hand side of the chart. If it is estimate the population mean or its probable range, move down the right-hand side. The next consideration is the nature of the data: different types of data require different tests.

1.7.2 Goodness-of-fit: Data in the form of measurements

A question about a single population is often one of **goodness-of-fit**: has the sample been drawn from a population with a specified distribution shape? Suppose, for example, that one has a sample of measurements and wishes to ascertain whether these have been drawn from a normal population. Figure 6 shows that the **Kolmogorov-Smirnov test** is appropriate for this purpose.

1.7.3 Goodness-of-fit: Nominal data

Suppose a researcher wants to know whether 5-year-old children of a certain age show a preference for one of two toys (A or B). The choices of one hundred 5-year-olds are noted. Here the population comprises the choices (A or B) of 5-year-olds in general. Of the hundred children in the study, 60 choose toy A and 40 toy B. The null hypothesis states that the probability of choosing A (or B) is 0.5: more formally, it states that we have sampled 100 times from a Bernoulli population with $p = 0.5$. Does this theoretical distribution fit our data? Figure 6 indicates that a **binomial test** can be used to test this hypothesis.

If, in the foregoing example, there were three or more toys to choose from, the **chi-square test for goodness-of-fit** can be used to test the null hypothesis that the children have no preference for any particular toy.

1.7.4 Inferences about the mean of a single population

Suppose we want to know whether the performance of a group of schoolchildren on a standardised test is typical of those in their age group. Figure 6 shows that a **one-sample t-test** can be used to test the null hypothesis that the population mean has the putative 'population' value. Often, however, as when the researcher is working with an unstandardised test, it may not be possible to specify any null hypothesis. Suppose that a lecturer wishes to ascertain the typical reaction speed of first year university students within a certain age group. The lecturer may have data on, say, two hundred first year students; but the research question, being about the reaction speeds of first year students <u>in general</u>, concerns the <u>population</u> of reaction times. The sample mean is a **point estimate** of the unknown population mean. The t-distribution can also be used to build a **confidence interval** around the sample mean, so that the researcher has a range of values within which the true population mean is likely to lie.

1.7.5   Nominal data: Testing a coin for fairness

When we toss a coin a large number of times to ascertain its fairness, we obtain a sample from the (infinite) population of such tosses. We might find that the coin turned up heads on 58 out of 100 tosses. Is the coin 'fair': that is, in the population, are the relative frequencies of heads and tails both 0.5?

The **binomial test** can be used to test the hypothesis that the population proportion is ½ (or, indeed, that it is any other specified proportion). A **confidence interval** can also be constructed on the sample proportion to give a range of values within which we can be confident that the true population proportion lies.

A test for randomness: The Runs test

Since each toss of a coin can have only one of two outcomes, a series of coin tosses can yield a set of nominal data carrying the information that in, say, 100 tosses, there were so-many heads and so-many tails. A continuous record of the experiment, however, also contains sequential information, such as the longest sequence of heads (or tails). A very long sequence of either heads or tails suggests a lack of randomness. The **Runs test** (Chapter 6) can be used to test for randomness in such situations.

1.8   FINDING LATENT VARIABLES: FACTOR ANALYSIS

Suppose that 300 people are measured on twenty tests of ability. It is likely that if the correlations between each test and every other test are arrayed in a **correlation matrix (R)**, there will be substantial positive correlations among the tests in the battery.

Factor analysis (see Chapter 15) is a set of techniques which, on the basis of the correlations in an R matrix, classify all the tests in a battery in terms of relatively few underlying dimensions or **factors**. The reader will have noticed that the term factor has more than one meaning in statistics, because it has already occurred in the context of analysis of variance (ANOVA), where it denotes an independent variable that is manipulated either experimentally or statistically by the experimenter. Actually, the two meanings are not quite so disparate as might first be supposed. Arguably, the factors that emerge from factor analysis are also independent variables, since they contribute to performance on tests in the battery, which can therefore be regarded as dependent variables. However, the factors emerging from factor analysis can never be directly measured or controlled by the researcher, and in this sense are 'latent' variables.

In **exploratory factor analysis**, the object is to find the minimum number of latent variables, or **factors**, necessary to account for the correlations among the psychological tests. In **confirmatory factor analysis**, specified models are compared to see which gives the best account of the data.

1.9   A FINAL COMMENT

In this chapter, we have offered some advice about the circumstances in which one might consider using formal statistical tests to support the researcher's claim that what is true of a particular data set is likely to be true in the population. At this point, however, a word of warning is appropriate.

Formal tests, statistical models and their assumptions

The making of a formal statistical test of significance always presupposes the applicability of a statistical **model**, that is, an interpretation (usually in the form of an equation) of the data set as having been generated in a specified manner. The model underlying the one-sample t-test, for example, assumes that the data are from a normal population. To some extent, statistical tests have been shown to be **robust** to moderate violations of the assumptions of the models upon which they are based: that is, the actual error rates are not markedly different from the nominal values. But there are limits to this robustness, and there are circumstances in which a result, declared by an incautious user to be significant beyond, say, the 0.05 level, may actually have been considerably more probable than that. There is no way of avoiding this pitfall other than by thoroughly exploring the data first (see Chapters 4 and 5) to ascertain their suitability for specified formal tests.

See
Chaps.
4 & 5

CHAPTER 2

WINDOWS OPERATIONS FOR SPSS

2.1   WORKING WITH WINDOWS

2.2   PROPERTIES OF WINDOWS

2.3   FINDING PROGRAMS AND FILES

2.4   FILE AND FOLDER OPERATIONS

2.5   OPENING AND CLOSING SPSS

2.1 WORKING WITH WINDOWS

We can assume that the user with the exclusive use of a PC with **Windows** is already familiar with the system, at least to some extent. However it may be useful to outline those Windows procedures that we have found to be essential when running SPSS. Although there are several excellent comprehensive texts on Windows, these tend to be rather formidable tomes; whereas to use SPSS, a few basic Windows procedures are all that is required.

There are currently several versions of Windows available, most recently Windows ME, NT and 2000. Although this chapter concentrates on Windows NT, much of what follows is common to all versions. There are some important differences too, however, and we shall draw your attention to these as they arise.

2.1.1 The Windows NT operating system

An **operating system** such as Windows creates a computing environment, or **interface**, within which the user accesses or runs **applications** such as SPSS and word processors. Windows creates a **graphical interface**, in which applications and other user-accessible software appear on the screen as small graphical symbols known as **icons**. When icons are activated and opened, commands can be given by using a device such as a **mouse** to make selections from lists of choices known as **menus**.

When Windows is first accessed, the screen shows an array in which several icons appear against a homogeneous coloured background known as the **Desktop**. (This is not, of course, to be confused with the real surface on which the computer is actually standing and over which the user may be moving a mouse.) Part of a typical Desktop configuration is shown in Figure 1.

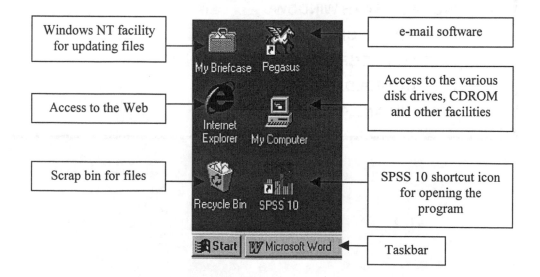

Figure 1. Part of the Desktop showing some of the icons

There will be some variation in the icons displayed, depending on the selection of software that has been installed and the characteristics of the network. Some icons, such as the one labelled SPSS 10, have a little arrow in the bottom left-hand corner (see Figure 1). This arrow indicates that the icon is a **short-cut** and can be used as a quick access to an item that is actually located elsewhere in the system.

When an item is opened, its contents appear in a rectangular box superimposed on the desktop. This box is called a **window**. There are different kinds of windows, each kind having its own special function. Some contain arrays of icons; others invite the user either to adjust pre-set values or to enter further information. (The second type of window is known as a **dialog box**.) Details of the features of a window will be given in Section 2.2.

2.1.2   The screen pointer: Handling the mouse

The screen pointer

The screen pointer makes it first appearance on the **Desktop**, when Windows has just been opened. Initially, the pointer has the form of an arrow pointing diagonally upward to the left (↖). The pointer retains the arrow shape wherever it may be moved on the desktop. In other circumstances, however, it assumes different shapes, depending on its location and the current activity of the computer.

Sometimes it assumes the shape of a small hour-glass, which indicates that 'something is going on', and the user should do nothing until the shape changes. The hour-glass will be seen when Windows is first being accessed; thereafter it appears whenever processing is taking place. Since PCs vary enormously in their capacity to process information, the user of a less powerful computer will be more aware of the hour-glass, because processing takes longer. In any case, the user should always bear in mind that *processing takes time*.

The other common screen pointer shapes are: a cross; a girder or I-beam **I** ; a horizontal double-arrow ⟺; a vertical double-arrow ⇕; and a diagonal double-arrow ⤢ . Each of these has its significance and is a useful cue, but we shall consider the meaning of each pointer shape as the need arises.

Positioning the screen pointer

The position of the screen pointer is controlled by the mouse (or a mouse analogue, such as a trackball or a touch-pad). Running the mouse around on the surface of the desk (or, preferably, a high-friction **mouse-mat**) changes the position of the pointer on the screen.

Should you run out of space on the mouse-mat

Sometimes, the user may find that the mouse has been moved to the edge of the available space on the desk (or mouse-mat) before the pointer has reached the desired position on the screen. In that case, simply lift the mouse and reposition it on the surface.

The mouse buttons

On the upper side of the traditional mouse are two buttons, left and right. When the screen pointer has been positioned at the desired spot on the screen, clicking (or sometimes double-clicking) the left button of the mouse transmits the user's choice to the computer. **Double-clicking** means pressing the left button down twice in quick succession: an insufficiently rapid double-click will not have the desired effect. The same result, however, can be achieved by a **single click** followed by a press of the **Return** (↵) key. In **click-and-drag** operations (see below), the left button is held down while the mouse is moved. The right button of the mouse is also used occasionally to open additional menus.

In Windows, it is also possible to give commands by pressing keys. In fact, as the user becomes accustomed to Windows, key pressing, which is quicker than manipulating the mouse, often becomes the preferred mode of operation.

Clicking an icon to activate it

Move the mouse so that the pointer lies on one of the **Desktop** icons. If you click the left mouse button, the title of the icon will change colour. The icon has been **activated** and certain operations can now be carried out such as relocating it. If you double-click the icon, the underlying application will start: for example, double-clicking the SPSS icon will run the SPSS program.

Relocating an icon: The click-and-drag operation

Position the pointer on one of the Desktop icons. Press the mouse button and keep it held down, while moving the mouse. The original icon remains in place, but a dotted outline of the icon, known as a **ghost**, moves with the arrow to whatever new location the user chooses. When the mouse button is released, the original icon jumps to the new position. This is known as a **click-and-drag** operation. Note, however, that computers linked in a network often have a fixed initial layout for the Desktop and so will not retain the new position of an icon after a user has logged off. Should you run out of mat space in the middle of a click-and-drag operation, keep the left button pressed down, lift the mouse off the mat and put it down again in a more suitable place on the mat.

2.1.3 Keeping more than one application open

One useful feature of **Windows** is that the user can keep several applications open at the same time. It is therefore quite possible to be writing a report of an experiment in a word-processing application and, while doing so (when SPSS is also running), to import computing output from SPSS into the same document file. Be careful not to have too many applications open simultaneously because their performance may suffer as a consequence.

If more than one application has been opened, clicking the appropriate button on the **Taskbar** (normally at the foot of the screen but it can be moved to either side or even the top of the screen) will transfer control to that application. Alternatively, holding down the **Alt** key and pressing **Tab** repeatedly will enable the user to cycle through all the applications that are currently open.

2.2 PROPERTIES OF WINDOWS

The **Desktop** remains available (though not necessarily visible) throughout a Windows session. Windows, however, must be specially opened. Each of the icons visible on the **Desktop** can be opened to show its own window by double-clicking its icon. To confirm this, try double-clicking any of the icons on the **Desktop**.

The icons in the window that represent the folders and files on the hard disk are of two types.

1. Yellow **folder icons** 📁 resemble the folders in a filing cabinet, each with a protruding 'label' at the top left. (An open folder is shown as 📂 .)

2. White **file icons** bear a variety of designs, depending on the type of file. For example, a WORD file has the icon 📄, whose 'dog-ear' at the top right corner represents a much-thumbed letter or other document.

As an illustration of the features of a window, we shall examine the window of the folder *SPSS10 book*, which lists the first few chapters of this book (Figure 2). The figure shows the files in **Details** format with their text names and details of their size, type and last modification date and time. An alternative format (**Large Icons**) shows only the file icons and their names. These formats can be selected from the **View** drop-down menu.

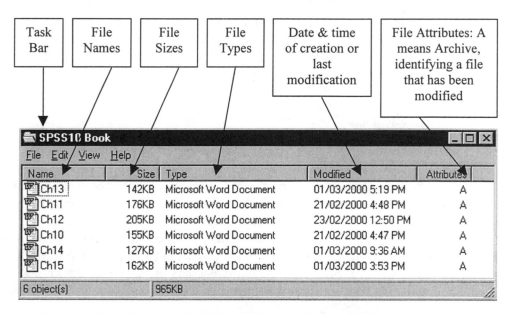

Figure 2. The window for the folder SPSS10 Book with the files in Details format

The title bar

Across the top of the window is the blue **Title Bar**, with the title of the window on the left.

Maximising, minimising, restoring and closing a window

On the right side of the **Title Bar** are three buttons, whose functions are to minimise, maximise, restore or close the window, depending on whether the window has already been maximised (i.e. occupies the whole screen) or is smaller. When a window has been made smaller, the three buttons (top right of Figure 2) are **Minimise**, **Maximise** and **Close**. When a window has been maximised, the middle button changes to **Restore** (Figure 3).

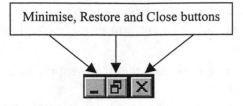

Figure 3. Icons at the right of the Title Bar when a window has been maximised

To maximise the size of the window so that it occupies the whole screen, click the **Maximise** button. The window will now expand to full size and the middle button will be replaced by the **Restore** button (Figure 3). Click the **Restore** button, and the window will return to its original (smaller) size.

When the **Minimise** button is activated, the window disappears from view. At the bottom of the screen, however, in the **Taskbar**, a button labelled with the name of the folder SPSS10 book. appears. Clicking that button will restore the window to the screen. If the window is that of a file such as Ch2, activation of the minimise button produces a small icon with the name of the file Ch2 at the foot of the Microsoft Word window.

To close the window completely, click **Close** X . Alternatively, a window can be closed by clicking the **File** drop-down menu in the **Menu bar** and selecting **Close**. If the **Desktop** is obscured by open windows, it will be necessary to minimise them all in order to see it.

The scroll bar

Notice the grey border running down inside the right hand edge of the window between the two arrowheads. This is known as a **scroll bar**. This scroll bar can be used to change the 'view' through the window, that is, move up or down through the list of items, so that new sections of the list can be seen. (If a folder contains many items or the items are too wide, its window will also have a *horizontal* scroll bar along the bottom of the window, which is useful for viewing items to the right or left of those that are visible at present.) A scroll bar has an arrow at either end, and contains a darker rectangle known as a **scroll box**.

By clicking one of the arrows ▲ or ▼ at either end of the vertical scroll bar, the window can be made to shift a little in the indicated direction, so that a few more file names come into view; and correspondingly, a few of those initially in view disappear. To scroll through the contents even faster, click once within the vertical scroll bar either above or below the scroll box depending on which direction you wish to move. Even greater scrolling speed can be achieved (for example, within a multi-paged document such as a WORD file) by clicking-and-dragging the scroll box within the scroll bar. Page-by-page scrolling can also be achieved by using the **Page Up** and **Page Down** keys on the keyboard.

Controlling the position and size of a window

Fine control of the position and size of a window can be achieved by **clicking-and-dragging** operations (Section 2.1.2). The **position** of the entire window can be adjusted by clicking-and-dragging on the window's **title bar**. The **height** or **width** of a window can be adjusted separately by clicking-and-dragging on a border. To change **both height and width**, click-and-drag on any of the corners of the window. The success of a **click-and-drag** window-shaping operation depends upon the shape of the screen pointer, which must assume the double-arrow shape: horizontal for an adjustment of width; vertical for an adjustment of height; diagonal for an adjustment of both width and height.

The menu bar

In the window shown in Figure 2, the **menu bar** beneath the title bar contains four drop-down menus: **File**, **Edit**, **View** and **Help**. Other windows may have additional items in the menu bar.

Notice that one of the letters of each of these words is underlined. This means that each menu can also be accessed by pressing and holding down **Alt** and typing the underlined letter. Pressing **Alt** with **F**, for example, will obtain the **File** drop-down menu. Clicking the menu's title caption will have the same effect.

A drop-down menu such as **File** 'hangs down' in front of part of the window, partially hiding it. In the menu, each item on the list may be a pointer to a **sub-menu** or a **command** that is run either by clicking its name in the menu or by pressing the underlined letter (do not press **Alt** this time). Among the items in the **File** menu, for example, is **Close**, which we have already discussed as an alternative method of closing a window. (Note: Hereafter, we shall describe mouse operations only: the equivalent key presses are given in the menus, and will not be described here.)

2.3   FINDING PROGRAMS AND FILES

It cannot be assumed that the application icons that are visible on the **Desktop** necessarily represent all the applications in the system. Should the icon of an application that is supposed to be available not appear on the desktop or be obscured by the window of another open application, click **Start** to open the menu shown in Figure 4.

- Highlighting **Programs** with the cursor will obtain a list of programs.
- Highlighting **Find** and then clicking **Files or Folders** will open the **Find: All Files** dialog box (see Figure 5).

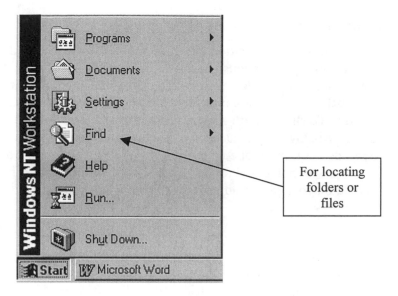

Figure 4. The Windows NT menu

There are occasions on which you may be unable to remember the name of the folder in which a file has been stored. Sometimes, too, a saving operation can go wrong, and the item may have been saved in a folder other than the one intended. There are various ways of locating such files, two of which are the **Find** procedure (see Figure 4) and using the **Windows Explorer**, which is accessed through the **Programs** option.

- To use the **Find** procedure, choose

  Find

      Files or Folders

  to open the **Find: All Files** dialog box (Figure 5).

- Type in the name (or part of the name) of the file and click **Find Now**.

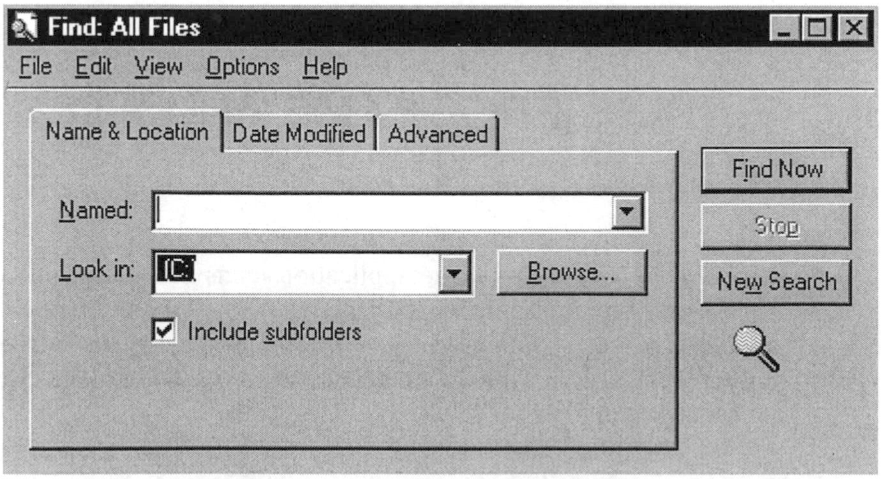

Figure 5. The Find: All Files dialog box

If such a name exists in one or more file names, a list of the files will appear in the lower section of the dialog box, together with their folders, sizes and types. The **Look in:** subdirectory and the **Browse** button enable the user to restrict the search to a particular disk drive (here it is C:) or even, to a particular folder within a disk drive, avoiding a large list of irrelevant files.

Another useful procedure for finding a file of a particular type (e.g. an SPSS data file) is to type in ***.sav**, where * means any file name and **.sav** is the conventional extension for SPSS data files. This will produce a list of all the files with a .sav extension. Double-clicking a file name in the list will result in the file being opened in whatever application is appropriate (e.g. a WORD file in WORD, an SPSS data file in SPSS, and EXCEL file in EXCEL, and so on).

- To use the **Windows Explorer**, choose

  Programs

      Windows Explorer

  to open a 'tree' of drives, folders and files (Figure 6).

Here within the highlighted folder *Book* there are several files (some of the chapters of this book) listed in the right-hand pane. Also specified (but not shown in Figure 6) are the size, type, and date of the last modification of each file.

In the left-hand pane of Figure 6, notice the ⊟ and ⊞ boxes to the left of the disk drive and folder names. A ⊟ box (e.g. beside *My Computer*) indicates that an item has been opened to show its contents (e.g. disk drives, folders, files). A ⊞ box indicates that although an item has contents, it has not yet been opened to display them. Clicking its box will produce, immediately below it, a list of its contents; and at the same time, the ⊞ will change to ⊟. Folders without a box (e.g. *Book*) have no constituent folders.

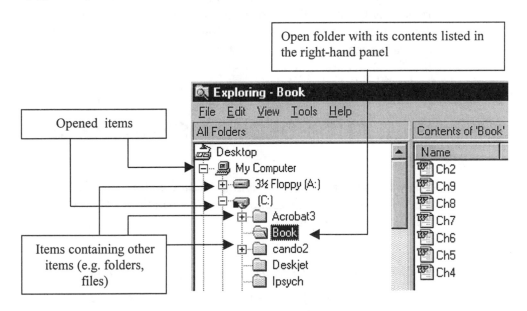

Figure 6. Part of the Explorer facility for listing drives, folders and files

Yet another way of locating a file is to double-click the **My Computer** icon. This operation will obtain a list of folders, the contents of any of which can be accessed by double-clicking the folder's icon.

Accessing an application quickly from the Desktop: Creating short-cut icons

There will certainly be some files and programs (such as SPSS) that are so frequently used that the user will want immediate access to them, rather than first having to select **Programs** and then choose the program concerned. Such rapid access is arranged by the operation known as **creating a shortcut**. A

shortcut is a copy, on the **Desktop**, of the icon of an application, folder or file that enables the user to access the item immediately, however deeply it may be stored within the hierarchy of folders. For example, to create a **shortcut** to the folder *spssdata*, proceed as follows:

- Locate the folder by using one of the methods described in the previous section.
- Activate the icon by clicking it.
- Within the **File** menu, select **Create Shortcut**, and click it. Note that in **Windows Explorer**, the file or folder has to be selected from the right-hand section.
- An icon will now appear which can be dragged to the **Desktop**.

On the **Desktop**, there is now an icon which is an exact replica of the icon for the original folder, except it has the caption **Shortcut to spssdata**, and there is a small arrow indicating that a shortcut has been created.

Clicking this icon will immediately open the *spssdata* folder window, which shows the files that the folder contains. Clicking one of the these files will immediately open SPSS and, in the case of a data file, load the data into the SPSS **Data Editor** window (see below). Note that the shortcut facility may not be available on networked computers.

2.4 FILE AND FOLDER OPERATIONS

There are several ways of copying, deleting and moving files and folders within the Windows system using mouse or key operations. Here we outline the use of the **Windows Explorer**.

Copying a file or folder to and from a floppy disk or another folder

Copying a file or folder to and from a floppy disk or another folder is a very simple operation in Windows Explorer.

- Open **Windows Explorer** as described in the previous Section and locate the file or folder to be copied (e.g. if the file were *Ch8* as in Figure 6, it would be necessary to click the folder *book* in order to show the icon for *Ch8* in the right-hand pane).
- Click the file or folder name so that it is highlighted.
- Select
  Edit
  > **Copy**
  to copy the file or folder.
- Locate the destination for the copied file. If it is to be copied into a floppy disk, locate **3½ Floppy (A:)** in the left-hand pane of Windows Explorer and click it to highlight it. The right-hand pane will then list the contents (if any)

of the floppy disk. If it is to be pasted into another folder, locate that within Windows Explorer and highlight it.

- Select
Edit
>> **Paste**

to copy the file or folder into the new destination. Its name will then appear in the right-hand pane.

Deleting a file

- Open **Windows Explorer** as in the previous Section, then locate and highlight the file to be deleted.
- Select
File
>> **Delete**

to delete the file. You will be asked to confirm the deletion.

Copying the contents of an entire floppy disk

- Select **My Computer** from the **Desktop** window and then highlight the floppy disk icon **3½ Floppy (A:)** by clicking it once (not double else the **3½ Floppy (A:)** window will open).
- Select **Copy Disk...** from the **File** drop-down menu and follow the subsequent prompts.

Creating new folders

- Open **Windows Explorer**, then locate the drive or folder for the new folder (e.g. **(C:)**).
- Choose
File
>> **New**
>>> **Folder**

and type the name of the folder over the words NEW FOLDER. Finally move the cursor away from the new name and click the mouse. If desired, folders can be created within folders, in a many-layered, hierarchical storage system.

2.5   OPENING AND CLOSING SPSS

Given that SPSS has been loaded into your machine or is available on your network, two conditions must be met before you can use the package:

- (1)   the **licence** must be current;
- (2)   there must be **sufficient memory** available to run SPSS and **free disc space** for work files.

Assuming that both these conditions have been met, there are several ways of accessing SPSS. If an SPSS shortcut icon (such as one of those in Figure 1) is available on the **Desktop**, double-click it to run the application. Alternatively, run SPSS either by double-clicking an SPSS file or with the **Start** menu on the **Task Bar**.

2.5.1 Accessing the Data Editor

When SPSS is opened by clicking the SPSS icon, a dialog box with the question: **What would you like to do?** appears (Figure 7).

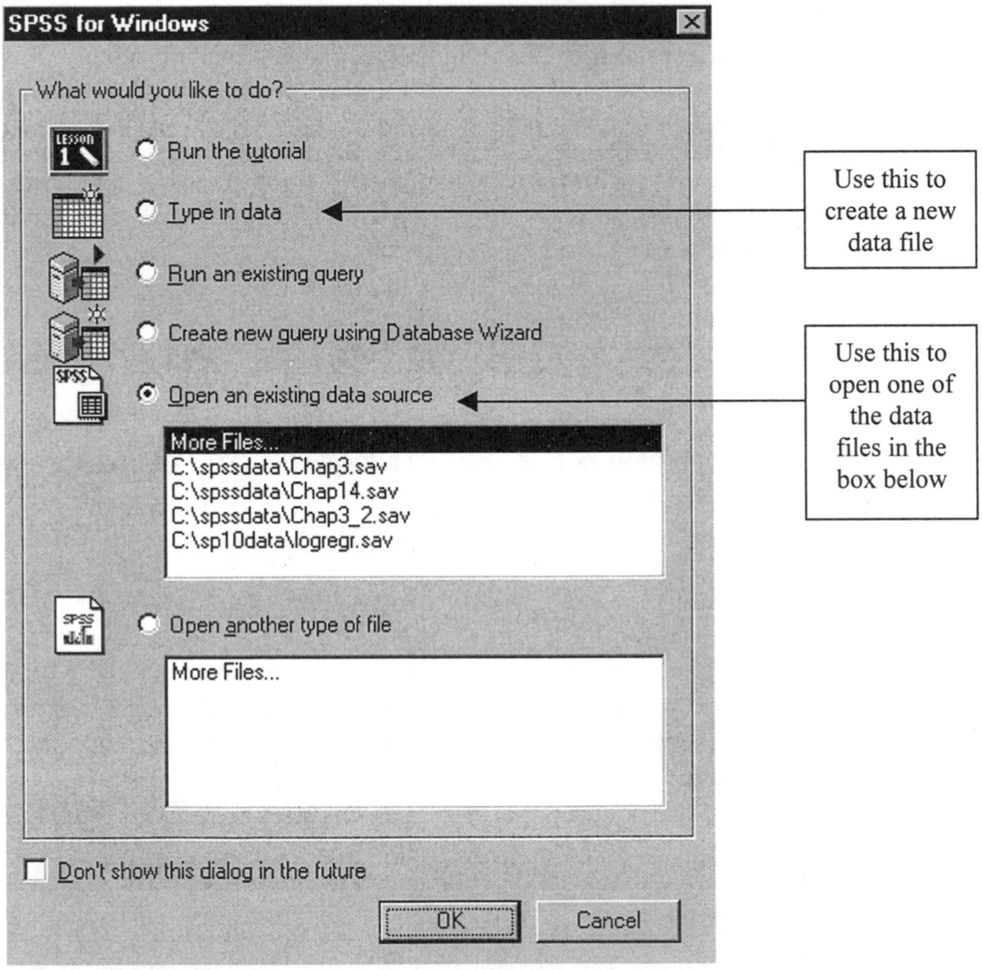

Figure 7. The opening SPSS for Windows dialog box

Users of a stand-alone computer can prevent this dialog box from appearing by clicking the **Don't show this dialog in the future** box.

If the user is entering new data, click the **Type in data** radio button (Figure 7) and then on **OK** to bring **Variable View** to the screen (Figure 8). (Should **Data View** appear first, simply click the tab labelled **Variable View** at the bottom left-hand side of the window to open **Variable View**.) Fuller details of how to name and specify the variables will be supplied in Chapter 3, Section 3.2.4; here we shall illustrate the procedure with a very simple data set consisting of people's ages, heights and weights.

A previously saved data file can be restored to **Data View** by clicking the **Open an existing data source** radio button and selecting the appropriate file in the list underneath. Note that networked computers may not list the user's data files, in which case clicking **More Files...** will open a directory box for locating the disk drive or folder required.

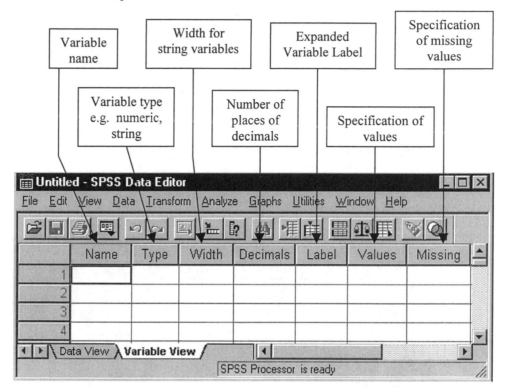

Figure 8. Variable View. (For this Figure, the columns have been narrowed. Others, headed Columns, Align, & Measure have been omitted.)

The **Data Editor** in SPSS10 works in two modes: **Variable View** for naming and specifying the characteristics of the variables; **Data View** which is a spreadsheet for entering the data into SPSS.

Although it is possible to enter data directly into **Data View**, it is more usual to start in **Variable View** by naming and specifying the variables and then switch to **Data View** to enter the data into columns already bearing the names of the previously specified variables.

To name the variables *age*, *height* and *weight*, type *age* into the first cell of the first row (in the column headed **Name**) of **Variable View** and then press the ↓ cursor key to move the highlighting (a thick black line around the cell) down to the cell below. Then type *height* into the highlighted cell and press the ↓ cursor key again to move the highlighting down to the third row. Finally type in *weight* and press the ↓ cursor key to move the highlighting down to the next row. **Variable View** will now appear as in Figure 9.

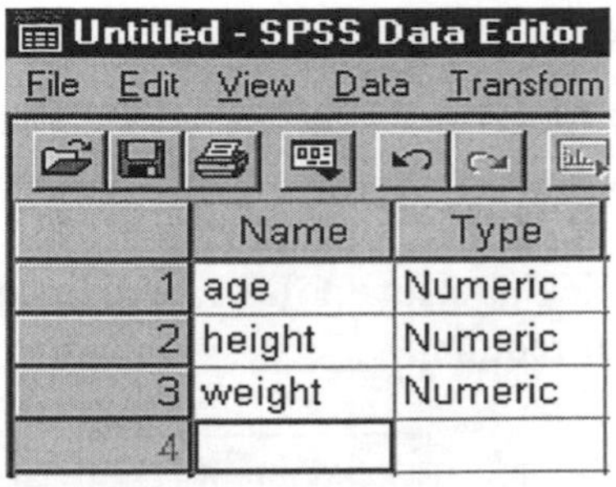

Figure 9. The appearance of the left-hand side of Variable View after entering the three variable names age, height and weight

Once the user has entered the details of the variables into **Variable View**, clicking the **Data View** tab at the bottom of the window (Figure 8) will bring **Data View** to the screen (Figure 10).

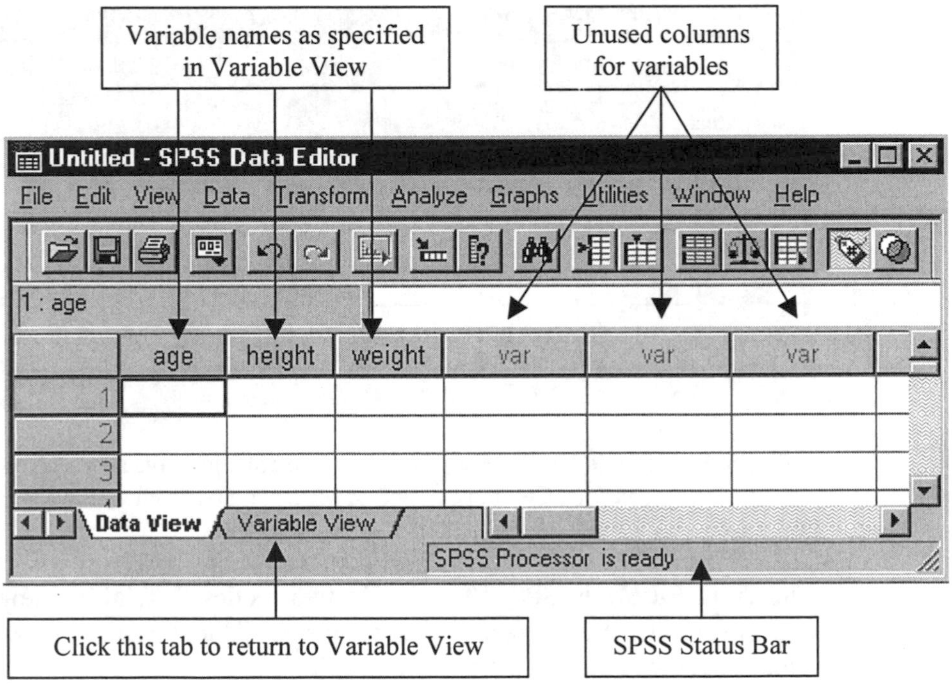

Figure 10. Data View with variables named age, height and weight

In an SPSS data set, each row represents a single case, or subject, and each column represents a **variable**. Within very generous limits, there can be any number of subjects and variables. Notice that in Figure 10 the rows are numbered and the first three columns have the names of variables previously entered in Variable View. The remaining columns have the dimmed label **var** at the top, because no other variable names have been specified. Notice also that, at this point, the window bears the title **Untitled - SPSS Data Editor** in the **Title Bar.**

Running along the bottom of the window is a horizontal band, in which various messages appear from time to time. When SPSS is accessed, the message reads: 'SPSS Processor is ready'. The horizontal band is known as the **Status Bar**, because it reports not only upon whether SPSS is ready to begin, but also on the stage that a procedure has reached. If, for example, a large data set is being read from a file, progress is continually monitored, case by case, in the status bar.

This **case counter** is one of several useful types of message that appear: there is also information about the weighting of cases (**weight status**), the selection of specified portions of the data set (**filter status**), and whether the data have been split into separate groups for analysis (**split file status**).

Note that at any time it is possible to return to **Variable View** by clicking the **Variable View** tab in order to name more variables or to add extra details about existing variables such as value names (e.g. 1 = Male, 2 = Female).

Now the values of *age*, *height* and *weight* for each person can be entered with a new row for each participant, thus:

	age	height	weight
1	18.00	1.82	85.00
2	22.00	1.75	75.00
3			

Fuller details about how to enter data into **Data View** will be given in Chapter 3, Section 3.2.5.

2.5.2 Closing SPSS and Windows

SPSS is closed by choosing **Exit** within the **File** menu. If the user has not yet saved the data file, a dialog box will appear with the question: **Save contents of data editor to untitled?**. The user must then click the **Yes**, **No** or **Cancel** button. Likewise, if any output (such as descriptive statistics) has been generated, the question **Save contents of output viewer to Output 1?** appears and again the user clicks on **Yes**, **No** or **Cancel**.

If the computer session is being terminated, it is usual to close Windows as well before logging off. In Windows NT, Windows 95 and Windows 98, this is done by first clicking **Start** in the bottom left-hand corner, then selecting **Shut Down**, and finally clicking one of the radio buttons for shutting down the computer.

2.5.3 Resuming work on a saved data set

There are several ways of resuming work on a saved data set, either for the purpose of carrying out statistical analysis, or adding more data. After starting SPSS, the quickest way is to click the radio button **Open an existing data source** in the opening SPSS for Windows dialog box (Figure 7). A list of saved files with the extension *.sav* will appear in the **More Files** window: select the appropriate file and click **OK**. The data file will then appear in Data View. Alternatively, after starting SPSS, click the **Type in data** radio button (Figure 7) and select **Open** in the **File** menu to open the **Open File** selection box, from which the appropriate file can be selected. (Note that in networked systems such as classrooms, these methods may not be applicable.) Finally a quick method without having to open SPSS first is to double-click the icon of a saved data file in the Windows **Find** menu (Figure 5). This will immediately start up SPSS and load the data file into **Data View**.

EXERCISE 1

SOME BASIC WINDOWS OPERATIONS

BEFORE YOU START

Before you begin the first exercise, there are one or two preliminaries which require your attention.

Read Chapter 2

Even if you already have some experience of computing, we strongly recommend that you study Chapter 2 closely before proceeding with this practical.

Arrange access to a network

We assume that most of our readers will be users of a network, rather than owners (or exclusive users) of a PC. Assuming you have access to a network, there may be an identification, or logging in, procedure. If so, make sure you have organised your number and password.

IF YOU HAVE NOT USED A COMPUTER BEFORE

If you are already an experienced user of a PC, you can ignore this section and pass on to the next.

Boot up the machine if necessary

The details of booting up a computer vary enormously. Seek help if necessary.

Logging in

Log in to the computer in the required manner.

GETTING INTO WINDOWS (Section 2.1)

You may or may not be transferred directly to **Windows** on booting up the machine: a menu may appear on the screen, or the **DOS** prompt, to which you must respond by typing **win** and pressing ↵. Read about the Windows operating system in Section 2.1.1.

The Desktop (Section 2.1.1)

Typically the **Desktop** is similar to that in Chapter 2, Figure 1, but will appear with different icons depending on what facilities and programs have been installed.

The parts of a window

From the Desktop, open a window Window such as **My Computer** by double-clicking its icon. You have already read the descriptions of the various parts of a window. Now look for these in the display before you. **Windows** offers the user a very flexible environment, and windows may be sized, shaped and positioned in many ways.

Title bar

The **title bar** is always the top structure in a window. Here the title bar contains the title **My Computer**.

Menu bar

Just underneath the **title bar** is the **menu bar**, which offers a range of drop-down menus labelled **File, Edit, View, Help**.

Minimising, maximising and closing the window

At the right-hand end of the title bar are three buttons ▣ for minimising, maximising and closing the window. Click the **Maximise** button (the middle of the three) to make the window occupy the whole screen. When this happens, the maximise icon is replaced by the **Restore** icon ▣. Click the **Restore** button (the middle of the three) and the window will become smaller. If you were to click the **Close** button (the rightmost of the three), the window would close (i.e. disappear).

Reducing a window to an icon

Click the **Minimise** button (the leftmost of the three buttons). The effect is dramatic: the window disappears from sight but its icon and title will appear in the **Taskbar** along the bottom of the screen to the right of 〽Start. Restore the **My Computer** window by double-clicking the icon at the foot of the screen.

Clicking-and-dragging operations

Notice what happens when the screen pointer touches a border or corner of a window: the pointer changes from a diagonally upward-pointing single arrow to a double-headed arrow. Only when the double-headed arrow appears, can the window by re-sized by clicking-and-dragging on the border (or corner) with the mouse.

Scrolling

If there are scroll bars present (this depends on the number of items in the folder), try scrolling down or across the window.

Closing the window

Close the **My Computer** window by clicking **Close** at the right-hand end of the Title Bar.

FINISHING THE SESSION

Close down Windows by clicking **Start** at the end of the Taskbar at the foot of the screen and select **Shut Down**. In the next dialog box, select the radio button for **Shut down the computer?**. In the case of a networked computer, **Close all programs and log on as a different user?** is the correct choice.

CHAPTER 3

DATA HANDLING IN SPSS

3.1   INTRODUCTION

Before any exploration of data or statistical analyses can take place, it is necessary to input the data to SPSS in a suitable form and to check that they have been correctly transcribed either by inspecting them on the screen or by printing them out using **Case Summaries** (see Section 3.5.2). Any corrections or modifications can then be made by invoking one of the editing procedures. In this chapter, the operations of inputting, editing, saving, listing, printing, selecting and case-weighting will be fully explained and demonstrated with examples.

3.2   ENTERING DATA

3.2.1   Data from a between subjects experiment

A between subjects experiment

In an experiment on the relative efficacy of two mnemonic methods for the recall of verbal material, each individual in a pool of 30 participants is randomly assigned to one of three equal-sized groups:

(1)   a **control** group, which receives no training;
(2)   a group trained to use the **Galton's Walk** method (**Mnemonic A**);
(3)   a group trained to use the **Peg** method (**Mnemonic B**).

Each participant is presented with verbal material and asked (at a later stage) to reproduce it in free written recall. The dependent variable is the number of words recalled. In this experimental design, the independent variable is Mnemonic Training Method with three levels (Control, Mnemonic A, and Mnemonic B).

The results of the experiment are shown in Table 1.

Table 1. The numbers of words recalled by participants with different mnemonic training methods.									
Control Group	3	5	3	2	4	6	9	3	8	10
Mnemonic A	10	8	15	9	11	16	17	17	7	10
Mnemonic B	20	15	14	15	17	10	8	11	18	19

Setting out the data in a form suitable for entry into SPSS

In Chapter 2, we saw that data for processing by SPSS are entered into a display called **Data View**, in which each row represents a participant and each column represents a variable or characteristic on which that person has been measured.

To make them suitable for analysis with SPSS, the results of an experiment or survey may have to be recast in a new format. In Table 1, for example, where each row represents the scores of ten participants, the data do not conform to the requirement that each row of **Data View** must contain the data from only one person.

When constructing an SPSS data set in **Data View**, it is an excellent practice to have, as the first variable, one with a name such as *case*, which records the participants' original case numbers: 1, 2, ..., and so on. Since the rows are numbered anyway, the merits of creating a variable *case* which duplicates these numbers might seem unclear. Suppose, however, that some cases subsequently have to be eliminated at a later stage. The row numbers of several participants' data would change; but the variable *case* would preserve each participant's original case number. This is very useful. For example, should the accuracy of the transcription of a participant's data into SPSS later be called into question, that person's data can always be identified and checked throughout the entire process of analysis.

We shall need a **grouping variable** to code the Mnemonic Training Method factor. We can use the second column for this. The column will contain code numbers indicating the method (Control, Mnemonic A or Mnemonic B) under which the participant was tested: 1s (for the control group), 2s (for the Mnemonic A group) and 3s (for the Mnemonic B group). Note that these numbers are merely *category labels*: they are not *measurements* of the degree to which some property is possessed. The variable can be named *group*. (An SPSS variable name must not exceed 8 characters, and there must be no gaps - see Section 3.2.2 for fuller details.) Finally, the third column will contain the scores of all the participants in the experiment, under the variable name *score*.

In Table 2, the results in Table 1 have been recast to reflect this re-organisation of data, so that each row now contains the data from a single participant.

Table 2. The data of Table 1 recast in a form suitable for entry into SPSS (the shaded items have been included for explanation only: they are not actually entered into SPSS)

Variable Names			
case	group	score	
1	1	3	
2	1	5	
...	...	...	Group 1: The Control Group
9	1	8	
10	1	10	
11	2	10	
12	2	8	
...	...	...	Group 2: Mnemonic A
19	2	7	
20	2	10	
21	3	20	
22	3	15	
...	...	...	Group 3: Mnemonic B
29	3	18	
30	3	19	

We are now ready to begin entering the data into SPSS. This is done in two stages:

(1) Specify the name, type and other characteristics of each variable in **Variable View**.

(2) Entering the data for each variable in **Data View**.

The first task is to assign names to the variables and (for the grouping variable) explanatory labels to the code numbers (or values). Ideally, these names need to be intelligible while conforming to the rules for variable names detailed below. Since there is a limit of eight characters for a variable name, it is not always possible to achieve intelligibility. For output purposes, longer labels can be assigned.

A notational convention

In this book, we shall use *italics* to indicate those variable names and values that are to be typed into **Variable View**. Note that whether we type in lower or upper case, **Variable View** will show (at the head of the appropriate column) a name in lower case only: for example, if we type *Field*, the name will be recorded as *field*. This is not true, however, of variable labels and values in the SPSS output which will appear as they are entered. We shall use a **bold** typeface for the names of menus, the names of dialog boxes and the items therein. Emboldening will also be used for emphasis and for technical terms.

3.2.2 Rules for naming variables

There are six rules for naming variables. A variable name:

(1) Must not exceed **eight characters**. (A **character** is a letter, a digit or a symbol.)

(2) Must **begin with a letter or @**.

(3) Must **not end with a full stop**.

(4) **Can** contain letters, digits or any of the characters @, #, _, or $.

(5) Must **not** contain either of the following:
   (i) a blank;
   (ii) special characters, such as !, ?, and *, other than those listed in (4).

(6) Must **not be** one of the keywords (such as AND, NOT, EQ, BY and ALL) that SPSS uses as special computing terms.

The names we have chosen, *group* and *score,* clearly comply with the rules. Note, however, that while the name *group1* would also have been satisfactory, *group 1* would not, because it contains a space, violating rule 5. The name *1group* would violate rule 2 since it does not start with a letter. Be careful about length, too (rule 1): *red_cube* is satisfactory; but *red_cubes* is not, because the total number of characters (including the underline symbol) exceeds the permitted limit of 8.

3.2.3 Obtaining Variable View

See Section 2.5.1

Variable View (Figure 1) is accessed by using one of the procedures described in Section 2.5.1. For a user intending to build a new data file, this is most likely to be done by clicking the radio button **Type in data** in the opening SPSS window (see Chapter 2, Figure 9). (Should **Data View** appear first, click the **Variable View** tab at the bottom to obtain **Variable View**.)

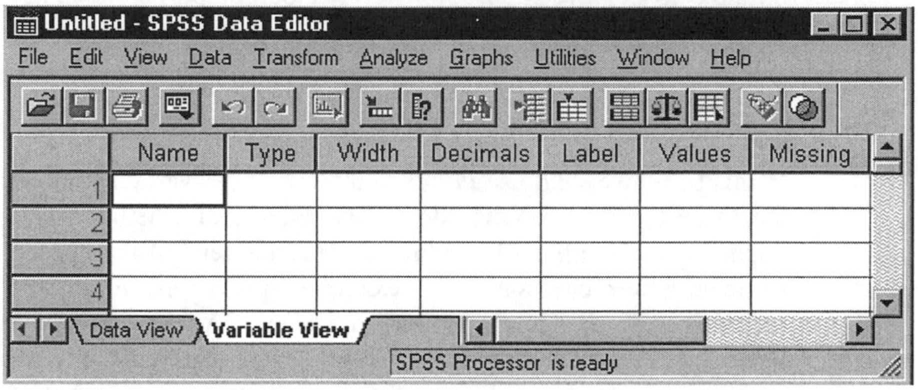

Figure 1. Variable View mode of the Data Editor

3.2.4 Using Variable View

*Entering the chosen variable names(the **Name** column)*

Type the first variable name (here it is *case*) into the first cell of the column headed **Name** and press the ↓ cursor key. **Variable View** will now appear (Figure 2).

Name of first variable specified as case

Highlighted cell ready for name of second variable

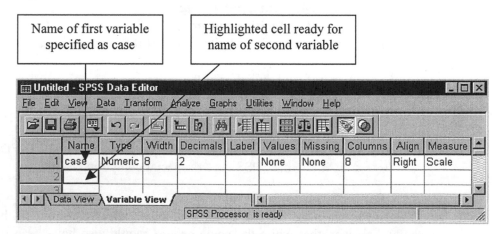

Figure 2. The appearance of Variable View after entering the first variable name and pressing the ↓ cursor key

All the default aspects of the variable appear in the columns to the right (e.g. it is a **Numeric** variable, appears in a column with a width of 8 characters and not more than 2 places of decimals, and there are no specified values or missing data values). Any of these default aspects can be changed. It is also possible to change the default aspects globally so that each time a new variable name is entered, the same default aspects appear. The way to do this will be described in the subsection *Changing the global default aspects of variables* at the end of the Section 3.2.4.

If the default aspects for the first variable are acceptable, the user can type the name of the second variable into the highlighted first cell of the second row. The same process is used for the remaining variables.

For this example we shall want to remove the decimal places from the case values so that our cases appear as 1, 2, 3 etc. rather than 1.00, 2.00, 3.00 etc.. It will also be nicer if the decimals are removed from the other variables as well. This is done in the column labelled **Decimals** (see below).

*Changing the type of variable (the **Type** column)*

By default, the variable type, shown in the column labelled **Type**, is numeric, but there are other types of variable available in SPSS.

Suppose we had wanted to record the names of all the participants taking part in the learning experiment and that the longest name did not exceed 20 characters in length. *Name* would be a **string variable**, (i.e. a qualitative variable whose categories are entered into the **Data Editor** as strings, rather than numbers). A **string** is a sequence of characters (letters, symbols, blanks, digits) which is treated as a label by the system. Thus a string can be a simple letter M, a word such as French, or a person's name such as Abraham Lincoln.

To set up a string variable, do the following:
- After typing in the name of the variable, press ↵ or the → cursor key to highlight the item **Numeric** thus

- Move the cursor on to the three dots shaded in grey to the right of **Numeric** and click to open the **Variable Type** dialog box (Figure 3).

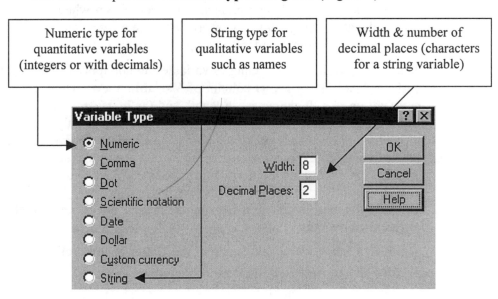

Figure 3. Variable Type dialog box

- In the dialog box is a list of eight variable types, each with a radio button. SPSS initially marks the **Numeric** button. Click the **String** radio button at the foot of the list. The **Width** and the **Decimal Places** boxes immediately disappear to be replaced with a box labelled **Characters**.
- Change the default value of 8 in the **Characters** box to some larger number such as 20 to accommodate the longest likely name. Do this by moving the cursor into the number box, deleting the 8 and typing in 20.
- The other types of variable are explained by clicking the **Help** button in the dialog box.
- Click **OK.** The variable type *String* will now appear in the **Type** column and 20 in the **Width** column.

*Changing the width and number of decimal places of variables (the **Width** and **Decimals** columns)*

In the case of our original variable *case*, there is no need to change the width of the column but we do wish to change the number in the **Decimals** column in order to display the case numbers as whole numbers. To do this, either click in the cell in the **Decimals** column or use the → cursor key to move the highlighting to there.

- Click the lower-pointing arrow to the right of the **Decimals** box

and continue clicking until 0 appears. The effect of this change will be to show all the case numbers as integers, and the data set will be much easier to read.
- Move the cursor to the next column to be changed and click, or to the **Name** column on the next row for entering the next variable's name.

*Entering a variable label (the **Label** column)*

As mentioned earlier, it is often advantageous to expand the sometimes cryptic variable name with a longer explanatory label. Even when a variable name is self-explanatory (e.g. *sex*), a short label (e.g. gender) will improve the appearance of the output after a descriptive command or statistical test is run.

The rules governing the naming of variables do not apply to the assignment of a variable label in the **Label** column of **Variable View**. Here, the label can be anything up to 120 characters in length and (as in *Mnemonic Training Method*) can include spaces. These variable labels often clarify tables and diagrams in the output. Moreover, unlike variable names in **Data View**, assigned variable labels in **Variable View** are case sensitive and are displayed exactly as they are entered. It should be borne in mind, however, that should a label with the maximum of 120 characters be chosen, fewer characters (usually the first 40) will actually be displayed in the output, though the precise number varies in different commands.

To enter a label, move the cursor to the **Label** column, click, and type in the label. Here we might enter *Case Number*.

*Values and value labels (the **Values** column)*

In the case of grouping variables such as our second variable *group*, we need to identify the various groups with values and labels. Let us assume that we have now moved to the second row of **Variable View**, entered *group* as the variable name, changed the number of decimals to 0 and entered *Mnemonic Training Method* as the variable label.

In Table 2, the second column contains the group numbers 1, 2 and 3 representing Controls, Mnemonic A and Mnemonic B respectively. Specification of these values and value labels is done using the **Values** column, thus:

- Move the cursor to the **Values** column and click.
- Click the three highlighted dots to the right of **None** to open the **Value Labels** dialog box (Figure 4).
- Type the lowest code number *1* into the **Value:** text box.
- In the **Value Label:** text box, type *Control.* This will embolden the **Add** button below.
- When **Add** is clicked, the following will appear in the lowest box:
      1 = "Control".

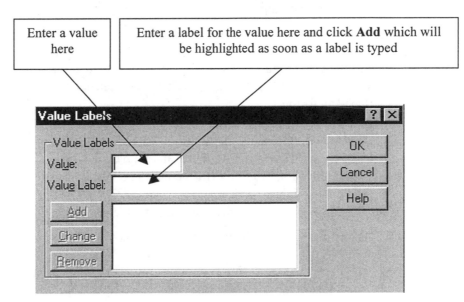

Figure 4. The Value Labels dialog box

- In a similar manner, proceed to label the values *2* and *3,* so that in the lowest box can be seen:
      1 = "Control"
      2 = "Mnemonic A"
      3 = "Mnemonic B"
- Now that all three values of the grouping variable have been labelled, click **OK**. The **Label** cell will now show {1, Control}. ... .

The completed **Value Labels** dialog box for *group* is shown in Figure 5.

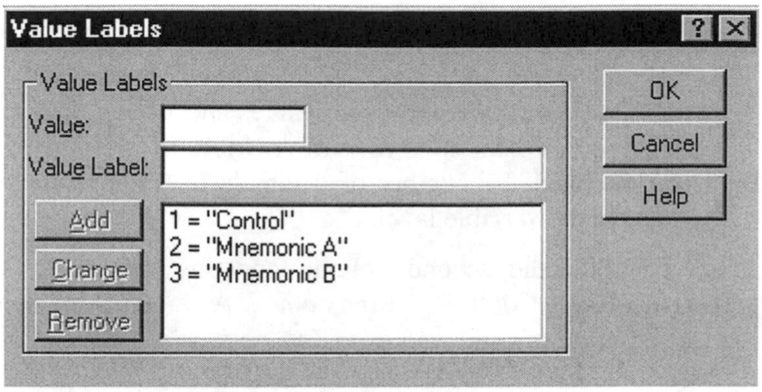

Figure 5. The Value Labels dialog box specifying the values and their labels for the variable *group*

Value labelling, like variable labelling, is governed by much looser constraints than is variable naming. A value label can be up to 60 characters in length, is case sensitive and can contain spaces. As with variable labels, however, fewer than the maximum of 60 characters (usually only about 20) will actually be displayed in the output.

A feature of **Variable View** is that the user can copy values and their labels from one variable to another. For example, one may have several variables using the same grading scheme of 1 for Excellent, 2 for Very Good, 3 for Good and so on. After specifying the values and their labels for one of the variables, proceed as follows:

- Ensure that the cell with the completed values and their labels within the **Values** column is highlighted.
- Click the **Edit** drop-down menu and then click **Copy**.
- Move the cursor to the **Values** column cell of the next variable to be assigned the copied values.
- Click the **Edit** drop-down menu and then click **Paste**.

This pasting procedure can be repeated for any number of variables.

*Missing values (the **Missing** column)*

In SPSS, there can be no empty cells within the data set, whose size is defined by the number of rows and columns. Hence if a cell has not had anything put in it by the user, SPSS supplies a **system-missing** value, which is indicated in the **Data Editor** by a full stop. SPSS will exclude system-missing values from its calculations of means, standard deviations and other statistics.

It may be, however, that for some purposes the user wishes SPSS to treat certain responses actually present in the data set as missing data. For example, suppose that, in a survey of political opinion, five categories are used (A, B, C, D & E), but category E was recorded when the person refused to answer and D was a category that indicated a failure to understand the question. The user wants SPSS to treat responses in both categories as missing, but to retain information about the relative frequencies of such responses in categories D and E in the output listings. In SPSS terminology, the user wants certain responses to be treated as **user-missing** values (as contrasted with **system-missing** values).

In analysing a set of exam results, for instance, the user might wish SPSS to treat as missing:

(1)   any marks between, say, 0 and 20;

(2)   cases where the candidate walked out without giving any written response. (A walk-out could be coded as an arbitrary, but salient, number, such as *-9*: the negative sign helps it to stand out as an impossible mark.)

To define such user-missing values:

- Move the cursor to the **Missing** column and click.

- Click the three highlighted dots to the right of **None** to open the **Missing Values** dialog box.

- Initially, the **No missing values** radio button is marked. The three text boxes underneath give the user the opportunity to specify up to three **Discrete Missing Values**, referred to in SPSS as *missing (1)*, *missing (2)*, and *missing (3)*. These may either be numerical, as with a grouping variable, or short string variables, but must be consistent with the original variable type. In the case of a string variable, the text is case sensitive. The other options in the dialog box are for quantitative variables: the user may define a missing value as one falling within a specified range, or one that falls either within a specified range or within a specified category.

- Click the **Range plus one discrete missing value** button, entering the values *0* and *20* into the **Low** and **High** boxes, respectively, and *-9* into the **Discrete value** box. The completed dialog box is shown in Figure 6.

- Click **OK.** The values will then appear in the **Missing** column cell.

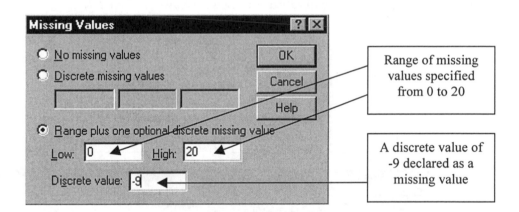

Figure 6. The completed Missing Values dialog box showing a range of missing values between 0 and 20 and a discrete value of -9

As in the case of a **Values** specification, a feature of **Variable View** is that the user can copy a **Missing Values** specification from one variable to another. For example, one may use the same missing values for several variables. After specifying the missing values for one of the variables, proceed as follows:

- Ensure that the cell with the completed missing values within the **Missing** column is highlighted.

- Click the **Edit** drop-down menu and then on **Copy.**

- Move the cursor to the **Missing** column cell of the next variable to be assigned the missing values.

- Click the **Edit** drop-down menu and then on **Paste.**

This pasting procedure can be repeated for any number of variables.

*Column width (the **Column** column)*

The width of a column in **Data View** can be altered using **Column**. In practice, this is hardly ever required. It is changed in a similar manner to the **Width** and **Decimals** columns.

*Data alignment (the **Align** column)*

The default alignment of data in **Data View** is the left margin but sometimes it is nicer to centre data or even align them to the right margin. This column enables this to be done by moving the cursor to the column and clicking, clicking the downward arrow to the right of **Left** and selecting **Right** or **Center**.

*Measurement level (the **Measure** column)*

The default measurement level is **Scale** for **Numeric** variables, and **Nominal** for **String** variables. However in the case of some chart-drawing commands, it is useful to be able to specify if measurement is nominal or ordinal.

Remaining variables for the Recall of Verbal Material experiment

In the case of the Recall of Verbal Material example, it only remains to add the third variable name *score* and variable label *Number of words recalled*. The final appearance of **Variable View** is then as shown in Figure 7.

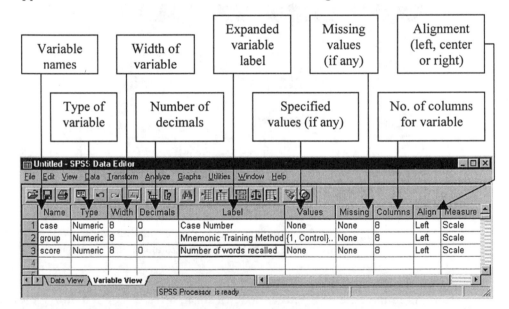

Figure 7. The final appearance of Variable View for the Recall of Verbal Material experiment

Changing the global default aspects of variables

If we want to enter several variables and display them all as whole numbers, it is more convenient to change the global aspects before entering any of the variable names. To do this:

- Click **Options** at the foot of the **Edit** drop-down menu to open the **Options** dialog box (Figure 8).

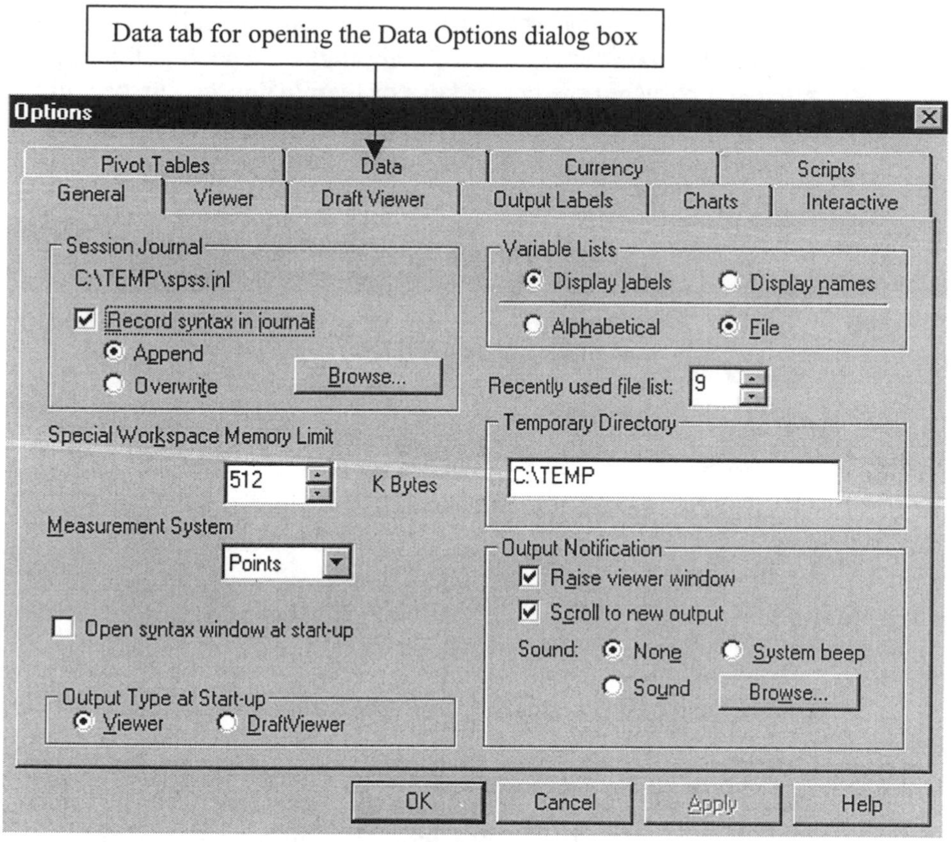

Data tab for opening the Data Options dialog box

Figure 8. The Options dialog box

- Click the tab labelled **Data** in the **Options** dialog box. Within the new dialog box is the **Display Format for New Numeric Variables** (Figure 9) in which the width and number of decimal places can be changed.

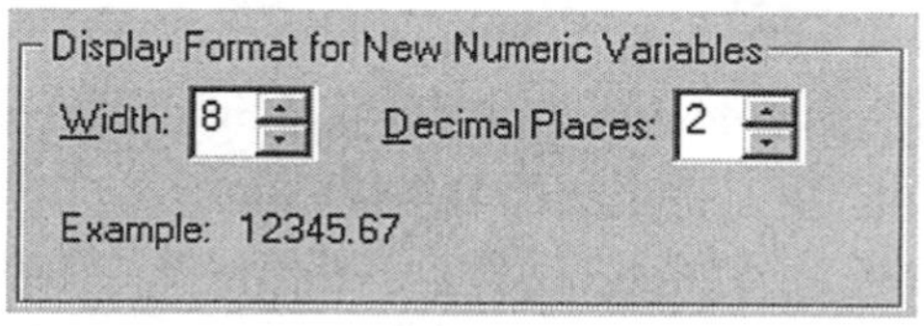

Figure 9. The Display Format for New Numeric Variables dialog box

- Click the downward arrow to the right of the box containing the number of **Decimal Places** until 0 appears. Click **OK** (or on **Apply** if some variables have already been defined and you want to change them as well).

There are many other SPSS aspects which can be changed in this **Options** dialog box but remember that they may not be permanent on networked systems.

3.2.5 Using Data View

When **Data View** is accessed by clicking the **Data View** tab at the foot of **Variable View**, the names of the variables entered in **Variable View** are reproduced at the heads of the columns (Figure 10). Just above the variable names, there is a grey bar showing *1:Case*, and a blank white bar to the right.

The white bar is the **cell editor**. The top left cell in the empty grid has a thickened black border, the **cell highlight**. The highlighting can readily be relocated by using the cursor keys or by moving the cursor with the mouse and clicking. The *1:case* shown in the grey bar indicates that the highlighting is presently in the first row of the variable *case*.

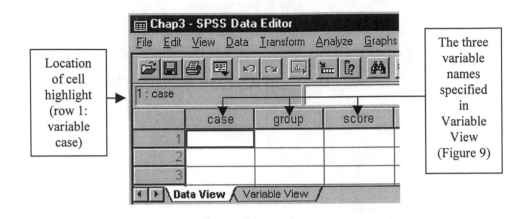

Figure 10. Part of Data View after naming the variables in Variable View

When a value is typed in from the keyboard, it will appear both in the highlighted cell and the cell editor. If a cursor key ($\rightarrow$ or $\downarrow$) or the ↵ key is pressed, this value (or its associated label as defined in the **Define Labels:** dialog box) is transferred permanently to the highlighted cell. Whether the value or its label appears is determined by the state of the toggle item **Value Labels** in the **View** drop-down menu: if the **Value Labels** command is ticked, then the label (if defined) will appear; if not, the value (i.e. the code number) will appear.

The subsequent location of the highlight depends upon which key is pressed: pressing the ↑ or ↓ highlights a cell above or below the original cell; if the ← or → cursor key is pressed, the highlight moves to the left or the right, respectively. An alternative way of moving down is to use ↵. The position of the cell highlight can also be controlled by using the mouse.

The position of the highlight determines which cell of the grid will receive the next number typed into the cell editor. Try entering a few numbers into the empty **Data View**. Once numbers have been entered in the window, the location of the cell highlight will be shown in an entry on the left of the cell editor. For example, the entry **2:group** locates the highlight at the cell in the *second* row of the column headed *group*. Try moving the highlight around with the → ↓ ← ↑ cursor keys and notice that the co-ordinates given in the cell editor change accordingly. Remove the numbers entered into the grid by clicking-and-dragging the cursor over the cells concerned to highlight them, and then pressing the **Delete** key.

Entering the data for the Recall of Verbal Material experiment

It is easiest to enter the data by columns in **Data View**.

In the first column labelled *case*, type in the case numbers identifying the participants. The numbers could be non-consecutive or even the names of the participants, provided the type of variable had been changed to **string** as described in Section 3.2.4. In the case of a large data set, there is a shortcut to typing in a sequence of numbers using the **Compute** command which will be more fully explained in Chapter 4. This command will automatically enter consecutive numbers in successive rows from 1 to the total number of rows in the data set.

In the second column labelled *group*, type in ten ones, ten twos and ten threes to identify the participants in the three treatment groups. (In Section 3.3, a quicker way of entering repeated numbers will be described.) Whether the entries in the column headed *group* appear as code numbers or value labels, depends upon whether there is a tick opposite the command **Value Labels** in the **View** menu. Notice that the numbers entered for the variable *group* have been replaced with the value labels previously defined in the **Value Labels:** dialog box. If the column is not wide enough for the whole label to be visible, it can be widened by moving the cursor to the right-hand edge of the box at the top of the column labelled *group* (where it will appear as a thick black line with an arrow protruding from both sides), holding down the left-hand mouse button and moving the cursor to the right until all the labels are fully visible. If necessary, the column can be narrowed by moving the cursor to the left.

The values in the third column *score* of Table 2 are entered as described for the case numbers. Parts of the final **Data View** are shown in Figure 11 (the reader should compare this with Table 2).

	case	group	score
1	1	Control	3
2	2	Control	5
3	3	Control	3
11	11	Mnemonic A	10
12	12	Mnemonic A	8
13	13	Mnemonic A	15
21	21	Mnemonic B	20
22	22	Mnemonic B	15
23	23	Mnemonic B	14

Figure 11. Parts of the completed Data View showing the first three participants in each group

More than one grouping variable

In this experiment there is just one grouping variable (**between subjects factor**). The entry procedure is easily extended to deal with several grouping variables.

Repeated measures (within subjects) designs

Notice particularly that data from an experiment having repeated measures (**within subjects factors**) are entered differently, because such data do not require any grouping variables at all (provided all the factors are within subjects). In this experimental design, the data from each of the levels of a within subjects factor are entered in a separate column as will be explained in the next Section.

Entering data into Data View before Variable View

It is possible to enter data into **Data View** without having previously entered details of the variables in **Variable View**. As soon as a value is typed into a cell, the variable heading at the top of the column will change from *var* to *var00001* (and if other columns have values typed into them, the variable names will become *var00002, var00003* and so on). If desired, the user can then click the **Variable View** tab, change var00001 to another variable name, and add any other variable specifications such as values and value labels. In other words, the two modes of the **Data Editor** are interchangeable in the order in which they are completed.

3.2.6   Data from a within subjects experiment

A within subjects experiment

Suppose ten participants participate in an experiment designed to investigate whether recognition of patterns is affected by the shapes of their perimeters. Each participant is tested on pattern recognition with three perimeter shapes: a triangle, a circle and a square. In this experiment, there is one treatment factor, Shape of Perimeter, comprising three levels, or conditions:

(1)   Triangle;
(2)   Circle;
(3)   Square.

The dependent variable is Recognition Time. The data are shown in Table 3.

Notice that, in contrast to the Recall of Verbal Material experiment, each participant is tested under all the three conditions making up the treatment factor. The factor Shape of Perimeter, therefore, has **repeated measures**: it is a **within subjects factor**.

	Table 3. Recognition times for three shapes of perimeter viewed by the same sample of participants		
	Levels of the factor: Shape of Perimeter		
Case	**triangle**	**circle**	**square**
1	220	300	260
2	250	290	300
3	260	280	290
4	230	340	190
5	190	300	250
6	220	270	240
7	250	320	270
8	280	290	260
9	270	340	250
10	240	300	350

Entering the variables into Variable View

Figure 12 shows how the variables are entered in **Variable View**. The first variable *case* identifies the participant. Observe that the heading Shape of Perimeter (the treatment factor in this experiment) is not entered in the **Data Editor**: only the conditions *triangle, circle, square* are entered as variable names.

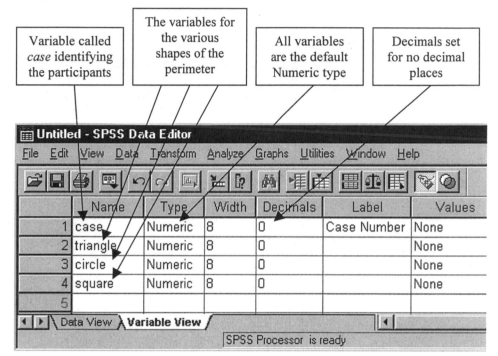

Figure 12. The variables for a within subjects design entered in Variable View

We have seen earlier that the **Data Editor** can accept only two kinds of variables:

(1) **grouping variables**, which identify (by codes) the condition under which each participant has been tested;

(2) **dependent variables**, comprising measurements.

At the moment, therefore, the **Data Editor** has no knowledge of the experimenter's interest in making comparisons among the three different shape columns. As far as the **Data Editor** is concerned, the data comprise **three dependent variables**. Later, we shall see that some statistical commands such as **Repeated Measures ANOVA** can be informed that the three variables are to be treated, not as separate dependent variables, but as comprising a single (within subjects) treatment factor with three levels.

After entering the variable names in **Variable View**, click the **Data View** tab and enter the data in the variable columns (Figure 13).

	case	triangle	circle	square
1	1	220	300	260
2	2	250	290	300
3	3	260	280	290

Figure 13. Part of Data View showing the first three cases of the within subjects data

Entering data with between subjects and within subjects variables

Data from an experiment with **both between subjects variables and within subjects factors** is entered in **Data View** as a combination of the procedures illustrated in this Section and those in Sections 3.2.4 and 3.2.5. For example, if the participants for the Recognition of Patterns experiment had been coded for sex, then all that would be required is an extra column for the variable *sex* with a code such as *1* for Males and *2* for Females (Figure 14).

	case	sex	triangle	circle	square
1	1	Male	220	300	260
2	2	Female	250	290	300
3	3	Female	260	280	290

Figure 14. Part of Data View showing the first three cases for a between subjects variable (sex) and the three levels of a within subjects variable

3.3 EDITING DATA

The **Data Editor** offers a range of functions, some of which are extremely useful, not only for amending data that are already in the **Data Editor**, but also for inputting data values that are to be repeated many times.

Notation

We shall adopt a notation for selecting items from a drop-down menu by showing the sequence of selections on successive lines with an indentation. Thus selecting the **Copy** item from the **Edit** drop-down menu will be shown as

Edit
>   **Copy**

Changing individual values

Enter a few numbers in **Data View**. Any of these can be changed at will by targeting the cell concerned with the black rectangle, typing a new value and pressing a cursor key or ↵ .

Blocking, copying and pasting

Initially, only one cell in **Data View** is highlighted. However, it is possible to highlight a whole row, column or block of cells. This **blocking** operation (when all the cells appear in inverse video i.e. the characters in white against a black background) is achieved very simply, either by clicking-and-dragging with the mouse or by proceeding as follows:

- A row or column: click a row number or a variable name and the whole row or column will then be highlighted.

- Block of cells in a column: highlight the first of the cells in the block with the cursor and clicking (or by moving the highlighting with the cursor keys), press and hold the **Shift** key, and then press the ↓ cursor key several times until the desired block has been highlighted. It will be seen that the whole block is now highlighted: the original cell and the new ones below.

The blocking operation can be used to copy the values in one column into another or to place them elsewhere in the same column.

- Highlight a column of values that you wish to copy and then choose
  Edit
  > **Copy**
- Next, highlight the cells of the target column and then choose
  Edit
  > **Paste**

The values in the source column will now appear in the target column. (Make sure that the number of highlighted target cells is equal to the number of cells copied.)

As an example, the repeated values 1, 2, 3 used for identifying the Mnemonic Training Method group could have been entered by using this copy-and-paste method.

- To enter the first (unshaded) column of values of Table 2 into the window, place the value *1* in the first (topmost) cell of the second column *group*. Move the black rectangle away from the cell to store the value and then return the highlight to the cell that now contains the value *1*.
- Choose
  Edit
  > **Copy**
  and highlight cells 2 to 10 in the second column using the **Shift** and downward cursor keys, or click-and-drag.

- It will be found that on choosing
  Edit
  > **Paste**,
  the value *1* will appear in each of the highlighted cells.
- Target the 11th cell in the second column and enter the value *2* in that cell.
- Proceed as above to enter the value *2* in all of the cells from 12 to 20, inclusive.
- In similar fashion, enter the value *3* in each of the cells from 21 to 30, inclusive.

Deletion of values

To delete the values in a cell (or block):
- Highlight the area concerned and press the **Delete** key.
- To delete a whole row of values, click the grey box containing the row number. This will highlight every cell in the row. Pressing the **Delete** key will remove the whole row from **Data View**.
- Similarly, clicking the grey box containing the name of a column will highlight all the cells in the column, and pressing the **Delete** key will remove the entire column of values from **Data View**.
- A variable can also be deleted from **Variable View** in the same manner.

Inserting additional variables and cases, and changing the order of variables

Additional variables (i.e. new columns) and additional cases (i.e. new rows) can always be added on to the present data set at the right and foot respectively. However, it is sometimes convenient to insert a new variable beside an existing variable within a large data set or to insert a new case (e.g. an additional male) at the end of a block of cases rather than at the foot of the entire data set. It can also be convenient to change the positions of variables so that certain variables are adjacent to one another.

All these operations are easily achieved in **Data View** as follows:
- Highlight the variable to the right of the position desired for the new variable or highlight the case above which the desired new case is to be inserted.
- Choose the **Data** drop-down menu and then select the appropriate item (**Insert Variable** or **Insert Case**). A blank column or a blank row will then be created.
- If a variable is to be moved to this new column, highlight the existing variable, select

  Edit
  >**Cut**

  and highlight the new column.
- Finally select

  Edit
  >**Paste**.

  The variable will then be pasted into its new position.

It is also possible to insert new variables in **Variable View**.
- Click the row number to highlight the whole row above which the new variable is to be inserted.
- Select

  Data
  >**Insert Variable**

  and a new variable with a name such as *var00001* will appear and displace all the remaining rows down one place.

3.4   SAVING AND RETRIEVING SPSS FILES

3.4.1 Saving a file

Suppose that we now have the results of the Recall of Verbal Material experiment in the **Data Editor**. We want to save this data set to a file named *learning*, and to store that file in a folder called *spssdata* on the hard disk (Drive C). It will be necessary to create this folder either through Windows using the **My Computer** icon or more directly from the SPSS **Save Data As** dialog box (to be described shortly). Alternatively, the user may wish to use an existing folder or save directly to a floppy disk in Drive A.

It is not good practice to save to the default folder *spss10* because this is used for several purposes and may be deleted if a new version of SPSS is installed. In some networked systems, *spss10* may be unavailable for storing files.

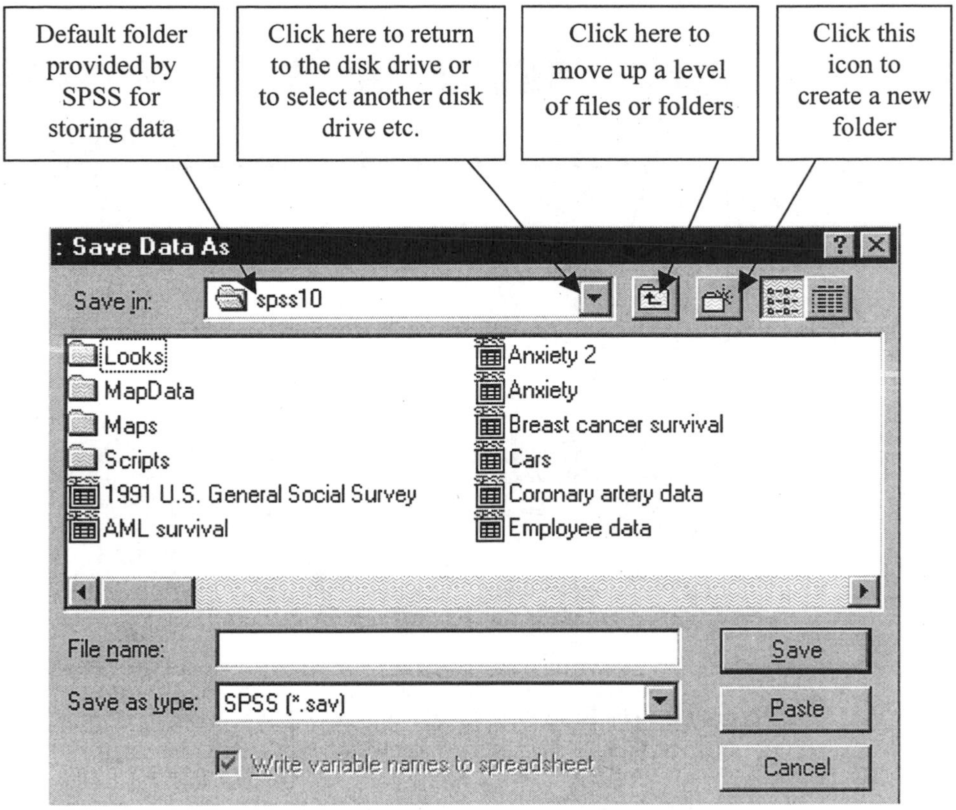

Figure 15. The Save Data As dialog box

- To save this data set as a data file, choose from the menu bar
  File
    Save as...
  to bring the **Save Data as** dialog box to the screen (Figure 15).
  There are three pieces of information that this dialog is looking for:
    (1) The *location* at which the file is to be saved (i.e. the **Save in:** box at the top).
    (2) The file's *name* (i.e. the **File name:** box near the bottom).
    (3) The *type* of file (i.e. the **Save as type:** box at the bottom).
- In the uppermost central rectangle is the default location folder *spss10* which is provided with the SPSS software. We recommend saving files to a different folder, either another existing one or one specially created for the purpose using the icon 🗁 to the right of the **Save in:** box. To find another existing folder (e.g. *spss10 data*), click ▼ to the right of *spss10,* moving up to the higher level (possibly a disk drive such as **Hard Disk (C:)**), and then select the desired folder. If the user wants to create a new folder for data within the higher level, click the icon 🗁 and then type in the desired name (e.g. *spss10 data*) in place of the words **New Folder** and then click **Save**.
- Click the desired folder for the file (e.g. *spss10 data*) and the original folder *spss10* will be replaced with the new folder - see Figure 16.
- Name the file by typing, in the **File name:** box, the name *learning* - see Figure 16.

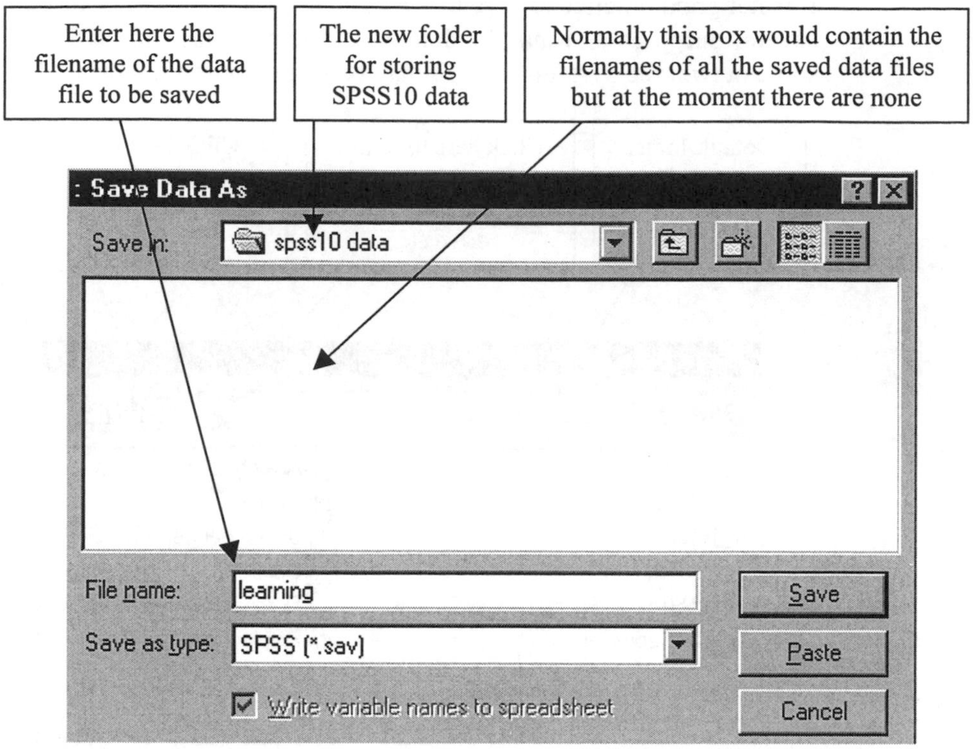

Enter here the filename of the data file to be saved

The new folder for storing SPSS10 data

Normally this box would contain the filenames of all the saved data files but at the moment there are none

Figure 16. The Save Data As dialog box with the new folder *spss10 data* located for storing the new data file called *learning*

- In the **Save as Type** rectangle at the bottom, the specification is the default **SPSS (*.sav)**. This choice will save the data in the form that preserves all the specifications of the data given to the **Data Editor** by the user.
- Click the **Save** button. The title in **Data View** and in **Variable View** will change from **Untitled** to *learning*.

Had the user wished to save the file to a floppy disk instead, it would have been necessary to change the drive in **Save in:** box to **3½ Floppy (A:)** using the arrow ▣ to the right of the box to open the choice of locations, the upward arrow to move up to **3½ Floppy (A:)**. Click this to paste it into the **Save in:** box.

The **Save Data As** dialog box is an example of a **directory dialog box**. Once a folder has several files in it, a list of those filenames will appear in the large white box. Similar boxes appear in all operations involving the saving or accessing of files or folders, and appear (in one form or another) whenever the user is working with any kind of SPSS material, whether data, output listings or command syntax. In the lowest box is a second directory dialog box **Save as Type** showing the data specification as **SPSS (*.sav)**. The new file will be saved as a SPSS data file with the extension .sav, and will be recognised as such by SPSS in future. If you click ▣ to the right of **SPSS (*.sav)**, you will see other specifications, such as **SPSS Portable Data [*.por]** , **Tab-delimited Data [*.dat]** , **Excel [*.xls]** and so on. These would save an SPSS data file that could be read by other SPSS versions, other applications, and an EXCEL spreadsheet respectively.

Saving other types of SPSS files

The **Save As** command is also used to save other kinds of SPSS material such as output and command syntax. Only the file extension will change.

Backing up files

It is often advisable to back up important files on floppy disk, especially if the user's computer is in a network. There are two ways of doing this:

(1)   Using the **Save As** dialog box a second time but this time nominating the location for the file as **3½ Floppy (A:)** and re-saving the file *learning* there.

(2)   After shutting down SPSS, return to the **Windows Explorer** (see Chapter 2, Section 2.4) and copy the file from the hard disk to the floppy disk.

3.4.2   Reading in SPSS files

As we saw at the end of Chapter 2 in Section 2.5.3, reading an SPSS data file into **Data View** is simplicity itself.

• When the opening SPSS window appears, select **Open an existing data source** in the **What would you like to do?** dialog box (Chapter 2, Figure 9).

• Select the appropriate file (it may be necessary in networked computers to click **More files ...** and locate the file or folder containing the file).

• Click **OK** to load the data file into **Data View**.

Alternatively, one of the following methods can be used:

• Click the radio button of the opening SPSS window labelled **Type in data** and then **OK** to bring **Data View** to the screen. Then select

> **File**
> > **Open**
> > > **Data**

to open the **Open File** dialog box. The target file can then be specified.

• If SPSS has not yet been opened, either locate the file using the Windows **Find** menu or the **My Computer** icon and double-click it: SPSS will automatically open with the data loaded in **Data View**. While data are being read into **Data View** from a file, the hour-glass will appear and messages will appear in the **Status Bar** at various stages in the operation. The message **SPSS Processor is ready** signals the end of the procedure.

3.4.3   Importing and exporting data

It is possible to import data from other applications or platforms such as Microsoft Excel and SPSS for Macintosh. It is also possible to import ASCII tab-delimited files, with values separated by tabulation symbols or fixed format files with variables recorded in the same column locations for each case.

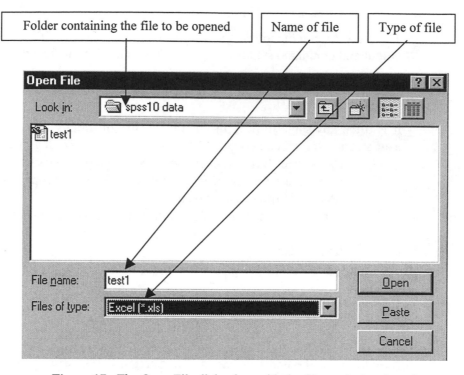

Figure 17. The Open File dialog box with the file test1.xls selected
in the folder spss10 data

For example, to import the **Excel** file called *test1.xls* stored in the folder *spss10 data*:

- Choose **File**
- Click **Open** to obtain the **Open File** dialog box and select the appropriate **Look in** folder (Figure 17).
- Click the directory of file types in the **Files of type:** box and highlight **Excel (*.xls)**.
- A list of files with the **.xls** extension will then appear in the white box above. Click the appropriate file and its name will appear in the **File name:** box.
- Click **Open** to open the **Opening File Options** dialog box (Figure 18). Turn on the check box for **Read variable names** in order to transfer the Excel variable names into the SPSS **Data Editor**.

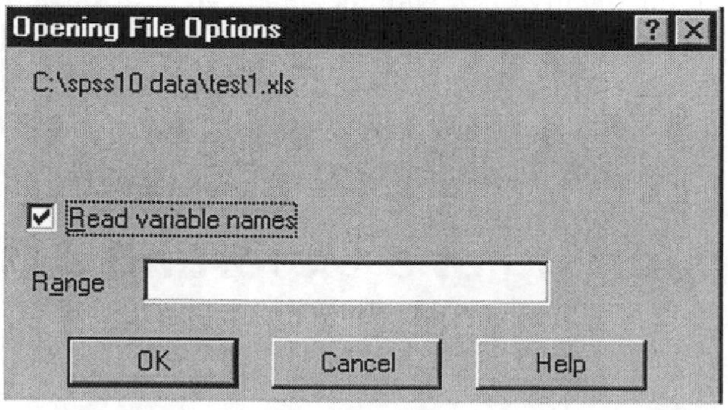

Figure 18. The Opening File Options dialog box with Read variable names selected

- If an error message appears stating that SPSS cannot load an Excel worksheet, it may be necessary to return to Excel and re-save the file in a different version of Excel or to copy and paste columns of data - see below.
- Click **OK** to transfer the file into SPSS. **Variable View** will list the variable names and their types, and **Data View** will show the transferred data and variable names (Figure 19).
- The file can then be saved as a SPSS data file.

	A	B	C	D			name	sex	age	score
1	**Name**	**Sex**	**Age**	**Score**	1	Brown, G	m	25.00	87.00
2	Brown, G	m	25	87	2	Green, F	m	18.00	78.00
3	Green, F	m	18	78	3	Mason, P	f	23.00	100.00
4	Mason, P	f	23	100	4	Sampson, G	m	24.00	67.00
5	Sampson, G	m	24	67	5	Winston, P	f	20.00	50.00
6	Winston, P	f	20	50						

Figure 19. Transfer of the Excel file (left) to SPSS (right)

It is also possible to copy columns of data from an Excel file by highlighting the data (but not the column headings), selecting **Copy** from the Excel **Edit** menu and then pasting them into **Data View** with **Paste** from the SPSS **Edit** menu. The variables can then be named in the usual manner within **Variable View**. If the Excel columns contain string material (e.g. names), change the **Type** of the SPSS column to **String** in **Variable View** before pasting. Other types of file can be transferred in a similar manner.

SPSS data can be exported in a format compatible with another application or platform by saving the file in a wide range of formats, such as **SPSS portable (*.por)**, before it is exported. Full details of importing and exporting files are available in the **Help** facility.

3.5 LISTING DATA

3.5.1 SPSS Viewer

All SPSS output (lists, tables, charts and graphs) appears in a single window, called the **SPSS Viewer**, consisting of two panes (Figure 20). The bar dividing the panes can be moved leftwards or rightwards to enlarge one or other pane by clicking-and-dragging it.

The left-hand pane lists the items of output in order of their appearance in the right-hand pane, each item having an icon and a title. The icon shows whether the item is visible (open-book icon) or invisible (closed-book icon). By double-clicking the icon, the item can be made visible or invisible in the right-hand pane, where all output is presented in full. The output can also be rearranged by moving the appropriate icons around in the left-hand pane by clicking-and-dragging them. A single click on an item in the left-hand pane will bring the item into view in the right-hand pane. It is also possible to delete unwanted items by highlighting them in the left-hand pane and pressing the **Delete** key. In this book, only selections from the right-hand pane will normally be reproduced.

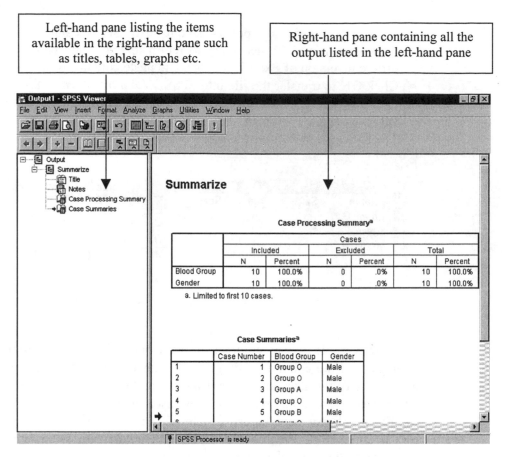

Figure 20. The SPSS Viewer showing the left-hand pane listing the items presented in the right-hand pane

The right-hand pane contains the titles, tables of data and statistics, charts and graphs. A feature of SPSS output is the ease with which it can be edited to improve the layout of materials in tables or to remove items which the user may not wish to reproduce in a document. After double-clicking anywhere within a boxed item, the item will be surrounded by a hatched box indicating that its contents can be edited (Figure 21).

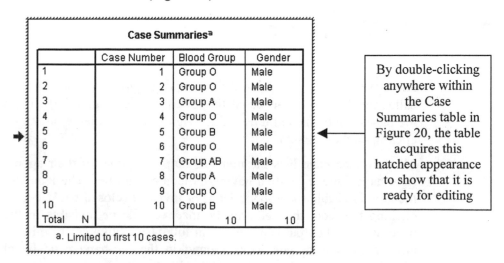

Figure 21. The table of Case Summaries made ready for editing by double-clicking anywhere within it

The arrow to the left of the hatched box in Figure 21 indicates that this item has been selected. Notice in Figure 20 that this arrow is also present to the left of the Case Summaries table in the right-hand pane as well as to the left of the Case Summaries icon in the left-hand pane.

Once a selected item is surrounded by a hatched box, the following editing changes can be made:

- To widen or narrow columns, move the cursor on to a vertical line in the table: a double arrow appears and it is then possible to slide the line sideways by clicking-and-dragging it.
- Items can be deleted by highlighting them and pressing the **Delete** key.
- Whole columns or rows can be deleted by highlighting them and pressing the **Delete** key.
- Text can be altered by double-clicking an item and deleting letters or typing in new ones.
- If values are listed, it is possible to alter the number of decimal places shown by highlighting the affected numbers in a block, pressing the right-hand mouse button, selecting the item **Cell Properties...** and making the appropriate change within the **Cell Properties** dialog box.

Several of the SPSS tables reproduced in this and later chapters have been edited in this manner. Much the best way of learning how to move around and use the **SPSS Viewer** is to choose:

Help
> **Tutorial**

and double-click to open the tutorial menu.

3.5.2 Case summaries

It is sometimes convenient to be able to list the data for a particular variable (or perhaps a few variables) rather than having to scan a particular column (or columns) in **Data View**. For example, although two variables may be several columns apart in **Data View**, the user might wish to see them side-by-side. Let us assume that a data set consisting of two quantitative variables *weight* and *height*, and two qualitative variables *sex* and *blood* (representing a person's blood group), has already been set up in **Data View** and you want to list only *sex* and *blood*.

- Choose
  Analyze
  > **Reports**
  >> **Case Summaries...**
  to open the **Summarize Cases** dialog box (the completed version is shown in Figure 22) to indicate which variables are to be listed.
- Select the variables of interest (here they are *sex* and *blood*) by clicking each variable name and then on ▶ to enter it into the **Variables** box.
- For illustrative purposes, we have chosen to list only the first ten cases by activating the **Limit cases to first** option and inserting *10* in the box.
- Click the check-box **Show case numbers** so as to include case numbers in the output.
- Click **OK**.

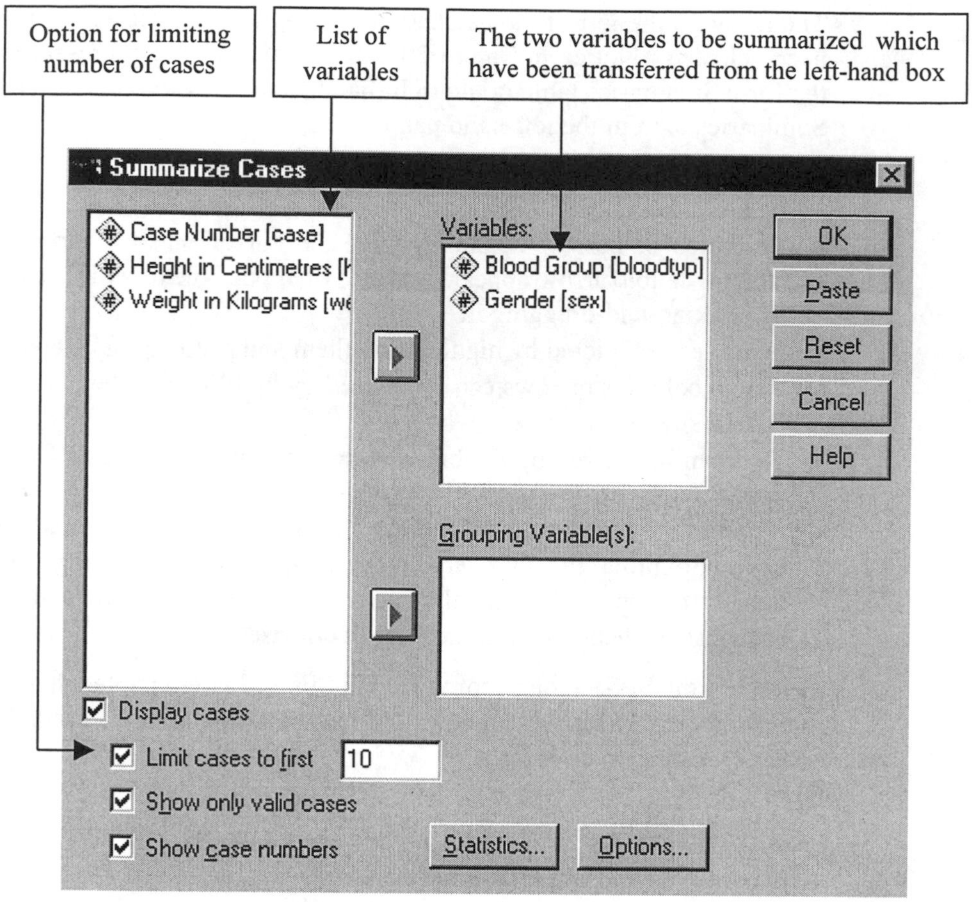

| Option for limiting number of cases | List of variables | The two variables to be summarized which have been transferred from the left-hand box |

Summarize Cases

Case Number [case]
Height in Centimetres [h
Weight in Kilograms [we

Variables:
Blood Group [bloodtyp]
Gender [sex]

OK
Paste
Reset
Cancel
Help

Grouping Variable[s]:

☑ Display cases
☑ Limit cases to first 10
☑ Show only valid cases
☑ Show case numbers

Statistics...   Options...

Figure 22. The Summarize Cases dialog box for Blood Group and Sex

The output is shown in Output 1.

Case Summaries [a]

	Case Number	Blood Group	Gender
1	1	Group O	Male
2	2	Group O	Male
3	3	Group A	Male
4	4	Group O	Male
5	5	Group B	Male
6	6	Group O	Male
7	7	Group AB	Male
8	8	Group A	Male
9	9	Group O	Male
10	10	Group B	Male
Total N		10	10

a. Limited to first 10 cases.

Output 1. Blood Group and Gender for the first 10 cases

The same command can be used for listing measurement variables (in this example *height* and *weight*) with the option of choosing some descriptive statistics (by clicking the **Statistics...** button). The statistics will be printed at the foot of the column for each variable.

3.5.3 Displaying data file information

It is useful to be able to see details of the variables in a data file (particularly a large one) such as their names, types, values and value labels. In the case of a file already in the **Data Editor**, this can be readily done by inspecting **Variable View**. To obtain a printed version, choose

Utilities
> **File Info...**

Details of the variables will immediately be listed in **SPSS Viewer** from where it can be printed though it may be necessary to resize the font and check the positions of page breaks.

In the case of a stored file not currently displayed in the **Data Editor**, choose

- **File**
  > **Display Data Info...**
  and select the appropriate file name from the **Display Data Info** dialog box.
- Click **Open** to implement the command, whose edited output (again resizing of the font and adjustment of page breaks may be needed - check by inspecting **Print Preview**) for the Blood Group data is shown in Output 2.

```
Total # of Defined Variable Elements: 5
# of Named Variables: 5
Data Are Not Weighted
Variable Information:
Name                                                       Position

CASE       Case Number                                        1
           Measurement level: Scale
           Format: F8  Column Width: 8  Alignment: Right
BLOODTYP   Blood Group                                        2
           Measurement level: Scale
           Format: F8  Column Width: 8  Alignment: Right
           Value     Label
               1        Group A
               2        Group B
               3        Group AB
               4        Group O
SEX        Gender                                             3
           Measurement level: Scale
           Format: F8  Column Width: 8  Alignment: Right
           Value     Label
               1        Male
               2        Female
HEIGHT     Height in Centimetres                              4
           Measurement level: Scale
           Format: F8  Column Width: 8  Alignment: Right
WEIGHT     Weight in Kilograms                                5
           Measurement level: Scale
           Format: F8  Column Width: 8  Alignment: Right
```

Output 2. Part of the output from Display Data Info for the Blood Group data file

The information in Output 2 includes the following:
- None of the variables was weighted (weighting is explained in Section 3.7.2).

- All the variables are Scale variables with up to eight non-decimal places and are aligned to the right margin.
- The variable BLOODTYP representing Blood Group has four defined values, together with their value names.
- The variable SEX has two defined values, together their value names.
- The other variables are CASE, WEIGHT and HEIGHT.

3.6 PRINTING IN SPSS

It is always reassuring to have a hard copy of important computer output. For example, after a series of complicated editing operations, the user may wish to print out **Data View** (in the present case, the data file *C:\spss10 data\Ch3 blood.sav*) to have a permanent record of the finalised data set but beware of the amount of paper which might be used for printing out a very large data set. It may be necessary to check that a suitable printer is connected to the computer (or to the network) by inspecting the information within the **Printer Setup** by choosing

File

    Print...

to open the **Print** dialog box (Figure 23). The appearance of the dialog will vary depending on the types of printers available. If there is a choice of printer, then clicking ▼ to the right of the **Name** box will reveal the list of available printers.

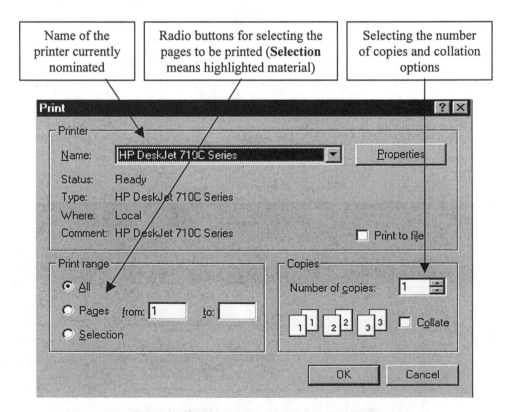

Figure 23. The Print dialog box for controlling the printing operation

70

The properties (e.g. the size and source of paper, or its orientation (portrait or landscape) can be changed if necessary by clicking the **Properties** box and changing the items in a number of dialog boxes selected by clicking various tabs.

Before finally giving the print command, it is advisable to look at the **Printer Preview** by choosing
File
     Print Preview

in order to see where the page breaks occur. Details of how to insert or remove page breaks will be given in Chapter 4 when we have more extensive output available for printing.

After checking that the right printer has been selected with the appropriate facilities (e.g. size of paper, orientation of image), make a selection from the **Print range** radio buttons (the default **All** is most often used). Extra copies can be selected by changing **Number of copies**. Finally click **OK**.

Bear in mind that only the contents of the **active** window will be printed: if the data set is to be printed out, the **Data Editor** must be active. Similarly, if part of the **SPSS Viewer** (i.e. the output) is to be printed, the **SPSS Viewer** window must be active. A window can be activated by clicking anywhere on it, or by selecting the appropriate window title from the **Window** drop-down menu.

If only parts of the output are to be printed, ensure that the relevant parts have been selected by holding down the **Ctrl** key and clicking the item titles in the left-hand pane of the **SPSS Viewer** so that all the relevant items are shown in the right-hand pane with boxes around them.

Printing out a selection from the data set

To print out only selected parts of the data set, use the click-and-drag method to define the target sections by blackening them. This requires a little practice; but it will be found that when the screen pointer touches the lower border of the window, the latter will scroll down to extend the blackened area to the desired extent. If the pointer touches the right border, the window will scroll to the right across the **Data Editor**. When the **Print** dialog box (Figure 23) appears, the marker will now be on **Selection**. Click **OK** to obtain a hard copy of the selected areas.

3.7   SOME SPECIAL OPERATIONS

So far, the emphasis has been upon the construction of a complete data set, the saving of that set to a file on disk, and its retrieval from storage. There are occasions, however, on which the user will want to operate selectively on the data. It may be, for instance, that only some of the rows comprising a data set are of interest (those contributed by the participants in one category alone, perhaps); or the user may wish to exclude participants with outlying values on specified variables. In this section, some of these more specialised manoeuvres will be described.

Transformation and recoding of data will be discussed in Chapter 4.

3.7.1 Case selection

Let us assume that we have the data of the Recall of Verbal Material experiment in **Data View**: there are three variables, *case*, *group* and *score*. Suppose, for example, that we want to analyse only the data from the two mnemonic groups (i.e. exclude the control group) from the experiment presented.

- Choose

    Data

    Select Cases...

    to **Select Cases** dialog box (see Figure 24). Obtain the **Select Cases: If** dialog box as shown.

Variable labels and names (in brackets) as specified in **Variable View**. To read hidden material, move the cursor on to the label	Select this radio button to activate the **If...** button and then click on it to open the **Select Cases: If** dialog box (Figure 25)

Select Cases

- Case Number [case]
- Mnemonic Training Me
- Number of words recal

Select
- ⦿ All cases
- ○ If condition is satisfied
    - [If...]
- ○ Random sample of cases
    - [Sample...]
- ○ Based on time or case range
    - [Range...]
- ○ Use filter variable:
    - [▶] [   ]

Unselected Cases Are
- ⦿ Filtered   ○ Deleted

Current Status: Do not filter cases

[OK] [Paste] [Reset] [Cancel] [Help]

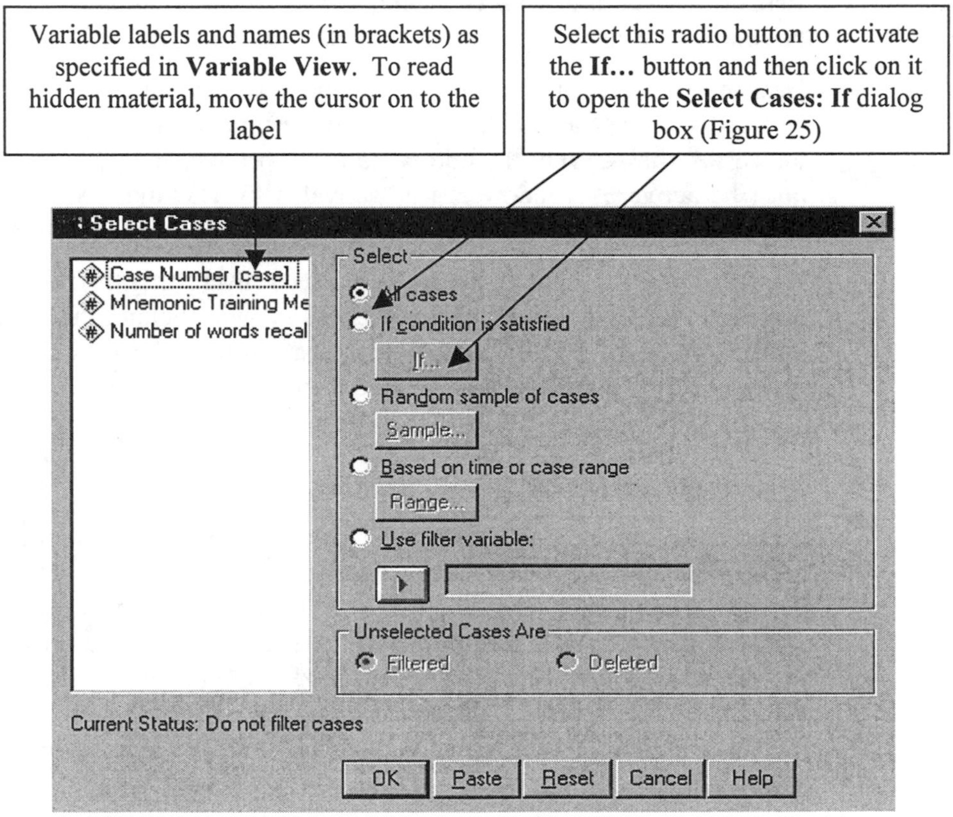

Figure 24. The Select Cases dialog box

- Complete the **Select Cases: If** dialog box as shown in Figure 25.
- If any variable label and variable name is partially hidden, it is easily seen in full by moving the cursor on to it, thus:

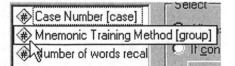

- When the conditional expression has been completed (Figure 25), click **Continue** and then **OK** to return to **Data View**, where it will be noticed that a new column labelled **filter_$** to the right of the other columns has appeared, containing the words *Not Selected* and *Selected* (Figure 26). If the

Value Labels option in the **View** menu is not ticked, *1*s and *0*s, will replace *Selected* and *Not Selected*.

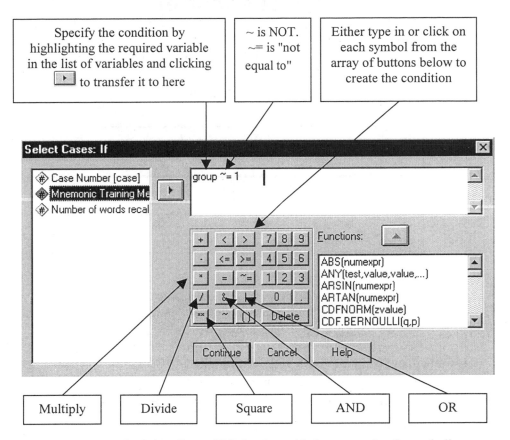

Figure 25. The Select Cases: If dialog box with the expression for excluding group 1 from the variable group

- The row numbers of the unselected cases have also been marked with an oblique bar. This is a useful indicator of **case selection status.** The status bar (if enabled at the foot of **Data View**) will carry the message **Filter On.** Any further analyses of the data set will exclude the cases within group 0.

	case	group	score	filter_$
8	8	Control	3	Not Selected
9	9	Control	8	Not Selected
10	10	Control	10	Not Selected
11	11	Mnemonic A	10	Selected
12	12	Mnemonic A	8	Selected
13	13	Mnemonic A	15	Selected

The oblique bars shows deselected cases

Figure 26. Part of Data View showing some of the deselected cases

Although filter_$ will then be listed as a variable in dialog boxes, it should not be selected.

The case selection can be cancelled as follows:
- Select the **Select Cases** dialog box and click **All cases**.
- Click **OK**.

3.7.2 The weighting of cases by their frequencies of occurrence

Suppose that fifty women and fifty men are asked whether they disapprove of a popular, but violent, television programme. Their responses can be summarised in what is known as a **contingency table** (Table 4).

	Disapprove	
Sex	**Yes**	**No**
Female	30	20
Male	10	40

Table 4. A contingency table

The purpose of constructing a contingency table is to bring out whatever relationship there may be between two qualitative or nominal variables. In the present example, the qualitative variables are Sex (Male and Female) and Disapprove (Yes and No). It is clear from Table 4 that there is indeed a relationship between the two variables: a markedly higher proportion of the female respondents disapproved of the programme.

As with the Mnemonic Training Method data in Table 1, a contingency table must be recast to make it suitable for entry into SPSS. Earlier, it was said that SPSS expects a data set in the form of a matrix whose rows are participants and whose columns are variables. Clearly, the arrangement of the data in Table 4 does not conform to this requirement: the two columns represent values of the same variable; and a row represents the responses of several participants.

The solution is to create two grouping variables (one for Sex and the other for Disapprove) and a third variable for cell frequencies as shown in Table 5.

Table 5. Recasting the data in Table 4 for entry into SPSS

Sex	**Disapprove**	**Cell Frequencies**
Female	Yes	30
Female	No	20
Male	Yes	10
Male	No	40

This meets the requirement that each column in **Data View** will relate to a single variable. In the present case, however, it must still be made clear to SPSS that the cell frequencies are not simply scores (compare the grouping variable and score variable used in Table 2 for the Mnemonic Training Method experiment) but represent the number of participants for each combination of the grouping variable levels. This is achieved by using **Weight Cases...** which will be described later.

To enter the data in Table 5, first specify the variables in **Variable View**:

- Name the first variable *sex* and assign the code values (*1* and *2*) with the labels *Female* and *Male* respectively in the **Values** column. Change the number of decimals to 0 in the **Decimals** column.
- Name the second variable *disapp* and assign the code values (*1* and *2*) with the labels *Yes* and *No* respectively in the **Values** column. Change the number of decimals to 0 in the **Decimals** column and add the variable label *Disapprove* in the **Label** column.
- Name the third variable *freq* and change the number of decimals to 0 in the **Decimals** column.

After specifying the variables in **Variable View**, click the **Data View** tab and enter the appropriate values and frequencies in **Data View**, thus

	sex	disapp	freq
1	Female	Yes	30
2	Female	No	20
3	Male	Yes	10
4	Male	No	40

Inspection of the data might suggest that they consist of two females and two males with one of each sex disapproving and approving of something, and scoring 30, 20, 10 and 40 respectively on something called *freq*. Actually, there are 30 disapproving females, 20 approving females, 10 disapproving males and 40 approving males. So how is SPSS to know this? The answer is to use **Weight Cases...** within the **Data** drop-down menu. The weighting of cases is an essential preliminary to the analysis of nominal data in the form of contingency tables, which is as described in Chapter 11.

To do this:

- Choose
  Data
  > **Weight Cases...**
  to open the **Weight Cases** dialog box.
- Follow the steps shown in Figure 27.
- Click **OK** to run the command.

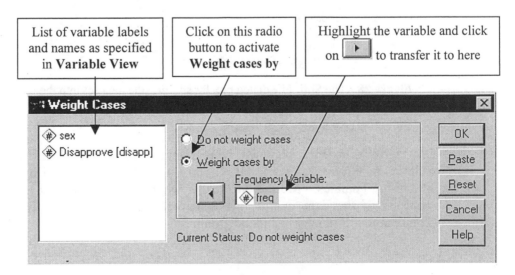

Figure 27. The Weight Cases dialog box weighting the cases by the variable *freq*

3.7.3 Splitting files

It is sometimes convenient to split a file by the levels of a grouping variable (or by combinations of more than one grouping variable) so that any subsequent exploratory data analysis or statistical analysis is conducted automatically on each level (or combinations of levels) separately. For example, the blood group data could be split by the levels of Gender and Blood Group.

*   Choose
    Data
        Split File...
    to obtain the **Split File** dialog box.
*   Follow the steps explained in Figure 28.
*   Click **OK** to complete the command.

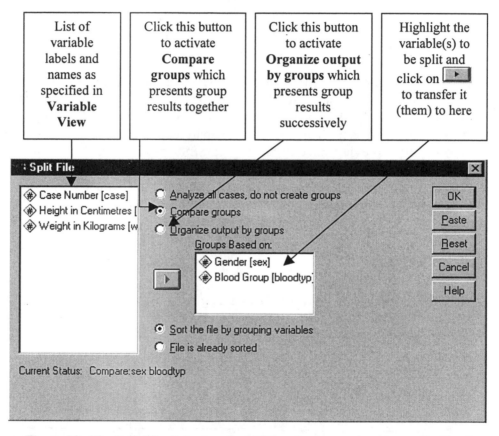

Figure 28. The Split File dialog box for splitting the data set into the two levels of Gender and the four levels of Blood Group

All the rows in **Data View** will be rearranged into blocks of each blood group (Group A, Group B, Group AB, Group O) for Males followed by each blood group for Females. More dramatically, when SPSS carries out any statistical analysis of the data in this file, there will be a separate analysis for each combination of gender and blood group.

3.8 COPYING SPSS DATA OR OUTPUT INTO OTHER APPLICATIONS (e.g. WORD PROCESSORS)

3.8.1 Copying data

See
Section
3.5.2

To copy data into a word processor such as WORD, use the procedure described in Section 3.5.2 to generate output which can then be copied using the steps described in the next Section.

3.8.2 Copying output

Output in the **SPSS Viewer** comes in two forms, tables and graphics. Pasting a graphic into another application is easier than pasting tables. However before copying any material from **SPSS Viewer**, it is advisable to edit it to remove any unnecessary columns or rows, to change legends or titles in graphics, or even to add titles using the procedure described in Section 3.5.1.

To copy an item of output, do the following:
- Ensure that the item of output in SPSS Viewer has a box around it by clicking the cursor anywhere within the table or graphic.
- Click **Copy** within **Edit**.
- Switch to the word processor and ensure that the cursor is located at the point where the item is to be positioned.
- If the item is a graphic, click **Paste**. The item can then be centred, enlarged or reduced by clicking it so that it acquires a box around it with the usual Windows tabs. To centre the box, click the centring icon. To enlarge or reduce the size of the graphic, drag one of the tabs in the appropriate direction.
- If the item is a table, click **Paste Special...** (if you click **Paste**, the table will be distorted) and when the **Paste Special** dialog box appears, select **Picture** and turn off the **Float over text** selection box. Click **OK**. When the table appears in the word processor, it can be centred, reduced or enlarged as described for a graphic.
- Alternatively in the case of a table, the **Formatted Text (RTF)** option in the **Paste Special** dialog box can be selected. The table can then be edited or formatted within the word processor (e.g. selecting a new font, a new font size, a new style of border, a shading for some of the boxes).

EXERCISE 2
QUESTIONNAIRE DATA

Introduction

Readers are strongly recommended to study Sections 2.5.1 and 3.2 before attempting this Exercise.

Exercises 2 to 7 are concerned with the preparation and entry of data into SPSS, and with various **exploratory data analysis (EDA)** procedures such as calculating descriptive statistics, drawing graphs, transforming and selecting data and so on. In this Exercise, the reader is asked to complete a short questionnaire and to enter the data from it into SPSS. In the next Exercise, this data will be merged with a larger data set, comprising the responses of 334 other people to the same questionnaire. Subsequently, the merged file will be used as the data set for the various EDA procedures described in later Exercises.

The questionnaire

Please complete the questionnaire below by entering the values or circling the appropriate options.

What is your age?		Years	
What is your sex?	Male 1	Female	2
What is your Faculty of study?	Arts 1	Science	2
	Medicine 3	Other	4
What is your status?	Undergraduate 1	MSc postgraduate	2
	PhD postgraduate 3	Other	4

What is your approximate weight? Use British or metric measures

British units	Stones	
	Pounds	
Metric units	Kilograms	

What is your approximate height? Use British or metric measures

British units	Feet	
	Inches	
Metric units	Metres (include two decimal places)	

Do you smoke?	Yes 1	No	2
		If so, how many a day?	

Opening SPSS

Log in to SPSS as described in Section 2.5.1. Select the radio button for **Type in data** from the opening SPSS window and click **OK**. If **Data View** appears first, click the **Variable View** tab to open **Variable View** as shown in Chapter 2, Figure 10 will then appear.

Entering the data into the Data Editor

As described in Sections 2.5.1 and 3.2, the task of entering data into SPSS includes two processes:

1. Within **Variable View**, specifying the variable name, variable type, optional value labels, and optional missing values for each variable in the data set (see especially Section 3.2.4).
2. Within **Data View**, entering the data into the named columns representing the variables previously specified in **Variable View** (see especially Section 3.2.5).

Normally variable names are a matter of individual preferences (provided they obey the rules given in Section 3.2.2) but here we have to take account of the fact that in the next Exercise, your data set will be merged with a much larger data set and this is much easier if both data sets have exactly the same **variable names** (though it is possible to change variable names prior to merging if it is discovered, for example, that one set uses the name *gender* and the other the name *sex* for males and females). It is also essential that you use the same **values** as in the larger data set (e.g. 1 for Male, 2 for Female). For this reason we ask you to use the following variable names and values:

case	(add a variable label Case Number - see below)
name	(specify it as a string variable - see below)
age	
sex	(add values and value labels: 1 for Male, 2 for Female - see below)
faculty	(add values and value labels: 1 for Arts, 2 for Science, 3 for Medicine, 4 for Other - see below)
status	(add values and value labels: 1 for Undergrad, 2 for MSc Postgrad, 3 for PhD postgrad, 4 for Other - see below)
stones	
pounds	
kilos	
feet	
inches	
metres	
smoker	(add values and value labels: 1 for Yes, 2 for No - see below)
npday	(add a variable label Number of Cigarettes per Day - see below)

Specify these variable names in the **Name** column of **Variable View** using the methods described in Section 3.2.4. Retain **numeric** format (the default type) for all the variables except *name* for which a **string** (i.e. alphanumeric - meaning letters and numbers) type is to be used. A string type is selected by clicking anywhere in the corresponding cell of the **Type** column and then clicking the three dots at the right-hand side to open the **Variable Type** dialog box. Select the **String** radio button and then click **OK** to return to **Variable View**. You should also expand the column labelled **Width** to, say, 20 and the column labelled **Columns** to, say, 20 to allow your name to be fully visible in **Data View** when you come to enter it.

Remember to assign the specified values and value labels when dealing with the numeric categorical variables *sex, faculty, status* and *smoker* in the **Values** column of **Variable View**. This will then allow you to enter numbers to indicate your sex, faculty, status and whether or not you smoke. (Incidentally, the assignation of value labels is not mandatory but it makes the interpretation of output tables, charts and graphs much easier, because items will be identified with the labels you have assigned. Labelling is also advantageous when you have a large data file, with many values assigned to a single variable.) It is also useful to include a fuller description of a variable in the **Label** column especially if the variable name is not very obvious (e.g. Case Number for *case*; Number of Cigarettes per Day for *npday*).

The data are much simpler to read if there are no decimals except for *metres* for which two decimal places will be required. Change the number in the **Decimals** column to 0 for all the variables except *metres* which should be 2. Note that, for those respondents giving their weights or heights in British units, two SPSS variables will be allocated to each measure: *stones* and *pounds* for weight, and *feet* and *inches* for height. Those responding in metric units will enter their data in the *kilos* and *metres* variables. In Exercise 5, we shall be transforming British Units into metric units so there is no need to worry about not knowing your metric measurements.

After specifying all the variables and their characteristics, click the **Data View** tab at the foot of **Variable View** to open **Data View**. Enter your data along the first row, putting a 1 for your *case*, typing in your name, age, a value for your sex, a value for your faculty and so on. For the variables with named values (e.g. sex, status), you will find that when you move into the appropriate cell with the → cursor key, the cell will appear as ☐☐☐☐☐ and clicking the arrow will show the choice of value names (e.g. for *sex* a box with Male and Female will appear) from which the desired selection can be made. Note that if you select **Value Labels** from the **View** drop-down menu in the Toolbar at the top of the screen, you can alternate between the actual values you have entered into **Data View** and the value labels you have assigned to them. If you do not smoke, do not enter anything in the *npday* column.

Saving the data

Once you have entered the data set and checked it for accuracy, select
File
     Save As
to obtain the **Save Data As** dialog box.

You then have to decide where the file is going to be saved (e.g. on the computer's own hard disk C, on a floppy disk in drive A, on a disk drive available on a networked system) and whether you want it to be saved in a folder such as **SPSSdata** which you might have to create beforehand by clicking the **Create New Folder** icon ☐ and typing in a name in the box alongside a folder icon. Having selected the appropriate drive and/or folder in the **Save in** box at the top of the **Save Data As** dialog box (if necessary, click ☐ at the right-hand end of the **Save in** box and select the drive, click it to open up a list of folders and finally click a folder icon so that its name is transferred to the **Save in** box), it remains to type a file name in the **File Name** box. We suggest you call the file *mydata*. Click **Save** to save your own questionnaire responses as the SPSS file *mydata*. You will be loading this file when you first open SPSS in the next Exercise.

Finishing the session

Close down SPSS and any other open windows before logging out of the computer.

CHAPTER 4

EXPLORATORY DATA ANALYSIS

4.1   INTRODUCTION

4.2   FINDING MENUS

4.3   DESCRIBING DATA

4.4   MANIPULATION OF THE DATA SET

4.1   INTRODUCTION

In recent years, statisticians have devised a set of statistical methods specially designed for the purpose of examining a data set. Together, they are known as **Exploratory Data Analysis (EDA)**. (For a readable account of EDA, see Howell, 1997). EDA has now found its way into all good statistical computing packages, including SPSS.

Suppose we have a set of measurements, say the heights in centimetres of a group of children. There are usually three things we want to know about such a data set:

(1)   the general **level**, or **average value**, of their heights;

(2)   the **dispersion** of height, i.e. the degree to which the individual scores tend to **vary** around or **deviate** from the average, as opposed to clustering closely around it;

(3)   the **distribution shape**, i.e. the relative frequencies with which heights are to be found in various regions of the total range of the variable.

We assume that the reader is familiar with the most common measures of level (the **mean**, the **median** and the **mode**) and of dispersion (the **standard deviation** and **quantile range** statistics). We also assume familiarity with terms relating to the distribution of the data set, such as **skewness**, **bimodality** and so on.

Different statistics are appropriate for data of different types: there is little point in finding the mean of a set of ranks, for example, because the resulting average would depend solely upon the number of people (or objects) in the sample. Should the reader be a little rusty on such matters, we strongly recommend that reading the relevant chapters of a good textbook on the topic, such as Gravetter & Wallnau (2000: chapters 1 to 4) or Howell (1997: chapters 1 and 2).

The influence of outliers and asymmetry of distribution

Statistics such as the mean and standard deviation are intended to express, in a single number, some characteristic of the data set as a whole: the former is intended to express the **average**, that is, the general level, typical value, or **central tendency**, of a set of scores; the latter is a measure of their **spread**, or **dispersion**. There are circumstances, however, in which the mean and standard deviation are very poor measures of central tendency and dispersion, respectively, as when the distribution of scores is markedly skewed, or when extreme values, or **outliers**, exert undue **leverage** upon the values of these statistics.

4.2 FINDING MENUS

Before considering the various exploratory statistical measures available on SPSS, it might be useful to remind the reader how to find the various menus, how to complete the dialog boxes, and how to amend the information that they contain.

In the **SPSS menu bar** are ten captioned drop-down menus:

| File | Edit | View | Data | Transform | Analyze | Graphs | Utilities | Window | Help |

Some items in the **Data Menu (Split File, Select Cases, Weight Cases)** have already been considered in Chapter 3. For this chapter, the relevant menus are **Transform, Analyze** and **Graphs** (Figure 1).

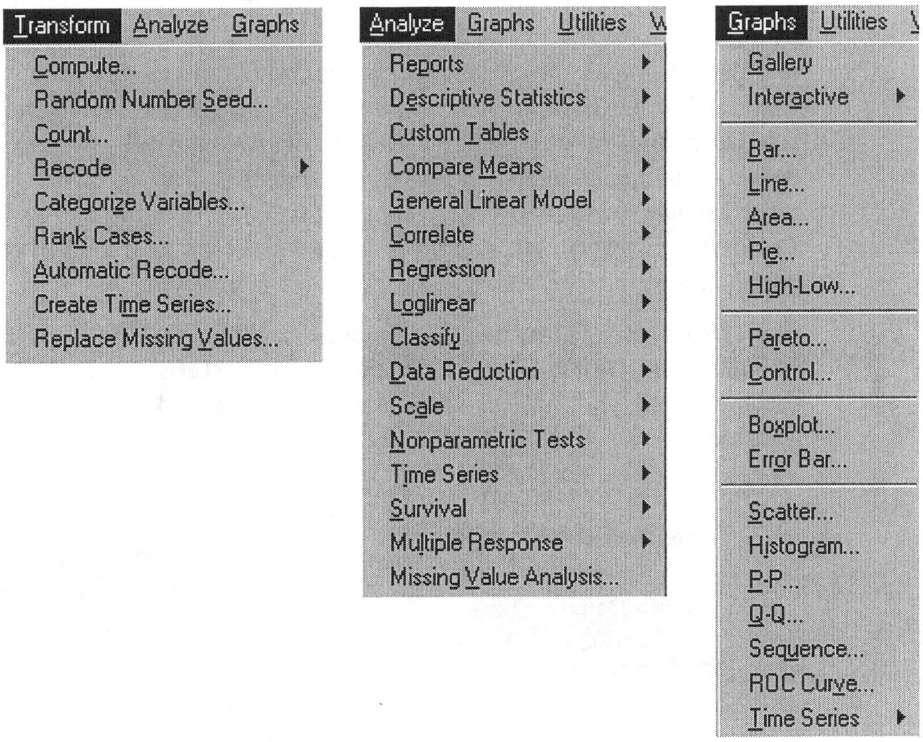

Figure 1. The Transform, Analyze and Graphs menus

In terms of exploring data, the most relevant submenus are those in **Analyze** and in **Graphs**. SPSS provides an abundance of overlapping choices for exploring data so it is not possible for a book of this type to cover all the possibilities for listing descriptive statistics or generating graphics. For example, many of the items in the **Analyze** menu include graphs and charts that are also available using the **Graphs** menu and there are several different ways of outputting descriptive statistics, some of which can be subdivided by categories of grouping variables (e.g. sex).

In the **Analyze** menu are **Reports, Descriptive Statistics, Custom Tables** and **Compare Means**. When the **Reports** or **Descriptive Statistics** are highlighted, the submenus shown in Figure 2 appear.

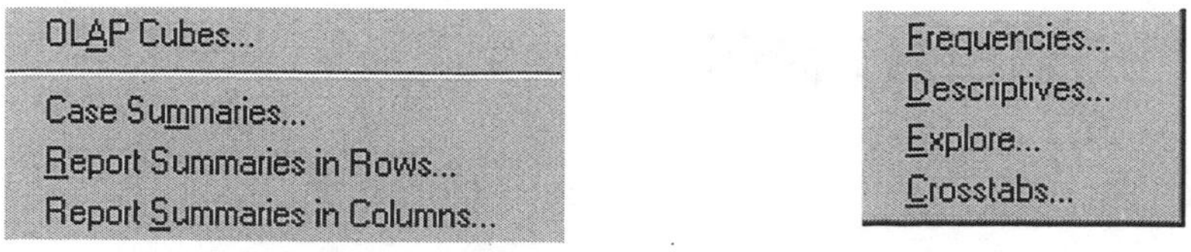

Figure 2. The submenus of Reports and Descriptive Statistics

The **Reports** submenu (left side of Figure 2) provides facilities for calculating various descriptive statistics of selected quantitative variables subdivided by categories of specified grouping variables. **OLAP Cubes** (Online Analytical Processing) initially outputs the selected statistics for selected quantitative variables summed across *all* categories of the grouping variables but the user can then select individual categories (or combinations of categories if there are two or more grouping variables) in the output in the **SPSS Viewer** and change the table of statistics accordingly. **Case Summaries** lists the values of selected quantitative variables for each case followed by a list of selected descriptive statistics for each combination of categories from selected grouping variables (e.g. for the data set of heights, weights, sex and blood group mentioned in Chapter 3, **Case Summaries** would list each height and weight for all males, all females and all cases with blood Group A followed by descriptive statistics such as the mean and standard deviation, and then the same for cases with each of the other blood groups, and finally for everyone). The output of **Row Summaries in Rows** or **Report Summaries in Columns** is not tabulated in boxes, so these commands are not recommended.

The **Descriptive Statistics** submenu (right side of Figure 2) includes **Frequencies, Descriptives, Explore,** and **Crosstabs.** All of these are highly recommended and will be described and illustrated in later sections of this Chapter.

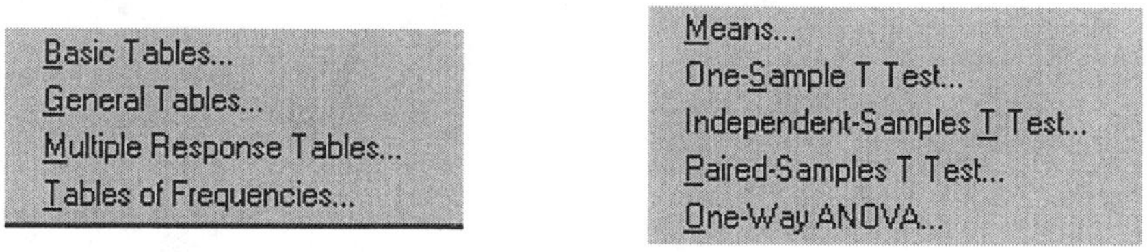

Figure 3. The submenus of Custom Tables and Compare Means

The **Custom Tables** submenu (left side of Figure 3) enables the user to display output in attractive tables, which can be pasted directly into reports of experiments or surveys. **Basic Tables** and **Tables of Frequencies** are particularly useful: they will be described and illustrated in later sections of this Chapter.

The **Compare Means** submenu (right side of Figure 3) contains just one item of relevance to exploring data, namely **Means**. This title is misleading because it can only be used for listing the means of variables subdivided by categories of grouping variables; other commands, such as one of the **Reports** or **Tables** items or **Descriptives** in the **Descriptive Statistics** menu, must be used for listing uncategorised means.

The items in the **Graphs** menu will form the material in the next Chapter, although we shall meet some of the items in this Chapter, since they are options that can be selected in several of the other exploratory commands.

Finally, in the **Transform** menu (Figure 4) there are several useful items which will be described and illustrated at the end of this Chapter.

```
Compute...
Random Number Seed...
Count...
Recode
Categorize Variables...
Rank Cases...
```

Figure 4. Useful items in the Transform menu

4.3   DESCRIBING DATA

The data that were introduced in Chapter 3 comprised two quantitative variables *weight* and *height*, and two qualitative variables *sex* and *bloodtyp*.   Let us assume the data have already been set up in **Data View** as shown in Table 1.

Table 1. The height, weight, sex and bloodgroup data

	bloodtyp	sex	height	weight		bloodtyp	sex	height	weight
1	Group O	Male	178	75	17	Group O	Female	163	60
2	Group O	Male	196	100	18	Group O	Female	142	51
3	Group A	Male	145	60	19	Group A	Female	150	55
4	Group O	Male	170	71	20	Group O	Female	165	64
5	Group B	Male	180	80	21	Group A	Female	160	53
6	Group O	Male	175	69	22	Group O	Female	175	50
7	Group AB	Male	185	78	23	Group O	Female	182	72
8	Group A	Male	190	90	24	Group B	Female	169	65
9	Group O	Male	183	70	25	Group O	Female	162	62
10	Group B	Male	182	85	26	Group B	Female	182	80
11	Group A	Male	170	72	27	Group O	Female	165	67
12	Group O	Male	160	77	28	Group A	Female	171	50
13	Group O	Male	170	95	29	Group O	Female	146	55
14	Group AB	Male	172	68	30	Group AB	Female	151	48
15	Group B	Male	190	120	31	Group O	Female	164	59
16	Group O	Male	180	75	32	Group B	Female	176	71

4.3.1   Describing nominal and ordinal data

Suppose we want to see the frequencies of the categories in the two grouping variables *sex* and *bloodtyp*. We might also want to see graphic representations of these such as a **bar chart** or **pie chart**. For measurements, such as heights or weights, we might want to see a **histogram**. There are several ways of obtaining such displays.

Frequencies (in **Descriptive Statistics**) gives frequency distributions for both nominal and ordinal data along with percentages and cumulative percentages. There are options for selecting graphics such as bar charts, pie charts and histograms. **General Tables** or **Tables of Frequencies** (in the **Custom Tables** menu), and **Crosstabs** (in the **Descriptive Statistics** menu) all provide a convenient two-way contingency table (e.g. rows of blood groups and columns of sex) but **Crosstabs** also supplies a column of totals. **Crosstabs** can also compute various statistics from contingency tables, such as **chi-square** and various **correlation coefficients**.

The following examples demonstrate the use of the descriptive statistics commands for Blood Group [*bloodtyp*] and Gender [*sex*].

- Choose
    Analyze
        Descriptive Statistics
            Frequencies...
    to open the **Frequencies** dialog box.
- Follow the steps shown in Figure 5.

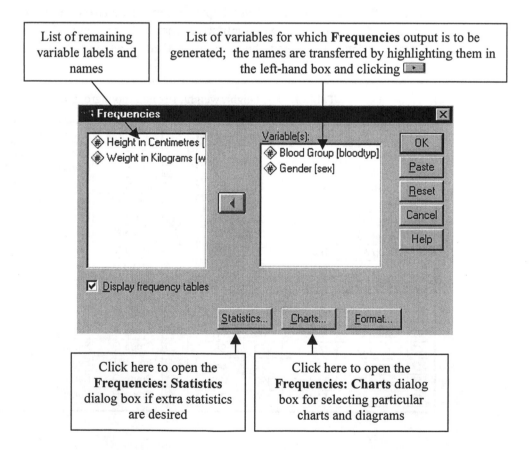

Figure 5. The Frequencies dialog box for blood group and gender

- Click **Charts** to obtain the **Frequencies: Charts** dialog box (Figure 6) and select the **Bar Chart(s)** radio button. There is also the choice of frequencies or percentages for the y axis in the **Chart Values** box.
- Click **Continue** to get back to **Frequencies** and then **OK**.

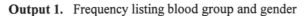

Figure 6. The Frequencies: Charts dialog box with Bar charts selected

The output consists of a couple of tables (Output 1) and the bar chart for Blood Group [*bloodtyp*] is shown in Output 2 (the bar chart for Gender has been omitted). Note that the bar chart can also be requested directly with the **Bar** item in the **Graphs** menu. It is possible to edit the bar chart to centre or change the axis labels, the title, the shading of the boxes and so on; more details about editing graphics will be given in the next chapter.

Blood Group

		Frequency	Percent	Valid Percent	Cumulative Percent
Valid	Group A	6	18.8	18.8	18.8
	Group B	6	18.8	18.8	37.5
	Group AB	3	9.4	9.4	46.9
	Group O	17	53.1	53.1	100.0
	Total	32	100.0	100.0	

Gender

		Frequency	Percent	Valid Percent	Cumulative Percent
Valid	Male	16	50.0	50.0	50.0
	Female	16	50.0	50.0	100.0
	Total	32	100.0	100.0	

Output 1. Frequency listing blood group and gender

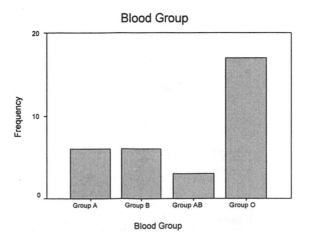

Output 2. Bar Chart for Blood Group

Contingency tables can be obtained with several commands. **Crosstabs** generates contingency tables from nominal or ordinal data. Here we illustrate its use with Blood Group [*bloodtyp*] and Gender [*sex*].

- Choose
  Analyze
     Descriptive Statistics
        Crosstabs...
  to open the **Crosstabs** dialog box.
- Transfer the variable names as shown in Figure 7 and click **OK**. If one of the variables has more than about four categories, it is better to use it for **Rows** rather than **Columns**, otherwise the output will be too wide for printing on a single page. In this example, a narrower table is produced if Blood Group [*bloodtyp*] is nominated for **Rows**.

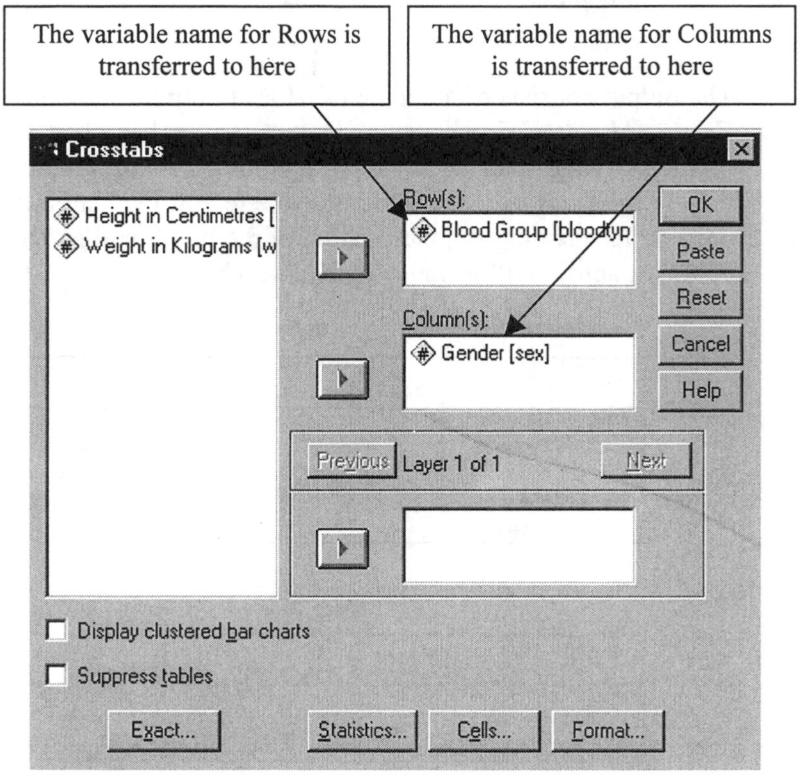

Figure 7. The completed Crosstabs dialog box

The output is shown in Output 3.

Blood Group * Gender Crosstabulation

Count

		Gender		
		Male	Female	Total
Blood	Group A	3	3	6
Group	Group B	3	3	6
	Group AB	2	1	3
	Group O	8	9	17
Total		16	16	32

Output 3. Contingency table from Crosstabs for Gender and Blood Group

Crosstabs is only applicable to contingency tables as described in Section 3.7.2 of Chapter 3: it should be requested only for nominal or ordinal data (i.e. categories or ranks) and not for measurements such as heights or scores.

Another command is **General Tables**.

- Choose
  Analyze
     Custom Tables
        General Tables…
  to open the **General Tables** dialog box.

- Transfer the variable names as shown in Figure 8 and click **OK**.

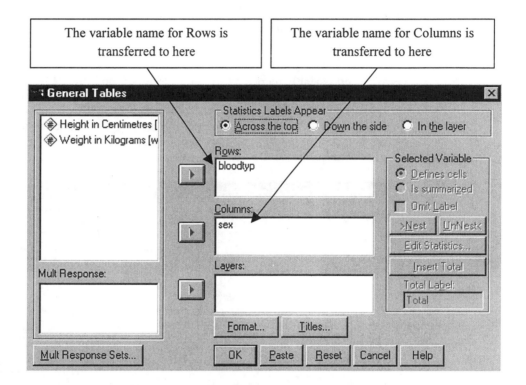

Figure 8. The completed General Tables dialog box

The output is shown in Output 4.

		Gender	
		Male	Female
Blood Group	Group A	3	3
	Group B	3	3
	Group AB	2	1
	Group O	8	9

Output 4. The Contingency table from General Tables for Gender and Blood Group

4.3.2 Describing measurements

There are many commands for describing and exploring data in the form of measurements.

Exploring variables without subdivision into categories of grouping variables

The most basic command is **Descriptives**.
- To list various descriptive statistics of height and weight, choose
  Analyze
      Descriptive Statistics
          Descriptives...
  to open the **Descriptives** dialog box.
- Transfer the variable names as shown in Figure 9 and click **OK**.

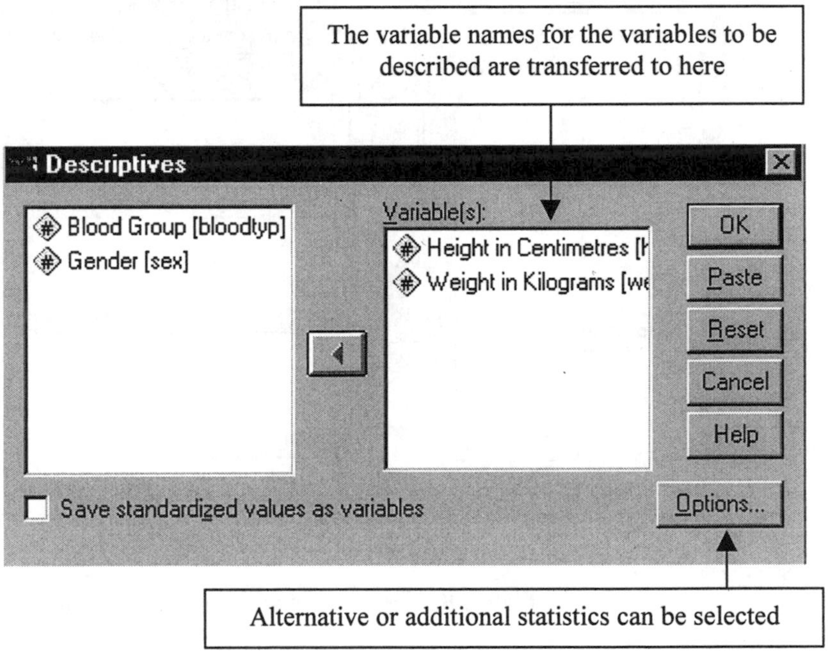

The variable names for the variables to be described are transferred to here

Alternative or additional statistics can be selected

Figure 9. The completed Descriptives dialog box

The output is shown in Output 5.

Descriptive Statistics

	N	Minimum	Maximum	Mean	Std. Deviation
Height in Centimetres	32	142	196	170.28	13.68
Weight in Kilograms	32	48	120	70.22	15.93
Valid N (listwise)	32				

Output 5. Descriptive statistics for height and weight

To obtain percentiles (e.g. quartiles), or to draw various graphics such as a boxplot, a stem-and-leaf table or a histogram, the appropriate commands are **Frequencies** and **Explore**.

The next example illustrates the use of **Frequencies** to draw a histogram, compute some descriptive statistics, and display some percentile values for the variable *height*. Proceed as follows:

- Choose
  Analyze
     Descriptive Statistics
        Frequencies...
- In the **Frequencies** dialog box (Figure 5), enter the variable name Height in Centimetres [*height*] into the **Variables** box. Check that the **Display frequency tables** checkbox is not showing ✓ , otherwise a full frequency table will be listed which for an extensive data set could be very long.
- Click **Charts** to open the **Frequencies: Charts** dialog box (Figure 6).
- In the **Chart Type** box, click the **Histograms** radio button, and mark the **With normal curve** box by clicking that also. Click **Continue**.
- Back in the **Frequencies** dialog box, click **Statistics** to open the **Frequencies: Statistics** dialog box and follow the steps shown in Figure 10.
- Click **Continue** to get back to the **Frequencies** dialog box and click **OK**.

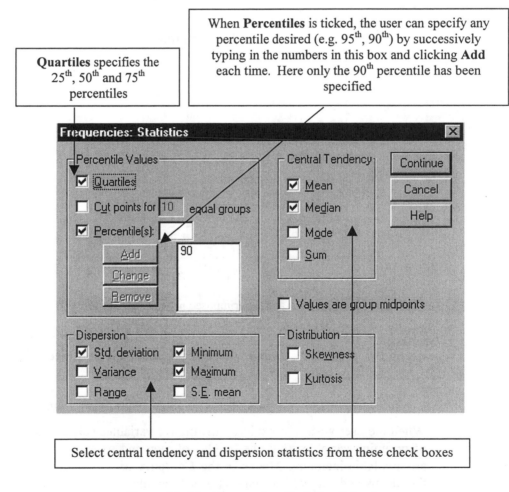

Quartiles specifies the 25th, 50th and 75th percentiles

When **Percentiles** is ticked, the user can specify any percentile desired (e.g. 95th, 90th) by successively typing in the numbers in this box and clicking **Add** each time. Here only the 90th percentile has been specified

Select central tendency and dispersion statistics from these check boxes

Figure 10. The Frequencies: Statistics dialog box

The statistical output is shown in Output 6 and the edited histogram in Output 7.

Statistics

Height in Centimetres

N	Valid	32
	Missing	0
Mean		170.28
Median		170.50
Std. Deviation		13.68
Minimum		142
Maximum		196
Percentiles	25	162.25
	50	170.50
	75	181.50
	90	188.50

The three quartiles requested by ticking the **Quartiles** box

The 90th percentile requested by ticking the **Percentiles** box and specifying 90

Output 6. The requested percentiles and descriptive statistics for height

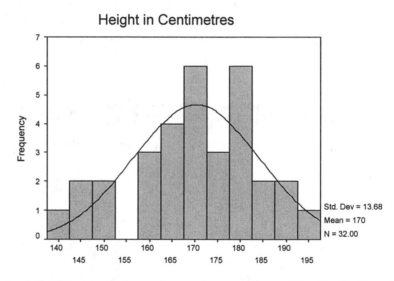

Height in Centimetres

Std. Dev = 13.68
Mean = 170
N = 32.00

Output 7. Histogram and superimposed normal curve of the distribution of height

Explore also produces stem-and-leaf displays and boxplots (see below).

Exploring variables with subdivision into categories of grouping variables

When the user wishes to explore quantitative variables subdivided by categories of grouping variables (e.g. the heights of men and women), several commands are available including **Means** in the **Compare Means** menu. This calculates the means and standard deviations of sub-populations (as defined by the values of a grouping variable). There is also the option of a one-way analysis of variance. Note especially that **Means** cannot be used for variables that have not been grouped by another variable: for such variables, **Descriptives** must be used instead. **Explore** in the **Descriptive Statistics** menu contains a large variety of graphs and displays (also available directly from the **Graphs** drop-down menu), as well as a variety of statistics.

The next example shows the use of **Means** to compute statistics such as the mean and standard deviation when one variable has been grouped by categories of another (e.g. height grouped by gender). Proceed as follows:

- Choose
  Analyze
     Compare Means
        Means...
  to open the **Means** dialog box.
- Follow the steps in Figure 11 and then click **OK**.

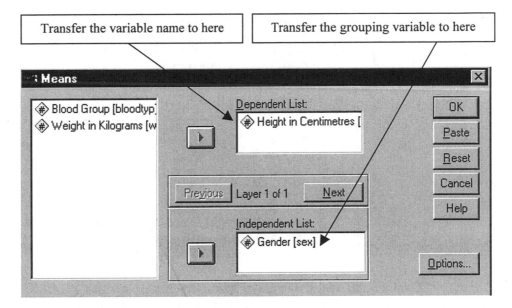

Figure 11. The Means dialog box for height categorised by gender

The output is listed in Output 8. The **Means** command has computed statistics such as the mean and standard deviation for the male and female participants separately.

Height in Centimetres

Gender	Mean	N	Std. Deviation
Male	176.63	16	12.46
Female	163.94	16	12.06
Total	170.28	32	13.68

Output 8. The mean height for each level of gender requested with Means

Breaking down the data with two or more classificatory variables: Layering

In Figure 11, notice the centrally located box containing two sub-dialog buttons **Previous** and **Next,** as well as the caption **Layer 1 of 1.** Here a **layer** is an independent (grouping) variable, such as *sex*. If you click **Next**, you can add another independent variable such as Blood Group [*bloodtyp*], so that the data are classified thus:

1st Layer	*sex*	Male	Female
2nd Layer	*bloodtyp*	A AB B O	A AB B O

The output tabulates the mean height (and standard deviation) for all combinations of *sex* and *bloodtyp* as shown in Output 9. Note that if you had not clicked on **Next** before adding the second classificatory variable, the output would have consisted of *height* by *sex* and of *height* by *bloodtyp* separately (i.e. only a single layer would have been used for each analysis).

Height in Centimetres

Gender	Blood Group	Mean	N	Std. Deviation
Male	Group A	168.33	3	22.55
	Group B	184.00	3	5.29
	Group AB	178.50	2	9.19
	Group O	176.50	8	10.66
	Total	176.63	16	12.46
Female	Group A	160.33	3	10.50
	Group B	175.67	3	6.51
	Group AB	151.00	1	.
	Group O	162.67	9	12.47
	Total	163.94	16	12.06
Total	Group A	164.33	6	16.33
	Group B	179.83	6	7.00
	Group AB	169.33	3	17.16
	Group O	169.18	17	13.35
	Total	170.28	32	13.68

Output 9. The use of layering to compute the mean height (and standard deviation) for all combinations of gender and blood type

Explore (in the **Descriptive Statistics** menu) can be regarded as a general exploratory data analysis (EDA) command. **Explore** offers many of the facilities already illustrated with other commands, and (like **Means** and **Compare Means**) allows quantitative variables to be subdivided by the categories of a qualitative variable such as gender. If, for example, a data set contains the heights of 50 men and 50 women collected into a column headed *height* and (in another column) code numbers making up the grouping variable *sex*, the command **Explore** will produce statistical summaries, graphs and displays either for the 100 height measurements considered as a single group, or the heights of males or females (or both) considered separately.

A useful first step in the analysis of data is to obtain a picture of the data set as a whole. **Explore** offers three kinds of graphs and displays:
- (1) **histograms**;
- (2) **stem-and-leaf displays**;
- (3) **boxplots**.

Readers unfamiliar with these can find, in Howell (1997), clear descriptions of histograms (and bar graphs) on pp17-20, of stem-and-leaf displays on pp21-23, and of boxplots on pp54-57.

The basis of all three types of graph is a table called a **frequency distribution**, which sets out either (in the case of nominal data) the categories comprising a qualitative variable and gives the frequency of observations in each category or (with measurements) divides the total range of values into arbitrary **class intervals** and gives the frequency of measurements that fall in each interval, that is, have values in the upper and lower **bounds** of the interval concerned. With data on height recorded in centimetres, for example, the total range could be divided into the class intervals (140-149, 150-159, 160-169, and so on), and the frequency distribution would give the **frequencies** of heights in each of these ranges.

A **bar graph** (SPSS calls this a 'bar chart': see Output 5) is suitable for qualitative (nominal) data, such as the numbers of people in a sample belonging to the various blood groups. In a bar graph, the bars are separated to clarify the fact that the horizontal axis contains no scale of measurement; in fact, the order of the bars in Output 5 is arbitrary, since the Group B bar could as well have followed the Group A bar. A **histogram** (see Output 7), on the other hand, is appropriate for measurements: the class intervals are stepped out on the horizontal axis; and on each interval a bar is erected, whose height represents the number of people whose heights fell in that interval. *In a histogram, in contradistinction to a bar graph, the bars touch one another: there are no spaces.*

To use the **Explore** command:

- Choose
  Analyze
     Descriptive Statistics
         Explore...
  to open the **Explore** dialog box.
- Follow the steps shown in Figure 12.

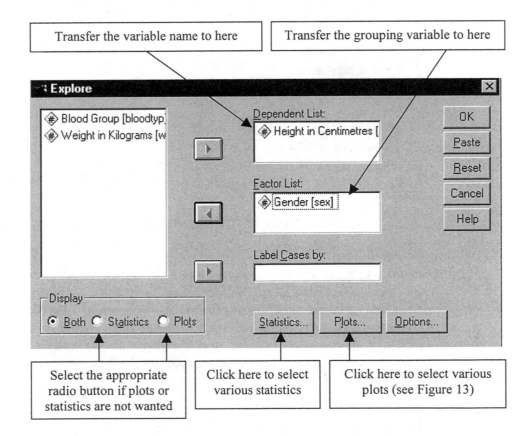

Figure 12. The Explore dialog box for height categorised by gender

- If there is a variable identifying the cases (e.g. *case*), then click *case* and on ![button] to transfer it to the **Label Cases by** box. Outliers or extreme values (these will be explained later) are identified in boxplots by their row numbers by default or by the identifier in the variable entered in the **Label Cases by** box.

- Click **Plots** to open the **Explore: Plots** dialog box and follow the steps shown in Figure 13. The default setting for the **Boxplots** is a side-by-side plot for each level of the factor (i.e. Female and Male). For **Descriptive**, the options are **Stem-and-leaf** and **Histogram**. Since we have seen the histogram earlier, we shall click **Stem-and-leaf** only.
- Click **Continue** and then **OK**.

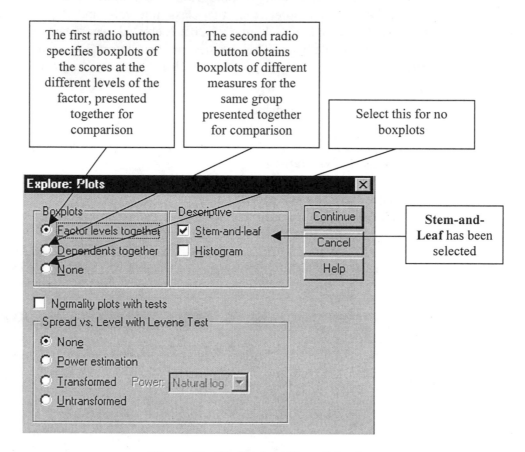

Figure 13. The Explore: Plots dialog box

Should one wish to have boxplots of two dependent variables side-by-side at each level of a classificatory variable (such as gender, or blood group), both dependent variables must be entered into the **Dependent List** box, and (in the **Boxplots** dialog box) the **Dependents together** radio button must be selected. In the present example, of course, it would have made no sense to plot boxplots of *height* and *weight* side-by-side at each level of gender, since height and weight measurements have quite different scales.

The tabular output and the boxplots are shown in Outputs 10 and 11.

The descriptive statistics and stem-and-leaf display of *height* for Males (one of the levels of *sex*) is shown in Output 11; the output for Females is not shown. In the **stem-and-leaf display**, the central column of numbers (16, 16, 17, 17, ..., 19), the **stem** of the display, represents the leading digit or digits (here they are hundreds and tens of centimetres). The numbers in the column headed **Leaf** are the final digits (centimetres). Each stem denotes the lower bound of the class interval: for example, the first number, 16, represents the lower bound of the class interval from 160 to 164, the second 16 from 165-169, the first 17 from

170 to 174 and so on. The column headed **Frequency** lists the number of cases in each stem. In stem 18, for example, there are four cases with a height between 180 and 184 centimetres. They are 180, 180, 182 and 183 since the leaves are listed as 0, 0, 2, 3. In addition, there is one case with a height between 185 and 189, namely 185. The display also shows extreme values: there is one value equal to or less than 145. The stem-and-leaf display is very useful for displaying small data sets, but for large sets, the histogram is generally preferred.

Descriptives

Gender				Statistic	Std. Error
Height in Centimetres	Male	Mean		176.63	3.12
		95% Confidence Interval for Mean	Lower Bound	169.98	
			Upper Bound	183.27	
		5% Trimmed Mean		177.31	
		Median		179.00	
		Variance		155.32	
		Std. Deviation		12.46	
		Minimum		145.00	
		Maximum		196.00	176.63
		Range		51.00	169.98
		Interquartile Range		14.50	183.27
		Skewness		-.95	177.31
		Kurtosis		1.64	179.00

```
Height in Centimetres Stem-and-Leaf Plot for
SEX= Male

 Frequency      Stem &  Leaf

     1.00 Extremes      (=<145)
     1.00         16 .  0
      .00         16 .
     4.00         17 .  0002
     2.00         17 .  58
     4.00         18 .  0023
     1.00         18 .  5
     2.00         19 .  00
     1.00         19 .  6

 Stem width:          10
 Each leaf:       1 case(s)
```

Output 10. Descriptive statistics, and stem-and-leaf display for height categorised by gender (only the output for Males shown here)

Output 11 shows the **boxplots** of the heights of the male and female subjects plotted side-by-side, for comparison. The structure of a boxplot is shown in Table 2. The box itself represents that portion of the distribution falling between the 25th and 75th percentiles, i.e. the **lower** and **upper quartiles** (in EDA terminology these are known as **hinges**). The xth percentile is the value below which x% of the distribution lies: so 50% of the heights lie between the 25th and 75th percentiles. The thick horizontal line across the interior of the box represents the median. The vertical lines outside the box, which are known as **whiskers**, connect the largest and smallest values that are not outliers or extreme values.

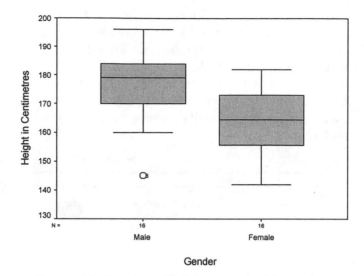

Output 11. Boxplots of height categorised by gender

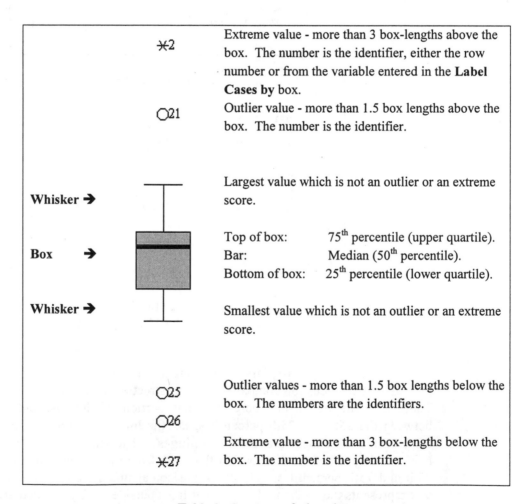

Table 2. Structure of a boxplot

An **outlier (o)** is defined as a value more than 1.5 box-lengths away from the box, and an **extreme value (*)** as more than 3 box-lengths away from the box. The number(s) alongside o and * are the case number(s). Note that they are not located in their real positions in relation to the scale on the ordinate (not shown in Table 2). The case numbers are either the row numbers in **Data View** by default, or the identifiers from the variable entered in the **Label Cases by** box. Skewness is indicated by an eccentric location of the median in the box. Notice that the distribution of heights for females is much more symmetric than that for males. The o^3 under the Male boxplot in Output 11 indicates the existence of an outlier and that it is the value for the case in row 3. This value (145cm) is well below the average height for males and its presence is also noted in the stem-and-leaf display in Output 10.

Boxplots are particularly useful for identifying outliers and extreme values in data sets, and can be requested directly by choosing
Graphs
    Boxplot....

Data screening

If any extreme values are present, the user should consider whether these case should be excluded from subsequent statistical analyses. Many statistical textbooks now have sections or chapters discussing data screening: for example, Tabachnick & Fidell (1996) have a chapter called Cleaning Up Your Act: Screening Data Prior to Analysis, in other words, removing extreme cases before engaging in further analyses. This is not "cooking the data" since any such exclusions must be mentioned in an experimental or research report. The simplest way of deselecting extreme cases is by the use of the **Select Cases** command discussed in Section 3.7.1. As well as deselecting cases, it may be desirable to transform the values of a variable to change the shape of its distribution (see below).

4.4   MANIPULATION OF THE DATA SET

4.4.1 Reducing and transforming data

After a data set has been entered into SPSS, it may be necessary to modify it in certain ways. For example, an exploratory data analysis may have revealed that atypical scores, or **outliers**, have exerted undue influence, or **leverage**, upon the values of statistics such as the mean and standard deviation. One approach to this problem is to remove the outliers and repeat the analysis with the remaining scores, on the grounds that it is better to have statistics that describe 95% of the data well than 100% of them badly. Cases can be dropped from the analysis by using the **Select Cases** command (Section 3.7.1).

Sometimes it is necessary to **transform** the values of a variable in order to satisfy the distribution requirements for the use of a particular statistic. Transformations, such as the square root or the logarithm, are easily made with the **Compute** command (Section 4.4.2).

Finally, it is sometimes convenient to combine or alter the categories that make up a qualitative or ordinal variable. This is achieved with the **Recode** command, which can construct a new variable with the new category assignments (Section 4.4.3).

4.4.2 The COMPUTE command

The **Compute** command computes values for a variable based on numeric transformations of other variables. It can be used either to create new variables or to replace the values of existing variables. The second procedure is dangerous and is not recommended, because the original values for the variable cannot be retrieved. Values can be computed selectively for subsets of data specified by logical conditions. There are over seventy built-in functions, including arithmetic functions, statistical functions, distribution functions, date and string functions.

Suppose, for example, that we want to look at the distribution of the square root of height. We shall call the new variable *roothght*. (The square root transformation is often used to make a distribution more symmetrical.)

- Choose
  Transform
      Compute...
  to open the **Compute Variable** dialog box (Figure 14).

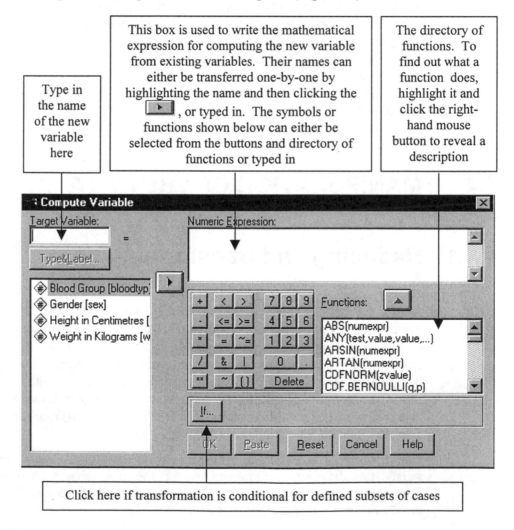

Figure 14. The Compute Variable dialog box

- Click in the **Target Variable** box at top left to locate control there and type in the name of the new variable, *roothght*. Click the **Type & Label** box just below and type in the **Label** box *Square-root of Height* and click **Continue**.
- Scroll down through the **Functions:** box on the right to find the square root function. Click **SQRT[numexpr]** and then ⬆ to paste it into the **Numeric Expression** box where it will appear as **SQRT[?]**.
- Click Height in Centimetres [*height*] and ▶ to make this variable the argument of the square root function (i.e. *height* replaces ?). The expression **SQRT[height]** will now appear in the **Numeric Expression** box. The final version of the dialog box is shown in Figure 15.
- Click **OK**.

A new column *roothght*, containing the square roots of the values of *height*, will appear in **Data View**. (It may be necessary to change some of its properties in **Variable View** - for example to reduce the number of decimal places - see Section 3.3.9.)

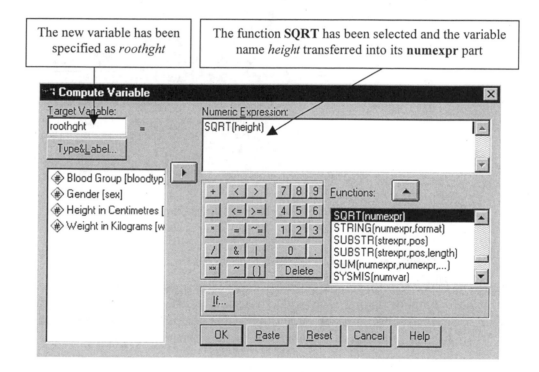

| The new variable has been specified as *roothght* | The function **SQRT** has been selected and the variable name *height* transferred into its **numexpr** part |

Figure 15. The Compute Variable dialog box for computing the square root of height

Compute can also be used to combine values of variables. For example, the command can compute a new variable *meanval* from the equation *meanval = (french + german + spanish)/3*, which sums the three scores and divides by three. If any value is missing, a system-missing result is recorded. Alternatively, the function *mean* can be used (e.g. *meanval = mean (french, german, spanish)*). *Mean* computes the mean of the valid values; the result is recorded as missing only if all three scores are absent.

Finally, conditional computations can be commanded by clicking **If...** in the **Compute Variable** dialog box and then **Include if case satisfies the condition**. A conditional statement, such as the one in Figure 16 specifying that the compute command applies only to Males (*sex* = 1) and Blood Group AB (*bloodtyp* = 3), can then be compiled in the box.

Click **Continue** to return to the **Compute Variable** dialog box where, for example, the **Target Variable** might be nominated as *group* and the **Numeric Expression** as *1*. All males with blood group AB will be categorised into value *1* of the variable *group*. Other values for *group* could be assigned by specifying other combinations of *sex* and *bloodtyp*.

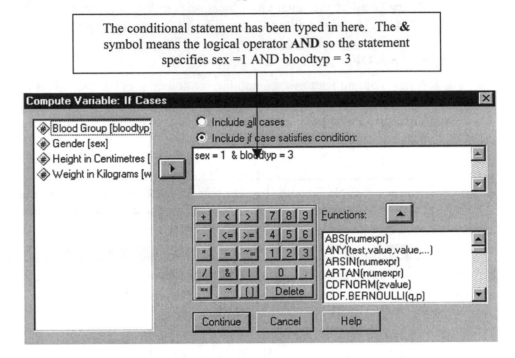

Figure 16. A conditional statement in the Compute Variable: If Cases dialog box

Using the Compute command for numbering cases

The **Compute** command can be used to enter a sequence of numbers for rows without having to type 1, 2, etc.. The data set must not be empty: it must already be in place or its future size determined by pasting a dummy number such as *1* down a column for as many rows as are needed.

• Choose
   Transform
      Compute...
to open the **Compute Variable** dialog box.

• Type *case* (or whatever variable name is wanted for the case numbers) into the **Target Variable:** box, *$casenum* into the **Numeric Expression:** box and then click **OK** (Figure 17).

A variable named *case* will appear in **Data View** with a succession of values starting with 1.

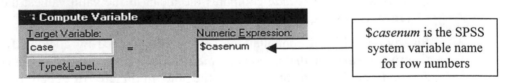

Figure 17. Part of the Compute Variable dialog box for generating case numbers

4.4.3 The RECODE command

We have seen that the **Compute** command operates upon one or more of the variables in the data set, so that there will be as many values in the transformed variable as there were in the original variable. Sometimes, however, the user may want to assign relatively few code numbers to values that fall in specified ranges of the variable rather than wanting a transformation that will convert all the values of a variable systematically.

For example, suppose we have a set of 18 children's examination marks on a scale from 0 to 100 (Table 3). If the pass mark is 50, it may be convenient to recode each child's mark into a Pass or a Fail. This can easily be done by using the **Recode** command.

Table 3. Children's Examination Marks					
Child	Mark	Child	Mark	Child	Mark
1	62	7	70	13	50
2	51	8	40	14	50
3	40	9	63	15	42
4	68	10	81	16	65
5	38	11	62	17	30
6	40	12	78	18	71

Enter the data into **Data View** in a variable named *marks* and then:
- Choose
  Transform
      Recode...
  and click **Into Different Variables** to open the **Recode into Different Variables** dialog box. Just as in the case of the **Compute** command, it is possible to change the values in the same variable to the recoded values but we recommend placing the recoded values in a new variable, perhaps *passfail*.
- Click *marks* and on ▶ to paste the name into the **Numeric Variable -> Output Variable** box.
- Type the name of the output variable *passfail* into the **Name** box and click **Change** to insert the name into the **Numeric Variable -> Output Variable** box (Figure 18).
- Click the **Old and New Values** box to open the **Recode into Different Variables: Old and New Values** dialog box (the completed dialog box is shown in Figure 19).
- Follow the steps in Figure 19 for defining the old and new values. These will categorise all exam marks less than 50 as *Fail* and all those of 50 and above as *Pass*.
- Click **Continue** and **OK**.

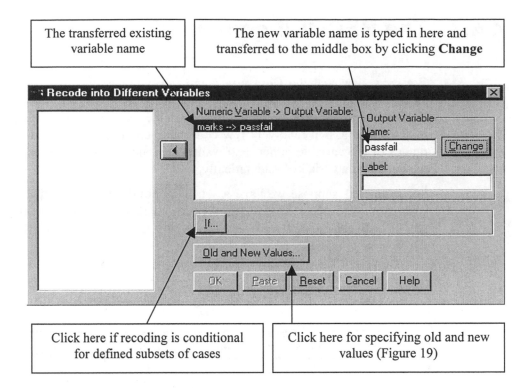

The transferred existing variable name

The new variable name is typed in here and transferred to the middle box by clicking **Change**

Click here if recoding is conditional for defined subsets of cases

Click here for specifying old and new values (Figure 19)

Figure 18. Part of the Recode into Different Variables dialog box showing the original variable and the one to which the recoded values will be placed

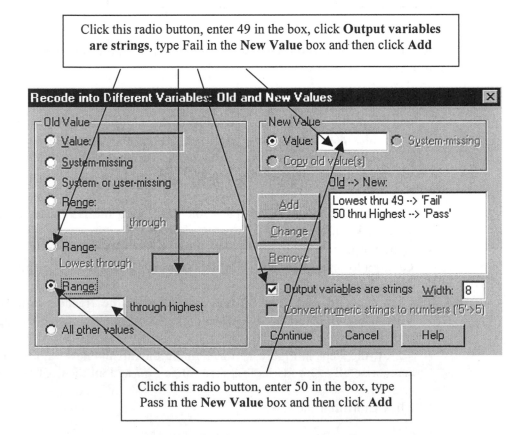

Click this radio button, enter 49 in the box, click **Output variables are strings**, type Fail in the **New Value** box and then click **Add**

Click this radio button, enter 50 in the box, type Pass in the **New Value** box and then click **Add**

Figure 19. The Recode into Different Variables: Old and New Values dialog box with defined ranges for Pass and Fail

A new string variable *passfail* containing the recoded labels *Pass* and *Fail*, will appear in **Data View** (Figure 20).

	child	marks	passfail
1	1	62	Pass
2	2	51	Pass
3	3	40	Fail
4	4	68	Pass
5	5	38	Fail
6	6	40	Fail
7	7	70	Pass
8	8	40	Fail
9	9	63	Pass
10	10	81	Pass

Figure 20. Part of Data View showing the new string variable *passfail* with the labels Pass and Fail

If a variable such as height has non-integer values, great care has to be taken in recoding the values into ranges such as *tall*, *medium* and *short*. For example, if *short* is to be defined as less than 1.6 metres, *medium* as 1.6 to 1.8 metres, and *tall* as more than 1.8 metres, then the ranges should be set in the **Recode** dialog box as follows (this time we show recoding into values rather than strings):

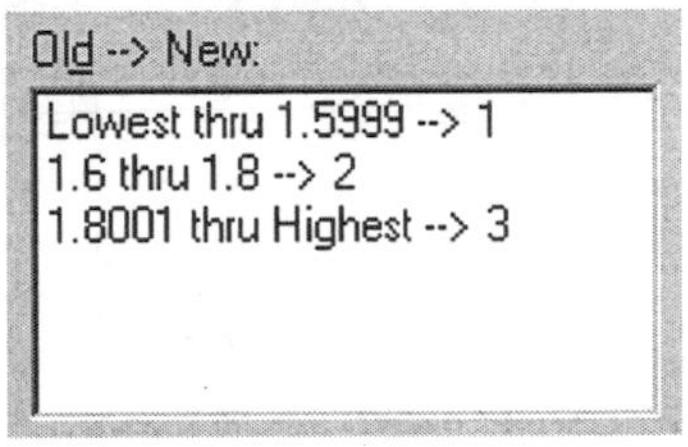

```
Old --> New:

Lowest thru 1.5999 --> 1
1.6 thru 1.8 --> 2
1.8001 thru Highest --> 3
```

The values *1*, *2* & *3* can then be given the labels *Short, Medium* & *Tall* by clicking the **Values** column of the new variable in **Variable View** and completing the dialog box as shown in Figure 21.

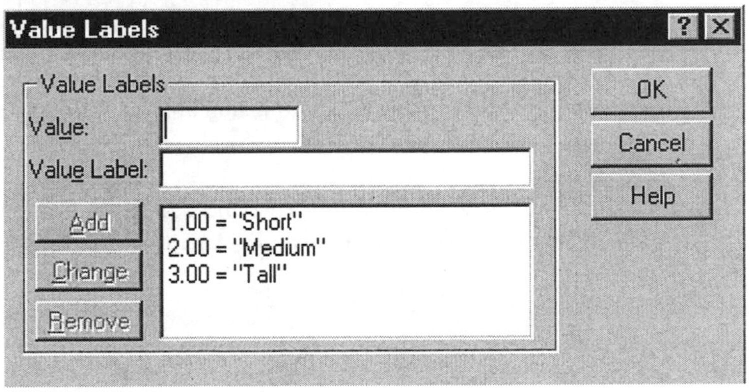

Figure 21. Value labels after recoding height into three ranges

Another procedure for splitting a continuous variable such as height into categories is presented in the next Section.

4.4.4 The Categorize Variables command

An alternative method for splitting a continuous variable into categories utilises the **Categorize Variables** command, which creates a new variable based on percentile groups, with each group containing approximately the same number of cases. For example, a specification of 4 groups would assign a value of 1 to cases below the 25th percentile, 2 to cases between the 25th and 50th percentile, 3 to cases between the 50th and 75th percentile, and 4 to cases above the 75th percentile.

To split height into three groups:

- Choose
  Transform
  >**Categorize Variables...**
  to open the **Categorize Variables** dialog box.

- Transfer the variable name Height in Centimetres [*height*] to the **Create Categories for:** box.

- Change the default value 4 into 3 in the **Number of categories:** box. The completed dialog box is shown in Figure 22.

- Click **OK**.

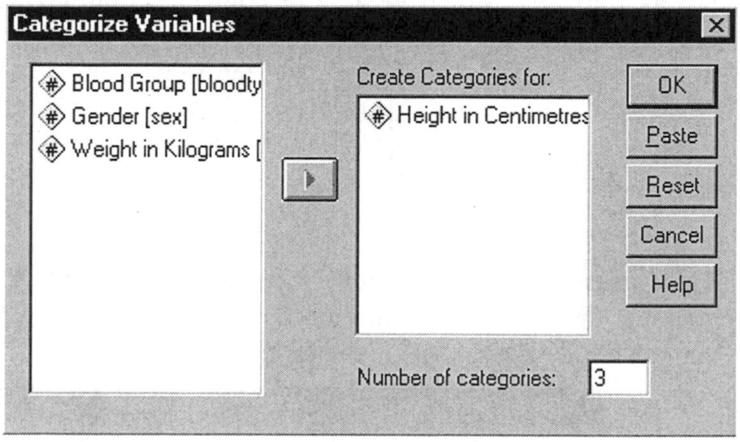

Figure 22. The Categorize Variables dialog box for splitting height into 3 categories

Data View will now show a new variable called *nheight* with the values 1, 2 or 3 for each case. Labels can be assigned to these values if desired in **Variable View**.

EXERCISE 3

QUESTIONNAIRE DATA (continued)

Introduction

This Exercise shows you how to open a saved file, how to merge your data with those of other users, how to obtain information about the structure of a data file, and how to print out a file. The relevant sections are 2.5.3 (resuming work on a saved data set), 3.4.2 (reading in SPSS files), 3.5.2 (displaying data file information) and 3.6 (printing in SPSS).

Opening your saved file in SPSS

Log in to SPSS as described in Section 2.5.1. Open the file that you saved under the name *mydata* from the previous Exercise by selecting the radio button **Open an existing data source** in the SPSS opening window and highlighting the appropriate filename. It may be necessary, especially in a networked computer, to select the **More Files...** option and select another disk drive or folder. Alternatively, select the **Type in data** radio button to open **Data View**, choose **File**, click **Open**, and finally **Data** to open the **Open File** selection box. Change the **Look in:** selection to the folder and/or disk drive where the file has been stored, click the filename so that it appears in the **Filename** box, and then click **Open**. Your file should then appear in **Data View**.

Locating the larger data set

The file containing the large data set with which you are going to merge your own data is to be found at the following WWW address:

http://www.psyc.abdn.ac.uk/teaching/spss/spssbook.htm

in the file labelled Exercise 3. If your instructor has not already downloaded this file on to a file server or hard disk drive for easier access, then enter WWW (you can minimise the SPSS window by clicking the minimise icon 🖻 in the top right-hand corner in order to see the appropriate icons for accessing WWW) and save the file to a more convenient place such as your hard disk drive.

Merging your data with the larger data set

To carry out the merger, select

Data

    Merge Files

        Add Cases

to obtain the **Add Cases: Read File** selection box, which prompts you to specify the file (the large data set) from which you want to merge other cases with your own. Locate the file *Exercise 3*, click it so that it is highlighted and *Exercise 3* appears in the **File Name:** box at the foot of the **Add Cases: Read File** dialog box. Click **Open**. A new dialog box labelled **Add Cases from**, together with the full name of the data file, will appear.

If you have entered the correct variable names in your own data file, the **Add Cases from** dialog box should show just one unpaired variable name in the **Unpaired Variables: box** (*name*) and all the corresponding variable names from both files in the **Variables in New Working Data File:** box (see

Figure 1). In fact the large data set does not contain the names of the participants - we included your name in Exercise 3 as an illustration of the use of a string variable.

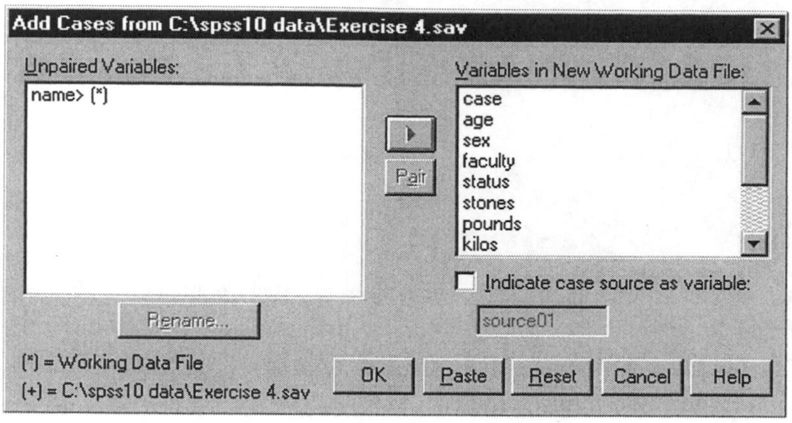

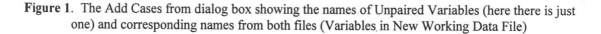

Figure 1. The Add Cases from dialog box showing the names of Unpaired Variables (here there is just one) and corresponding names from both files (Variables in New Working Data File)

Suppose, however, there had been a mismatch between one of the variable names you had typed into **Data View** and the name of the corresponding variable in the large data set. Suppose that, instead of typing *age* as the variable name, you had typed *aged*. The pair of variables, *aged* and *age*, would have appeared in the **Unpaired Variables:** box. You would then have had to select one of the variables and clicked **Rename** to obtain another dialog box, allowing you to rename the selected variable with the name of the other file. When this has been done, the desired variable name can be transferred to the right hand box, which shows the **Variables in the New Working Data File**.

Click **OK** to merge the files. Your variable *name* will disappear and you will notice that there are now two rows labelled with 1 in the *case* column (yours and Case 1 from the large data set). Obviously this ambiguity cannot be allowed to continue so you will need to renumber your case as 335 (there are 334 cases in the large data set - scroll down the file to check this). Do this by changing the first cell to 335 in **Data View**.

Sorting the cases in order of case numbers

The cases can then be sorted into sequence by selecting:
Data
>**Sort Cases...**

to open the **Sort Cases** dialog box. Select the variable *case* and click ▶ to transfer it into the **Sort by:** box (see Figure 2). Finally click **OK**. Your data will now appear as case 335 at the foot of the data set.

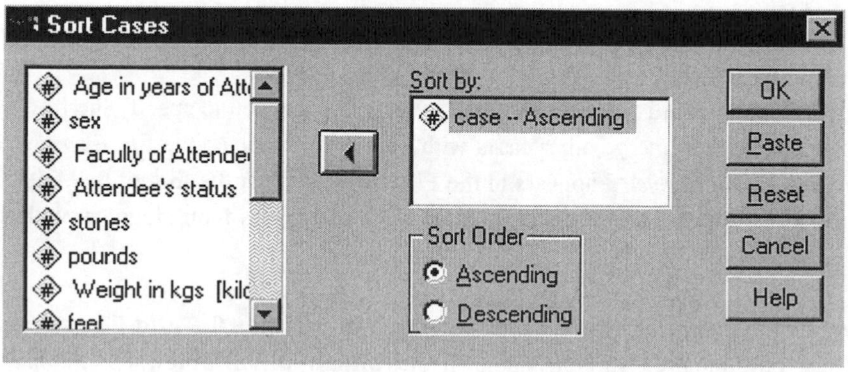

Figure 2. The Sort Cases dialog box completed for sorting based on the value in the variable case

Save the merged data file in the usual way using **Save As**, but this time call it *merged data*. You will be loading this file when you open SPSS in the next Exercise.

A warning

In the large data set, the categorical variable was of the numeric type, with values assigned as follows: 1 = Arts, 2 = Science, 3 = Medicine, 4 = Other.

Suppose that you had assigned the 1 to Science and the 2 to Arts, instead of the other way round, and that as a scientist, you had recorded a 1 in your own data set. SPSS will not warn you of the discrepancy. Instead, it will adopt your convention throughout the merged data set and all those people who recorded 1s in the larger original data set, will now be recorded as scientists, not arts students.

When two files are being merged, it is the value assignments of the first that determine those for the entire merged file, even when, as in the present example, the former contains only a single case.

Displaying data file information (Section 3.5.2)

It is often useful to be able to see a list of variable names, formats, values and value labels for a particular file not currently located in **Data View**. In the case of a file already in **Data View**, these details are readily seen in **Variable View**.

As an illustration, remove the data from **Data View** by selecting

File

    New

        Data.

Then select

File

    Display Data Info ...

which brings a directory dialog box. Locate and select the target file *merged data* by highlighting it. Then click **Open**. All the desired information appears in the **SPSS Viewer**, which will show the names and order of the variables in the data set, the value labels of category variables, and so on.

Finishing the session

Close down SPSS and any other windows before logging out of the computer.

CHAPTER 5

MORE GRAPHS AND CHARTS

5.1 INTRODUCTION

5.2 EDITING GRAPHS OR CHARTS

5.3 ERROR BAR CHARTS

5.4 PIE CHARTS

5.5 LINE GRAPHS

5.6 SCATTERPLOTS

5.1   INTRODUCTION

A wide range of graphs and charts (some of which we have already considered) are available for exploring and representing data. Here, before we go on to discuss some more graphical methods, we shall first outline some general aspects of graph-drawing in SPSS.

5.1.1   Requesting graphs and charts

The dialog boxes for specifying graphs and charts are accessed from the **Graphs** drop-down menu or from options within various procedures - for example, the **Frequencies** command contains an option **Charts**.

It is worth spending a few moments considering the variable names and labels that may be plotted in charts or graphs, in case the user might want to change some of them within the data file before going ahead with the chosen figure. If some data are missing from the data file, remember to specify whether (as in a bar chart, for example) missing data should be included in the plot. Missing data can be excluded by turning off the **Display groups defined by missing values** box in the **Options** dialog box.

If extensive editing is not anticipated, it is quicker to add a title (if desired) at this stage rather than at the editing stage (though for boxplots, titles can be added only at the editing stage) by clicking the **Titles** box and typing in the appropriate title.

It should be noted that not all boxes in a dialog box need necessarily be completed. For example, **Label Cases by** boxes can be left empty when that option is not required. (With a large data set, the use of **Label Cases by** can clutter the output with too many labels.) The critical test of whether enough information has been specified in a dialog box is whether **OK** is operative or not: if that is still dimmed, more information must be supplied before the command can be executed.

5.1.2   Seeing the graph or chart on screen

After a graph or chart has been completed by SPSS, it will appear in the window labelled **Output1 - SPSS Viewer**. It may be necessary to scroll down the window or, more quickly, to click its icon in the left-hand pane of **SPSS Viewer**. If the pointer is clicked on another window or another window is requested from the **Window** drop-down menu, the **SPSS Viewer** window will temporarily disappear. It can easily be retrieved, however, by reselecting it from the **Window** menu.

Users may wish to change the aspect ratio of the charts to make them narrower - the charts in this chapter have been drawn with an aspect ratio of 1 instead of the default value of 1.25.

To change the aspect ratio, select

Edit

    Options

        Charts

and then change the **Chart Aspect Ratio** value in the box to 1 and click **OK.**

5.2 EDITING GRAPHS OR CHARTS

SPSS provides a special **Chart Editor** for adding or amending graphic material.

5.2.1 The Chart Editor

After a graph or chart has appeared on the screen, the following options are available:

1. Accept the image as it is and save it, print it or copy it for pasting into a document.
2. Reject the image by clicking its icon in the left-hand pane and then pressing **Delete**. It is prudent to delete unwanted images in order to save memory.
3. Edit the image as described below.

It is tempting to save all relevant charts, but the reader should be aware that charts take up a lot of computer memory and disk space. If space is limited, save only the most important charts: it is easy to recreate them from saved data files later if necessary.

The **Chart Editor** allows a wide range of alterations and additions to be made to a graph or chart; though such editing is a slow process and proficiency takes some practice to acquire. The **Chart Editor** is invoked by double-clicking anywhere within the image: a single click will result in a simple frame appearing around the image but a double-click leads to the original image being shaded and a copy of it being displayed as shown in Figure 1, which shows a copy of the boxplot from the last Chapter.

We strongly recommend that the user works through the various tutorials on creating and editing charts provided by SPSS, which is accessed by clicking

Help

    Tutorial

and then double-clicking each of

Tutorials

    Creating and Editing Charts

        Modifying Charts

            Overview of chart editing features.

A series of annotated displays follows, covering many aspects of chart-editing.

The **Chart Editor** offers an array of menus, some of which include long lists of commands, and the user will need to experiment with these to learn how to apply them. The most important menus are **Gallery**, **Chart** and **Format**, details of which are shown in Figure 2. Note that some menus may be incomplete, since only items relevant to the type of chart being edited (e.g. boxplot, histogram, line graph, scatterplot) will be visible.

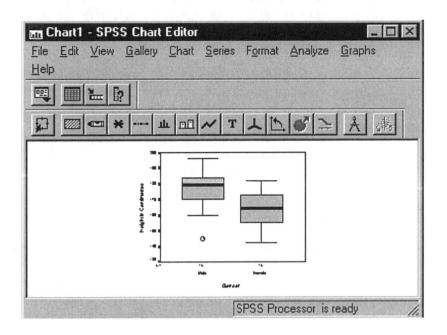

Figure 1. The Chart Editor as used for boxplots

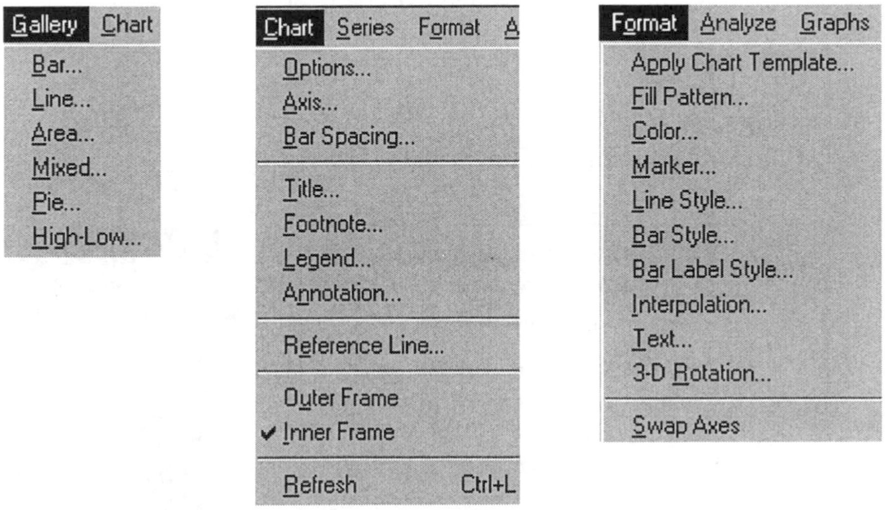

Figure 2. The Gallery, Chart and Format menus

- The **Gallery** menu offers various types of chart and a command **Mixed...** for producing hybrid graphs (see below).
- The **Chart** menu has commands for adding or altering labels, legends and titles, as well as changing the spacing between bars, putting frames around the graph, swapping axes, and so on.
- The **Format** menu has commands for changing the shadings of filled areas, the colours of bars and lines, point markers, line style and weight and so on. Most of these items also appear as icons beneath the menus.

When a chart is being edited, the item to be changed must first be selected by clicking it. Some items such as text will immediately appear with a box around them; others, such as lines on a graph or boxes in a boxplot, will appear with additional black markers at junctions or corners. The editing dialog box is then opened either by clicking a menu and selecting the appropriate item or by clicking an icon, if one is available. Alternatively, double-clicking the item itself (e.g. a legend on a graph axis) will open the appropriate editing dialog box.

If a series of similar graphs or charts is wanted, the reader should consider saving the edited first chart and then specifying this file with the **Chart Template** option for the second and subsequent charts.

In summary, it is possible to customise a graph or a chart to a considerable extent. It is also worth noting that in order to maximise clarity for reproduction by a monochrome printer, it is best to replace colours with uncoloured patterns.

Clustered bar charts

Several types of bar charts can be drawn. We have already considered the production of bar graphs showing the frequency distributions of gender or blood group considered separately. Now suppose that having constructed a bar graph of the frequency distribution of blood group in the sample of 32 people, we would like to be able to compare that distribution in the males with the same distribution in the females. In other words, instead of having a simple bar graph with a bar for each of the four blood groups, we want two clusters of bars, each cluster showing the frequencies of the different blood groups within either the males or the females in the sample.

To obtain such a clustered bar graph, proceed as follows.
- Choose
Graphs
    Bar...

to obtain the **Bar Charts** dialog box (Figure 3).

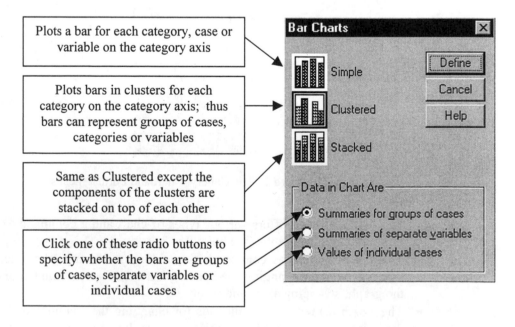

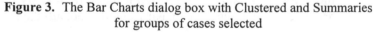

Figure 3. The Bar Charts dialog box with Clustered and Summaries for groups of cases selected

- Choose **Clustered** by clicking the middle diagram to get the black border (which, initially, will be round the **Simple** option) to move down to the **Clustered** diagram.
- Click **Define** to obtain another dialog box with the rather ponderous caption: **Define Clustered Bar: Summaries for Groups of Cases** (the completed dialog box is shown in Figure 4).

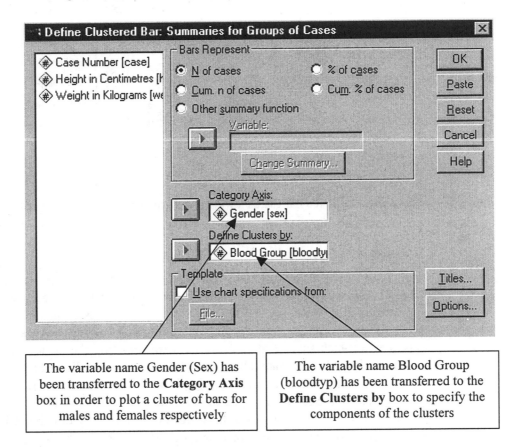

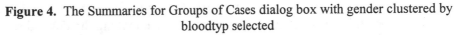

Figure 4. The Summaries for Groups of Cases dialog box with gender clustered by bloodtyp selected

- Transfer the variable names as shown in Figure 4.
- The uppermost box, **Variable**, will remain dim unless the lowest of the three radio buttons, **Other summary function**, is selected. For this exercise, however, the correct radio button is **N of cases**.
- Had we wanted, instead of frequencies, the mean height of the subjects in each of the six gender by blood group categories, we should have chosen the lowest radio button, **Other Summary Function**, and transferred the variable Height in Centimetres [*height*] into the text box there.
- Click **OK** to obtain a clustered bar chart similar to that shown in Output 1.
- If the chart is to be printed in black and white, it is best to use the chart editor to change the colours of the graph to shades of grey. In fact, we have found it most effective to change the fill colour to white and mark the bars with distinguishing fill patterns. Output 1 is such an edited chart, produced by procedures which will be described in the next Section.

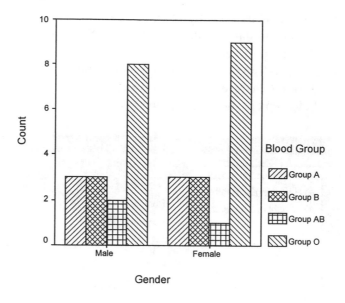
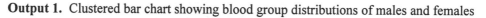

Output 1. Clustered bar chart showing blood group distributions of males and females

Editing a bar chart

If a colour printer is unavailable, it is advisable to improve reproduction clarity by replacing the default colour shadings of the boxes by white, grey or black, and introducing various fill patterns (i.e. the lines and cross-hatching in Output 2). This is most conveniently achieved by double-clicking the bars, which will appear with black squares at each corner, then selecting the ▣ icon to open the **Colors** dialog box (alternatively, select **Color...** from the **Format** menu). Click the desired colour and then click **Apply**. If other bars are to be altered, return to the bar chart and click the next set of bars; the same **Colors** dialog box can then be used for them. Finally close the **Colors** dialog box by clicking **Close**. The same procedure can be used for changing the fill pattern by selecting the ▨ icon (alternatively select the **Fill Pattern...** item from the **Format** menu) to open the **Fill Patterns** dialog box and then making the desired selections.

Several modifications are available for changing the positioning and width of bars in a chart as shown in the **Bar Spacing** dialog box in Figure 5, which is obtained by choosing the **Bar Spacing** item in the **Chart** menu. The settings can then be altered as desired. Other changes can also be made, such as alterations to the axis labels and bar identification key. For example, in Output 1, the positions of the axis labels were centred.

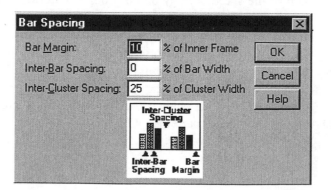

Figure 5. Options for altering the bar spacing and bar margins

5.3   ERROR BAR CHARTS

An alternative to a bar graph is what SPSS terms an **Error Bar chart**, in which the mean of the scores in a particular category is represented by a single point and the spread (confidence interval for the mean, multiples of the standard deviation or multiples of the standard error of the mean - the user can choose between these) is represented by a vertical line passing through the point.   The procedure is as follows:

- Choose
  Graphs
      Error Bar...
  to open the **Error Bar** dialog box.
- Select the default option of **Simple** and the default radio button **Summaries for groups of cases**, and click **Define** to open the **Define Simple Error Bar: Summaries for Groups of Cases** dialog box (the completed version is shown in Figure 6).

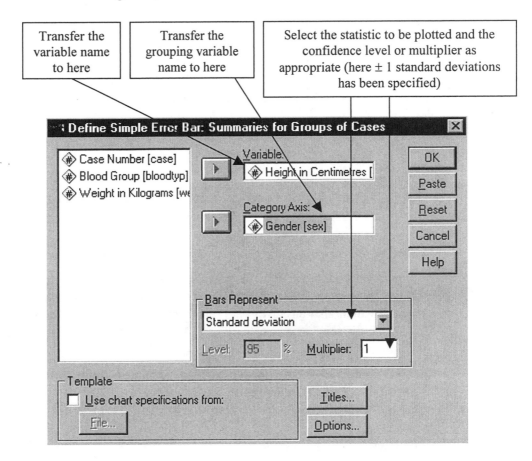

Figure 6. The Summaries for Groups of Cases dialog box for height categorised by gender

- Transfer the variable names and select the appropriate statistic (and the multiplier if needed) for the error bars as shown in Figure 6. Here we have selected **Standard deviation** and set the **Multiplier** to 1.
- Click **OK** to produce the **Error Bar Chart** (the edited version is shown in Output 2).

You will notice that in Output 2, there are no lines linking points across the sexes. This is entirely appropriate, since Female and Male are qualitatively distinct categories. In other circumstances, however, as when the categories are ordered, it may be desirable to join up the points with straight lines. This is easily achieved by choosing the **Interpolation** item from the **Format** menu and selecting the appropriate command (the correct choice is obvious from the icons in the dialog box).

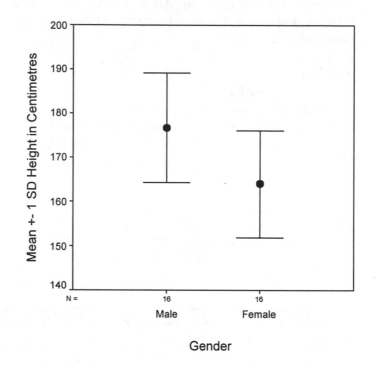

Output 2. Error bar chart showing means and standard deviations of the heights of the men and women

Producing hybrid graphical displays: Bar graphs with error bars

By appropriate choices from the menus, it is possible to produce graphs that combine features of different displays. For example, one may wish to produce a bar graph which also has error bars representing the spread of the scores around their mean for the various categories. An example of such a hybrid chart is shown in Output 3.

First, proceed as in the previous example to obtain the chart shown in Output 2. Then edit the chart, as follows:
- Double-click anywhere in the chart to open the **Chart Editor**.
- Select
   Gallery
      Mixed...
   to open the **Mixed Charts** dialog box. Select **Replace**.
- In response to a warning that the replaced chart cannot be changed back into an Error Bar chart, click **Yes**. You are now in the **Bar/Line/Area Displayed Data** dialog box (Figure 7).

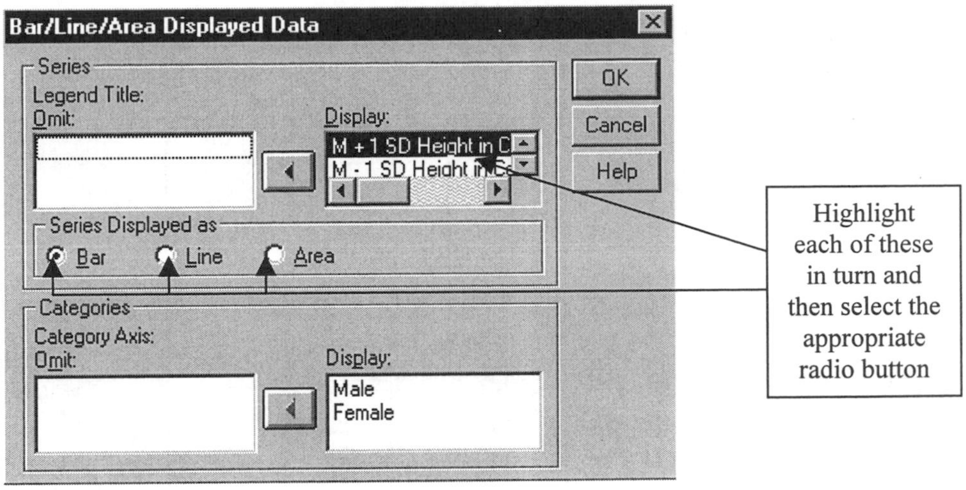

Figure 7. The Bar/Line/Area Displayed Data dialog box for selecting which items are to be represented by a bar or a line or an area

- In the **Display box**, you will see highlighted, **M + 1 SD Height in Centimetres** (in this example, we are using the variable *height*). In the **Series Displayed As** box below and to the left, click the **Line** radio button. Move the highlight to **M - 1 SD Height in Centimetres** and click the **Line** radio button again. Finally, highlight **Mean Height in Centimetres** and click the **Bar** radio button.
- Click **OK** to obtain a figure which looks like a combination of a bar graph and a line graph. This, however, is only an intermediate stage.
- Choose
  Format
       Interpolation...
  to obtain the **Line Interpolation** dialog box. The thick black border should be around the icon labelled **None**. Click **Apply All** and the **Close** box to obtain the next intermediate figure, which is a bar graph with two points along the vertical axis of each bar.
- Choose
  Chart
       Options...
  to obtain the **Bar/Line/Area Options** dialog box. In the **Line Options** box, select the **Connect markers within categories** check box and click **OK** to produce the **bar chart with error bars**.
- At this stage, perhaps with a view to printing in black and white, you might wish to change the colouring of the bars to grey and the lines and markers to black using the **Colors** option.
- The markers at the top and bottom of the ± 1 SD lines can be changed using the **Marker** option.
- Finally, the axis labels and legend labels can be altered by double-clicking each in turn and changing the items in the various dialog boxes.

The result is the chart shown in Output 3.

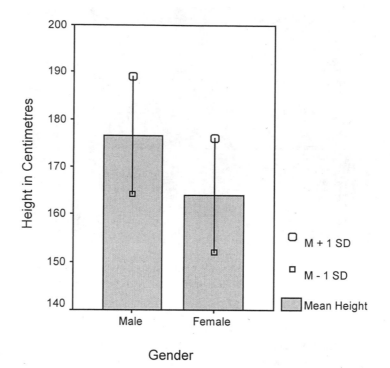

Output 3. A bar chart with error bars for ± 1 SD around the mean

5.4 PIE CHARTS

The **pie-chart** provides a picturesque display of the frequency distribution of a qualitative variable.

To draw a pie chart of the categories within Blood Group [*bloodtyp*]:

- Choose

  Graphs

  Pie...

  to open the **Pie Charts** dialog box (not reproduced here).

- Since the default option of **Summaries for groups of cases** is what we want, click **Define** to open the **Define Pie: Summaries for Groups of Cases** dialog box (the completed version is shown in Figure 8).

- Click Blood Group [*bloodtyp*] and on  to paste the name into the **Define Slices by** box.

- Click **% of cases** so that the slices represent percentages rather than the values of N.

- Finally, it is desirable to have a title: click **Titles** and type the desired title into the box (e.g. *Blood Group Distribution*), click **Continue** and then **OK** to draw the pie-chart, an edited version of which is shown in Output 4.

Transfer the variable name Blood Group (bloodtyp) to here in order to define the categories of the slices

Specify what the slices are to represent (here it is the percentage of cases)

: Define Pie: Summaries for Groups of Cases

Case Number [case]
Gender [sex]
Height in Centimetres [h
Weight in Kilograms [we

Slices Represent
○ N of cases   ● % of cases
○ Cum. n of cases   ○ Cum. % of cases
○ Other summary function

Variable:
▶
Change Summary...

Define Slices by:
◀   Blood Group [bloodtyp]

Template
☐ Use chart specifications from:
File...

OK
Paste
Reset
Cancel
Help
Titles...
Options...

Figure 8. The Summaries for Groups of Cases dialog box with bloodtyp selected for defining the slices

The pie-chart in Output 4 has been edited by changing the colours to grey, and changing the position of the slice labels. (Within the **Chart** menu, choose **Options**, and open the **Pie Options** dialog box. Select **Format**, obtaining the **Pie Options: Label Format** dialog box. For **Position**, opt for **Best fit**.)

It is also possible to rotate the pie if it is desired to make a particular slice near the top. A slice can also be "exploded" i.e. moved out a little from the circle for emphasis.

Blood Group Distribution

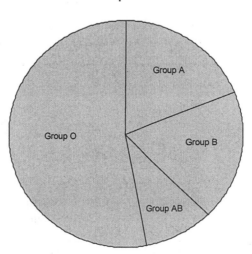

Output 4. Pie Chart of blood group distribution

5.5   LINE GRAPHS

See
Section
4.4.3

Suppose we wanted a **line graph** of mean weight against height. Such a line graph would consist of a number of mean weights plotted above the mid-points of their respective intervals of heights, and then joined successively with straight lines. The total range of heights of the participants is readily split into, say, five intervals by using the **Recode** command (see Section 4.4.3) to create a new variable *hghtcat* consisting of the intervals <155, 156-165, 166-175, 176-185, >185, and assigning these intervals the ordered category labels 1, 2, ..., 5, respectively. The key to the codes can be supplied by using the **Define Labels** dialog box from the **Define Variable** dialog box.

A line graph is obtained by choosing
Graphs
         Line...
and completing the **Line Charts** (choose **Simple** and click **Define**) and the **Define Simple Line: Summaries for Groups of Cases** dialog boxes (Figure 9).

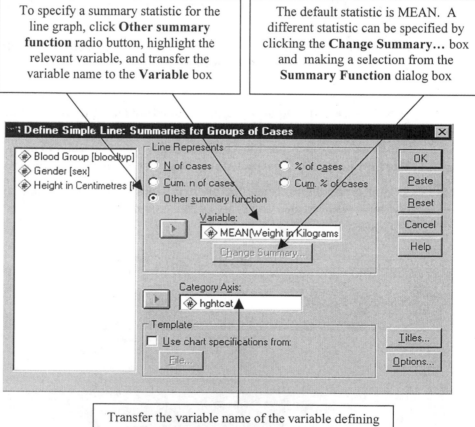

To specify a summary statistic for the line graph, click **Other summary function** radio button, highlight the relevant variable, and transfer the variable name to the **Variable** box

The default statistic is MEAN. A different statistic can be specified by clicking the **Change Summary...** box and making a selection from the **Summary Function** dialog box

Transfer the variable name of the variable defining the values of the x-axis of the line to here

Figure 9.   The Summaries for Groups of Cases dialog box for mean *weight* categorised by ranges of height (*hghcat*)

The edited line graph is shown in Output 5. The editing operations included centring the axis labels, adding circles to the line to mark the mean weights (using the **Interpolation** item within the **Format** menu and then ticking the

Display markers box in the **Line Interpolation** dialog box), and making the line black.

Output 5. Line graph showing mean weight against height category

5.6 SCATTERPLOTS

<table>
<tr>
<td>See
Chaps.
11 &
12</td>
<td>Another way of illustrating the pattern of weight against height is the scatterplot which is a plot of points representing the weight and height of each participant. It should always be plotted and examined before calculating a correlation coefficient (Chapter 11) or conducting a regression analysis (Chapter 12).</td>
</tr>
</table>

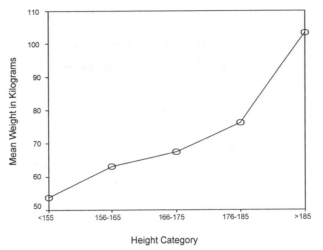

Transfer the variable names to these boxes

Figure 10. The Simple Scatterplot dialog box for weight against height

To obtain the scatterplot of weight against height:

- Choose
  Graphs
     Scatter...
  to open the **Scatterplot** dialog box (not shown here).
- Click **Define** to open the **Simple Scatterplot** dialog box.
- Transfer the variable names as shown in Figure 10.
- Click **OK**.

The edited version of the scatterplot is shown in Output 6. The changes included centring the axis labels, making the points black and changing their form to crosses.

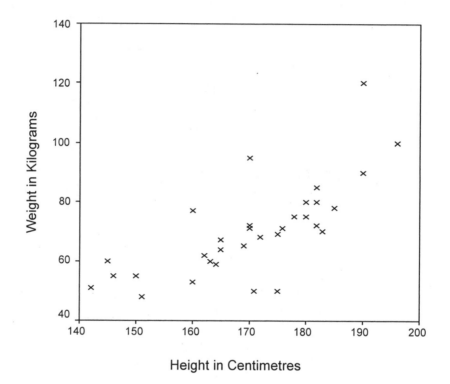

Output 6. The Scatterplot of weight against height

The overall trend of the points can be depicted by the addition of the **regression line** which is the best-fitting straight line drawn through, or as near, as many of the points as possible. Further examples of scatterplots (e.g. plotting bivariate data subdivided by a grouping variable such as sex; adding regression lines to the plots) will be considered in Chapters 11 and 12.

EXERCISE 4

EXPLORATORY DATA ANALYSIS (EDA)

This exercise explores the data in your saved file of merged data, consisting of the responses of 335 people (including yourself) to a questionnaire.

Opening SPSS

Open SPSS in the usual way, selecting the data file *merged data* which was saved in the previous Exercise. Ensure that the value labels (e.g. Female) are visible in **Data View** (if not, click **Value Labels** within the **View** drop-down menu).

Describing categorical data: Obtaining a frequency distribution

Use the **Frequencies** command described in **4.3.1** to obtain a frequency listing for the variable *smoker* in the Output window, remembering to click the **Charts...** box in order to be able to select **Bar Chart(s)** within the **Frequencies: Charts** dialog box.

Inspect the frequency table in the **SPSS Viewer**. Is it what you expected? Before taking any steps to remedy the situation, inspect the bar chart as well.

The bar chart

You will notice immediately that, although the variable *smoker* was supposed to consist only of Yes and No responses, the horizontal axis of the bar chart also shows a bar for 3. To investigate such a mishap, look at the frequency table again. There you will find that, as far as the variable smoker is concerned, in the 335 cases that were processed, there was one 3 entry and one missing value labelled System meaning that there is no entry in the data set as represented by a full stop in **Data View**. Return to **Data View** by clicking **merged data - SP...** in the **Task Bar** at the foot of the screen.

Notice in **Data View** that for the variable *smoker*, Case 10 has a 3 and Case 14 has no value. It is obvious that the 3 should be a 2 since there is no value in *npday* and that the missing value should have been a 1 for *Yes* since the case is recorded as smoking 5 cigarettes per day. Such mistakes are common when one is preparing large data sets and this is why exploratory data analysis (EDA) is important for detecting possible errors. Sometimes it is more convenient to find aberrant values by highlighting the appropriate variable in **Data View** and then selecting
Edit
      Find...
entering the value or symbol required (here it would be 3) in the **Find what** box and then clicking **Find Next**.

To remedy these faults, click 3 for Case 10 to get [3 ▼], click the arrow and select *No* from the choice of options. Do the same for Case 14 but select *Yes* from the choice of options.

Save the corrected data file, using the **Save As** item within the **File** drop-down menu, to a new file name *merged data2* (so that it is not confused with the unaltered data file *merged data*).

Now re-run the **Frequencies** command (remember to click the **Bar Chart** option within **Charts...**) and notice the differences in the output. The message is that EDA is useful for detecting any false data before more extensive statistical analyses are conducted.

Obtaining a bar chart from the Graphs drop-down menu

You can obtain a bar chart directly, without any additional statistics, by selecting

Graphs
Bar ...

to obtain the **Bar Charts** dialog box. You will find that the default settings are **Simple** and **Summaries for Groups of Cases**. This is quite correct for present purposes.

- Click **Define** to open the **Define Simple Bar: Summaries for Groups of Cases** dialog box. Check that in the **Bars Represent** box the **N of cases** option is selected, and then enter the variable name *smoker* into the **Category Axis** box.
- Click **OK** to obtain the bar chart, which will appear in the **SPSS Viewer**.

Editing a bar chart (Section 5.3)

Initially bar charts (and other graphics) will appear in colour on the screen. Such a screen image, however, does not print well in black-and-white. To make the image suitable for black-and-white printing, some editing will be necessary. Proceed as follows.

- Double-click anywhere within the bar chart to open the **SPSS Chart Editor** window. To edit any part of the figure, you must select that part of the screen figure. Highlight the bars by clicking one of them so that each corner has little black squares.
- Click the ⬚ icon to open the **Colors** dialog box. Click the desired colour (e.g. grey) and then click **Apply**.
- The same procedure can be used for changing the fill pattern by selecting the ▨ icon to open the **Fill Patterns** dialog box and then making the desired selections.

After completing the change of pattern, click anywhere in the **Chart** window to turn off the bar highlighting. It is possible to control many other features of charts and graphs by using the **Chart Editor**. For example, by double-clicking an axis, a dialog box will appear enabling you to label the axis and position the label either centrally or to right or left. There are many other adjustments that can be made; but the way forward is to try it yourself.

It is also possible to alter other aspects of the screen figure, such as the aspect ratio, and the spacing of bars and boxes in graphs. All this can be done while you are in the **Chart Editor**. The **aspect ratio** (the height of a graph divided by its width) can be changed from the **Options...** submenu of the **Edit** drop-down menu. Click

Edit
Options...

to open the **Options** dialog box. Click the **Charts** tab to bring the **Charts** dialog box into view.

The default setting for the **Chart Aspect Ratio** is usually 1.25. To improve the appearance of bars and boxes in SPSS graphs, it is well worth experimenting with aspect ratios such as 1 by changing the **Chart Aspect Ratio** to 1 in the box, and then clicking **OK**.

Back in the **Chart Editor**, the spacing of the bars is controlled by the **Bar Spacing** option within the **Chart** menu. There are two aspects of bar spacing:
(1) the **Inter-Bar Spacing** (expressed as a percentage of bar width, and which can vary from 0% to 100%);
(2) the **Bar Margin**, which is the distance of the outermost bars from the inner frame, an invisible rectangle with the horizontal and vertical axes of the graph as two of its sides.

Increasing the bar margin will make the bars narrower, since the inter-bar spacing has been fixed at a specified relative value. It is recommended that the reader experiment with varying combinations of aspect ratio, bar margin and inter-bar spacing.

When editing is finished, return to **SPSS Viewer** by clicking ☒ in the top right-hand corner.

To save your edited chart, ensure that it has a box around it; if not, click anywhere within the bar chart and a box will appear. Then select
File
> **Save**

to obtain a directory dialog box for selecting the disk drive and folder for the file.
Try printing out your chart, following the instructions in Chapter 3, Section 3.6.

Describing categorical data: Crosstabulation

Next we are going to produce some contingency tables, using the **Crosstabs** command (Section 4.3.1).
A crosstabulation is a table showing the frequency of observations in each combination of two categorial variables. Here we shall crosstabulate the *sex* and *faculty* of the cases in our merged data set.

Choose
Analyze
> **Descriptive Statistics**
>> **Crosstabs**

to open the **Crosstabs** dialog box. Enter one of the variables into the **Row(s)** box by clicking its name and then on ▸. Enter the other variable into the **Column(s)** box. Click **OK**.

To save the crosstabulation output, click the second subtable containing the crosstabulation and then select **Save**, and complete the dialog box.

Finishing the session

Close down SPSS and any other windows before logging out of the computer.

EXERCISE 5

EDA (continued)

Opening SPSS

For this exercise, you should have available the corrected merged data set that you corrected in the course of the previous exercise and saved as ***merged data2***. Open SPSS with this data set in the usual way.

Describing interval data

Use the **Frequencies** command outlined in Section 4.3.2 to obtain a histogram with a superimposed normal curve and a table showing the mean, standard deviation and quartiles for *age*. Select the same options as in the **Frequencies: Statistics** dialog box (Figure 17) in Section 4.3.2. Remember to ensure that the **Display frequency tables** box is turned off. Save both the histogram and the table.

- **Edit the histogram to make it suitable for black-and-white printing**

- **Print the histogram.**

Manipulation of the data set - transforming variables

It is sometimes useful to change the data set in some way. For instance, in the current data set, some people have entered their weight in stones and pounds, and others in kilograms. Likewise, height has been entered both in British units (feet and inches) and in metres. In order to be able to produce useful data on weight and height, we must use the same units of measurement. In this exercise we shall adopt metric units (kilograms and metres). Thus we must convert any other measurements into metric measurements. Use the **Compute** command (Section 4.4.2) by selecting

Transform
> **Compute ...**

to obtain the **Compute Variable** dialog box. In the **Target Variable** box, type the name of the variable (*kilos*) which contains the kilograms data In the **Numeric Expression** box, enter the conversion factor. Thus you will enter **(stones*14 + pounds) * 0.453** to convert pounds to kilograms using the conversion factor that 1 pound is 0.453 kilograms and remembering to convert stones to pounds by multiplying by 14. Note that the symbol * is used for multiplication in computing.

There remains one further problem: what about cases whose weight is already in *kilos* and do not have any values in the *stones* and *pounds* variables? If the formula above were to be immediately applied, these people would end up with no values in the *kilos* column. Therefore to convert only the cases with stones and pounds measurements, you must select the **If** box in the **Compute Variable** dialog box, then the **Include if case satisfies condition** box and enter the following expression **stones > 0** which tells the program to calculate the kilograms if the entry in *stones* is greater than 0 (we assume that no-one has a weight of less than 1 stone!). Select **Continue** and then **OK**. You will see a message which asks **Change existing variable?**. Select the **OK** option. Now the program will calculate all the missing *kilos* data and enter them in the data set. Check that it has done this. Save the file using the **Save As** option, giving the amended file a new name (e.g. ***metric data***). This ensures that you still have a copy of the old file, in case you have made any mistakes in calculation and you wish to retrieve the old data at some future time. (It is often regarded as a safer procedure to recode data into a new variable since it allows one to check that the correct recoding command has been requested. We have not done that here, because we wanted to preserve the values already present for some cases in *kilos*.)

Now do a similar conversion for the height data, converting feet and inches to metres. To do this you will need to know that there are 12 inches in a foot and 1 inch is 0.0254 metres. Work out a conversion factor with this in mind. Remember to change the condition to **feet >0**. When you have converted the height data, save the file again, this time by simply clicking **Save** rather than **Save As** since you have already nominated a new file name of *metric data*.

Describing interval data - means of cases categorised by a grouping variable

We can obtain a table of means for one variable at different categories (or combinations) of another variable (or variables). Use the **Means** command described in Section 4.3.2 to obtain a two-way table of means for *metres* by *sex*. Then use the same command to obtain a three-way table of *kilos* by *sex* by *faculty*. (Look carefully at Section 4.3.2 to see how to layer the variables, using the **Next** facility, to produce the three-way table).

- **Print the listing output of this exercise.**

Finishing the session

Close down SPSS and any other windows before logging out of the computer.

EXERCISE 6

MORE CHARTS AND GRAPHS

Opening SPSS

This exercise shows you how to request various charts and graphs. Open SPSS with the data file *metric data* saved in the previous Exercise.

Charts and graphs
1) Stem-and-leaf plot and boxplot

It is often useful to present data in a graphical form, which is easily read and conveys the information quickly and effectively. Use the **Explore** command (Section 4.3.2) to produce stem-and-leaf plots and boxplots of *metres* categorised by *sex*. Remember to click the **Plots** radio button to suppress the Statistics output. Click **Plots...**, ensure that **Stem-and-leaf** has been selected (if not, click the checkbox) and return to the **Explore** dialog box by clicking **Continue**. Enter the variable name *case* into the **Label Cases by...** box.

The **stem-and-leaf plot** provides more information about the original data than does a histogram. As in a histogram, the length of each row corresponds to the number of cases that fall into a particular interval. However, the stem-and-leaf plot represents each case with a numeric value that corresponds to the actual observed value. This is done by dividing observed values into two components - the leading digit or digits, called the **stem**, and a trailing digit, called the **leaf**. For example, the value 64 would have a stem of 6 and a leaf of 4. In the case of heights in metres, the stems are the metres expressed to the first decimal place, the leaves are the second decimal place. Thus the modal height (i.e. the most frequent height) for males is shown with a stem of 17 (1.7 metres), the leaves being the second decimal place. If there is a large number of values for a particular stem, then the stem is repeated on successive rows for different groups of leaves.

The **boxplot** is another type of display, which is more fully explained in Section 4.3.2. The main box spans 50% of the cases (those between the upper and lower quartiles) and the extensions (**whiskers**) cover the remaining cases, provided they are not deemed to be outliers (shown as o's) or extremes (shown as asterisks).

- **Prepare the boxplot for printing in black-and-white, and print the Output.**

- **Within the female group, which stem contains the most leaves?**

Examine the boxplot for males and note the case numbers of the outliers so that you can check their actual heights in the data set. There is a command for locating a specific case in the data set. Select
Data
> **Go to case ...**

to obtain the **Go to Case** dialog box. You then enter the required case number and click **OK**.

- **Write down the actual heights of the males denoted by the outliers on the box plots.**

2) Bar charts

Draw a bar chart of *kilos* and *metres* by *sex* using the **Bar** option within the **Graphs** drop-down menu.

Choose
Graphs
> **Bar**
>> **Clustered**

and select the radio button for **Summaries of Separate Variables** in the **Data in Chart Are** box. Click **Define** and then enter *kilos* and *metres* into the **Bars Represent** box and *sex* into the **Category Axis** box.

- **Study the chart produced. Does this seem a sensible graphic representation of the two variables? If not, why not? You do not need to print the chart, but make a note of why the representation is not appropriate and what would be a better way of displaying the mean heights and weights of subjects split by sex.**

The moral behind this is that you must always consider what your output is likely to be. SPSS will produce the graph that you ask for, but the end result may not be a sensible representation of the data. It is best to draw by hand a rough representation of what you expect the graph to look like before requesting SPSS to do so.

Transposing data on a graph or chart

It is possible to transpose data on graphs and charts which have more than one variable or factor plotted so that the lines or bars are replotted in a transposed manner. This will become clearer with an example.

Plot a new bar chart of the mean number of cigarettes smoked (*npday*) categorised by *sex* and by *faculty*. Do this by choosing
Graphs
> **Bar**
>> **Clustered**

and select the radio button for **Summaries for groups of cases** in the **Data in Chart Are** box (this is the default selection). Click **Define** and then click **Other summary function** within the **Bars Represent box**. Then enter *npday* into the **Variable** box (it will appear as **MEAN(Number of cigarettes per day [npday])**), *sex* in the **Category Axis** box, and *faculty* in the **Define Clusters by** box.

You should then see in the **SPSS Viewer** window a bar chart arranged by sex, with each cluster consisting of bars representing the three Faculties and Missing (apparently no female in Missing smokes). Suppose, however, that you would rather see a chart with four clusters (Faculties) of two (sex) instead of two clusters (sex) of four (Faculties). This could be done by returning to the dialog box and changing *sex* and *faculty* around, but a quicker method is to use the **Chart Editor** as described in Section 5.2.1.

To get into the **Chart Editor**, double-click anywhere within or near the barchart. A new window labelled **SPSS Chart Editor** will appear together with a new range of drop-down menus along the top.

Select
Series
    Transpose Data
and a rearranged barchart will appear.

Return to the untransposed by clicking again on **Transpose Data** within the **Series** menu.

To change the cumbersome captions in the legend to the right of barchart, select
Chart
    Legend...
and then delete *Mean Number of cigarettes per day* after each category of Faculty of Attendee in the two lines of the **Selected Label** boxes within the **Legend** dialog box, clicking the **Change** box each time.

The user might also wish to change the colours into different varieties of **Fill Patterns**. This is a two-stage procedure involving changing each colour to white and then selecting a different fill pattern for each. Follow the steps described at the end of Section 5.2.1.

A title can be added using
Chart
    Title...
and then entering a title into the **Title 1:** box and changing the justification to **Centre**.

Finally return the edited barchart to the **SPSS Viewer** by closing the **Chart Editor** (click ☒ in the top right-hand corner). If desired, the edited barchart can be printed from **SPSS Viewer**.

Pie chart

Another way of presenting data is in the form of a **pie chart**. Draw a pie chart (see Section 5.4) for *status* and give the chart a title, including your **own** name in the title (e.g. Pie Chart of Status produced by Mary Smith) by selecting
Graphs
    Pie...
to open the **Pie Charts** dialog box.

Edit the chart to show actual percentages for each slice. You can do this by double-clicking near the pie chart to open the **SPSS Chart Editor** window and then selecting
Chart
    Options
and selecting **Percents** in the **Pie Options** dialog box. You could also click **Formats** and change the **Position:** option to **Best Fit** which will then put the label and percentages inside each slice.

Try for yourself the following:

- **Edit the chart to make it suitable for black-and-white printing.**

Return the edited pie chart to **SPSS Viewer** by closing the **Chart Editor** in the usual way.

- **Print the pie chart.**

Finishing the session

Close down SPSS and any other windows before logging out of the computer.

EXERCISE 7

RECODING DATA; SELECTING CASES; LINE GRAPH

Aim

This exercise shows you how to recode data, select cases and draw a line graph..

Opening SPSS

Open SPSS with the data file **metric data** saved in an earlier Exercise.

Recoding data

Sometimes you may wish to recode values or categories within a variable (e.g. you might want to combine more than one value or category into a single new value or category). Suppose that you are not particularly interested in whether people are doing a MSc degree or a PhD degree, but just want to know whether they are postgraduates. You can change the database to give you this information, either within the original variable, *status*, or by creating a new variable containing the recoded information. In this session we are going to use a new variable, since this retains the original variable *status* for checking that the recoding has been done correctly. It also maintains the original values in the data set.

Use the **Recode** (Section 4.4.3) command to recode the status codes *MSc Postgrad* and *PhD Postgrad* (i.e. categories 2 and 3) into a new category 1 and the codes *Undergrad* and *Other* (i.e. categories 1 and 4) into a new category 2. You will need to follow the section carefully. The **Recode** command creates a new variable which you are asked to name: we suggest *new_stat* containing the underline, not the hyphen, symbol. An underline is allowed in a variable name but a hyphen or a space is not. To do this, you will have to choose the **Recode into Different Variables** option within the **Recode** command.

- Choose
  Transform
  Recode
  Into Different Variables
  to open the **Recode into Different Variables** dialog box.
- Highlight Attendee's Status [status] and click ▶ to transfer it into the **Input Variable → Output Variable** box.
- Type *new_stat* in the **Name** box within the **Output Variable** box and click **Change**. The new variable name *new_stat* will now appear alongside *status*.
- You might also type *New Status* into the **Output Variable Label** box as a label for the new variable *new_stat*.
- Click **Old and New Values** and then fill in the corresponding values in the **Value** box of **Old Value** and in the **Value** box of **New Value**, clicking **Add** each time. The following should then appear in the right-hand box: $1 \rightarrow 2$, $2 \rightarrow 1$, $3 \rightarrow 1$, $4 \rightarrow 2$.
- Finally click **Continue** and **OK**.

When you have followed this command, check that you have the new variable at the far right of your data set. Now you should clarify the values by adding suitable labels. To do this, switch to **Variable View** and then click **None** in the cell in the **Values** column for the row of the new variable *new_stat*. When the grey box with three dots appears, click it to open the **Values Labels** dialog box. Complete this box in the usual way by assigning *Postgrad* to value 1 and *Others* to value 2, and finally click **OK**. To see whether this has worked, switch to **Data View** and check the data for the new variable *new_stat*.

Save the data file again.

We shall now use the **Recode** command to recode the heights of people as tall, medium or short. When the **Recode** dialog box re-appears, be sure to click **Reset** to remove the previous information. Give the new variable the name *new_ht* containing the underline, not the hyphen, symbol.

Use the following table for recoding the heights into values (we shall attach the labels later):

Range	Value	Label
Under 1.7 metres	1	Short
Between 1.7 and 1.8 metres	2	Medium
Over 1.8 metres	3	Tall

You will need to use the **Range Lowest through** facility for short people, the **Range** facility for medium people, and the **Range through highest** facility for tall people, taking particular care to ensure that there is no ambiguity about the group into which a height will be assigned. SPSS recodes values from the smallest upwards. Thus 1.7 will be included in Short unless it is defined as **Lowest thru 1.6999**. Re-read the end of Section 4.4.3 for extra help.

Check your data to make certain that they have all been classified in the manner that you planned. Note that although you may see only two decimal places in the **Data Editor**, so that a value such as 1.71 may in fact be 1.7068. If the value is highlighted, the true value will appear in the **Cell Editor** box above the variable names.

Once the new variable *new_ht* has been created, switch to **Variable View** and add the labels *Short*, *Medium* and *Tall* to values 1, 2 and 3 respectively. Click **OK**. These labels should then appear in **Data View**.

Pie chart

Produce a pie chart with a title showing what percentages of the cases are tall, medium or short. Edit the pie chart to show the percentage for each slice using the **Pie Options** dialog box (see Exercise 6 if you need to refresh your memory).

- **Edit the pie chart to prepare it for black-and-white printing. Print the pie chart.**

Select cases

It is also useful to be able to select the cases you want to analyse. Suppose, for example, that you wished to consider only the data relating to females. Use **Select Cases** (Section 3.7.1) to specify that only the female cases will be analysed.

Now suppose that, since smoking is said to suppress appetite, you wanted to see whether female smokers were lighter in weight than non-smokers. Use the **Compare Means** (Section 4.3.2) command to do this. Remember the Dependent variable will be *kilos* and the Independent variable *smoker*.

- **Print the Report table produced. Note that as a result of the Select Cases command you have just followed, this table will apply to the female respondents only.**

- **Are there any differences between the smokers and the non-smokers? Comment briefly on any differences you find. (When you think about this, bear in mind the difference in size between the smoking and non-smoking groups)**

Line graph

A **line graph** is suitable when there is an interval or ordinal scale for one of the variables with not more than about ten values. When the scale is nominal, a bar chart is preferable. Now that we have an ordinal scale of height with three values in the variable *new_ht*, we can draw a line graph of *sex* against *new_ht*.

First, however, the selection of females in the previous section must be reversed by returning to the **Select Cases** dialog box and clicking the **All cases** radio button. Then choose

> **Graphs**
>> **Line**
>>> **Multiple**
>>>> **Summaries for groups of cases**

to open the **Define Multiple Line: Summaries for Groups of Cases** dialog box. Then insert the variable *new_ht* into the **Category Axis** box and *sex* into the **Define Lines by** box. Click **Options** and deselect **Display groups defined by missing values** (this stops the missing data for height being plotted). Click **Continue** and then **OK** to plot the lines. A two-line graph should then appear, one line for Male and one line for Female, with the points on the abscissa labelled Short, Medium and Tall.

In order to differentiate the sexes clearly in the printed graph, change one of the lines to a discontinuous line using the editing facility (see Section 5.5). Double-click anywhere on the graph to open **the SPSS Chart Editor**. Click one of the lines so that it acquires black rectangles and then select ▦ to open the **Line Styles** dialog box, select the interrupted line and click **Apply**.

Prepare the graph for black-and-white printing by changing the colours of the lines to black as described for barcharts in Exercise 4.

You may also wish to show the markers for the different categories, in which case, select ◿ to open the **Line Interpolation** dialog box. Select **Straight**, ensure that the checkbox for **Display markers** is ticked (click it if it is not) and click **Apply All**. If desired, you can change the shape or the size of the markers by entering the Markers dialog box with the ✱ icon.

Save the chart in the usual way.

- **Print out the line graph.**

Finishing the session

Close down SPSS and any other windows before logging out of the computer.

CHAPTER 6

COMPARING AVERAGES: TWO-SAMPLE AND ONE-SAMPLE TESTS

6.1 INTRODUCTION
6.2 PARAMETRIC METHODS: THE T-TESTS
6.3 NONPARAMETRIC EQUIVALENTS OF THE T-TESTS
6.4 ONE-SAMPLE TESTS

6.1 INTRODUCTION

See
Section
1.2

In Chapter 1 (Section 1.2), five types of research situation were identified. In the first, the researcher has two samples of scores and wants to know whether the difference between sample averages is significant. In the decision chart for the selection of an appropriate statistical test (Chapter 1, Figure 2), the first question is how many conditions there are. This chapter is partly concerned with the use of SPSS to carry out the tests recommended in the flow chart when there are only two conditions. In the fifth research situation described in Chapter 1, the researcher has only a single sample of scores, on the basis of which he or she wishes either to make an inference about the mean of the population or decide whether the distribution of the sample is sufficiently well fitted by a theoretical distribution for it to be safe to assume that the sample is indeed from a population with that distribution (Chapter 1, Figure 6). This chapter will also describe the use of SPSS to make appropriate one-sample tests to make inferences about the population mean and to test for goodness-of-fit.

6.1.1 SPSS commands for two-sample tests

Table 1 shows the SPSS menus and sub-menus for various two-sample tests. The left half of Table 1 identifies **parametric tests**, i.e., tests that make assumptions about population distributions. The right half of the table specifies **non-parametric tests**, which do not make such assumptions. Each half of the table is subdivided according to whether the samples are independent or related (SPSS refers to related samples as **paired samples** in the case of the t-test, but as **related samples** for nonparametric tests).

Table 1. SPSS menus and submenus within the Analyze drop-down menu for various two-sample situations

Data derived from populations assumed to have normal distributions and equal variances		No specific assumptions about the population distributions	
Independent samples	**Paired samples**	**Independent samples**	**Related samples**
Compare Means	Compare Means	Nonparametric Tests	Nonparametric Tests
↓	↓	↓	↓
Independent Samples T Test…	Paired Samples T Test…	2 Independent Samples…	2 Related Samples…

↓ indicates that the item below is part of the submenu of the item above

6.1.2 SPSS commands for one-sample tests

Table 2 shows the SPSS menus and sub-menus for various one-sample tests. The left side of the table shows the one-sample t-test; the right side lists some non-parametric tests.

Table 2. SPSS menus and submenus within the Analyze and Nonparametric Tests drop-down menus for various one-sample situations				
Data derived from a population assumed to have a normal distribution	**No specific assumptions about the population distributions**			
Analyze	Nonparametric Tests			
↓	↓	↓	↓	↓
Compare Means	Chi-Square…	Binomial…	Runs…	1-Sample K-S*…
↓				
One-Sample T Test…				

↓ indicates that the item below is part of the submenu of the item above

*K-S stands for Kolmogorov-Smirnov

6.1.3 One-tailed and two-tailed tests

See Section 1.1

The **experimental hypothesis** is a prediction about the effect of an experimental treatment. A t-test (or any other formal statistical test), however, tests the negation of the experimental hypothesis, which is known as the **null hypothesis**. Sometimes, in exploratory work especially, the experimental hypothesis can simply be that there may be a difference: that is, the hypothesis is **non-directional**. In that case, the corresponding null hypothesis is simply that there is no difference, and a large difference in either direction would be evidence against it. Accordingly, a **two-tailed test**, which rejects the null hypothesis if the value of the test statistic falls within either tail of the distribution, is appropriate. This means that if we set the significance level at .05 (or 5%), a value of the test statistic in either the top or the bottom 2.5% of the distribution will result in the rejection of the null hypothesis.

Usually, however, the experimental hypothesis specifies the direction of the difference: Group A is expected to perform better than Group B, or vice versa. The negation of this **directional** hypothesis is the null hypothesis that Group A is no better than Group B. Only a large difference in favour of Group A will count as evidence against this null hypothesis: should there be a difference in the opposite direction, the hypothesis must be accepted. In this situation, arguably, a **one-tailed test** is appropriate, with the region of rejection as the top 5% of the distribution, rather than the top and bottom 2.5%, as in a two-tailed test.

6.2   PARAMETRIC METHODS: THE T-TESTS

If you are not familiar with the t-test, we strongly recommend that you read the relevant sections of a good statistical text: e.g. Gravetter & Wallnau (2000; chapters 9-11) give a lucid account.

6.2.1   Assumptions underlying the use of the t-test

With independent samples, the t statistic is calculated by dividing the difference between the sample means by an estimate of the standard deviation of the distribution of differences, which is known as the **standard error of the difference**. Should the sample variances have similar values, it is common practice to work with a pooled estimate of the supposedly constant population variance (hence the term **pooled t-test**); but if the variances are markedly disparate, the pooled estimate is not used and a **separate variance t-test** is made. The precise value of t needed for significance depends upon the **degrees of freedom** of the distribution, which in turn depends upon the sizes of the samples in the experiment; but a value of t greater than or equal to 2 is usually significant, unless the samples are very small.

The model underlying a t-test assumes that the data have been derived from normal distributions with equal variance. Computer simulations, however, have shown that even with moderate violations of these assumptions, one may still safely proceed with a t-test, provided the samples are not too small, do not contain outliers (atypical scores), and are of equal (or nearly equal) size. Should a preliminary exploration of the data (as recommended in Chapter 4) indicate that the assumptions of a t-test model have been seriously violated, an alternative test could be chosen from the portfolio of **non-parametric** tests in the **Non-parametric Tests** menu. Another approach is to remove the outliers and apply the t-test to the reduced data set.

6.2.2   The paired-samples t-test

In an experiment on lateralisation of cortical functioning, a participant looks at a central spot on a computer screen and is told to press a key on recognition of a word that may appear on either side of the spot. The experimental hypothesis is that words presented in the right visual field will be more quickly recognised than those in the left visual field, because the former are processed by the left cerebral hemisphere, which is thought to be more proficient with verbal information. Notice that this is a **directional hypothesis**, for which we shall make a **one-tailed test** of the null hypothesis that recognition is not faster for words in the right visual field.

For each participant, the median response time to forty words in each of the right and left visual fields is recorded, as indicated in Table 3.

Table 3. Paired data: Median word recognition times in milliseconds for words in the left and right visual fields

Case	Left Field	Right Field
1	323	304
2	512	493
3	502	491
4	385	365
5	453	426
6	343	320
7	543	523
8	440	442
9	682	580
10	590	564

See
Section
3.2

Prepare the data file from the paired data in Table 3 as follows:

- Using the techniques described in Chapter 3 (Section 3.2), open **Variable View** and name the variables *case*, *leftfld* and *rightfld* (adding fuller labels, such as *Left Visual Field* and *Right Visual Field*).

- Now switch to **Data View** (which will show the variable names) and enter the data.

Exploring the data

See
Section
5.6

To check for anomalies in the data before running the t-test, construct a scatterplot. Use the **Scatter** item in the **Graphs** menu (Chapter 5, Section 5.6), entering Left Visual Field [*leftfld*] in the **Y Axis** box and Right Visual Field [*rightfld*] in the **X Axis** box. The scatterplot is shown in Output 1.

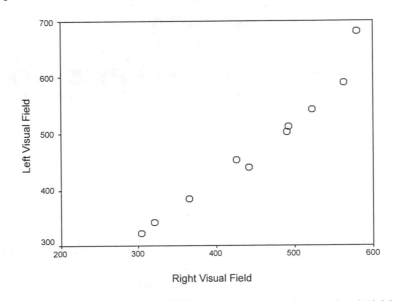

Output 1. The scatterplot of Left Visual Field against Right Visual Field

No outlier appears in the scatterplot. It should be noted that the presence of an outlying pair of scores, even one showing a difference in the same direction as the others, can have the effect of increasing the denominator of the t statistic more than the numerator and so reduce the value of t to insignificance. This effect is illustrated in one of the Exercises. The vulnerability of the standard deviation to the leverage exerted by outliers derives from the fact that the elements of the variance are the **squares** of deviations from the mean, and large deviations thus continue to have a disproportionate influence, even after the square root operation has been carried out.

When outliers are present, the user can either consider removing them or choose a nonparametric method such as the **Sign test** or the **Wilcoxon matched pairs test**. The former is completely immune to the influence of outliers; the latter is much more resistant than the t-test. Should there be no contra-indications against the use of the t-test however, the parametric t-test is preferable to a nonparametric test because the latter would incur the penalty of a loss of power.

Running the t-test

Proceed as follows:
- Choose
  Analyze (see Figure 1)
        Compare Means
              Paired-Samples T Test ...
  to open the **Paired-Samples T Test** dialog box (the completed version is shown in Figure 2).

Figure 1. The Compare Means menu

- Transfer the variable names to the **Paired Variables** box as described in Figure 2.
- Click **OK**.

Since it is possible to run t-tests for several pairs of variables at the same time, the output specifies the **Pair** under consideration in each sub-table. In this example, there is only one pair. The output table, **Paired Samples Statistics**, tabulates statistics for each variable.

Paired Samples Statistics

		Mean	N	Std. Deviation	Std. Error Mean
Pair 1	Left Visual Field	477.30	10	112.09	35.45
	Right Visual Field	450.80	10	97.09	30.70

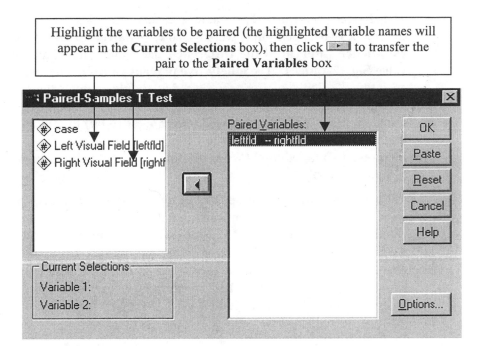

Figure 2. The Paired-Samples T Test dialog box for pairing Left and Right Visual Fields

The second output table, **Paired Samples Correlations,** gives the value of the correlation coefficient, which is 0.97.

Paired Samples Correlations

		N	Correlation	Sig.
Pair 1	Left Visual Field & Right Visual Field	10	.97	.00

The final table (Output 2), **Paired Samples Test,** tabulates various statistics and their p-values.

Paired Samples Test

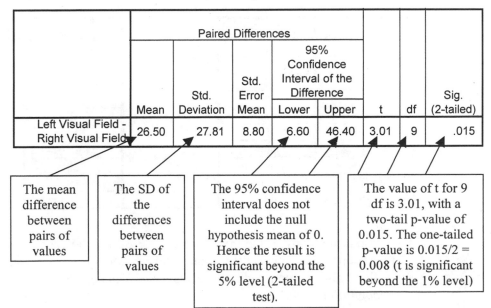

Output 2. T-test output for paired samples

The **Paired Samples Test** table presents statistics of the distribution of differences between the paired scores (**Paired Differences**), the **95% confidence Interval of the Difference**, the **t** value, its **df** and its two-tailed p-value **Sig. (2-tailed)**. The **ninety-five percent confidence interval (95% CI)** is an interval calculated from the data that should include the true value of the parameter (in this case the mean difference in the population) in 95% of samples. Here the interval ranges from **Lower** (6.60) to **Higher** (46.40). Since this interval does not include the H_0 value of 0, t is significant beyond the .05 level on a two-tailed test. (We know, therefore, that t must also be significant on a one-tailed test.)

The most important result appears in the last three columns. We see that the value of the test statistic **t** (on 9 degrees of freedom) is 3.01, and that the 2-tail p-value, **Sig. (2-tailed)**, is 0.015. Since we are testing a **directional hypothesis**, we **halve the two-tailed p-value**, obtaining a value of 0.008. Thus the null hypothesis can be rejected at the 1% level (.01). Accordingly, the scientific hypothesis that words presented in the right visual field will be more quickly recognised than those in the left visual field is confirmed. Write this result as:

$$t (9) = 3.01; p < 0.01,$$

where the value in brackets is the number of degrees of freedom and p is the p-value.

6.2.3   The independent samples t-test

Now suppose that **different** participants had been tested with words in the right and left visual fields. The data table might appear as in Table 4.

Case	Left Field		Case	Right Field
1	500		11	392
2	513		12	445
3	300		13	271
4	561		14	523
5	483		15	421
6	502		16	489
7	539		17	501
8	467		18	388
9	420		19	411
10	480		20	467

Table 4. Independent samples: Median word recognition times in milliseconds for words in the left and right visual fields

- In **Variable View**, name the variables as *case* for the case number, *field* for the grouping (independent) variable, and *rectime* for the dependent variable.
- In the **Label** column, add the labels *Case Number*, *Visual Field* and *Word Recognition Time*.

- In the **Values** column, define the values and their labels (e.g. 1 = Left Field, 2 = Right Field) for *field*.
- Open **Data View** and type in the case number, value label and recognition time for each participant.

Exploring the data

See
Section
4.3.2

Before running the t-test, it is important to check the data for anomalies such as extreme values or skewed distributions. Since this data set contains a grouping variable, the **Explore** command (Chapter 4, Section 4.3.2) is appropriate.
- Choose
  Analyze
  >   **Descriptive Statistics**
  >   **Explore...**
  to open the **Explore** dialog box (see Chapter 4, Figure 20).
- Transfer the dependent variable Word Recognition Time [*rectime*] in the left-hand box to the **Dependent List:** box. Transfer the grouping variable Visual Field [*field*] to the **Factor List:** box.
- Click **Plots...** to open the **Explore: Plots** dialog box, deselect the **Stem-and-leaf** check box and select **Histogram** check box. Click **Continue** to return to the **Explore** dialog box.
- Click **OK** to run the **Explore** command.

See
Table
2,
Chap.
4

The output is extensive. In Output 3, the Left Field boxplot shows an extreme value of 300ms for case 3 (*3 means, 'Case 3 is an extreme value'). In Output 4, which shows histograms of the same distributions, the same extreme value appears as the isolated left-hand box in the Left Field histogram. Another score, 271ms for Case 13, appears as the isolated left-hand box in the Right Field histogram though it is not flagged as an outlier in the boxplot.

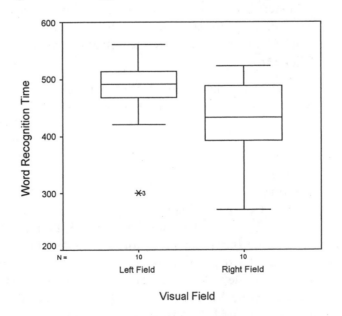

Output 3. The boxplots from the Explore command

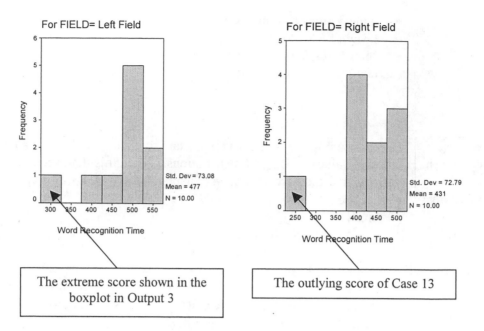

Output 4. The histograms from the Explore command

See Section 3.7.1

In view of these findings, it is advisable to deselect Cases 3 and 13 before running the t-test. This is easily done using the **Select Cases** command described in Chapter 3, Section 3.7.1.

- Choose
    Data
        Select Cases...
    to open the **Select Cases** dialog box (see Chapter 3, Figure 22).
- Click the **If condition is satisfied** radio button and then on **If...** to open the **Select Cases: If** dialog box.
- Transfer Word Recognition Time [*rectime*] to the conditional statement box. Type in an expression such as >300 to select all times greater than 300 ms. Click **Continue** to return to the **Select Cases** dialog box.
- Click **OK**.

Inspection of the data in **Data View** will show that cases 3 and 13 have been deselected. Now we can continue with the t-test.

Running the t-test

- Choose
    Analyze
        Compare Means
            Independent-Samples T Test ...
    to open the **Independent-Samples T Test** dialog box.
- Transfer the dependent variable Word Recognition Time [*rectime*] to the **Test Variable(s)** box. Transfer the grouping variable Visual Field [*field*] to the **Grouping Variable** box. At this point the **Grouping Variable** box will appear with **field [? ?]** as shown in Figure 3.

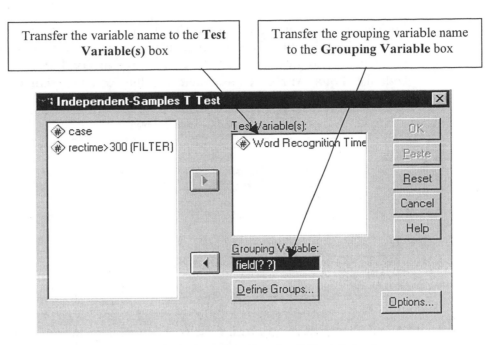

Figure 3. The Independent-Samples T Test dialog box

- Define the values of the groups by clicking **Define Groups** to obtain the **Define Groups dialog box** (Figure 4).

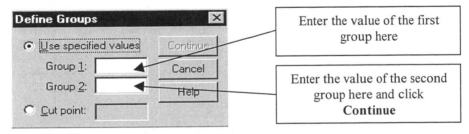

Figure 4. The Define Groups dialog box before defining the values of the two groups

- Type the value *1* into the **Group 1** box and the value *2* into the **Group 2** box, and click **Continue**. The values 1, 2 will then appear in brackets after *field* in the **Grouping Variable** box:

Grouping Variable:
field(1 2)

- Click **OK** to run the t-test.

Firstly, in the output there is a table, **Group Statistics**, listing some statistics of the two samples, including the means (496.11 and 448.56). The means look different; but is this difference significant?

Group Statistics

	Visual Field	N	Mean	Std. Deviation	Std. Error Mean
Word Recognition Time	Left Field	9.00	496.11	41.01	13.67
	Right Field	9.00	448.56	49.14	16.38

The answer to this question is shown in the second table (Output 5), **Independent Samples Test**, which tabulates the value of **t** and its p-value, **Sig. (2-tailed)**. Also given are the **95% Confidence Interval of the Difference** for both the **Equal variances assumed** and the **Equal variance not assumed** situations.

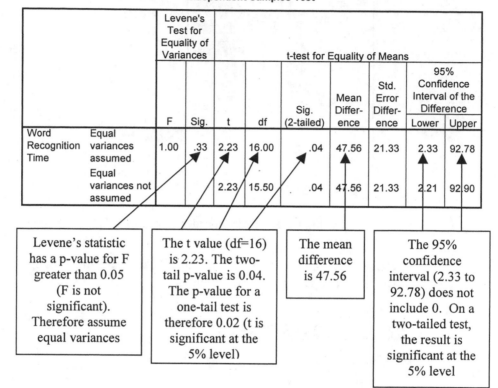

Independent Samples Test

Output 5. T-test output for Independent Samples

Notice **Levene's Test for Equality of Variances**, which is a test for homogeneity of variance. Provided Levene's test is **not significant** (p > 0.05), the variances can be assumed to be homogeneous and the **Equal Variances** line of values for the t-test can be used. (This is the **pooled t-test** mentioned earlier.) In summary:

- If p > 0.05, the homogeneity of variance assumption is tenable, and the equal-variance (pooled) t-test (**Equal variances assumed**) is used.
- If p < 0.05, the homogeneity of variance assumption has been violated and the separate variance t-test (**Equal variances not assumed**) is used.

The reader will have observed that in this example, both the p-values and t-values for **Equal variance assumed** and **Equal variance not assumed** are identical. That would not have been the case had the variances been heterogeneous: the two t-tests can lead to different decisions about the null hypothesis. In this example, the Levene Test is not significant (p > 0.05), so the t value calculated with the pooled variance estimate (**Equal variances assumed**) is appropriate.

The most important result is that the value of **t** (df = 16) is 2.23, with a two-tail p-value, **Sig. (2 tailed)** of 0.04. For a one-tail test, we must halve this value to obtain a p-value of 0.02 (2%): *t* is significant at the 5% level. Thus, the hypothesis that words presented in the right visual field will be more quickly recognised than those in the left visual field is confirmed. Write this result as:

$$t(16) = 2.23; \; p < 0.05.$$

The **95% Confidence Interval of the Difference** is 2.33 to 93.78 which does not include 0, the value under H_0. Had the lower value been negative, the result of the two-tailed t-test would have been not significant.

Recall that this t-test has been run on a reduced data set. The reader might wish to re-run the test on the complete data set. In that case,

$$t(18) = 1.401; \; p > 0.05.$$

The t-test fails to show significance because the two low scores have the effect of increasing the standard error of the difference (the denominator of t) from 21.33 to 32.62, thereby reducing the value of t.

6.3 NONPARAMETRIC EQUIVALENTS OF THE T-TESTS

When there are serious violations of the assumptions of the t-test, nonparametric tests can be used instead. They should not be used as a matter of course, however, because should the data meet the requirements of the t-test, the comparable nonparametric test may lack the **power** to reject the null hypothesis, should that be false. (The **power** of a statistical test is the probability that the null hypothesis, if false, will be rejected.) It is best, therefore, to consider the parametric test first, resorting to the nonparametric alternative only if the data seriously violate the requirements.

SPSS offers a wide selection of nonparametric tests in the **Nonparametric Tests** submenu of **Analyze**. The **Sign** and **Wilcoxon** tests are nonparametric counterparts of the paired samples t-test; the **Mann-Whitney** test is an alternative to the independent samples t-test. Most nonparametric methods use statistics, such as the median, that are resistant to outliers and skewness. In the tests described here, H_0 states that, in the population, the two **medians** are equal.

6.3.1 Related samples: Wilcoxon, Sign and McNemar tests

With the data from Table 3 in the **Data Editor**,
* Choose
  Analyze
  > **Nonparametric Tests**
  > > **Related Samples ...**
  to obtain the **Two-Related-Samples** dialog box (Figure 5).
* Transfer the variable names Left Visual Field [*leftfld*] and Right Visual Field [*rightfld*] to the **Test Pair(s) List:** box, where they will appear joined by dashes as shown.
* Click **OK**.

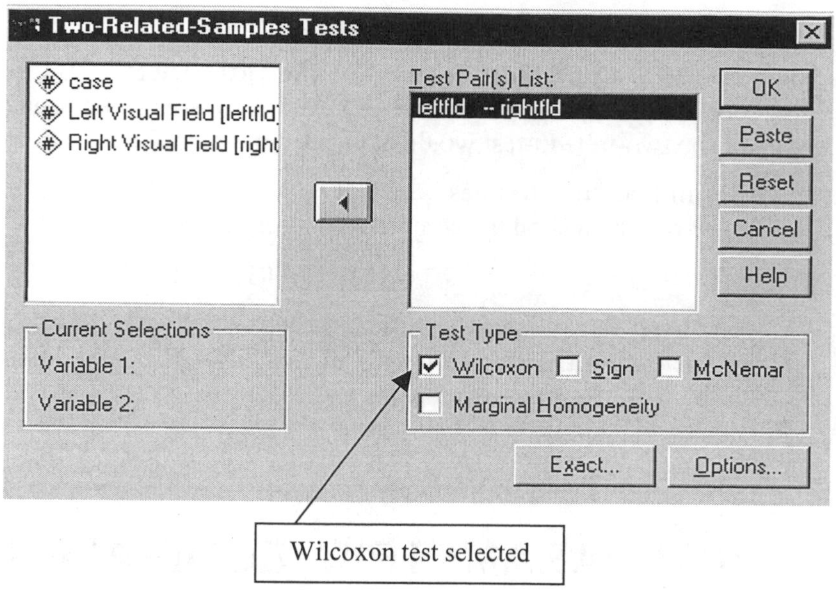

Figure 5. Two-Related-Samples Tests dialog box for Left - Right Visual Fields with Wilcoxon Test selected

The first table in the output, **Ranks**, shows the sums of the positive and negative ranks.

Ranks

		N	Mean Rank	Sum of Ranks
Right Visual Field - Left Visual Field	Negative Ranks	9[a]	6.00	54.00
	Positive Ranks	1[b]	1.00	1.00
	Ties	0[c]		
	Total	10		

a. Right Visual Field < Left Visual Field

b. Right Visual Field > Left Visual Field

c. Left Visual Field = Right Visual Field

The second table (Output 6), **Test Statistics**, gives the value of the test statistic, whose p-value, **Asymp. Sig. (2-tailed),** is less than 0.01.

Test Statistics[b]

	Right Visual Field - Left Visual Field
Z	-2.70[a]
Asymp. Sig. (2-tailed)	.01

a. Based on positive ranks.

b. Wilcoxon Signed Ranks Test

The z value derived from the smaller absolute value of the two Sums of Ranks is -2.70 with a two-tailed p-value of 0.01. For a one-tail test, halve the p-value to obtain 0.005. The difference is therefore significant at the 1% level

Output 6. The output for the Wilcoxon test

As in the case of the t-test, simply halve the given, two-tail p-value for a **one-tail test**. The result confirms the t-test result: there is a significant difference between the visual fields. Write this as:

$$z = 2.70; \quad p < 0.01.$$

Other non-parametric alternatives to the paired t-test

Although the **Wilcoxon test** assumes neither normality nor homogeneity of variance, it does assume that the two samples are from populations with the same distribution shape. It is therefore also vulnerable to the influences of outliers - though not to nearly the same extent as the t-test. The **Sign test**, which is even more robust than the Wilcoxon, can be requested by clicking its check box. The **McNemar test** is applicable to paired qualitative data.

6.3.2   Independent samples: Mann-Whitney test

Here we will use the complete data set rather than the reduced set we used for the t-test. With the data from Table 4 in **Data View**,

- Choose
  Analyze
  > **Nonparametric Tests**
  >> **Independent Samples ...**
  to obtain the **Two-Independent-Samples** dialog box.
- Transfer the test (dependent) variable Word Recognition Time [*rectime*] to the **Test Variable List** box. Transfer the grouping variable Visual Field [*field*] to the **Grouping Variable** box. Click **Define Groups** and add the group numbers *1* and *2* in the usual way (Figure 6).
- Click **Continue** and then **OK** to run the test.

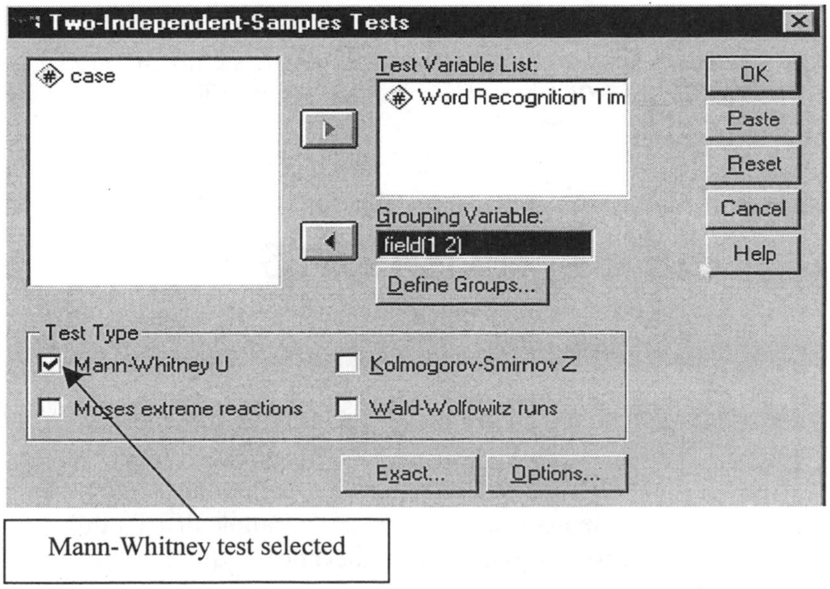

Mann-Whitney test selected

Figure 6. The Two-Independent-Samples dialog box for Word Recognition Time categorised by Visual Field with the Mann-Whitney U Test selected

The first table in the output, **Ranks**, tabulates the sums of ranks for the Left and Right Fields.

Ranks

	Visual Field	N	Mean Rank	Sum of Ranks
Word Recognition Time	Left Field	10	12.65	126.50
	Right Field	10	8.35	83.50
	Total	20		

The second table (Output 7), **Test Statistics**, gives the values of various statistics, including **Mann-Whitney U** and its p-value, **Asymp. Sig. (2-tailed)**.

Test Statistics[b]

	Word Recognition Time
Mann-Whitney U	28.500
Wilcoxon W	83.500
Z	-1.626
Asymp. Sig. (2-tailed)	.104
Exact Sig. [2*(1-tailed Sig.)]	.105[a]

a. Not corrected for ties.

b. Grouping Variable: Visual Field

The z value derived from the Mann-Whitney statistic is -1.626 with a two-tail p-value of 0.104. For a one-tailed test, halve this value giving 0.053. U is not significant

Output 7. The output for the Mann-Whitney test

For a **one-tail test**, we halve the p-value, obtaining 0.053. Since this p-value is greater than 0.05, this test does not confirm the scientific hypothesis that words presented in the right visual field will be more quickly recognised than those in the left. Write the result of the Mann-Whitney test as follows:

$$z = 1.63; \ p > 0.05$$

The reader might wish to run the Mann-Whitney test with the reduced data set used for the t-test. Now the value of z is significant after halving the two-tailed p-value of 0.064 ($z = -1.86$; $p < 0.05$), matching the result of the t-test.

6.4   ONE-SAMPLE TESTS

In Section 1.7 of Chapter 1, two situations were identified in which a researcher might wish to make a one-sample test:

(1)   One may wish to compare a sample distribution with a hypothetical distribution, such as the normal distribution. In technical terms, this is a question of the **goodness-of-fit**.

(2)   One may wish to make **inferences about the parameters of a single population from the statistics of a sample**, either for the

purpose of ascertaining whether the sample is from a known population or estimating the parameters of an unknown population. For example, if one has the heights of a hundred children in a certain age group, what can be said about the <u>typical</u> height of children in that age group?

The scope of goodness-of-fit tests extends far beyond ascertaining normality of distribution. With nominal data, for example, goodness-of-fit tests can be used to confirm preferences among a range of choices, or the fairness of a coin or a die.

So far in this chapter, we have been concerned with comparisons between the means of two samples. Yet, as we shall see presently, in the case of paired data, a one-sample test can be used to make such a comparison. In fact, the **t-test for two related samples** that we described earlier in this chapter is actually a special case of a **one-sample test**.

6.4.1 Goodness-of-fit: Data in the form of measurements

A researcher has a sample of measurements (say the heights of 100 people) and wishes to ascertain whether these have been drawn from a normal population. Testing for normality of distribution is one of the commonest applications of a goodness-of-fit test. The **Kolmogorov-Smirnov test** is appropriate for this purpose.

The histograms of the relative frequencies of some variables such as height and IQ are bell-shaped, indicating that they have an approximately normal distribution. The area under such a curve between two points on the horizontal axis represents the probability of a value within that particular range. In the distribution of IQ, the mean (which lies under the highest point of the curve) is 100 and the standard deviation is 15. The probability of an IQ in the range from 100 to 115, that is between the mean and a value one standard deviation above the mean, is approximately 0.3. This probability is the area under the curve between the uprights on the values 100 and 115 on the horizontal axis.

The **cumulative probability** of any particular value in a distribution is the probability of obtaining a value less than or equal to that value. For example, the cumulative probability of an IQ of 100 is 0.5, because in a symmetrical distribution, the mean splits the population (and the total area under the curve) into two equal parts. If we construct a table giving the cumulative probabilities of the IQs in the range from, say, 40 to 140 in steps of ten units, and plot a histogram, we shall have a picture of the **cumulative distribution** of the IQ variable. The cumulative normal distribution is not bell-shaped, but has the shape of a flattened S, rising slowly at first, accelerating as the mean is approached, slowing down as the mean is passed, and eventually flattening out at the upper end of the distribution.

Table 5. A sample of 50 IQ scores drawn from a normal population with µ=100 and σ = 15									
104.6	101.1	122.5	116.5	87.7	105.9	71.7	107.4	92.4	107.3
76.4	90.5	98.6	99.3	118.5	85.7	118.5	107.1	81.8	104.3
91.4	90.7	128.7	118.7	103.7	123.0	102.7	95.3	105.0	70.7
100.3	100.0	117.1	135.1	111.0	90.8	81.8	103.1	112.1	116.8
84.4	96.4	120.6	92.1	118.3	93.7	112.3	100.9	88.7	104.5

The **Kolmogorov-Smirnov test** for goodness-of-fit compares the cumulative probabilities of values in your data set with the cumulative probabilities of the same values in a specified theoretical distribution. If the discrepancy is sufficiently great, the test indicates that your data are not well fitted by the theoretical distribution. The **Kolmogorov-Smirnov statistic** is the greatest difference in cumulative probabilities across the entire range of values. If its value exceeds a cut-off level, the null hypothesis that your sample is from the specified population is rejected. Table 5 shows some fictitious IQ data that were selected randomly by SPSS from a normal population with a mean of 100 and a standard deviation of 15.

In **Variable View**, name a variable *iq* (assign the label Intelligence Quotient). Enter the data in **Data View**. Run the **Kolmogorov-Smirnov test** for goodness-of-fit to a normal distribution as follows:

- Choose
  Analyze
      Nonparametric Tests
          1-Sample K-S...
  to obtain the dialog box for the **One-Sample Kolmogorov-Smirnov Test** (Figure 7).
- Transfer Intelligence Quotient [iq] to the **Test Variable List:** box and notice that the default **Normal** checkbox has been selected.
- Click **OK**.

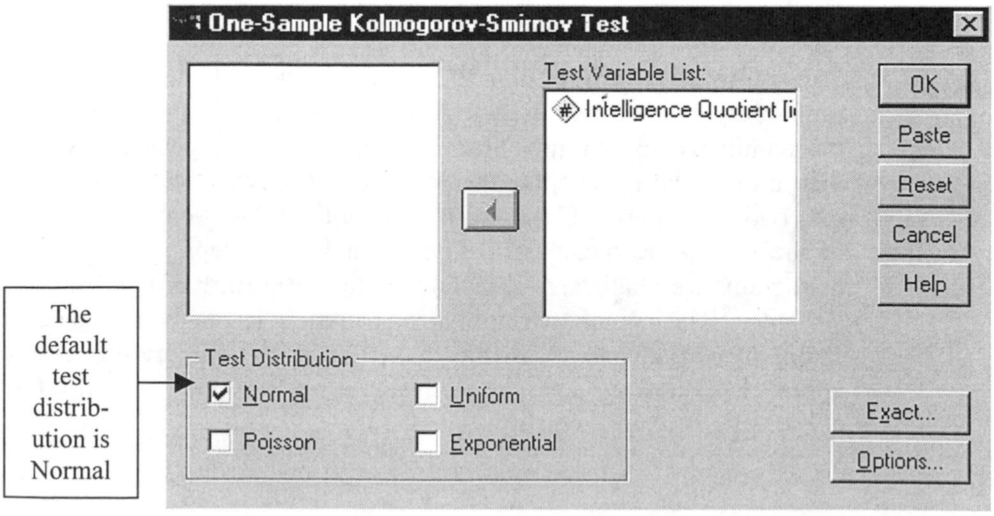

The default test distribution is Normal

Figure 7. The One-Sample Kolmogorov-Smirnov dialog box

The results of the test are shown in Output 8.

One-Sample Kolmogorov-Smirnov Test

		Intelligence Quotient
N		50.00
Normal Parameters [a,b]	Mean	102.15
	Std. Deviation	14.55
Most Extreme Differences	Absolute	.08
	Positive	.06
	Negative	-.08
Kolmogorov-Smirnov Z		.55
Asymp. Sig. (2-tailed)		.92

z = 0.55 with a p-value of 0.92 (i.e. the result is not significant)

a. Test distribution is Normal.

b. Calculated from data.

Output 8. The Kolmogorov-Smirnov goodness-of-fit test to a normal distribution

The most important item is in the last row: **Asymp. Sig. (2-tailed)**, the two-tail p-value. The high p-value, 0.92, means that there is no evidence against the null hypothesis that the sample has been drawn from a normal distribution. That is exactly what one would expect, because we know that the data set has indeed been drawn from a normal population. The result of the test is written as follows:

The distribution can be assumed to be normal:
Kolmogorov-Smirnov Z = .55;   p = 0.92.

6.4.2 Goodness-of-fit: Nominal data

Dichotomous nominal data

Suppose a researcher wants to know whether 5-year-old children of a certain age show a preference for one of two toys (A or B). The choices of one hundred 5-year-olds are noted. Of the hundred children in the study, 60 choose toy A and 40 toy B. As another example, suppose that, in order to determine whether a coin is 'fair' (that is, heads and tails are equally likely to occur), we toss a coin 100 times, and find that the coin turns up heads on 58 tosses.

In both examples, the null hypothesis states that the probability of choosing A (or B) on each trial is 0.5. The term **Bernoulli trials** is used to denote a series of events or experiments with the following properties:

(1) The outcomes of every trial can be divided into the same two dichotomous categories, one of which can be regarded as a 'success', the other as a 'failure'.

(2) The outcomes of the trials are independent.

(3) The probability of a 'success' is the same on all trials.

Note that (1) does not imply that there are only two outcomes, only that we can divide the outcomes into two categories. Suppose that a candidate sitting a multiple-choice examination with six alternatives per question were to choose the answer by rolling a die each time. In that case, although there are six outcomes per question, they can be classified dichotomously into 'pass' (with a probability of 1/6) and 'fail' (with a probability of 5/6).

Where, as in the foregoing examples, we have Bernoulli trials, the **Binomial test** can be used to test the null hypothesis that the probability of a success on any trial has a specified value. In the case of coin-tossing, that specified probability will usually be 0.5. The binomial test, however, can be used to test the hypothesis that the population proportion has <u>any</u> specified value.

To illustrate the binomial test, we shall use our first example of the children's choices between two toys. Of the 100 five-year-olds studied, 60 chose toy A and 40 chose toy B. Proceed as follows:

- Assign code numbers to the two choices, say 1 to toy A and 2 to toy B.
- In **Variable View**, name a variable *toy* and assign the values 1 to Toy A and 2 to Toy B.
- Name a second variable *freq* for the number of choices.
- Enter the data in **Data View**.
- Select **Weight Cases...** in the **Data** menu to obtain the **Weight Cases** dialog box (see Section 3.7.2), select the **Weight Cases by** radio button, transfer *freq* to the **Frequency Variable:** box and click **OK**.
- Select
  Analyze
        Nonparametric Tests
             Binomial ...
  to open the **Binomial Test** dialog box (Figure 8).
- Transfer *toy* to the **Test Variable List:** and click **OK** to run the Binomial test.

See Section 3.7.2

Figure 8. The Binomial Test dialog box with toy selected for the Test Variable List

Notice the small **Test Proportion:** box on the right, containing the default value 0.5. This is appropriate for the present test, because if the experiment was conducted properly and the children have no preference, the probability of each choice is 0.5. In other situations, however, that would not be the case, as when a candidate is guessing the correct answers to the questions in a multiple-choice examination, in which case, if there were four choices, the Test Proportion would be 0.25. The **Weight Cases** procedure ensures that the two choices will be weighted by their frequencies of occurrence.

The output is shown in Output 9.

Binomial Test

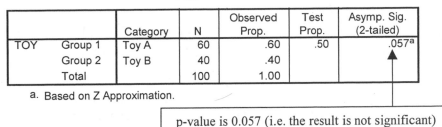

		Category	N	Observed Prop.	Test Prop.	Asymp. Sig. (2-tailed)
TOY	Group 1	Toy A	60	.60	.50	.057[a]
	Group 2	Toy B	40	.40		
	Total		100	1.00		

a. Based on Z Approximation.

p-value is 0.057 (i.e. the result is not significant)

Output 9. The output for the Binomial Test

The important item here is the rightmost entry, headed **Asymp.Sig (2-tailed)**. Since this p-value exceeds 0.05 (in fact, it is almost 0.06), the null hypothesis is accepted. The result of the test is written as follows:

Although more children chose toy A than toy B, a binomial test failed to reject the hypothesis that there is no preference: p > 0.05.

Small numbers of trials: Omitting the Weight Cases procedure

Should we have only the outcomes of a few Bernoulli trials, as when a coin is tossed twenty times, it is easier to enter the result of each toss directly, rather than aggregate the data and use the **Weight Cases** procedure. In **Variable View**, name one variable *toss* with two values (1 is a Head, 2 a Tail), enter the data in **Data View**, and complete the **Binomial Test** dialog box by transferring the variable name *toss* to the **Test Variable List:** box.

A test for randomness: The Runs test

One may carry out a binomial test on the results of a set of Bernoulli trials and find no evidence against the null hypothesis. But suppose that, in trying to ascertain whether a child has understood a rule that should enable him or her to choose correctly from box A and box B, we find that the sequence of choices is:

ABABABABABABABABABAB

or perhaps

AAAAAAAAAABBBBBBBBBB.

Such outcome sequences would cast serious doubt on the randomness assumption. A very long sequence of either heads or tails suggests a lack of randomness; but so also does the absence of <u>any</u> such sequences, as when the outcome categories alternate from trial to trial. The **Runs Test** can be used to test for randomness in such situations. Here, where the outcome is either dichotomous or can be made so in some way, as by a median split, the term **run** denotes a succession of outcomes in one category. The size of a run can vary from 1 to the longest possible sequence over the specified number of trials. If there are, say, twenty trials, a run could have any discrete value from 1 (as when there are twenty heads in twenty tosses) to 20 (as when heads and tails alternate). Note that SPSS's version of the **Runs Test** requires that <u>there must</u>

be at least two runs before the test can be carried out.

Suppose that we have been informed that the results of twenty tosses of a coin are as follows:

H T H T H T H T H T H T H T H T H T H T

Although there are ten heads and ten tails (which is consistent with the hypothesis that the coin was 'fair', in the sense that heads and tails have come up equally often), the alternation between heads and tails looks far from random.

To use the **Runs Test** on these data:

- In **Variable View**, name a variable *outcome* with values 1 for Heads and 2 for Tails.
- Enter the data (which will consist only of 1's and 2's) into **Data View**.
- Select
  Analyze
  　　Nonparametric Tests
  　　　　Runs...
  to open the **Runs Test** dialog box (Figure 9).
- Transfer the variable name *outcome* to the **Test Variable List:** box.
- Click **OK**.

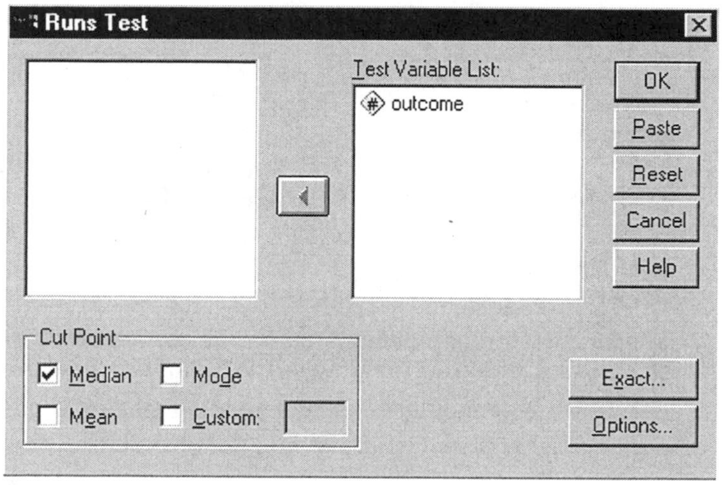

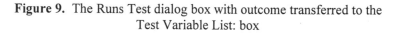

Figure 9. The Runs Test dialog box with outcome transferred to the Test Variable List: box

Notice the check boxes under **Cut Point** at bottom left. The user must choose a value such that the data in **Data View** will be classified either as greater or less than the value, reflecting the outcomes of the coin tosses. In this example, selecting the box marked **Median** (the default setting) will achieve this.

The results are shown in Output 10. The output shows that there were 20 runs and the row labelled **Aymp. Sig. (2-tailed)** indicates that the tail probability is less than .0005. Thus the null hypothesis of randomness is rejected, since $p < 0.05$. The result of the test is written as follows:

A runs test indicated that the sequence is non-random: $Z = 3.905$; $p < 0.01$.

Runs Test

	OUTCOME
Test Value [a]	1.50
Cases < Test Value	10
Cases >= Test Value	10
Total Cases	20
Number of Runs	20
Z	3.905
Asymp. Sig. (2-tailed)	.000

a. Median

z =3.905 with a p-value of less than 0.0005 (significant at the 1% level)

Output 10. The listing for the Runs Test

Goodness-of-fit test with three or more categories

If, in the foregoing example, there were three or more toys to choose from, the **Chi-square goodness-of-fit test** can be used to test the null hypothesis that the children have no preference for any particular toy.

As an example, suppose that, in an experiment similar to an earlier example, there were three toys, A, B and C. Of 90 children tested, the numbers choosing the three toys were 20, 41 and 29, respectively. The **Chi-square goodness-of-fit test** is run as follows:

- In **Variable View** define the variables *toy* and *freq*, the former with three levels: 1 for A, 2 for B, 3 for C.
- Enter the data in **Data View**.
- Use **Weight Cases...** (See Section 3.7.2) to weight the values in *freq*.
- Choose
  Analyze
  > **Nonparametric Tests**
  > > **Chi-Square...**
  to open the **Chi-Square Test** dialog box (Figure 10).
- Transfer the variable name *toy* to the **Test Variable List:** box.
- Click **OK**.

See Section 3.7.2

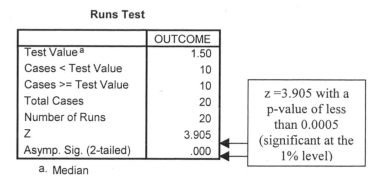

Figure 10. The Chi-Square Test dialog box with toy transferred to the Test Variable List box

The first table in the output shows the observed and expected frequencies. Any transcription errors will immediately be apparent here. Notice that the expected frequencies are 30 for each choice, because if there is no preference, the three choices are equally likely, and we should have approximately equal numbers of children choosing A, B and C.

TOY

	Observed N	Expected N	Residual
A	20	30.0	-10.0
B	41	30.0	11.0
C	29	30.0	-1.0
Total	90		

The next table (Output 11) tabulates the results of the chi-square goodness-of-fit test.

Test Statistics

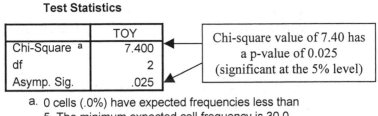

	TOY
Chi-Square [a]	7.400
df	2
Asymp. Sig.	.025

> Chi-square value of 7.40 has a p-value of 0.025 (significant at the 5% level)

a. 0 cells (.0%) have expected frequencies less than 5. The minimum expected cell frequency is 30.0.

Output 11. The output for the Chi-square goodness-of-fit test

The first table showed marked discrepancies between the expected and observed frequencies, and it is not surprising that the p-value (**Asymp. Sig.**) in the second table is small (.025). The Chi-square goodness-of-fit test, therefore, confirms the discrepancies shown in the first table. The result is written as

$$\chi^2(2) = 7.4; p < 0.05$$

In the term $\chi^2(2)$, the degrees of freedom (2) is the number of categories in the classification minus one.

6.4.3   Inferences about the mean of a single population

The mean and standard deviation of the 50 IQ scores in Table 5 (Section 6.4.1) are 102.2 and 14.6 respectively. (You can confirm this with **Descriptives...** within the **Descriptive Statistics** submenu in the **Analyze** menu.) What can we infer about the population mean?

On the sample mean, a **95% confidence interval** can be constructed, that is, a range of values within which the population mean will usually lie. To do this (assuming the data have already been entered in a variable named *iq* in **Data View**):
- Choose
  Analyze

Descriptive Statistics
Explore…

to obtain the **Explore** dialog box (Figure 11).

- Transfer the variable name Intelligence Quotient (*iq*) to the **Dependent List:** box.
- If you click **Statistics…** (not the **Statistics** radio button), you will obtain the **Explore: Statistics** subdialog box, in which it can be seen that the **Descriptives** check box has been selected, and a 95% Confidence Interval for Mean has already been specified by default. (The user may wish to specify a higher confidence level, such as 99%.)
- Click **Continue** to return to the **Explore** dialog box.
- Click **OK**.

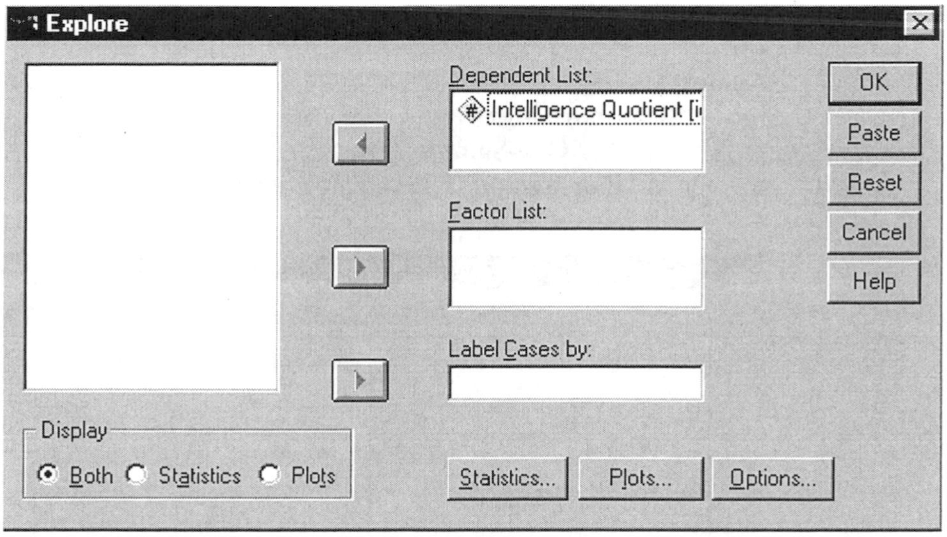

Figure 11. The Explore dialog box with iq transferred to the Dependent List box

An edited version of the output is shown in Output 12. The output gives the sample mean as 102.15 and the 95% Confidence Interval for Mean as extending from 98.02 to 106.29. Not surprisingly, the actual population mean (100) lies within this range since, as we have seen, the data were actually generated by commanding SPSS to select 50 scores from a normal population with a mean of 100 and a standard deviation of 15. Note, incidentally, that, because of sampling variability, the sample mean is not *exactly* 100.

Descriptives

			Statistic	Std. Error
Intelligence Quotient	Mean		102.15	2.06
	95% Confidence Interval for Mean	Lower Bound	98.02	
		Upper Bound	106.29	

Output 12. An edited version of the Output the 95% Confidence Interval for the Mean

Using a confidence interval to test a hypothesis about the mean of a single population

A hypothesis about the mean of a single population can be tested by constructing a confidence interval on the sample mean. If the hypothetical mean value lies outside the confidence interval, the null hypothesis can be rejected beyond the .05 level (for the 95% confidence interval) and the .01 level (for the 99% confidence interval). In the present case, the null hypothesis that the population mean IQ is 100 must be accepted, which is the correct decision.

Using a one-sample t-test to test a hypothesis about the mean of a single population

We have claimed that the fifty IQ scores are a random sample from a normal population with a mean of 100 and a standard deviation of 15. We have seen that one way of testing this hypothesis is to construct a 95% confidence interval on the mean and reject the hypothesis if the sample mean falls outside this interval. Another approach is to make a **one-sample t-test** of the null hypothesis that the mean is 100. To do so:

- Choose
  Analyze
        Compare Means
              One-Sample T Test...
  to open the **One-Sample T Test** dialog box (Figure 12).

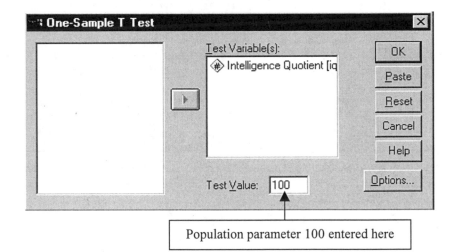

Figure 12. The One-Sample T Test dialog box with iq transferred to the Test Variable(s) box and 100 entered for the Test Value

- Transfer the variable name *iq* to the **Test Variable(s):** box and type 100 (the null hypothesis value for the mean) into the **Test Value:** box.
- Click **OK**.

The first table in the output, **One-Sample Statistics**, tabulates some descriptive statistics.

One-Sample Statistics

	N	Mean	Std. Deviation	Std. Error Mean
Intelligence Quotient	50	102.15	14.55	2.06

The second table (Output 13) includes the t-test results and the 95% Confidence Interval. It can be seen from the table that the null hypothesis must be accepted.

This result is written as

$$t(49) = 1.05; p = .3.$$

One-Sample Test

	Test Value = 100				95% Confidence Interval of the Difference	
	t	df	Sig. (2-tailed)	Mean Difference	Lower	Upper
Intelligence Quotient	1.05	49	.30	2.15	-1.98	6.29

With t = 1.05 and df = 49, the p-value of 0.30 shows that the observed mean difference is not statistically significant assuming μ = 100.

The 95% confidence interval from -1.98 to 6.29 includes the population mean difference of 0. Thus the observed mean difference is not significant.

Output 13. The output for the one-sample t test

EXERCISE 8

COMPARING THE AVERAGES OF
TWO INDEPENDENT SAMPLES OF DATA

Aim

The previous exercises have used data from a questionnaire. The next few exercises will be based on data from experiments designed to test experimental hypotheses. In real experiments, of course, a larger number of participants would have been used.

Before you start

Before proceeding with this exercise, we suggest you read Chapter 6 carefully. In this Exercise, we shall be making an **independent samples t-test** (Section 6.2.4). In the next Exercise, we shall be making a **paired-samples t-test** (Section 6.2.3). Finally in Exercise 10, we shall be making **one-sample tests** (Section 6.4).

An investigation of the effects of a drug upon performance

The data we are going to explore in this exercise might have been produced by the following project. A team of investigators has good reason to believe that a small dosage of a certain drug changes the speed with which people can make decisions. They decide to try to confirm this by carrying out an experiment in which the decision times of 14 people who have ingested the drug are compared with those of a control group of 14 other people who have performed the task under a placebo condition. The experimenters expect that the decision times of the experimental group will differ from those of the placebo group. The results are shown in Table 1.

Table 1. Decision times of the experimental and placebo groups in the drug experiment							
DRUG GROUP				PLACEBO GROUP			
Case	Time	Case	Time	Case	Time	Case	Time
1	390	8	425	15	446	22	440
2	494	9	421	16	749	23	471
3	386	10	407	17	599	24	501
4	323	11	386	18	460	25	492
5	660	12	550	19	390	26	392
6	406	13	470	20	477	27	578
7	345	14	393	21	556	28	398

Opening SPSS

In the opening window of SPSS, select the **Type in data** radio button. If **Data View** appears, click the tab **Variable View** to open **Variable View**.

Constructing the SPSS data set

Construct the data set as described in Section 3.2. In **Variable View**, the first variable, *case*, will represent the participants. The second is the grouping variable (i.e. the type of treatment - drug or placebo). Call the grouping variable *group* and name the values. The third variable, which can be named *score*, contains all the participants' scores on the dependent variable. Notice that the *score* variable includes the scores for **both** treatments. The grouping variable *group* is needed to enable the computer to identify the group to with a score belongs. Since there are no decimals in the data, ensure that the values in the **Decimals** column are all 0.

Click the **Data View** tab and enter the data of Table 1 into **Data View** in the manner described in Section 3.2.5. When the data have been entered, save them to a file with a name such as ***Drugs***.

Exploring the data

The first step is always to examine the data set to see whether there are any odd features.

Means and standard deviations

We shall want a table of means and standard deviations, together with indicators of distribution shape such as stem-and-leaf displays and boxplots. The statistics for the subgroups are most easily obtained with the **Means** procedure. (The plots are obtained with the **Explore** command.) Follow the instructions in Section 4.3.2, remembering that the dependent variable name is *score* and the independent variable name is *group*.

- **Write down the values of the means and standard deviations**

(Note that the **Means** procedure requires the presence of a grouping variable in the data set. Should the mean and standard deviation of a set of ungrouped data be required, use the **Descriptives** procedure.)

Graphical displays of the data

To draw the boxplots, proceed as described in Section 4.3.2. The dependent variable is *score*, the factor is *group*, and the **Labels Cases by** is *case.* (This choice labels any outliers or extreme scores in the boxplots with the number of the case, which is more useful than the default row number, especially if some cases have been deselected). Remember to click the **Plots** radio button in the **Display** section of the **Explore** dialog box, thus turning off the **Both** radio button and ensuring that the descriptive statistics tables are omitted. Click **Plots**, select **Stem-and-leaf**, click **Continue** and finally **OK**.

The output in **SPSS Viewer** begins with the usual **Case Processing Summary** listing the number of valid cases in each group. Then it shows **Stem-and-leaf Plots** and **Boxplots** for the two groups.   The boxplots show two outliers with the identifying numbers of the participants concerned (because you specified the participants' numbers in the **Label Cases by** box in the **Explore** dialog box).

When there is a marked discrepancy between the mean and median of a set of scores, the distribution is probably skewed or otherwise asymmetrical. Atypical scores, or **outliers** can also pull the value of the mean away from that of the median. Read Section 4.3.2 carefully for an explanation of SPSS's stem-and-leaf and boxplot displays.

- **Identify any outliers by means of their identifiers, which are numbers in the variable *case*.**

Printing the output

If you want a hard copy of the output, follow the procedure described in Section 3.6. The precise details will depend upon your local set-up.

The independent samples t-test

Run an independent samples t-test on the full data set as described in Section 6.2.4.

Output for the independent samples t-test

Guidance on how to interpret the output is given in Section 6.2.4. We suggest you study that section and try to answer the following questions.

- **On the basis of the Levene test p-value, which row of the t-test results will you use?**

- **Write down the value of t and its tail probability. Is the p-value evidence against the null hypothesis? Remember that if the result is sufficiently unlikely (i.e. p < 0.05) under the null hypothesis, it is regarded as evidence against the null hypothesis and hence in favour of the experimental hypothesis.**

- **Write down your interpretation of the result of the test: has the t-test confirmed the pattern shown by the means of the two groups?**

- **If the hypothesis had been one-tailed (e.g. that decision times of the experimental group will tend to be shorter than those of the control group), then the appropriate p-value would be obtained by dividing the two-tailed p-value by 2. What would be the one-tailed p-value in that case?**

A nonparametric equivalent of the independent samples t-test: The Mann-Whitney U test

The running of the **Mann-Whitney** test on SPSS is described in Section 6.3.2. Run the command as described in that section.

Output for the Mann-Whitney test

The output gives the values of the statistics U and W (the W statistic belongs to a test by Wilcoxon which is the exact equivalent of the Mann-Whitney), followed by a standard normal deviate score Z and a 2-tailed probability value corrected for ties. An exact 2-tailed probability value not corrected for ties concludes the table. If the p-value is less than 0.05, the null hypothesis can be rejected and the groups declared to differ significantly.

- **Write down the results of the Mann-Whitney test, including the value of U and its p-value. State whether the result is significant and whether the Mann-Whitney test confirms the result of the t-test. In what circumstances would you expect the p-values of U and t to differ?**

Printing the output

To obtain a hard copy of the output, proceed as described in Section 3.6.

Re-running the tests after deselecting the two outliers

Deselect the two outliers using the **Select Cases...** procedure (see Section 6.2.4) by entering score <600 in the **Select Cases** dialog box. Then re-run the t-test and the Mann-Whitney test.

- **Write down the new value of t and its p-value (assuming a two-tail test). Is the conclusion different from what it was with the complete data set?**

- **Write down the results of the Mann-Whitney test (assuming a two-tail test), including the value of U and its p-value. Is the conclusion different from what it was with the complete data set?**

- **Write down your interpretation of the effects on each test of eliminating the outliers.**

Finishing the session

Close down SPSS and any other windows before logging out of the computer.

EXERCISE 9

COMPARING THE AVERAGES OF TWO RELATED SAMPLES OF DATA

Before you start

The methods described in the previous exercise, (the **independent samples t-test** and the **Mann-Whitney** test), are appropriate for data from a between subjects experiment, that is, one with independent samples of participants in the two groups. Suppose, however, that the data had come from an experiment in which the same participants had been tested under both the experimental and control conditions. Such a within subjects experiment would yield a set of paired (or related) data. In this exercise, we shall consider some methods for comparing the averages of the scores obtained under the experimental and control conditions when we have a set of paired data (SPSS calls this **paired samples**), rather than independent samples. Before proceeding with this exercise, the reader should review the material in Sections 6.2.2 and 6.2.3.

THE PAIRED SAMPLES T-TEST

An experiment on hemispherical specialisation

In an experiment investigating the relative ease with which words presented in the left and right visual fields were recognised, participants were instructed to fixate a spot in the centre of the field. They were told that, after a short interval, a word would appear to the left or the right of the spot and they were to press a key as soon as they recognised it. In the trials that followed, each word was presented an equal number of times in each field, though the order of presentation of the words was, of course, randomised. From the results, a table of median decision times was constructed from the participants' reactions to presentations of 40 words in each of the two visual fields (Table 1).

Table 1. Median decision times for words presented to the right and left visual fields					
Case	Right visual field	Left visual field	Case	Right visual field	Left visual field
1	323	324	8	439	442
2	493	512	9	682	683
3	502	503	10	703	998
4	376	385	11	598	600
5	428	453	12	456	462
6	343	345	13	653	704
7	523	543	14	652	653

Do these data support the experimental hypothesis that there is a difference between the response times for words in the left and right visual fields? Before proceeding with this exercise, we strongly urge you to read Section 6.2.3, which describes the procedure for a paired samples t-test.

Opening SPSS

In the opening window of SPSS, select the **Type in data** radio button. If **Data View** appears first, click the tab labelled **Variable View** to open **Variable View**.

Preparing the SPSS data set

In the data set for the independent samples t-test, one of the variables must be a grouping variable, showing which participants performed under which conditions. With the paired samples t-test, however, there are no groups, so no coding variable need be constructed.

After naming a variable *case*, name two more variables: *rvf* with the label *Right Visual Field* in the **Label** column, and *lvf* with the label *Left Visual Field* in the **Label** column. Since there are no decimals in the data, ensure that the values in the **Decimals** column are all 0.

Select **Data View** and enter the data in the usual way, as described in Section 3.2.5.

Exploring the data

As always, it is wise to explore the data, rather than automatically pressing ahead with a formal test. Use **Scatter** in the **Graphs** menu for a *Left Visual Field* against *Right Visual Field*. From inspection of the scatterplot, it is quite clear that there is a glaring outlier. It is instructive to ascertain the effect of its presence upon the results of the t-test, in comparison with the nonparametric **Wilcoxon** and **Sign** tests.

Running the paired samples t-test

Run the **paired samples t-test** by following the procedure described in Section 6.2.3.

Output for the paired samples t-test

From the details given in the t-test output, it is clear that there are contra-indications against the use of the paired samples t-test for the data in the present experiment. There is marked discrepancy between the standard deviations of the scores obtained under the *rvf* and *lvf* conditions, which arises from the presence of an outlier, which showed up dramatically in the scatterplot.

- **Write down the value of *t* and its p-value. Is *t* significant? Write down, in terms of the research hypothesis, the meaning of this result.**

What has happened here? You should find the t-test result paradoxical to say the least. You might find another clue by examining the distribution of differences between the scores. Use **Compute** to calculate a difference between *Left Visual Field* and *Right Visual Field*, putting the answer in a variable called *diffs*.

- **What do you notice about the magnitude of the differences in *diffs*?**

NONPARAMETRIC ALTERNATIVES TO THE PAIRED SAMPLES T-TEST

The Wilcoxon matched pairs test

Now carry out the **Wilcoxon matched pairs** test, following the procedure described in Section 6.3.1.
- **Write down the value of the statistic and its p-value. Compare the p-value with that for the t-test. Relate the result of the Wilcoxon test to the experimental hypothesis.**

The Sign test

This test is based very simply on how many positive and negative differences there are between pairs of data, assuming that the value of one variable is consistently subtracted from the value of the other. It is a straightforward application of the binomial model to paired data, such as the results of the visual field experiment above. To merely record the signs (rather than the magnitudes) of the differences between the times for the left and right visual fields is certainly to lose a considerable amount of information. Indeed, when paired data show no contraindications, the related t-test is preferable to the Sign test, for to use the latter in such circumstances would be to make a needless sacrifice of power. The great advantage of the Sign test, however, is its robustness to the influence of outliers; moreover, there are no requirements about bivariate normality in the original paired data.

The procedure is very similar to that for the Wilcoxon test except that within the **Test Type** box, the **Wilcoxon** check box should be clicked off and the **Sign** check box clicked on. Click **OK** to run the test.

- **Write down the results of the Sign test, including the p-value. Is the result significant? Compare this with the result of the paired samples t-test and explain any discrepancy.**

Eliminating the outliers

When there are contra-indications for the **paired samples t-test**, the use of a nonparametric test is not the only alternative available. Another approach is to consider the possibility of eliminating some of the data. In the present set of paired data, there is one difference in *diffs* that is much larger than all the others. This may have arisen because case 10 had special difficulty in recognising words in the left visual field. At any rate, that participant's performance is quite atypical of this sample of participants and certainly calls into question the claim that he or she was drawn from the same population as the others. It is instructive to re-analyse the data after excluding the scores of Case 10. This is done by using the **Select Cases** procedure (Section 3.7.1). Follow the procedure described in that section to eliminate case 10 from the data. (Hint: give the instruction to select cases if *case* ~= 10. The sign ~= means "not equal to".)

Now re-run the **paired samples t-test**, and run both the **Wilcoxon** and the **Sign** test on the reduced data set. Examine the new output.

- **Write down the value of t and its tail probability. Write down your interpretation of this new result. Similarly give the statistics and their p-values for the Sign and Wilcoxon tests. Explain your findings**

Finishing the session

Close down SPSS and any other windows before logging out of the computer.

EXERCISE 10

ONE-SAMPLE TESTS

Before you start

Before beginning this exercise, the reader should study Section 6.4.

The Kolmogorov-Smirnov test for goodness-of-fit

A researcher wishes to ascertain whether response latencies have been drawn from a normal population. The **Kolmogorov-Smirnov test** is an appropriate goodness-of-fit test for this purpose. Table 1 shows the decision-making response latencies of fifty young adults.

Table 1. Response latencies of fifty young adults (ms)									
910	1013	921	895	879	906	892	902	902	858
874	900	894	872	909	878	935	878	849	969
879	926	877	861	876	906	897	860	887	968
896	905	876	906	928	899	899	899	889	903
977	900	899	892	986	891	881	879	850	874

Name a variable *latency* and enter the data. Then draw a histogram of the distribution along with a normal curve using

Analyze
> **Descriptive Statistics**
>> **Frequencies...**

to open the **Frequencies** dialog box. Click **Charts...** and select **Histograms**, together with the checkbox **With normal curve**. Return to the original dialog box by clicking **Continue** and then ensure that the tick in **Display frequency tables** has been turned off. Finally click **OK**.

- **From inspection of the histogram, would you expect the Kolmogorov-Smirnov test to accept or reject the null hypothesis of normality of distribution?**

Run a **Kolmogorov-Smirnov** test for goodness-of-fit on the data in Table 1, as described in Section 6.4.1.

- **Write out the result of the Kolmogorov-Smirnov test**
- **Is the result what you had expected?**

Nominal data: The binomial test

A die is rolled ten times, during which 6 sixes turn up. Have we grounds for suspecting that the die is unfair? Note that the probability of obtaining a six from the roll of a die is 1/6 (0.17). This is the null hypothesis value to enter as the **Test Proportion** in the **Binomial Test** dialog box (see Section 6.4.2).

Use the procedure described in Section 6.4.2 to enter the data but modified so that the grouping variable is *die* with values 1 for Six and 2 for Not Six. Remember to apply **Weight Cases...** to the second variable *freq* and to change the value of **Test Proportion** in the **Binomial Test** dialog box.

- **Write out the result of the binomial test**
- **Do we have grounds for suspecting that the die is unfair?**

Nominal data: The chi-square test for goodness-of-fit

One hundred 5-year-old children are asked which of five toys they prefer. Their choices are as in Table 2.

Table 2. Toy preference				
Toy A	Toy B	Toy C	Toy D	Toy E
40	25	15	15	5

Is there evidence for any preferences among the five toys?

Enter the data as in Section 6.4.2 except that there are five categories here instead of three. Remember to apply **Weight Cases...** to the second variable *freq.*
- **Write down the result of the chi-square test for goodness-of-fit**
- **Referring to this result, write down your answer to the question**

The one sample t-test

Table 3 contains the heights of fifty 18-year-old female college students, measured in the year 2000. Past records, which ended in 1910, showed that over the previous decade, the mean height of women in the same college was 160 cms. No data on spread (or dispersion) are available. Do the present data suggest that women going to this college are taller (or shorter) nowadays?

Table 3. Heights of female college students (cms)									
162	157	166	157	168	177	168	166	168	166
168	166	161	158	162	167	175	161	171	173
166	178	177	174	178	166	159	175	168	168
166	167	163	173	166	172	166	177	171	168
156	166	165	172	168	162	163	160	169	170

The directional question of whether today's college women are taller than their predecessors can be approached by making a one sample t-test on the data of Table 3. Enter the data into a variable such as *height*.
Choose
Analyze
> **Compare Means**
>> **One-Sample T Test...**
to obtain the **One-Sample T Test** dialog box. For the **Test Value**, enter the value 160. Click **OK** to run the test.
- **Write out the result of the one-sample t test**
- **Does the result of the test indicate that today's college women are taller?**

Finishing the session

Close down SPSS and any other windows before logging out of the computer.

CHAPTER 7

THE ONE-FACTOR BETWEEN SUBJECTS EXPERIMENT

7.1   INTRODUCTION

Suppose that an experiment has been carried out to compare the performance of two groups of subjects: an **experimental** group and a **control** group. Provided the data have certain characteristics (i.e., the samples have approximately normal distributions and comparable variances), an independent samples t-test can be used to test the null hypothesis (H_0) of equality of the two population means. If the test shows significance, we reject H_0: we conclude that there is a difference between the two population means, which is equivalent to the conclusion that the experimental manipulation does have an effect.

The same null hypothesis, however, can also be tested by using one of the set of techniques known as **analysis of variance** (**ANOVA** for short). Despite its name, the ANOVA, like the t-test, is concerned with the testing of hypotheses about **means**. In fact, if the ANOVA and the (pooled) t-test are applied to the data from a simple, two-group experiment, the tests will give the same result: if the t-test shows the difference between the means to be significant, then so will the ANOVA and vice versa.

The ANOVA, however, is more versatile than the t-test. Suppose that in an investigation of the effects of mnemonic training method upon recall, three groups of subjects were tested:
  (a)   a group trained in Mnemonic Method A;
  (b)   a group trained in Mnemonic Method B;
  (c)   a Control group, who were asked only to memorise the material as
         well as possible.

The **one-way ANOVA** can test the null hypothesis that all three population means are equal. The t-test, on the other hand, cannot be used to evaluate a hypothesis about three or more population means: it can substitute for ANOVA only if there are two groups in the experiment.

A lucid account of the rationale of the one-factor between subjects (one-way) ANOVA is given in Gravetter & Wallnau (2000), Chapter 13. Basically, the rationale is this. A group mean is taken to be an estimate of people's typical level of performance under that particular condition. But individual performance can vary widely and at times deviates markedly from the group mean. Think of this **within group** variability as background noise, or **error**. It may be, however, that mnemonic groups A and B achieved higher average levels of performance than did the control group: in other words, there is high variability **between (i.e. among) groups**. The **ANOVA F statistic** is calculated by dividing an estimate of the variability **between groups** by the variability **within groups**:

$$F = \frac{\text{variance between}}{\text{variance within}}$$

The between groups variance estimate is determined completely by the values of the group (treatment) means. Its value, however, reflects not only population differences among the group means, but also error. The within groups estimate is the average of the variances of the scores in the different groups. It is, in fact, a pooled estimate of the supposedly constant population variance of the scores at all levels of the single treatment factor. The within groups variance estimate, therefore, reflects only error.

If there are substantial differences among the treatment means, the numerator of F (and therefore F itself) will be inflated and the null hypothesis is likely to be rejected. If, on the other hand, there are no differences in the population, the numerator and denominator of F both reflect error alone. In that case, they should have similar values, giving an F close to unity. A high value of F, therefore, is evidence against the null hypothesis of equality of all three population means.

There remains a problem, however. If H_0 states that all the means are equal, the alternative hypothesis is simply that they are not. If the ANOVA F test is significant, we may conclude there is probably a difference **somewhere** among the means, but that does not justify us in saying that any **particular** comparison is significant. Further analysis is necessary to confirm whatever differences there may be among the individual treatment means.

The question of exactly how one should proceed after finding a significant F test is not a simple one, and an adequate treatment of it earns an extensive chapter in many statistical texts (e.g. Kirk, 1982, Chapter 3; Howell, 1997, Chapter 12). It is important to distinguish between those comparisons that were **planned** before the data were actually gathered, and those that are made as part of the inevitable process of unplanned **data-snooping** that takes place after the results have been obtained. Planned comparisons are often known as **a priori** comparisons. Unplanned comparisons should be termed **a posteriori** comparisons, but unfortunately the misnomer **post hoc** is generally used.

SPSS offers the user both planned comparisons and an assortment of unplanned data-snooping tests, such as **Tukey's test**, **Scheffé's test**, and so on. If these are unfamiliar to you, we urge you to read the relevant chapters in the books we have cited.

7.2 THE ONE-WAY ANOVA

7.2.1 The mnemonics experiment revisited

In Chapter 3 (Section 3.2.1), an experiment was described in which the performance of two groups of subjects, each trained in a different mnemonic method (Mnemonic A or Mnemonic B), was compared with that of a group of untrained controls. The results are shown in Table 1, which is a reproduction of Table 1 in Chapter 3.

Table 1. The numbers of words recalled by participants using different mnemonic training methods

Control Group	3	5	3	2	4	6	9	3	8	10
Mnemonic A	10	8	15	9	11	16	17	17	7	10
Mnemonic B	20	15	14	15	17	10	8	11	18	19

Section 3.2.1 described how this set of results is recast into a form suitable for entry into SPSS. The first variable *case* contains the case numbers, the second variable *group* identifies the Control, Mnemonic A, and Mnemonic B groups, and the third variable *score* contains the participants' scores. These variable names together with longer labels were defined in **Variable View** along with the values and their labels for the grouping variable *group*.

Exploring the data

See
Section
4.3.2

Before embarking on the ANOVA, it is important to check the data for anomalies such as extreme values or skewed distributions. This can be done with the **Explore** command (see Chapter 4, Section 4.3.2) used in the previous Chapter for the independent samples t-test, or more simply with the **Boxplot...** command in the **Graphs** menu. The boxplots are shown in Output1 where it can be seen that the data set has no extreme values or outliers. We can therefore proceed with the ANOVA without deselecting any cases.

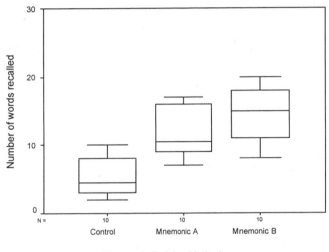

Output 1. The boxplots for the Mnemonic Training Methods experiment

7.2.2 Procedure for the one-way ANOVA

The one-way analysis of variance is selected by proceeding as follows:
- Choose
  Analyze
     Compare Means (Figure 1)
        One-Way ANOVA...
  to open the **One-Way ANOVA** dialog box (the completed box is shown in Figure 2).
- Transfer the variable names as shown in Figure 2.
- Should the user not want to use all the levels in a grouping variable, it would be necessary to invoke the **Select Cases** command to identify the levels for the analysis.

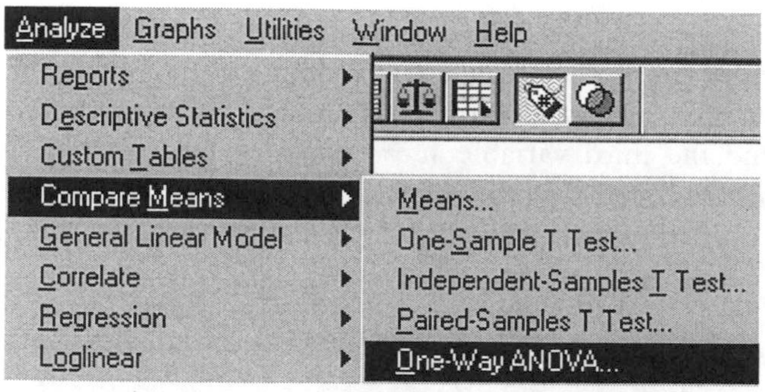

Figure 1. The Compare Means menu

- Unplanned multiple pairwise comparisons among the means can be obtained by clicking the **Post Hoc** button to obtain the **One-Way ANOVA: Post Hoc Multiple Comparisons** dialog box (Figure 3). Click the check box opposite **Tukey**.
- Descriptive statistics, Levene's test of homogeneity of variance and a plot of the means can be obtained by clicking **Options** to obtain the **One-Way ANOVA: Options** dialog box (Figure 4). Click the check boxes opposite **Descriptive, Homogeneity-of-variance** and **Means plot**.
- Click **Continue** to return to the **One-Way ANOVA** dialog box.
- Click **OK**.

The results are shown in Output 2 (page 176).

One-way ANOVA can also be requested by clicking **Options** in the **Means** dialog box and then **Anova table and eta**.

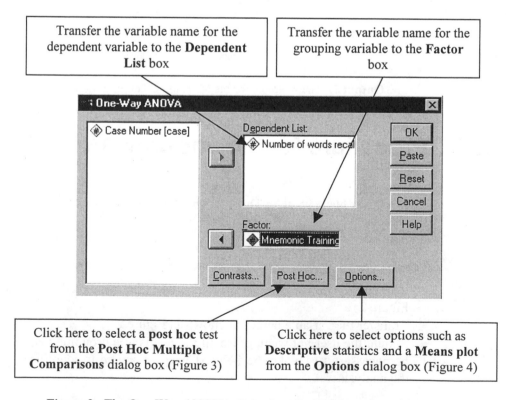

Transfer the variable name for the dependent variable to the **Dependent List** box

Transfer the variable name for the grouping variable to the **Factor** box

Click here to select a **post hoc** test from the **Post Hoc Multiple Comparisons** dialog box (Figure 3)

Click here to select options such as **Descriptive** statistics and a **Means plot** from the **Options** dialog box (Figure 4)

Figure 2. The One-Way ANOVA dialog box for Number of words recalled by levels of Mnemonic Training Method

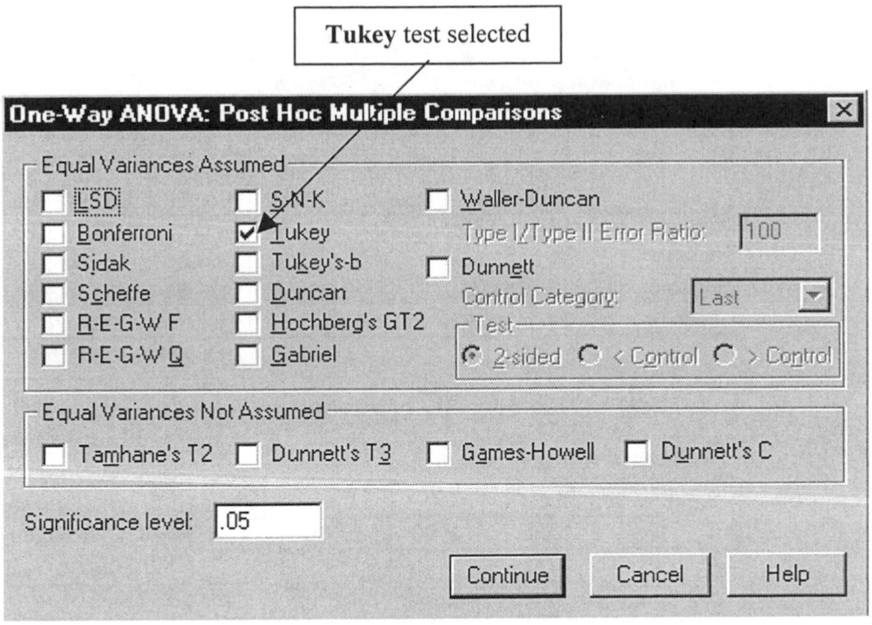

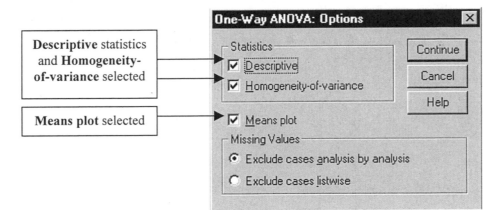

Figure 3. The Post Hoc Multiple Comparisons dialog box with Tukey selected

Figure 4. The Options dialog box with Descriptive and Means plot selected

7.2.3 Output for the one-way ANOVA

Descriptive statistics for a one-way ANOVA

Output 2 tabulates the requested Descriptive and Homogeneity-of-variance statistics.

The Descriptive statistics include Means, Standard Deviations, Standard Errors, 95% Confidence Intervals for the Mean and extreme values (Minimum and Maximum).

The non-significance of the **Levene Statistic** for the **Test of Homogeneity of Variances** indicates that the assumption of homogeneity of variance is tenable.

Descriptives

Number of words recalled

	N	Mean	Std. Deviation	Std. Error	95% Confidence Interval for Mean		Minimum	Maximum
					Lower Bound	Upper Bound		
Control	10	5.30	2.83	.90	3.28	7.32	2	10
Mnemonic A	10	12.00	3.86	1.22	9.24	14.76	7	17
Mnemonic B	10	14.70	4.00	1.27	11.84	17.56	8	20
Total	30	10.67	5.31	.97	8.68	12.65	2	20

Test of Homogeneity of Variances

Number of words recalled

Levene Statistic	df1	df2	Sig.
1.01	2.00	27.00	.38

The p-value (Sig.) for the Levene Statistic is 0.38 (not significant). Thus there is no evidence for heterogeneity of variance

Output 2. Descriptive and homogeneity-of-variance statistics

The plot of means

The plot of the means is shown in Output 3.

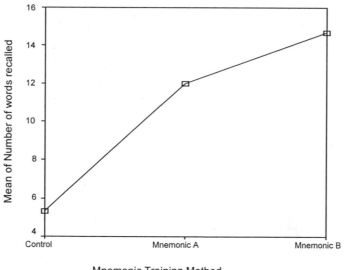

Mnemonic Training Method

Output 3. The plot of the means

The ANOVA summary table

The summary table for the one-way ANOVA is shown in Output 4.

The p-value (**Sig.**) for the F ratio of 18.06 is listed as .00, which means that it is less than .005. Therefore, H_0 is rejected. It is worth noting that in a scientific paper, it is not acceptable to write, 'p = .00'. The results of the present ANOVA F test would be reported in the format:

$$F(2, 27) = 18.06; \ p < 0.01,$$

where the bracketed numbers are the degrees of freedom of the numerator (the Between Groups df) and the denominator (the Within Groups df) of the F ratio.

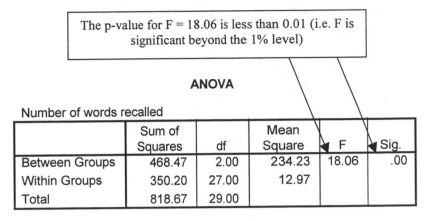

The p-value for F = 18.06 is less than 0.01 (i.e. F is significant beyond the 1% level)

ANOVA

Number of words recalled

	Sum of Squares	df	Mean Square	F	Sig.
Between Groups	468.47	2.00	234.23	18.06	.00
Within Groups	350.20	27.00	12.97		
Total	818.67	29.00			

Output 4. The Summary Table for One-Way ANOVA

Unplanned multiple comparisons with Tukey's HSD test

The results of the **Tukey** test are tabulated in Outputs 5 and 6.

Post Hoc Tests

Multiple Comparisons

Dependent Variable: Number of words recalled

Tukey HSD

(I) Mnemonic Training Method	(J) Mnemonic Training Method	Mean Difference (I-J)	Std. Error	Sig.	95% Confidence Interval Lower Bound	95% Confidence Interval Upper Bound
Control	Mnemonic A	-6.70*	1.61	.00	-10.69	-2.71
	Mnemonic B	-9.40*	1.61	.00	-13.39	-5.41
Mnemonic A	Control	6.70*	1.61	.00	2.71	10.69
	Mnemonic B	-2.70	1.61	.23	-6.69	1.29
Mnemonic B	Control	9.40*	1.61	.00	5.41	13.39
	Mnemonic A	2.70	1.61	.23	-1.29	6.69

*. The mean difference is significant at the .05 level.

These differences are significant since the p-value is less than 0.01

These differences are not significant since the p-value is greater than 0.05

Output 5. The Tukey test output

Output 5 lists the differences between means (**Mean Difference (I-J)**), their standard errors, p-values (**Sig.**) and 95% Confidence Interval for each pair. Inspection of the p-values shows that the Control group differs significantly (p <

0.05) from both Mnemonic A and Mnemonic B groups but mnemonic A does not differ significantly from Mnemonic B ($p > 0.05$).

This is more clearly shown by Output 6, in which the groups are divided into homogeneous subsets, thus showing which means do *not* differ from one another (i.e. the members within each subset). Here the Control group, which differs significantly from Mnemonic A and from Mnemonic B is in a separate subset from the other two groups, which do not differ significantly from one another.

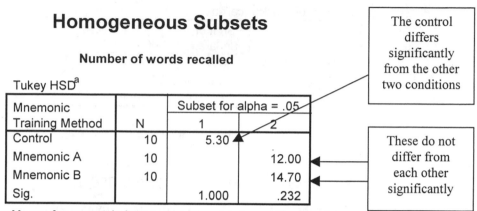

Homogeneous Subsets

Number of words recalled

Tukey HSD[a]

Mnemonic Training Method	N	Subset for alpha = .05	
		1	2
Control	10	5.30	
Mnemonic A	10		12.00
Mnemonic B	10		14.70
Sig.		1.000	.232

Means for groups in homogeneous subsets are displayed.

a. Uses Harmonic Mean Sample Size = 10.000.

The control differs significantly from the other two conditions

These do not differ from each other significantly

Output 6. The homogeneous subsets from Tukey's test

The rationale of **Tukey's HSD** test is that if the treatment means are arranged in order of magnitude, and the smallest is subtracted from the largest, the probability of obtaining a large difference increases with the size of the array of means. For a pairwise difference to achieve significance on the Tukey test, it must exceed a **critical difference (CD)**, which is given by the formula

$$CD = q_{critical} \sqrt{\frac{MS_{error}}{n}}$$

where $q_{critical}$ is the critical value of a special statistic known as the **Studentized Range Statistic q** (a table of its critical values is given in Howell, 1997; pp 680-681), MS_{error} is the mean square for the error term of the one-way ANOVA, and n is the number of scores in each treatment group.

The **One-Way ANOVA: Post Hoc Multiple Comparisons** dialog box (Figure 3) listed several other tests for making unplanned comparisons. There is a discussion of various *post hoc* tests in Howell (1997) pp369-383.

7.3   NONPARAMETRIC TESTS

Should the data be unsuitable for ANOVA (as when there is marked heterogeneity of variance, or the data are highly skewed), one should consider using **nonparametric** tests, which assume neither homogeneity of variance nor a normal distribution. With inherently ordinal data, the parametric ANOVA cannot be used in any case (see Chapter 5).

7.3.1 The Kruskal-Wallis test

The nonparametric equivalent of the one-way (between subjects) ANOVA is the **Kruskal-Wallis Test**. To run this test, proceed as follows:

- Choose
Analyze
   Nonparametric Tests
      K Independent Samples... (Figure 5)
to open the **Tests for Several Independent Samples** dialog box (the completed version is shown in Figure 6).

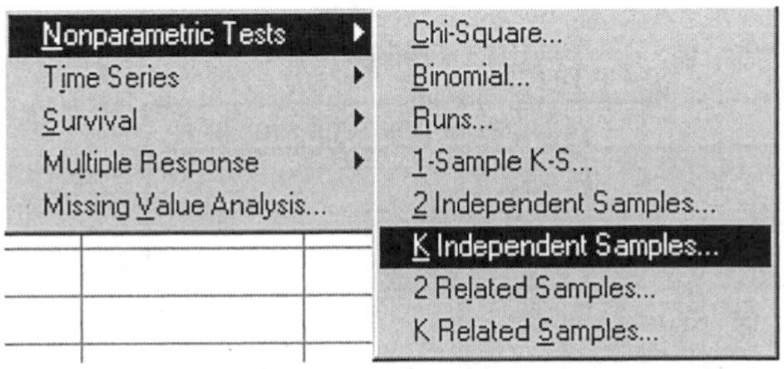

Figure 5. Part of the Analyze menu showing Nonparametric Tests and its submenu with K Independent Samples selected

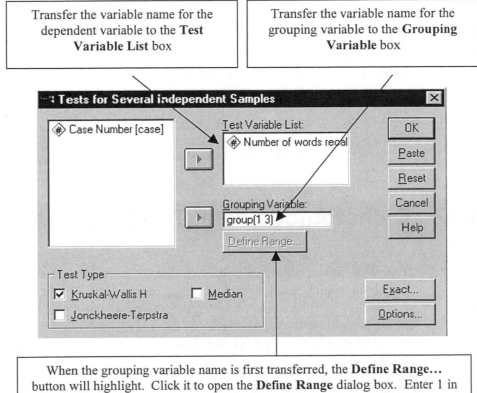

Transfer the variable name for the dependent variable to the **Test Variable List** box

Transfer the variable name for the grouping variable to the **Grouping Variable** box

When the grouping variable name is first transferred, the **Define Range...** button will highlight. Click it to open the **Define Range** dialog box. Enter 1 in the **Minimum** box and 3 in the **Maximum** box, and click **Continue**

Figure 6. The Tests for Several Independent Samples dialog box

- Transfer the variable names and define the range of the grouping variable as shown in Figure 6.
- Click **OK**.

The test results are shown in Output 7.

Kruskal-Wallis Test

Ranks

	Mnemonic Training Method	N	Mean Rank
Number of words recalled	Control	10	6.60
	Mnemonic A	10	17.80
	Mnemonic B	10	22.10
	Total	30	

Test Statistics[a,b]

	Number of words recalled
Chi-Square	16.63
df	2.00
Asymp. Sig.	.00

The p-value associated with a Chi-square value of 16.63 is less than 0.01 (i.e. the test is significant at the 1% level)

a. Kruskal Wallis Test

b. Grouping Variable: Mnemonic Training Method

Output 7. The Kruskal-Wallis One-Way ANOVA output

The first subtable, **Ranks**, tabulates the mean rank for each group. The second subtable, **Test Statistics**, lists the value of Chi-Square, its df and its p-value (**Asymp. Sig.**). Since the p-value is much smaller than 0.01, the Kruskal-Wallis test agrees with the parametric test that the three groups do not perform equally well. We can write this result as:

$$\chi^2 (2) = 16.63; p < 0.01,$$

where the value in brackets is the number of degrees of freedom and p is the p-value.

7.3.2   Dichotomous data: The Chi-square test

If three groups of participants attempt a problem under different conditions, and it is noted whether each individual managed to solve it, the result will be a set of nominal data. With such a data set, the **chi-square test** can be used to test the null hypothesis that, in the population, there is no tendency for the problem to be solved more often in some conditions than in others. The procedure is described in Chapter 11.

EXERCISE 11

ONE-FACTOR BETWEEN SUBJECTS ANOVA

Before you start

We suggest that you review the material in Chapter 7 before working through this practical exercise.

The purpose of a one-factor between subjects ANOVA

In one-factor between subjects ANOVA, the **F ratio** compares the spread among the treatment means with the (supposedly uniform) spread of the scores within groups about their group means. The purpose of this exercise is to help clarify the rationale of the F ratio by showing how its value is affected by various manipulations of some (or all) of the data. Before proceeding with this exercise, we ask you to suppose that a one-factor ANOVA has been carried out upon a set of data and yields an F value of, say, 7.23. Now suppose we were to multiply every score in the experimental results by a constant, say 10. What would happen to the value of F: would it still be 7.23? Or would it increase? Or decrease?

We also invite you to speculate upon the effect that adding a constant (say 10) to all the scores in just one of the groups would have upon F: suppose, for example, we were to add 10 to all the scores in the group with the largest mean. Would F stay the same, increase or decrease in value? Would the effect be the same if the constant were added to the scores of the group with the smallest mean?

As a first approach to answering these questions, we shall carry out a **one-factor ANOVA** on a set of data. Then we shall see what happens to the value of F when the data are transformed as described in the previous paragraphs.

Some data

Suppose a researcher is interested in how well non-Chinese-speaking students can learn Chinese characters using different kinds of mnemonic. Independent groups of participants are tested under three conditions: *No Mnemonic*, *Mnemonic 1* and *Mnemonic 2*. The dependent variable is the number of Chinese characters that are correctly recalled. The data are shown in Table 1.

Table 1. Results of a completely randomised experiment on the effects of different mnemonic systems upon recall of logographic characters									
No Mnemonic **(10 control subjects)**	4	6	4	3	5	7	10	4	9	11
Mnemonic 1 **(10 subjects trained in Mnemonic 1)**	11	9	16	10	12	17	18	16	8	11
Mnemonic 2 **(10 subjects trained in Mnemonic 2)**	21	16	15	16	18	11	9	12	19	20

Opening SPSS

Open SPSS and select the **Type in data** radio button in the opening window. If **Data View** appears first, click the **Variable View** tab to open **Variable View**.

Construction of the SPSS data set

Recast the data of Table 1 into a form suitable for analysis by SPSS by following the procedure described in Chapter 3. In **Variable View**, name the variables *case, group, score*, remembering to change the value in the **Decimals** column to 0 each time. The variable *group* will need appropriate values and value labels specified in the **Values** column. It is also recommended that variable labels should be entered in the **Label** column e.g. Case Number, Learning Group.

Switch to **Data View** and enter the data. The easiest way of entering the case numbers is to wait until all the other data have been entered. Then access **Compute** and enter *case* as the **Target Variable** and *$casenum* as the **Numeric Expression**. All the case numbers will automatically appear in the *case* column of **Data View**.

Save the data set to a file such as ***Mnemonics***.

Exploring the data

As always, we recommend a preliminary exploration of the data set before any formal testing is carried out, in case there are problems with ANOVA. As in Exercise 8, use the **Means** procedure for descriptive statistics and **Explore** for checks on the distributions of the scores within the groups. (Remember to click the **Plots** radio button to suppress the **Statistics** output. This will save you from being swamped with superfluous statistics).

The output for **Means** begins with a **Case Processing Summary** table, followed by a table labelled **Report** listing the means, number of cases (N) and standard deviations for the three groups. After that, side-by-side boxplots appear.

- **Examine the Output for the Means procedure. Do the means appear to differ? Are the standard deviations similar in value?**

The output for **Explore** begins with a **Case Processing Summary** table, followed by the stem-and-leaf displays for the three groups. The final item is the side-by-side boxplots.

- **Do the boxplots suggest any anomalies in the distributions of the data in any of the three groups? Write a statement assessing the suitability of the data for ANOVA.**

Procedure for the one-way ANOVA

The procedure for the one-way ANOVA is described in detail in Section 7.2.2. Remember to click the **Post-Hoc...** button, select **Tukey** and click **Continue** to return to the **One-way ANOVA** dialog box. This is because if the ANOVA F-ratio is significant, you will want to know which pairs of levels differ significantly (see Section 7.1).

Click **OK** to run the ANOVA and the multiple comparisons procedure.

Output for the one-way ANOVA

Examine the **ANOVA Summary Table**.

- **Write down the value of F and its associated p-value. Is F significant? What are the implications of this result for the experimental hypothesis?**

Look at the table of **Multiple Comparisons**.

- **Construct your own table showing clearly which pairs of levels are significantly different and which are not.**

RE-ANALYSIS OF TRANSFORMED DATA SETS

In this section, we return to the question of the effects of transforming the data upon the ANOVA statistics.

1) Multiplying every score by a constant

We recommend that whenever you have occasion to transform the values of a variable in an original SPSS data set, you should construct a new target variable, rather than change (perhaps irreversibly) the original data. Use the **Compute** procedure (Section 4.4.2) to multiply each value in the data set by a factor of 10. Follow the instructions in that section, choosing, for the target variable, a mnemonic name such as *allbyten*. Now change the **One-way ANOVA** dialog box so that the dependent variable is *allbyten* instead of *score* and click **OK** to run the analysis.

- **Write down the value of F and its associated p-value. Is F significant? What are the implications of this result for the experimental hypothesis?**

In the output, you will see that both the between groups and within groups variance estimates have increased by a factor of 100. It is easy to show algebraically that when each of a set of scores is multiplied by a constant, the new variance is the old variance times the square of the constant. Since, however, the factors of 100 in the numerator and denominator of the F ratio cancel out, the value of the F ratio remains unchanged.

2) Adding a constant to the scores in only one group

This time, we want a dependent variable that contains, for two of the three groups, the original scores. In the third (Mnemonic 2) group, however, every score must be increased by 10. First use **Compute** to copy the values in *score* to a new target variable *newscore*. Use **Compute** again to add *10* to the numbers in this new variable only when the grouping variable has the value *3*. To do this, type *newscore* into the **Target Variable** box and *newscore +10* in the **Numeric Expression** box. Click **If** to open the **Compute Variable: If Cases** dialog box. Transfer the grouping variable name *group* into the box and add the expression *=3*. Click **Continue** and **OK** to run the procedure. In **Data View**, check that the values in *newscore* for the third group have changed but the rest have their original values. Now re-run the **one-way ANOVA**, using *newscore* as the dependent variable.

- **Write down the value of F and its associated p-value. Is F significant? What are the implications of this result for the experimental hypothesis?**

You will see that the effect of adding a constant of *10* to all scores in the *Mnemonic 2* group has no effect at all upon the within groups variance estimate. Adding the same constant to all the scores in a set has no effect upon the *spread* of the scores - it merely shifts the mean. The between groups mean square, however, computed from the values of the treatment means alone, has increased considerably. The within groups mean square, on the other hand, is the average of the variance estimates of the scores within groups and is quite independent of the spread among the group means. Consequently, it is quite possible to change the value of the former without affecting that of the latter and vice-versa. The effect of increasing the mean of the third group is to increase the spread of the three treatment means. This increases the value of $MS_{between}$, while leaving MS_{within} unaltered. The result is an increase in F.

Finishing the session

Close down SPSS and any other windows before logging out of the network.

CHAPTER 8

FACTORIAL EXPERIMENTS (BETWEEN SUBJECTS)

8.1 INTRODUCTION

8.2 FACTORIAL ANOVA

8.3 EXPERIMENTS WITH MORE THAN TWO TREATMENT FACTORS

8.1   INTRODUCTION

Experiments with two or more factors are known as **factorial** experiments. In the simplest case, there is a different sample of participants for each possible combination of conditions. This arrangement is known as a **between subjects** (or **completely randomised**) factorial design.

Suppose that a researcher is commissioned to investigate the effects upon simulated driving performance of two new anti-hay fever drugs, A and B. It is suspected that at least one of the drugs may have different effects upon fresh and tired drivers, and the firm developing the drugs needs to ensure that neither has a deleterious effect upon driving performance.

The researcher decides to carry out a two-factor experiment, in which the factors are:

(1)   **Drug**, with levels **Placebo**, **A** and **B**;

(2)   **Alertness**, with levels **Fresh** and **Tired**.

All participants are asked to take a flavoured drink which contains either (in the A and B conditions) a small dosage of a drug or (in the control, or **Placebo** condition) no drug. Half the participants are tested immediately on rising; the others are tested after twenty hours of sleep deprivation. A different sample of ten participants is tested under each of the six treatment combinations: (Fresh, Placebo); (Fresh, Drug A); (Fresh, Drug B); (Tired, Placebo); (Tired, Drug A); (Tired, Drug B).

Notice that in this design, each level of either factor is to be found in combination with every level of the other: the two factors are said to **cross**. There are designs in which the factors do not cross: that is, not all combinations of conditions (or groups) are present, but those will not be considered in this book. The two-factor between subjects factorial design can be represented as a table in which each row or column represents a particular level of one of the treatment factors, and a **cell** of the table (i.e. a single rectangle in the grid) represents one particular treatment **combination** (Table 1). In Table 1, the cell on the bottom right represents the combination (Tired, Drug B). The Group 6 participants were tested under that treatment combination.

Table 1. A completely randomised, two-factor factorial experiment on the effects of two factors upon simulated driving performance.			
		Levels of the Drug factor:	
Levels of the Alertness factor:	Placebo	Drug A	Drug B
Fresh	Group 1	Group 2	Group 3
Tired	Group 4	Group 5	Group 6

The mean scores of the participants are shown in Table 2. The row and column means, which are known as **marginal means**, are the mean scores at each level of either factor considered separately, ignoring the other factor in the classification.

	Placebo	Drug A	Drug B	Means
Table 2. Mean scores achieved by the participants in the drugs experiment				
Fresh	21.0	12.0	22.0	18.3
Tired	10.0	18.0	16.0	14.7
Means	15.5	15.0	19.0	16.5

Main effects and interactions

In a two-factor experiment, there are two kinds of possible treatment effects:
  (1) **main effects**;
  (2) an **interaction**.

The column marginal means in Table 2 represent the mean scores of the participants who were tested at each level of the Drug factor, *ignoring the other experimental factor (Alertness)*. Similarly, the row marginal means in Table 2 represent the mean scores of the fresh and tired participants, *ignoring the Drug factor.*

Should the differences among the means for the three levels of the drug factor be sufficiently great as to indicate a difference in the population, the Drug factor is said to have a **main effect**. Similarly, a large difference between the two row means would indicate that the Alertness factor also has a main effect. Since there are indeed marked differences among both row and column marginal means, there may be main effects of both factors.

Turning now to the cell means in Table 2, another striking feature of the results emerges. If we look at the fresh participants only, we see a sharp dip in performance with Drug A: that is, a dose of this drug actually has a deleterious effect upon the performance of fresh participants. Drug B, on the other hand, has no such effect: the mean performance of the participants under that condition is much the same as that of the placebo group. The corresponding means for the tired participants show a different pattern. Under Drug A, their performance is almost as good as that of the fresh placebo group. Drug B also appears to improve performance. It would appear, therefore, that the researcher's suspicions were well founded: Drug A may improve the performance of tired drivers; but it seems to have an adverse effect upon fresh drivers.

Definition of an interaction

The effect of one treatment factor (such as Drug) at one particular level of another factor (e.g. the Fresh participants only) is known as a **simple main effect**. The Alertness factor has different simple main effects at different levels of the Drug factor: its effect is diminished with Drug B and actually reversed with Drug A. When one treatment factor does not have the same simple main effects at all levels of another, the two factors are said to **interact**.

The analysis of variance of data from a factorial experiment offers tests not only for the presence of main effects of each factor considered separately but also for interactions between (or among) the factors.

The interaction we have just described can be pictured graphically, as plots of the cell means against Drug group for the Fresh and Tired participants (see

Figure 1). There is thus a **Fresh** participants' profile, which is V-shaped, and a **Tired** participants' profile below it, which rises to a plateau under the Drug A and Drug B conditions. **The presence of an interaction is indicated by profile heterogeneity across the levels of one of the factors, that is, by profiles that are not parallel.** An interaction between two factors A and B is often indicated by a multiplication sign: **A × B**, often abbreviated to **AB**.

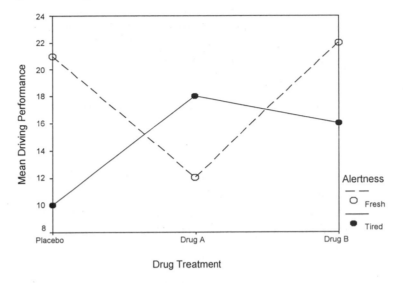

Figure 1. A pattern of cell means suggestive of an interaction

Algebraically, main effects and interactions are independent, so it is quite possible to obtain significant main effects without any significant interaction between the factors, and it is also possible to have significant interactions without any significant main effects.

The rationale of the ANOVA tests for the presence of main effects and an interaction is lucidly described in Gravetter & Wallnau (2000, Chapter 15). If you are unfamiliar with such ANOVA terms as **sum of squares**, **mean square** and **degrees of freedom**, we urge you to read their earlier ANOVA chapters also.

8.2   FACTORIAL ANOVA

Table 3 shows the raw data from the two-factor factorial **Drug × Alertness** experiment.

	Levels of the Drug factor:		
Levels of the Alertness factor:	**Placebo**	**A**	**B**
Fresh	24 25 13 22 16 23 18 19 24 26	18 8 9 14 16 15 6 9 8 17	27 14 19 29 27 23 19 17 20 25
Tired	13 12 14 16 17 13 4 3 2 6	21 24 22 23 20 13 11 17 13 16	21 11 14 22 19 9 14 11 21 18

Table 3. Results of the Drug × Alertness factorial experiment

8.2.1 Preparing the data for the factorial ANOVA

Since there are two factors, *two* **grouping variables** will be required to specify the treatment combination under which each score was achieved. If the grouping variables are *alert* and *drug*, and performance in the driving simulator is *drivperf*, the data file will consist of a column for case numbers, two for the grouping variables, and one for *drivperf*.

Proceed as follows:

See Section 3.2

- Name the variables in the **Name** column of **Variable View** as described in Chapter 3, Section 3.2.
- Display whole numbers only by changing the values to 0 in the **Decimals** column.
- Add labels in the **Label** column such as Case Number, Alertness, Drug Treatment, and Driving Performance.
- Add values and labels in the **Values** column for the grouping variables, such as *1* and *2* (with labels *Fresh* and *Tired*, respectively) for the variable *alert* and *1*, *2*, and *3* (with labels *Placebo*, *Drug A*, and *Drug B*, respectively) for the variable *drug*.
- Click the **Data View** tab at the foot of **Variable View** and enter the data in **Data View**. To display the labels for the values entered for the grouping variables, ensure that **Value Labels** is ticked in the **View** menu.
- Part of the completed data set is shown in Figure 2. Note that the values for the grouping variables have been replaced by their corresponding labels (e.g. for case 28, *1* has been replaced by *Fresh* for the variable *alert* and *2* has been replaced by *Drug B* for the variable *drug*. Likewise, in case 31, *2* has been replaced by *Tired* and *1* by *Placebo* in the *alert* and *drug* cells, respectively. The values in the column *driveperf* are the Driving Performance scores.

	case	alert	drug	drivperf
27	27	Fresh	Drug B	19
28	28	Fresh	Drug B	17
29	29	Fresh	Drug B	20
30	30	Fresh	Drug B	25
31	31	Tired	Placebo	13
32	32	Tired	Placebo	12
33	33	Tired	Placebo	14
34	34	Tired	Placebo	16

Figure 2. Part of Data View showing some of the data from Table 3.

8.2.2 Exploring the data: Obtaining boxplots

Before running the ANOVA, it is important to explore the data to check for any problem with the distributions.

To obtain the boxplots under each of the six treatment combinations, proceed as follows:

- Choose
  Graphs
     Boxplot...
  to open the **Boxplot** dialog box.
- Select **Clustered** by clicking the icon and click **Define** to open the **Define Clustered Boxplot: Summaries for Groups of Cases** dialog box.
- Transfer the variable names as shown in Figure 3.
- Click **OK**.

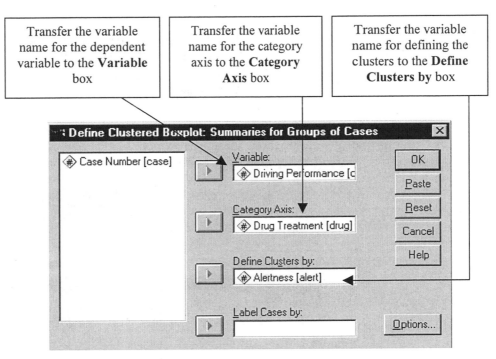

Figure 3. The Define Clustered Boxplot: Summaries for Groups of Cases dialog box

The boxplots are shown in Output 1.

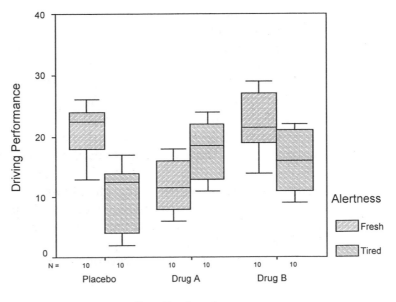

Output 1. The boxplots clustered for the levels of Drug Treatment across each level of Alertness

189

See
Table 2
in
Ch. 4
These boxplots show no extreme cases, which would have been flagged with an asterisk. (See Chapter 4, Table 2, for details of the structure of a boxplot.). None of the distributions is markedly skewed. There is therefore no need to remove any cases or apply a transformation to symmetrise the distribution. We can safely proceed with the ANOVA.

8.2.3 Choosing a factorial ANOVA

For ANOVA designs that are more complex than the one-factor experiment, SPSS applies the **General Linear Model (GLM)**. Both multiple regression (Chapter 12) and ANOVA can be viewed as applications of the GLM. However, in order to simplify the complexity of the GLM dialog boxes, SPSS offers three options within the **General Linear Model** menu (Figure 4): **Univariate** (the subject of this chapter), **Multivariate** (which is not considered in this book), and **Repeated Measures** (which is discussed in the next chapter).

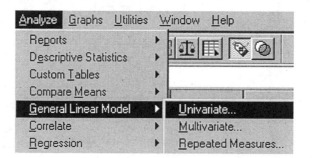

Figure 4. The General Linear Model menu leading to Univariate

- To run a factorial ANOVA, choose
  Analyze
  　　General Linear Model
  　　　　Univariate...
  to open the **Univariate** dialog box.
- Transfer the variables in the usual manner. The **Dependent Variable:** is Driving Performance [*driveperf*] and the **Fixed Factor(s):** (see below for an explanation) are the grouping variables Alertness [*alert*] and Drug Treatment [*drug*]. The completed version is shown in Figure 5.
- Various optional additions to the output can be selected. To obtain a table of means and standard deviations for each level and each combination of levels of the factors, click **Options...** , select the **Descriptive statistics** check box and click **Continue**.
- To obtain a profile plot of the means, click **Plots...** to open the **Univariate: Profile Plots** dialog box. Select Drug Treatment [*drug*] for the **Horizontal Axis:** box and Alertness [*alert*] for the **Separate Lines:** box. Click **Add** to add the plot to the **Plots:** list (the completed dialog box is shown in Figure 6). Click **Continue** to return to the **Univariate** dialog box.

Transfer the variable name for the dependent variable to the **Dependent Variable** box

Transfer the variable names of the grouping variables to the **Fixed Factor(s)** box

For random factor grouping variables (most grouping variables are not random factors)

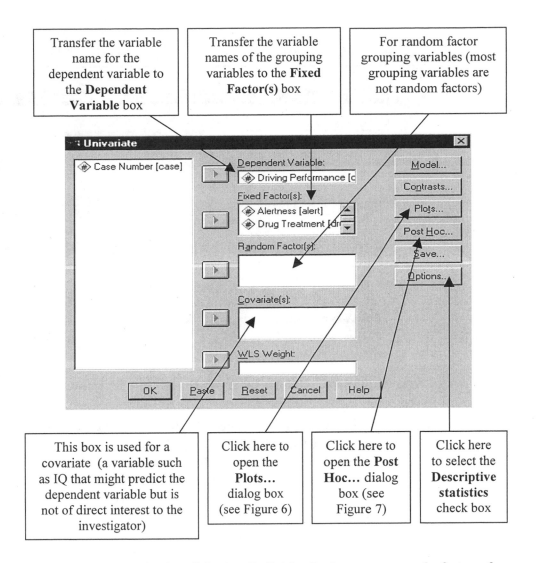

This box is used for a covariate (a variable such as IQ that might predict the dependent variable but is not of direct interest to the investigator)

Click here to open the **Plots...** dialog box (see Figure 6)

Click here to open the **Post Hoc...** dialog box (see Figure 7)

Click here to select the **Descriptive statistics** check box

Figure 5. The Univariate dialog box for Driving Performance across the factors of Alertness and Drug Treatment

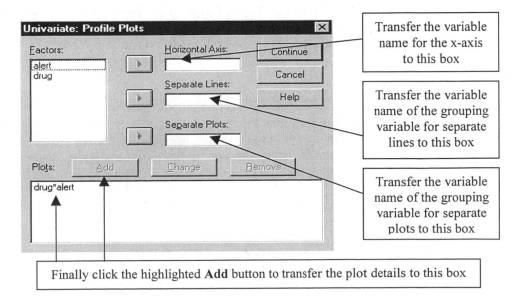

Transfer the variable name for the x-axis to this box

Transfer the variable name of the grouping variable for separate lines to this box

Transfer the variable name of the grouping variable for separate plots to this box

Finally click the highlighted **Add** button to transfer the plot details to this box

Figure 6. The completed dialog box for plotting Drug Treatment along the Horizontal Axis with the lines representing the levels of Alertness

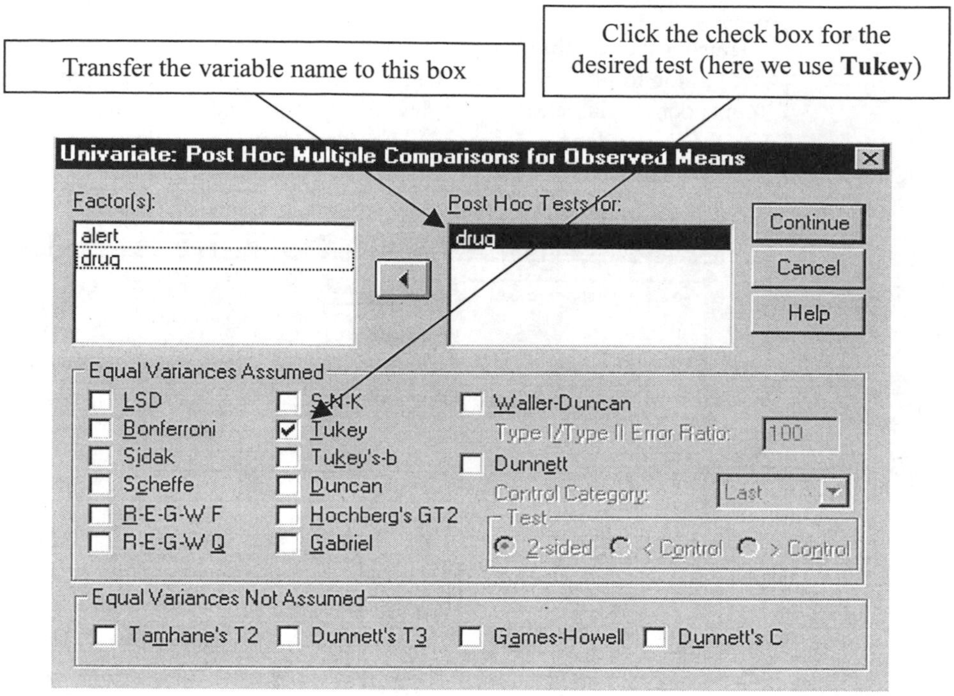

Transfer the variable name to this box

Click the check box for the desired test (here we use **Tukey**)

Univariate: Post Hoc Multiple Comparisons for Observed Means

Factor(s):
alert
drug

Post Hoc Tests for:
drug

Continue
Cancel
Help

Equal Variances Assumed
- [ ] LSD
- [ ] Bonferroni
- [ ] Sidak
- [ ] Scheffe
- [ ] R-E-G-W F
- [ ] R-E-G-W Q
- [ ] S-N-K
- [x] Tukey
- [ ] Tukey's-b
- [ ] Duncan
- [ ] Hochberg's GT2
- [ ] Gabriel
- [ ] Waller-Duncan

Type I/Type II Error Ratio: 100
- [ ] Dunnett
  Control Category: Last
  Test
  ( ) 2-sided ( ) < Control ( ) > Control

Equal Variances Not Assumed
- [ ] Tamhane's T2 [ ] Dunnett's T3 [ ] Games-Howell [ ] Dunnett's C

Figure 7. The completed post-hoc dialog box for Drug Treatment using the Tukey test

- If one-way post-hoc tests are desired, click **Post-Hoc...** to open the **Univariate Post-Hoc Multiple Comparisons for Observed Means** dialog box. Select *drug* for the **Post Hoc Tests for:** box (there is no point in running a post-hoc test for *alert* because it has only two levels) and click the check box for **Tukey** (the completed dialog box is shown in Figure 7). Click **Continue** to return to the **Univariate** dialog box.
- Click **OK** in the **Univariate** dialog box.

WLS Weight

The **WLS Weight** box in Figure 5 is used for identifying a variable containing weights for weighted least-squares analysis. We do not consider this type of analysis in this book.

Factors with Fixed and Random effects

The box labelled **Random Factor(s)** in Figure 4 is used only if the levels of a factor are a random sample of possible levels. In practice, this is rare, and most treatment factors have **fixed effects**. In the present example, *alert* and *drug* are fixed effects factors.

Covariates

The box labelled **Covariate(s)** in Figure 4 is used for identifying any covariates. A **covariate** is a variable which, although not of direct interest in the investigation, could be expected to correlate (co-vary) with the dependent variable. For example, suppose that our participants all belonged to an organisation which collected their IQ test scores. It would be interesting to know whether the mean IQs of the various experimental groups were similar in value, otherwise, genuine treatment effects could be confounded with differences in intelligence. There are techniques known as **Analysis of Covariance (ANCOVA)** that essentially remove the effects of covariates and perform ANOVA on a 'purified' data set. The advantage is often a reduction of 'data noise' and a resulting increase in the power of the ANOVA tests. To run an ANCOVA, transfer the variable name(s) of the covariate(s) into the covariate box.

8.2.4 Output for a factorial ANOVA

The results are shown in Output Listings 2-5. The table in Output 2, **Between Subjects Factors**, summarises the factor names and level labels, together with the number of cases at each level.

Between-Subjects Factors

		Value Label	N
Alertness	1	Fresh	30
	2	Tired	30
Drug Treatment	1	Placebo	20
	2	Drug A	20
	3	Drug B	20

Output 2. The table of Between-Subjects Factors

Output 3 is the table of descriptive statistics requested from **Options...** .

Descriptive Statistics

Dependent Variable: Driving Performance

Alertness	Drug Treatment	Mean	Std. Deviation	N
Fresh	Placebo	21.00	4.29	10
	Drug A	12.00	4.42	10
	Drug B	22.00	4.94	10
	Total	18.33	6.35	30
Tired	Placebo	10.00	5.66	10
	Drug A	18.00	4.64	10
	Drug B	16.00	4.78	10
	Total	14.67	5.97	30
Total	Placebo	15.50	7.47	20
	Drug A	15.00	5.38	20
	Drug B	19.00	5.65	20
	Total	16.50	6.38	60

Output 3. The table of descriptive statistics

The table in Output 4, **Tests of Between-Subjects Effects**, tabulates the source of variation, the sums of squares, degrees of freedom (df), mean square, F ratio and p-value (Sig.). Note that each F ratio is the Mean Square for the source divided by the Error Mean Square (23.15).

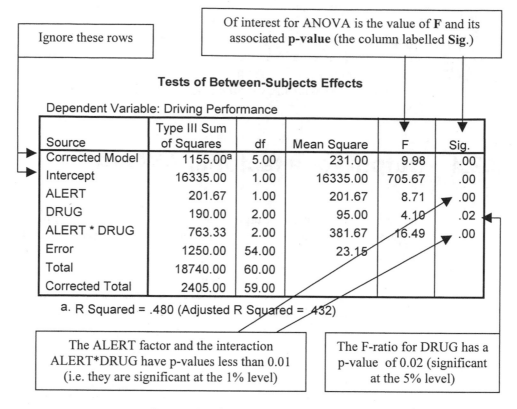

Output 4. The ANOVA Summary Table

This table was edited in **SPSS Viewer** to reduce three decimal places to two. This is done by double-clicking the whole table so that it shows a hashed border, highlighting the five columns of numbers so that they are shown in inverse video, clicking the right-hand mouse button to show a menu, selecting the item **Cell Properties...**, selecting in the **Format** box the item. #.#, changing the number of decimals shown in the **Decimals** box to 2, and finally clicking **OK**.

The terms **Corrected Model** and **Intercept** refer to the regression method used to carry out the ANOVA and can be ignored. The three rows, ALERT, DRUG, ALERT*DRUG, are of most interest, since these report tests for the two main effects and the interaction. Note the **Sig.** (i.e. p-value, or tail probability) for each F ratio. There are significant main effects for both the *alert* and *drug* factors: the former is significant beyond the 0.01 level, the latter beyond the 0.05 level, but not beyond the 0.01 level. In addition to main effects of both treatment factors, there is a significant interaction. The p-value is given as *0.00*, which means that it is less than *0.005*. Clearly, the *drug* factor has different effects upon Fresh and Tired participants. To ascertain the nature of these effects, however, we shall need to examine the pattern of the treatment means more closely.

These results should be reported by specifying the name of the factor followed by the value of the F ratio (with the df of the numerator and denominator separated by a comma in brackets) and the p-value e.g.

"There was a significant main effect of the Alertness factor: $F(1,54) = 8.71$; $p < 0.01$."

Optional post-hoc test

The optional Tukey post-hoc test results for the factor Drug Treatment are shown in Output Listings 5-6. It can be seen that Drugs A and B differ significantly from one another, but neither differs significantly from Placebo.

Multiple Comparisons

Dependent Variable: Driving Performance

Tukey HSD

(I) Drug Treatment	(J) Drug Treatment	Mean Difference (I-J)	Std. Error	Sig.
Placebo	Drug A	.50	1.52	.942
	Drug B	-3.50	1.52	.064
Drug A	Placebo	-.50	1.52	.942
	Drug B	-4.00*	1.52	.029
Drug B	Placebo	3.50	1.52	.064
	Drug A	4.00*	1.52	.029

Based on observed means.

*. The mean difference is significant at the .05 level.

The only difference with a p-value (**Sig.**) less than 0.05 is Drug A and Drug B. Note these rows are highlighted with *

Output 5. The multiple comparisons of the Tukey Post Hoc test for the Drug factor.

Homogeneous Subsets

Driving Performance

Tukey HSD [a,b]

Drug Treatment	N	Subset 1	Subset 2
Drug A	20	15.00	
Placebo	20	15.50	15.50
Drug B	20		19.00
Sig.		.942	.064

Means for groups in homogeneous subsets are displayed.
Based on Type III Sum of Squares
The error term is Mean Square(Error) = 23.148.

a. Uses Harmonic Mean Sample Size = 20.000.

b. Alpha = .05.

Levels within a column do not differ significantly. The only levels in different columns are Drug A and Drug B which therefore do differ significantly

Output 6. The homogeneous subsets of the Tukey Post Hoc test for the factor Drug Treatment

Optional profile plot

The optional profile plot is shown in Output 7 (this is a repeat of Figure 1). It has been edited in **SPSS Viewer** to change coloured lines to black, to change one of the lines into dashes, and to represent the means as black discs.

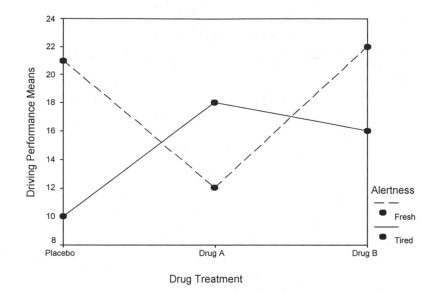

Output 7. Profile plots of Alertness across the levels of Drug Treatment

The graph shows several important results.
  (1)   Fresh participants given a Placebo score more highly than Tired participants.
  (2)   Drug A causes a deterioration in the performance of Fresh participants but enhances the performance of Tired participants.
  (3)   Drug B, while slightly enhancing performance for Fresh participants, also enhances the performance of Tired participants; though not to the same extent as Drug A.

Notice that the most interesting results from this experiment are to be found in the analysis of the cell means following the discovery of a significant interaction between the two factors Drug Treatment and Alertness. As is so often the case in factorial experiments, the presence of an interaction draws attention away from main effects (which, as we have seen, are apparent from considerations of the marginal means). In the present example, it is of relatively little interest to learn that the mean level of performance of drugged participants is somewhat higher than that of undrugged participants, because the three Drug profiles are so disparate; nor is it surprising to find that Fresh participants outperform tired ones.

Often, having made a preliminary graphical exploration of the cell means, the user will wish to make some unplanned pairwise comparisons among selected cell means to confirm the patterns evident in the graph. For example, Figure 7 suggests that the simple fact of tiredness led to a deterioration in performance. That would be confirmed should a comparison between the means for the combination (Placebo, Fresh) and (Placebo, Tired) prove significant. To confirm that Drug A actually has deleterious effect upon the performance of Fresh participants, we should need to find a significant difference between the means for the (Placebo, Fresh) and (Drug A, Fresh) conditions. It is possible, too, that the apparent enhancement by Drug B of the performance of Fresh

Placebo participants may not be significant. That would be confirmed by a non-significant difference between the means for conditions (Placebo, Fresh) and (Drug B, Fresh).

Since the Alertness factor comprises only two conditions, the answer to the question of whether tiredness alone produces a significant decrement in performance is answered by a test for a **simple main effect** of Alertness at the Placebo level of the Drug Treatment factor. Tests for simple main effects are available on SPSS, but the user must know the syntax of the SPSS control language. Another approach is to perform an ANOVA only upon the data at the level of the qualifying factor concerned. If we go back to **Data View**, select the data only from the Placebo condition using the **Select Cases** procedure in the **Data** menu and request a one-way ANOVA with Alertness as the single factor, we shall find that $F(1, 18) = 23.99$; $p = .0001$. This confirms the simple main effect of Alertness at the Placebo level of the Drug factor and hence that the difference between the means for the (Placebo, Fresh) and (Placebo, Tired) conditions is indeed significant.

Some of the other questions mentioned can only be answered by directly making pairwise comparisons between specified treatment means. Since many such comparisons are possible, it is necessary to protect against inflation of the *per family* type I error rate by using a conservative method such as the **Tukey** test, described in the following section.

Unplanned multiple pairwise comparisons with Tukey's test

Following a significant main effect or interaction, the user will often want to make unplanned comparisons either among the marginal means (to compare levels in a main effect) or among the cell means (to investigate an interaction).

In the present case, the ANOVA showed significant main effects of both the Drug Treatment and Alertness factors. However, since there were only two levels of Alertness, it is only meaningful to scrutinise the pairwise differences among the three treatment means of levels of Drug Treatment. This has already been shown in Output 4. Should an interaction prove significant (as in the present example), it will often be illuminating to make comparisons among the **cell means** rather than the marginal means. The **Univariate** dialog box does not offer a post-hoc test for an interaction so another procedure has to be adopted. The solution is to apply the **Tukey** test from the **One-Way ANOVA** procedure to all the cell means in the original two-way table of results. To achieve this, we must construct a new grouping variable *cellcode*, containing a code number for each of the combinations of the levels of the grouping variables. Use the **Compute** command as follows:

- Click **Transform** and **Compute...** to obtain the **Compute Variable** dialog box (Figure 8). In the **Target Variable:** box, type the name of the new variable *cellcode*.
- Transfer *alert* into the **Numeric Expression:** box and type in *10 and +. Transfer *drug* into the box so that the whole expression is *alert*10 + drug*. Click **OK** to create in **Data View** the new variable *cellcode* with values of 11, 12, 13, 21, 22 and 23.
- To label the cell codes, click the **Variable View** tab to switch from **Data View** to **Variable View** and click the **Values** column for the variable *cellcode* to open the **Values Labels** dialog box. Fill in each number in turn

along with their corresponding condition (e.g. 11 is labelled Fresh, Placebo; 12 is labelled Fresh, Drug A; and so on).

- Click **OK**.

Back in **Data View**, these labels should have replaced the numbers. If they have not, click **Value Labels** in the **View** drop-down menu.

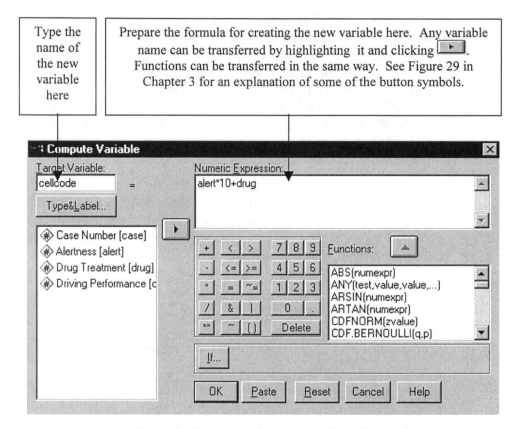

| Type the name of the new variable here | Prepare the formula for creating the new variable here. Any variable name can be transferred by highlighting it and clicking ▶. Functions can be transferred in the same way. See Figure 29 in Chapter 3 for an explanation of some of the button symbols. |

Figure 8. Creation of the new variable *cellcode*

Now run the **One-Way ANOVA** command with the **Tukey Post Hoc** test.
- Select
  Analyze
  > **Compare Means**
  >> **One-Way ANOVA...**
  to open the **One-Way ANOVA** dialog box. Transfer Driving Performance [drivperf] to the **Dependent List:** box and *cellcode* to the **Factor:** box.
- Click **Post Hoc...** and select the **Tukey** test. Click **Continue**.
- Click **OK**.

Part of the output showing the homogeneous subsets from the Tukey test is reproduced in Output 8. Items in the same subset are not significantly different from one another, whereas items across subsets (provided they are not repeated) are. These subsets show that there are five significant differences: (1) between (Tired, Placebo) and (Tired, Drug A); (2) between (Tired, Placebo) and (Fresh, Placebo); (3) between (Tired, Placebo) and (Fresh, Drug B); (4) between (Fresh, Drug A) and (Fresh, Placebo); and finally (5) between(Fresh, Drug A) and (Fresh, Drug B). Notice that (Tired, Drug B) is not significantly different from any of the other combinations.

Homogeneous Subsets

Driving Performance

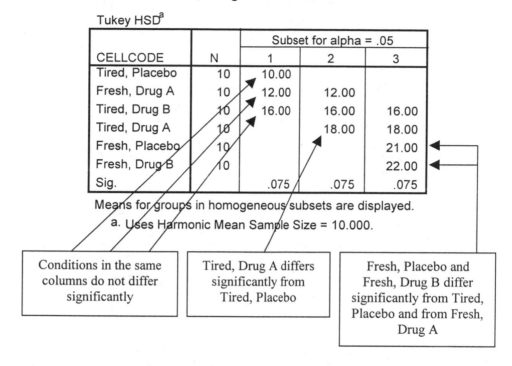

Tukey HSD[a]

CELLCODE	N	Subset for alpha = .05		
		1	2	3
Tired, Placebo	10	10.00		
Fresh, Drug A	10	12.00	12.00	
Tired, Drug B	10	16.00	16.00	16.00
Tired, Drug A	10		18.00	18.00
Fresh, Placebo	10			21.00
Fresh, Drug B	10			22.00
Sig.		.075	.075	.075

Means for groups in homogeneous subsets are displayed.

a. Uses Harmonic Mean Sample Size = 10.000.

Conditions in the same columns do not differ significantly	Tired, Drug A differs significantly from Tired, Placebo	Fresh, Placebo and Fresh, Drug B differ significantly from Tired, Placebo and from Fresh, Drug A

Output 8. Part of the Tukey test listing for the interaction of *drug* and *alert*

Unplanned multiple comparisons following the ANOVA of complex factorial experiments: Some cautions and caveats

In considering the making of unplanned multiple comparisons to explore a significant interaction, we have touched upon a difficult and contentious area. In the writings of the most respected statistical authorities, the reader will look in vain for a set of rules and procedures on which there is complete consensus. Few, however, would dispute the following statements.

(1) The making of unplanned multiple comparisons (and other *a posteriori* analyses following the initial ANOVA) carries a heightened risk of Type I error, that is, obtaining a significant difference (or pattern) which has merely arisen through sampling variability. Accordingly, the user must take precautions to prevent the *per family* (or *experiment-wise*) error rate from rising to unacceptable levels.

(2) The more complex the experiment, the greater the risk of Type I errors.

(3) The risks are greatly increased if the researcher follows an indiscriminate 'dredging' strategy, whereby every possible statistical test is automatically carried out: simple main effects of A at the various levels of B, simple effects of B at the different levels of A, comparisons between very possible pair of cell means, and so on. We have seen that only some comparisons are informative. In the present example, for instance, we should learn little from a comparison of (Placebo, Tired) with (Fresh, Drug A), because it

would be impossible to say which factor was responsible for the difference.

(4)   Whatever strategy one adopts, formal testing should be driven by substantive, theoretical considerations, rather than a desire to milk the data to the maximum possible extent in the hope of finding significance somewhere.

The **Tukey test** assumes that every possible paired comparison will be made. Since, however, the discriminating user will only wish to make selected comparisons, it may be felt that the Tukey test is unduly conservative. Certainly, with more complex factorial designs, with many treatment combinations, the Tukey criterion for a significant difference is a very exacting one. For this reason, some authors (e.g. Keppel, 1973; p244) suggest that a preliminary test for a simple main effect can justify defining the comparison family more narrowly, and carrying out a Tukey test only on the means relating to the simple main effect concerned. For example, returning to our current example of the effects of drugs upon fresh and tired participants, the significant ANOVA interaction could be followed by tests of the simple main effects of the Drug factor at the Fresh and Tired levels of the Alertness factor.

8.3   EXPERIMENTS WITH MORE THAN TWO TREATMENT FACTORS

SPSS can readily be used to analyse data from more complex factorial experiments, with three or more treatment factors. We should warn the reader, however, that experiments with more than three factors should be avoided, because interpretation of complex interactions involving four or more factors is often extremely difficult. Here we illustrate how easily an analysis of a three factor ANOVA can be run with SPSS. Suppose the driving simulation data had included *sex* as an additional factor, as shown in Table 4.

		Levels of the Drug factor:		
Levels of the Alertness factor:	Levels of the Sex factor:	Placebo	A	B
Fresh	Male	24 25 13 22 16	18 8 9 14 16	27 14 19 29 27
Fresh	Female	23 18 19 24 26	15 6 9 8 17	23 19 17 20 25
Tired	Male	13 12 14 16 17	21 24 22 23 20	21 11 14 22 19
Tired	Female	13 4 3 2 6	13 11 17 13 16	9 14 11 21 18

Table 4. Results of a three-way factorial experiment

The data set in **Data View** would now have to include three grouping variables (*alert*, *sex*, and *drug*), as well as a column for the dependent variable *drivperf*. Figure 9 shows a section of **Data View** with the new grouping variable *sex* added.

	case	alert	drug	drivperf	sex
1	1	Fresh	Placebo	24	Male
2	2	Fresh	Placebo	25	Male
3	3	Fresh	Placebo	13	Male
4	4	Fresh	Placebo	22	Male
5	5	Fresh	Placebo	16	Male
6	6	Fresh	Placebo	23	Female
7	7	Fresh	Placebo	18	Female
8	8	Fresh	Placebo	19	Female
9	9	Fresh	Placebo	24	Female
10	10	Fresh	Placebo	26	Female

Figure 9. Part of Data View showing some of the data in Table 4

To run the three-factor ANOVA, proceed as follows:
- Open the **General Linear Model - Univariate** dialog box and complete it as in Figure 5, but adding variable Sex [*sex*] to the **Fixed Factor(s):** box.
- Select the optional **Descriptive statistics** check box from **Options...** and the **Tukey Post-hoc** test for *drug* from **Post-Hoc...** , clicking **Continue** each time to return to the **Univariate** dialog box.
- Click **OK**.

The first table in the output lists the number of cases for each level of the variables (Output 9).

Between-Subjects Factors

		Value Label	N
Alertness	1	Fresh	30
	2	Tired	30
Drug Treatment	1	Placebo	20
	2	Drug A	20
	3	Drug B	20
Sex	1	Male	30
	2	Female	30

Output 9. The table of Between-Subjects Factors

The next table (Output 10) shows the descriptive statistics requested in **Options...**

Descriptive Statistics

Dependent Variable: Driving Performance

Alertness	Drug Treatment	Sex	Mean	Std. Deviation	N
Fresh	Placebo	Male	20.00	5.24	5
		Female	22.00	3.39	5
		Total	21.00	4.29	10
	Drug A	Male	13.00	4.36	5
		Female	11.00	4.74	5
		Total	12.00	4.42	10
	Drug B	Male	23.20	6.42	5
		Female	20.80	3.19	5
		Total	22.00	4.94	10
	Total	Male	18.73	6.67	15
		Female	17.93	6.22	15
		Total	18.33	6.35	30
Tired	Placebo	Male	14.40	2.07	5
		Female	5.60	4.39	5
		Total	10.00	5.66	10
	Drug A	Male	22.00	1.58	5
		Female	14.00	2.45	5
		Total	18.00	4.64	10
	Drug B	Male	17.40	4.72	5
		Female	14.60	4.93	5
		Total	16.00	4.78	10
	Total	Male	17.93	4.33	15
		Female	11.40	5.68	15
		Total	14.67	5.97	30
Total	Placebo	Male	17.20	4.78	10
		Female	13.80	9.40	10
		Total	15.50	7.47	20
	Drug A	Male	17.50	5.66	10
		Female	12.50	3.89	10
		Total	15.00	5.38	20
	Drug B	Male	20.30	6.13	10
		Female	17.70	5.10	10
		Total	19.00	5.65	20
	Total	Male	18.33	5.54	30
		Female	14.67	6.73	30
		Total	16.50	6.38	60

Output 10. Descriptive statistics for each combination of levels

With three factors, the ANOVA summary table (Output 11) is considerably longer than in the two-factor case. As before, there are main effects. This time, however, there are three different main effects, one for each of the three factors in the experiment. In the two-factor experiment, there can be only one two-way interaction; but in the three-factor experiment, there are three and here all are significant except DRUG * SEX. Moreover, in the three-factor table a new interaction appears, ALERT * DRUG * SEX. This is known as a **three-way**, or **three-factor interaction**. A three-factor interaction is said to occur when there is heterogeneity of the interaction between two factors across the levels of a third. There is, however, no evidence of a significant three-factor interaction in the present data set:

$$F(2, 48) = 1.93; \text{NS.}$$

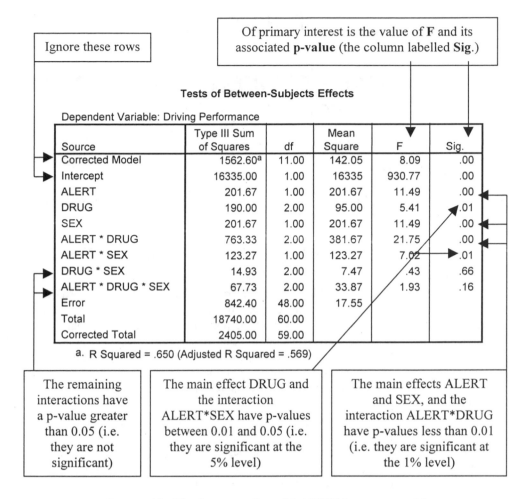

Ignore these rows

Of primary interest is the value of **F** and its associated **p-value** (the column labelled **Sig.**)

Tests of Between-Subjects Effects

Dependent Variable: Driving Performance

Source	Type III Sum of Squares	df	Mean Square	F	Sig.
Corrected Model	1562.60ᵃ	11.00	142.05	8.09	.00
Intercept	16335.00	1.00	16335	930.77	.00
ALERT	201.67	1.00	201.67	11.49	.00
DRUG	190.00	2.00	95.00	5.41	.01
SEX	201.67	1.00	201.67	11.49	.00
ALERT * DRUG	763.33	2.00	381.67	21.75	.00
ALERT * SEX	123.27	1.00	123.27	7.02	.01
DRUG * SEX	14.93	2.00	7.47	.43	.66
ALERT * DRUG * SEX	67.73	2.00	33.87	1.93	.16
Error	842.40	48.00	17.55		
Total	18740.00	60.00			
Corrected Total	2405.00	59.00			

a. R Squared = .650 (Adjusted R Squared = .569)

The remaining interactions have a p-value greater than 0.05 (i.e. they are not significant)

The main effect DRUG and the interaction ALERT*SEX have p-values between 0.01 and 0.05 (i.e. they are significant at the 5% level)

The main effects ALERT and SEX, and the interaction ALERT*DRUG have p-values less than 0.01 (i.e. they are significant at the 1% level)

Output 11. The three-way factorial ANOVA summary table

In conclusion, in addition to the significant main effects and interaction noted in Output 4, there are now also a significant main effect *sex* and a significant interaction of *sex* and *alert*.

EXERCISE 12

FACTORIAL BETWEEN SUBJECTS ANOVA (TWO-WAY ANOVA)

Before you start

Before proceeding with this practical, please read Chapter 8. The following exercise assumes a knowledge of the standard **factorial ANOVA** terminology.

An experiment on the memories of chess players

'Must have a marvellous memory!'. This is something often said of a good chess player; but do good chess players necessarily have better short-term memories than those who are mediocre? To find out, a psychologist tested chess players at three levels of proficiency on their ability to reconstruct board positions they had just been shown. Some of the positions used were from real games selected from tournaments; but others were merely random placings of the same pieces. The psychologist predicted that whereas the better players would show superior reconstructions of real board positions, this superiority would disappear when they tried to reproduce random placements. The dependent variable in this experiment was a participant's *score* on reconstruction. There were two independent variables (factors):

      (1)   Competence   (Novice, Average, Good).
      (2)   Position   (Real, Random).

An important feature of the design of this experiment was that a different sample of participants performed under each of the six treatment combinations: that is, each group of players at a given level was subdivided into those reconstructing Real positions and those reconstructing Random positions.

What the psychologist is predicting is that, when performance is averaged over Random and Real positions, the better players will achieve higher performance means; but this will turn out to be because of their superior recall of Real board positions only, and the beginners will be just as good at reconstructing Random positions. The **two-factor ANOVA**, therefore, should show a significant interaction between the factors of Competence and Position, as well as (possibly) a main effect of Competence. The latter might be expected to arise because the better players' much superior performance in reconstructing real board positions pulls up the mean value of their performance over both Real and Random positions, even though they may not excel beginners on the Random task.
The results of the experiment are shown in Table 1.

Table 1. Results of the experiment on the reconstruction of positions by chess players															
	Competence														
Position	Novice					Average					Good				
Real	38	39	42	40	40	65	58	70	61	62	88	97	79	89	89
Random	50	53	40	41	36	50	40	43	37	38	41	40	50	42	41

Opening SPSS

Open SPSS and select the **Type in data** radio button in the opening window. If **Data View** opens first, click the **Variable View** tab to open **Variable View**.

Preparing the SPSS data set

Recast the data of Table 1 into a form suitable for entry into SPSS along the lines of the description in Section 8.2.1. You will need a variable for cases (there are 30 participants) as well as two grouping variables, *compet* and *position*, with appropriate values and value labels specified in the **Values** column, and one dependent variable, *score*. Ensure that the values in the **Decimals** column have been reduced to 0. We also recommend you to use the **Label** column to assign fuller labels to the variables: e.g. Case Number, Competence, Position of Pieces.

Switch to **Data View** and enter the data, leaving the values for *case* until last, when you can use **Compute** to enter them automatically, making *case* the **Target Variable** and *$casenum* the **Numeric Expression**.

As always, save the data set with a suitable name.

Exploring the data

Before proceeding with the ANOVA, it is important to explore the data. Look at the boxplots (see Section 8.2.2) using

Graphs
> **Boxplot....**

to open the **Boxplot** dialog box.

- **What do you notice about the distribution of data among the three levels of Competence and between the two levels of Position?**

Procedure for the two-way ANOVA

Choose
Analyze
> **General Linear Model**
>> **Univariate...**

to open the **Univariate** dialog box. Then complete the dialog box as described in Section 8.2.3, specifying a plot of the means using the **Plots...** dialog box, selecting **Descriptive statistics** using the **Options...** dialog box, and a post-hoc **Tukey** test for *competence* (ignore *position* since it has only two levels) using the **Post-Hoc...** dialog box .

Output for the two-way ANOVA

Construct a table of means to include the cell and marginal means from the descriptive statistics table.

- **From inspection of the marginal means, is there likely to be a main effect? Do the cell means form a pattern suggestive of an interaction?**

The ANOVA summary table gives F ratios for the main effects of *compet* and *position* and also for the interaction between the two factors.

- **Write down the values of F (and the associated p-values) for the main effect and interaction tests. Do these results confirm your predictions from inspection of the output from the Means procedure? Relate these results to the experimental hypothesis about the short-term memory of chess players.**

Post-hoc comparisons among the levels of competence

Inspect the output for the post-hoc comparisons of the levels of competence.

- **Construct your own table showing clearly which pairs of levels are significantly different and which (if any) are not.**

Graph of cell means

Inspect the graph.

- **What do you conclude from the plot?**

Post-hoc comparisons among the cell means

Since the interaction is significant, make pairwise comparisons among all six cell means using the procedure described in Section 8.2.4 by using the **Compute** and **Recode** commands to create six categories. Remember to create new labels for each of these means in **Variable View**. Then, to these six means, apply the **Tukey** post-hoc test within the **One-Way ANOVA** from the **Compare Means...** menu.

- **What do you conclude from the output?**

Finishing the session

Close down SPSS and any other windows before logging out of the computer.

CHAPTER 9

WITHIN SUBJECTS EXPERIMENTS

9.1   INTRODUCTION

A potential problem with between subjects experiments (Chapters 7 & 8) is that if there are large individual differences in performance, searching for a meaningful pattern in the data can be like trying to listen to a radio programme against a loud background crackle of interference. For example, in the Mnemonic Training Method experiment described in Chapter 7, some of the scores obtained by participants in the control condition may well be higher than those of participants who were trained to use a mnemonic: there are some people who, when asked to read through a long list, can, **without any training at all**, reproduce most of the items accurately; whereas others, even after training, would recall very few items. Individual differences, therefore, can introduce considerable **noise** into the data from between subjects experiments.

In the **within subjects experiment** (see Chapter 1), each participant is tested at all levels of every treatment factor in the design. Each participant, therefore, serves as his or her own control, making it possible, in the within subjects ANOVA, to remove the variance associated with individual differences in overall ability and make a more powerful F test.

Another drawback with the between subjects experiment is that it is wasteful of participants: if the experimental procedure is a short one, a participant may spend more time travelling to and from the place of testing than actually performing the experiment. The within subjects experiment allows the researcher to make fuller use of the participant's time and trouble.

In summary, therefore, the within subjects experiment has two advantages over the between subjects experiment:
(1)   It cuts down data noise.
(2)   It makes more efficient use of time and resources.

The within subjects experiment, however, also has disadvantages, which in some circumstances can outweigh considerations of convenience and the maximisation of the signal-to-noise ratio.

Where participants are tested on not one but several tasks, their performance on the later tasks may improve through a **practice effect**. Practice effects, however, are only one type of **carry-over**, or **order effect**. Not all carry-over effects are positive: e.g., recall of the items in a list is vulnerable to interference from items in previous lists (proactive interference). In within subjects experiments, carry-over effects are potential **extraneous variables**, whose effects may be confounded with those of the treatment factor.

The possibility of confounding carry-over effects is reduced by the procedure known as **counterbalancing**, in which the conditions making up a within subjects factor is varied from participant to participant, in the hope that carry-over effects will balance out across conditions. Counterbalancing is not always sensible, however, as in the mnemonics experiment, where (as we have seen) it would make little sense to have the control condition coming last. Such matters must be considered carefully before deciding to perform an experiment with repeated measures on its treatment factors.

A statistical test always assumes that the data have been generated in a certain manner, as specified by a statistical **model**. For example, the ANOVA for between groups experiments (Chapters 7 and 8) requires that there must be homogeneity of variance from group to group. The model for the within subjects ANOVA makes additional specifications, over and above those made by the between groups models. The most important of these is that the covariances among the scores at the various levels of the within subjects factor are homogeneous. This requirement is known as the assumption of **homogeneity of covariance** (or **sphericity**). If this assumption is violated, the true type I error rate (i.e. the probability of rejecting H_0 when it is true) may be inflated.

SPSS tests for homogeneity of covariance with the **Mauchly sphericity test**. Should the data fail the sphericity test (i.e. p-value < 0.05), the ANOVA F test can be modified to make it more *conservative* (less likely to reject the null hypothesis). SPSS offers three such tests, varying in their degree of conservativeness: the **Greenhouse-Geisser**, the **Huynh-Feldt**, and the **Lower-bound**. All three tests reduce the degrees of freedom of the numerator and the denominator of the F ratio, thus increasing the value of F required for significance.

9.2   A ONE-FACTOR WITHIN SUBJECTS ANOVA

Suppose that in an experiment on aesthetics, each participant was asked to produce three pictures, using just one of three different materials for any one picture: Crayons, Paints or Felt-tip pens.

The dependent variable was the rating a picture received from a panel of judges. The independent variable was the type of implement used to produce the picture. Since the participants would certainly vary in artistic ability, it was decided to ask each to produce three pictures, one with each type of implement. (In an attempt to neutralise carry-over effects, the order in which the three implements were used was counterbalanced across participants.) The data are shown in Table 1.

	Table 1. Results of a one-factor within subjects experiment		
	Levels of factor: Implement		
Case	**Crayon**	**Paint**	**Felt-tip**
1	10	12	14
2	18	10	16
3	20	15	16
4	12	10	12
5	19	20	21
6	25	22	20
7	18	16	17
8	22	18	18
9	17	14	12
10	23	20	18

9.2.1 Entering the data

To enter the data of Table 1 into **Data View**, no grouping variable is required, since the participants have not been subdivided into groups. In **Variable View**, using the procedures described in Section 3.2, define the variables *case*, *crayon*, *paint*, and *felttip*. Using the **Label** column, expand the cryptic variable names to Case Number, Crayon Pencil, Paintbrush and Felt-tip Pen. In **Data View**, enter the data from Table 1 into the first four (pre-labelled) columns.

9.2.2 Exploring the data: Boxplots for within subjects factors

To draw boxplots of the data at the various levels of a within subjects factor, select

> **Graphs**
>> **Boxplot...**

to open the **Boxplot** dialog box (Figure 1).

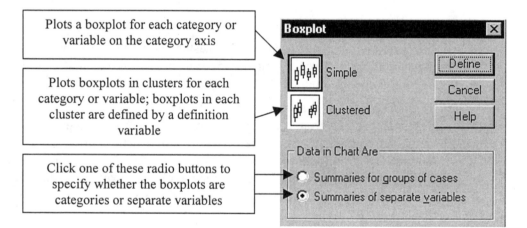

Figure 1. The Boxplot dialog box with Summaries of separate variables selected

- In the **Data in Chart Are** box, activate the **Summaries of separate variables** radio button. Click the **Define** button (Figure 1) to open the **Define Simple Boxplot: Summaries of Separate Variables** dialog box (the completed version is shown in Figure 2).
- Transfer the variable names to the **Boxes Represent** box as shown in Figure 2.
- Click **OK** to obtain the boxplots (the edited version is shown in Output 1). (Editing is described in Chapter 5, Section 5.2.

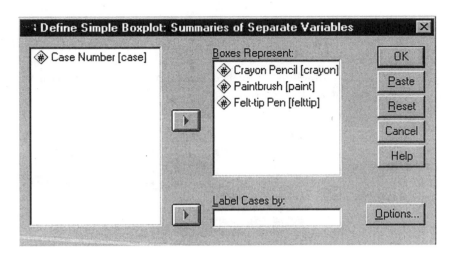

Figure 2. The Summaries of Separate Variables dialog box with the three variables selected

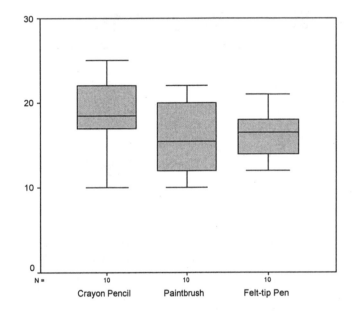

Output 1. Boxplots of the data at each level of the factor *implem*

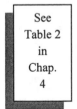

See Table 2 in Chap. 4

The boxplots reveal no extreme cases (which would have been flagged by * - see Table 2 in Chapter 4 for details of the structure of a boxplot). None of the distributions is markedly skewed. There is therefore no need to remove any cases or apply any transformation to symmetrise the distribution. We can carry on with the ANOVA.

9.2.3   Running the within subjects ANOVA

The within subjects ANOVA is selected as follows:
• Choose
  Analyze
    General Linear Model

211

Repeated Measures... (Figure 3)
to open the **GLM - Repeated Measures Define Factor(s)** dialog box (Figure 4).

- Follow the steps described in Figure 4. Click on **Add** to obtain the dialog box shown in Figure 5.

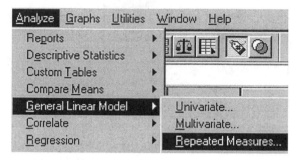

Figure 3. The General Linear Model menu

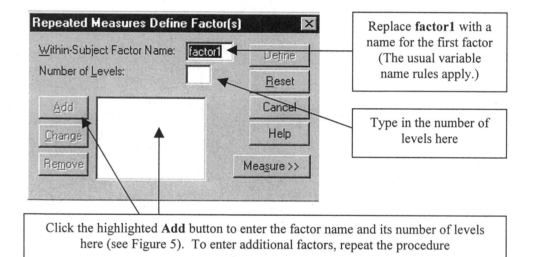

Figure 4. The Repeated Measures Define Factor(s) dialog box

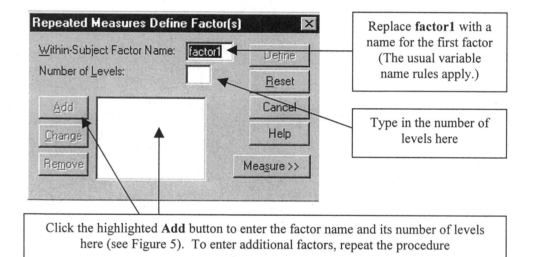

Figure 5. The Repeated Measures Define Factor(s) dialog box for three levels of *implem*

- Click **Define** to open the **Repeated Measures ANOVA** dialog box (the upper half of which is shown in Figure 6).
- You will see that the uppermost variable name has been highlighted. Highlight the variables *crayon*, *paintbrush* and *felttip* by clicking-and-

dragging the cursor down over them and clicking ▶ to transfer all three into the **Within Subjects Variables: [implem]** box. The question marks will be replaced by the variable names as shown in Figure 7.

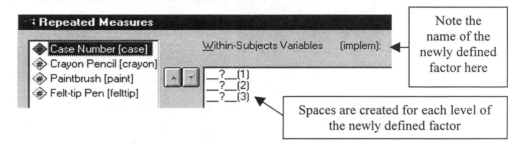

Figure 6. The upper half of the Repeated Measures dialog box after defining the Within-Subjects Variables factor as *implem* with three levels

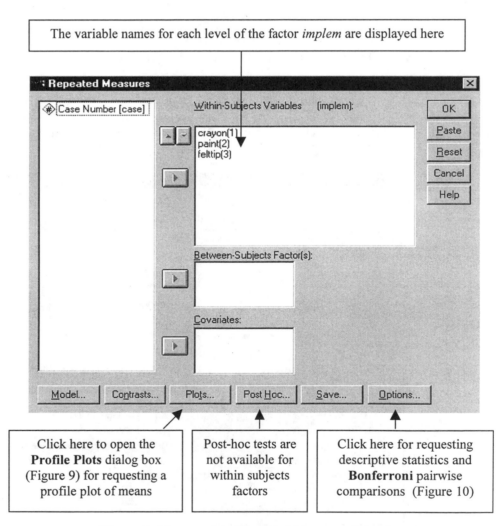

Figure 7. The completed Repeated Measures dialog box

- It is recommended that the user also request a number of options associated with a within subjects (repeated measures) ANOVA. For example, obtain a profile plot of the levels of the within subjects factor by clicking **Plots...** and following the steps shown in Figure 8. Click **Continue** to return to the original dialog box.

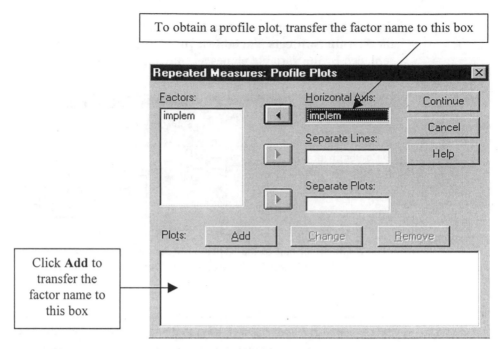

Figure 8. The Profile Plots dialog box for a plot at each level of a factor

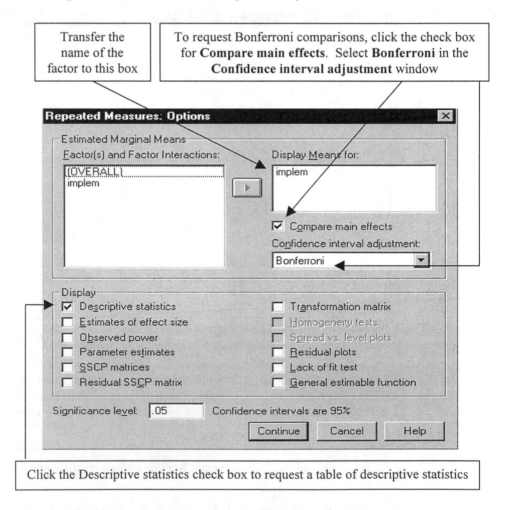

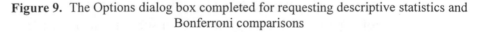

Figure 9. The Options dialog box completed for requesting descriptive statistics and
Bonferroni comparisons

- A table of descriptive statistics and a table of Bonferroni adjusted pairwise comparisons among the levels of the within subjects factor are requested by clicking **Options...** in the **Repeated Measures** dialog box and following the steps shown in Figure 9. Click **Continue** to return to the original dialog box.
- Click **OK**.

9.2.4 Output for a one-factor within subjects ANOVA

The output is extensive, and not all of it is required for a within subjects ANOVA. Output 2 shows the left-hand pane of the **SPSS** Viewer, in which are itemised the various subtables that appear in the right-hand pane. Three of the tables should be deleted immediately by highlighting each in turn and pressing the **Delete** key on the keyboard: **Multivariate Tests**; **Tests of Within-Subjects Contrasts**; **Tests of Between-Subjects Effects** (in this example, there are no between subjects factors). The **Multivariate Tests** in **Estimated Marginal Means** can also be deleted.

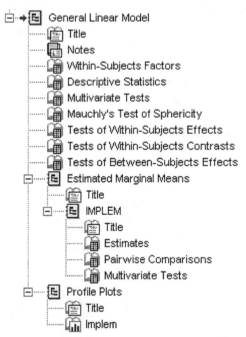

Output 2. The left-hand pane of the SPSS Viewer for the Repeated Measures (within subjects) analysis

Output 3 shows the **Title**, the **Within-Subjects Factors** list and the specially requested **Descriptive Statistics** table.

Within-Subjects Factors

Measure: MEASURE_1

IMPLEM	Dependent Variable
1	CRAYON
2	PAINT
3	FELTTIP

Descriptive Statistics

	Mean	Std. Deviation	N
Crayon Pencil	18.40	4.65	10
Paintbrush	15.70	4.27	10
Felt-tip Pen	16.40	3.06	10

Output 3. The Within-Subjects Factors list and Descriptive Statistics table

Output 4 reports the result of the **Mauchly's Test of Sphericity** for homogeneity of covariance (see Section 9.1).

- If the test result is not significant (i.e. **Sig.**, the p-value, has a value greater than 0.05), the p-value given in the rows labelled **Sphericity Assumed** in the ANOVA summary table (to be shown in Output 5) can be accepted.
- If the test result is significant (i.e. **Sig.**, the p-value, has a value less than or equal to 0.05), then one can make a more conservative test, such as the **Greenhouse-Geisser test** by reading the **Greenhouse-Geisser** rows in the ANOVA summary table (to be shown in Output 5).

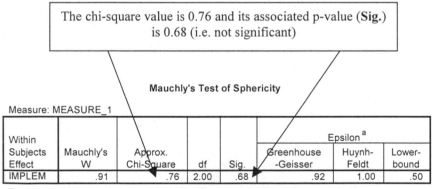

The chi-square value is 0.76 and its associated p-value (**Sig.**) is 0.68 (i.e. not significant)

Mauchly's Test of Sphericity

Measure: MEASURE_1

Within Subjects Effect	Mauchly's W	Approx. Chi-Square	df	Sig.	Epsilon [a] Greenhouse-Geisser	Huynh-Feldt	Lower-bound
IMPLEM	.91	.76	2.00	.68	.92	1.00	.50

Tests the null hypothesis that the error covariance matrix of the orthonormalized transformed dependent variables is proportional to an identity matrix.

a. May be used to adjust the degrees of freedom for the averaged tests of significance. Corrected tests are displayed in the Tests of Within-Subjects Effects table.

Output 4. Mauchly's Test of Sphericity and values of epsilon for conservative ANOVA F-tests

The conservative test only makes a difference when:
(1)   There is heterogeneity of covariance (i.e. Mauchly test is significant);

(2)   the F with unadjusted degrees of freedom (i.e. the values shown in the Sphericity Assumed rows) is barely significant beyond the 0.05 level.

Should F have a low tail probability (say p<0.01), the null hypothesis can safely be rejected without making a conservative test. In the present case, the Mauchly test gives a p-value of 0.68, so there is no evidence of heterogeneity of covariance. The usual ANOVA F test can therefore be used.

The ANOVA summary table for the within subjects factor Implement (*implem*) is shown in Output 5, which has been edited to reduce the number of decimal places to two and to narrow some of the columns.

Tests of Within-Subjects Effects

Measure: MEASURE_1

Source		Type III Sum of Squares	df	Mean Square	F	Sig.
IMPLEM	Sphericity Assumed	39.27	2.00	19.63	4.86	.02
	Greenhouse-Geisser	39.27	1.83	21.41	4.86	.02
	Huynh-Feldt	39.27	2.00	19.63	4.86	.02
	Lower-bound	39.27	1.00	39.27	4.86	.05
Error(IMPLEM)	Sphericity Assumed	72.73	18.00	4.04		
	Greenhouse-Geisser	72.73	16.50	4.41		
	Huynh-Feldt	72.73	18.00	4.04		
	Lower-bound	72.73	9.00	8.08		

Since the Mauchly result was not significant, the **Sphericity Assumed** rows apply. The other rows could be deleted in the Output Viewer

For F = 4.86 with a p-value (**Sig.**) of 0.02, the factor is significant at the 5% level

Output 5. The ANOVA summary table for the within-subjects effects

Note that the p-value for F (**Sig.**) in the **Sphericity Assumed** row is *0.02*: that is, the obtained value of F is significant beyond the five per cent (.05) level, but not beyond the 0.01 level. We can therefore conclude that the type of implement used does affect the ratings that a painting receives. We can write this result as:

$$F(2,18) = 4.86; \ p < 0.05.$$

The value of 18 for the error df can be seen in the row labelled **Error (IMPLEM) Sphericity Assumed**.

In the present case, there was no need to make a conservative F-test because the Mauchly test was insignificant. It is apparent from the **Sig.** column that *in this particular example* the conservative tests make no difference to the result of the ANOVA F-test.

See Section 9.2.6

The next table (Output 6) shows the pairwise comparisons adjusted according to the Bonferroni method (see the Section 9.2.6).

Pairwise Comparisons

Measure: MEASURE_1

(I) IMPLEM	(J) IMPLEM	Mean Difference (I-J)	Std. Error	Sig.[a]	95% Confidence Interval for Difference[a]	
					Lower Bound	Upper Bound
1	2	2.70*	.90	.04	.07	5.33
	3	2.00	1.01	.24	-.97	4.97
2	1	-2.70*	.90	.04	-5.33	-.07
	3	-.70	.78	1.00	-2.97	1.57
3	1	-2.00	1.01	.24	-4.97	.97
	2	.70	.78	1.00	-1.57	2.97

Based on estimated marginal means

*. The mean difference is significant at the .05 level.

a. Adjustment for multiple comparisons: Bonferroni.

> Only one comparison has a p-value (**Sig.**) less than 0.05

Output 6. The Bonferroni adjusted pairwise comparisons among the levels of the within subjects factor

The requested profile plot is shown in Output 7.

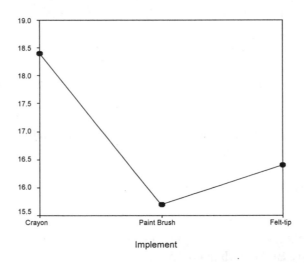

Output 7. The plot of means of the three types of implement

9.2.5 Unplanned multiple comparisons: Bonferroni method

There is some doubt as to whether, following significant main effects of within subjects factors, the Tukey test affords sufficient protection against inflation of the *per family* type I error rate. Other methods, therefore, have been recommended. In Section 7.1, we distinguished between planned and unplanned tests. Suppose it is planned to make exactly c pairwise comparisons among a set of treatment means resulting from a one-factor experiment. It is desired to keep the *per family* error rate at 0.05. In the **Bonferroni method**, ordinary t-tests are used for the pairwise comparisons, but the *per family* error rate is divided by the number of planned comparisons. To achieve significance, therefore, each t-test must show significance beyond (sometimes well beyond) the 0.05 level.

The Bonferroni method, although primarily intended for the making of planned comparisons, can also be used to make *unplanned* pairwise multiple comparisons among a set of k treatment means following a one-factor ANOVA.

In this case, however, the *per family* type I error rate must be divided by the number of possible pairs (c) that can be drawn from an array of k means, which is given by

$$c = \frac{k!}{2!(k-2)!}$$

where the symbol ! means **factorial** (e.g. 4! is $4 \times 3 \times 2 \times 1 = 24$). In the present example, the ANOVA has shown a significant main effect of the Implement factor. Here the number of treatment means (k) = 3, so c = 3. The Bonferroni t-tests, therefore, will have to show significance beyond the 0.05/3 = 0.02 level, approximately. The p-values (**Sig.**) given in Output 5 are the usual within subjects t-test p-values multiplied by 3 to reflect this adjustment for multiple comparisons.

9.3 NONPARAMETRIC TESTS FOR A ONE-FACTOR WITHIN SUBJECTS EXPERIMENT

As with the one-factor completely randomised experiment, nonparametric methods are available for the analysis of ordinal and nominal data.

9.3.1 The Friedman test for ordinal data

Suppose that six people rank five objects in order of 'pleasingness'. Their decisions might appear as in Table 2.

Table 2. Six people's ranks of five objects in order of 'pleasingness'					
	Object 1	Object 2	Object 3	Object 4	Object 5
Person 1	2	1	5	4	3
Person 2	1	2	5	4	3
Person 3	1	3	4	2	5
Person 4	2	1	3	5	4
Person 5	2	1	5	4	3
Person 6	1	2	5	3	4

If we assume that the highest rank is given to the most pleasing object, it would appear, from inspection of Table 2, that Object 3 is more pleasing to most of the raters than is Object 1. Since, however, the numbers in Table 2 are not independent measurements but ranks, the one-factor within subjects ANOVA cannot be used here. The Friedman test is suitable for such ordinal data. In **Variable View**, name the variables *object1, object2, ... object5* (with no spaces before the digits). In **Data View**, enter the data in the usual way.

To run the Friedman test:
- Choose
    Analyze
        Nonparametric Tests
            K Related Samples...
    to obtain the **Tests for Several Related Samples** dialog box (Figure 10).
- In the panel on the left, will appear a list of the variables. This list should include the items *object1, object2, ..., object5*, which will contain the numbers shown in Table 2. Simply transfer these names to the **Test Variables:** box in the usual way. Make sure the **Friedman** check box has been ticked.
- Click **OK**.

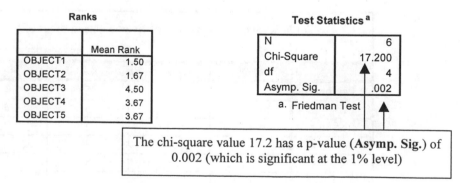

Figure 10. The Tests for Several Related Samples dialog box with the Friedman Test selected

The Friedman results are shown in Output 8.

Friedman Test

Ranks

	Mean Rank
OBJECT1	1.50
OBJECT2	1.67
OBJECT3	4.50
OBJECT4	3.67
OBJECT5	3.67

Test Statistics [a]

N	6
Chi-Square	17.200
df	4
Asymp. Sig.	.002

a. Friedman Test

The chi-square value 17.2 has a p-value (**Asymp. Sig.**) of 0.002 (which is significant at the 1% level)

Output 8. Friedman test results

Clearly the rankings differ significantly across the objects since the p-value (**Asymp. Sig.**) is less than 0.01. We can write this result as:

$$\text{Chi-square} = 17.2; \, df = 4; \, p < 0.01.$$

9.3.2 Cochran's Q test for nominal data

Suppose that six children are asked to imagine they were in five different situations and had to choose between Course of Action *A* (coded *0*) and *B* (coded *1*). The results might appear as in Table 3. From inspection of Table 3, it would seem that Course of Action B (i.e. cells containing *1*) is chosen more often in some scenarios than in others. A suitable confirmatory test is **Cochran's Q** test, which was designed for use with related samples of dichotomous nominal data.

	Scene 1	Scene 2	Scene 3	Scene 4	Scene 5
Table 3. Courses of action chosen by six children in five scenarios					
Child 1	0	0	1	1	1
Child 2	0	1	0	1	1
Child 3	1	1	1	1	1
Child 4	0	0	0	1	0
Child 5	0	0	0	0	0
Child 6	0	0	0	1	1

To run Cochran's Q test:
- Bring the **Test for Several Related Samples** dialog box to the screen (see previous section and Figure 12), click off the **Friedman** check box and click the **Cochran** check box. Click **OK**.

The results are shown in Output 9.

Cochran Test

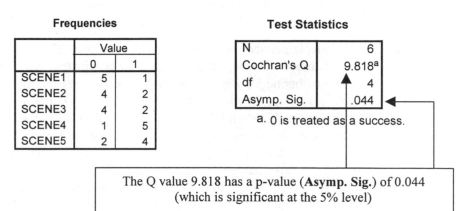

Frequencies

	Value	
	0	1
SCENE1	5	1
SCENE2	4	2
SCENE3	4	2
SCENE4	1	5
SCENE5	2	4

Test Statistics

N	6
Cochran's Q	9.818[a]
df	4
Asymp. Sig.	.044

a. 0 is treated as a success.

The Q value 9.818 has a p-value (**Asymp. Sig.**) of 0.044 (which is significant at the 5% level)

Output 9. Cochran test results

It is clear that the same course of action is not taken in all five scenarios:

Cochran Q = 9.82; df = 4; p < 0.05.

9.4 THE TWO-FACTOR WITHIN SUBJECTS ANOVA

An experiment is designed to investigate the detection of certain theoretically important patterns on a screen. The patterns vary in shape and solidity. The dependent variable (DV) is the Number of Errors made in responding to the pattern, and the two factors (IVs) are Shape (Circle, Square, or Triangle) and Solidity (Outline or Solid). The experimenter suspects that a shape's solidity affects whether it is perceived more readily than another shape. The same sample of participants is used for all the possible treatment combinations: that is, there are two within subjects (repeated measures) factors in the experiment. The results are shown in Table 4.

Table 4. Results of a two-factor within subjects experiment						
SHAPE:-	Circle		Square		Triangle	
SOLIDITY:-	Solid	Outline	Solid	Outline	Solid	Outline
Participant						
1	4	2	2	8	7	5
2	3	6	2	6	8	9
3	2	10	2	5	5	3
4	1	8	5	5	2	9
5	4	6	4	5	5	10
6	3	6	4	6	9	12
7	7	12	2	6	4	8
8	6	10	9	5	0	10
9	4	5	7	6	8	12
10	2	12	12	8	10	12

Extra care is needed when analysing data from experiments with two or more within subjects factors. It is essential to ensure that SPSS understands which data were obtained under which combination of factors. In the present example, there are six data for each participant, each datum being a score achieved under a different combination of the two factors. We can name the data variables as *circsol*, *circlin*, *squarsol*, *squarlin*, *triansol* and *trianlin*, representing all possible combinations of the shape and solidity factors. (While in **Variable View**, be sure to assign less cryptic variable labels as well.) Should there be many treatment combinations in the experiment, however, it would be very tedious to name the variables individually. In such cases, it is much more convenient to use the default variable names provided by the computer (e.g. *var00001*, *var00002*, *var00003* etc.), but a careful note must be kept about which combinations of levels of the within subjects factors are represented by which of these default variable names. This information must be borne in mind later when the user has accessed the **Repeated-Measures Define Variable(s)** dialog box and is naming the within subjects factors.

In the present example, remembering that the program initially treats each combination of levels of within subjects factors as a separate dependent variable, it can be seen that the sequence of names *circsol*, *circlin*, *squarsol*, *squarlin*, *triansol* and *trianlin*, represents successive columns of data in Table 4.

9.4.1 Preparing the data set

The first four rows of data in **Data View** appear as in Figure 11.

	case	circsol	circlin	squarsol	squarlin	triansol	trianlin
1	1	4	2	2	8	7	5
2	2	3	6	2	6	8	9
3	3	2	10	2	5	5	3
4	4	1	8	5	5	2	9

Figure 11. Part of Data View for the two-factor within subjects ANOVA

9.4.2 Running the two-factor within subjects ANOVA

- Select
  Analyze
  > **General Linear Model**
  > > **Repeated Measures...**
  and complete the various dialog boxes by analogy with the one-factor example, defining a second within subjects (repeated measures) factor.

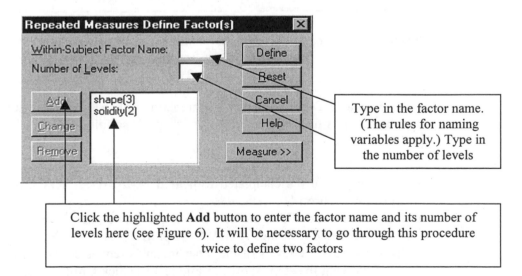

Figure 12. The Repeated Measures Define Factor(s) dialog box with two factors and their numbers of levels defined

- The completed **Repeated Measures Define Factor(s)** dialog box, with two generic names *shape* and *solidity* is shown in Figure 12.
- After **Define** has been clicked, the **Repeated Measures** dialog box appears with the six variables listed in alphabetical order on the left. (The top half is reproduced in Figure 13.)

On the right, in the box labelled **Within-Subjects Variables [shape, solidity]**, appears a list of the various combinations of the code numbers representing the levels of each of the two treatment factors. It will be noticed that, as one reads down the list, the first number in each pair changes more slowly than the second.

When there is more than one within subjects factor, it is inadvisable to transfer the variable names in a block from the left-hand box to the **Within-Subjects Variables** box by a click-and-drag operation, as in the one-factor situation. Care must be taken to ensure that the correct variable name is transferred to the correct slot. It is recommended that the variables be transferred one at a time, noting the numbers in the square brackets and referring to the names of the newly-defined within subjects factors (in this case *shape* and *solidity*) inside the square brackets in the caption above the Within-Subjects Variables box.

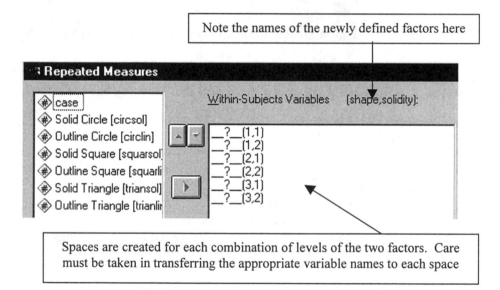

Figure 13. The top half of the Repeated Measures dialog box for two factors shape and solidity before transferring the variable names

A table such as Table 5 clarifies the numbering of the levels of within subjects variables. Thus the variable *circsol* is [shape 1, solidity 1] i.e. [1,1], *circlinl* is [1,2] and so on.

- The top half of the completed **Repeated Measures ANOVA** dialog box is shown in Figure 14.
- It is recommended that the user also request a number of options associated with a repeated measures ANOVA. A profile plot of the levels of one of the factors across the levels of the other factor is requested by clicking **Plots...** and following the steps shown in Figure 15. Click **Continue** to return to the original dialog box.

Table 5. Numbering of levels in within subjects variables						
Shape Factor	**Shape 1** (Circle)		**Shape 2** (Square)		**Shape 3** (Triangle)	
Solidity Factor	**Solidity 1** (Solid)	**Solidity 2** (Outline)	**Solidity 1** (Solid)	**Solidity 2** (Outline)	**Solidity 1** (Solid)	**Solidity 2** (Outline)
Variable name	*circsol*	*circlin*	*squarsol*	*squarlin*	*triansol*	*trianlin*

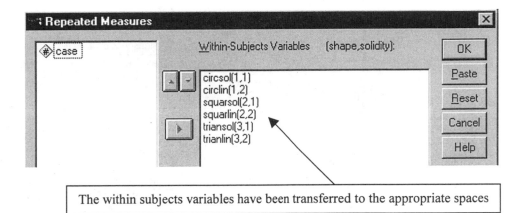

The within subjects variables have been transferred to the appropriate spaces

Figure 14. The Within-Subjects Variables section of the Repeated Measures dialog box after transferring the variable names

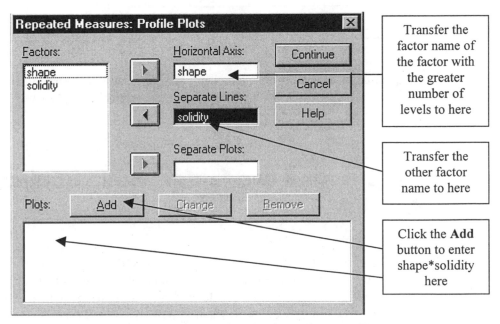

Transfer the factor name of the factor with the greater number of levels to here

Transfer the other factor name to here

Click the **Add** button to enter shape*solidity here

Figure 15. The dialog box for requesting a profile plot

- A table of descriptive statistics and a table of Bonferroni pairwise comparisons among the levels of within subjects factors with more than two levels are requested by clicking the **Options...** button in the **Repeated**

Measures dialog box and following the steps shown in Figure 16. Click **Continue** to return to the original dialog box.

• Click **OK**.

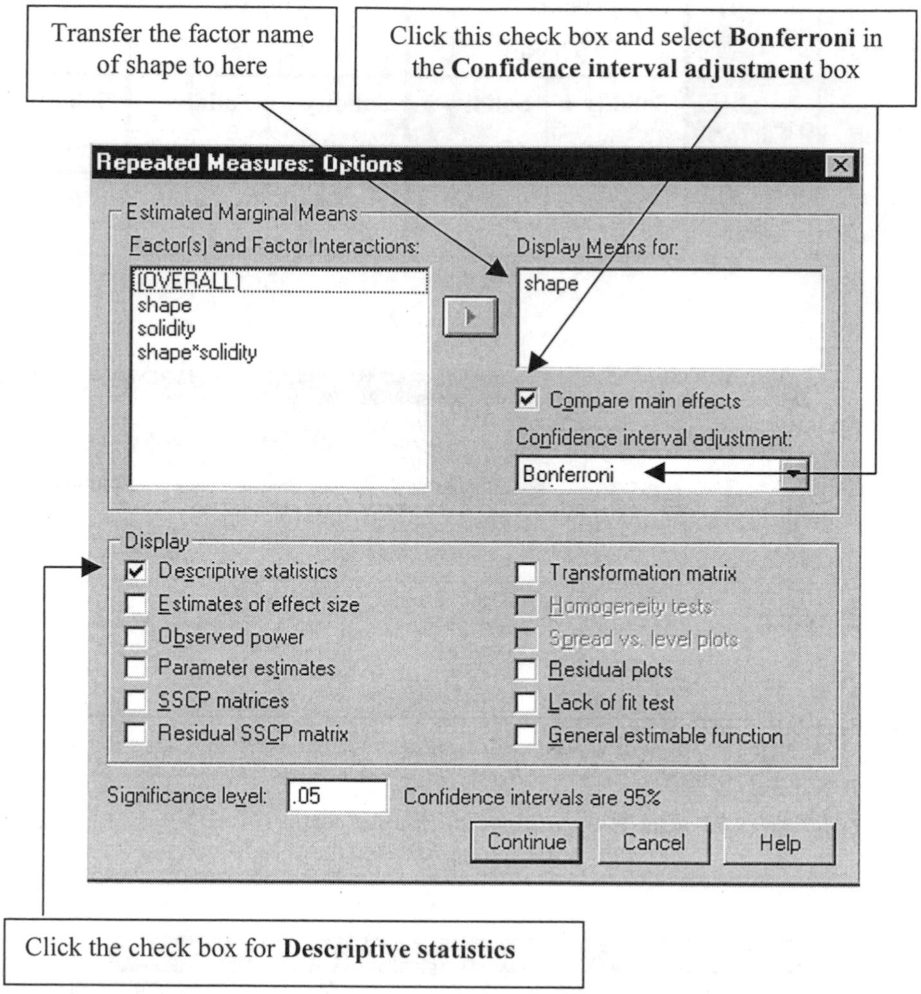

Figure 16. The completed Options dialog box for requesting descriptive statistics and Bonferroni pairwise comparisons among the levels of shape

9.4.3 Output for a two-factor within subjects ANOVA

As in the case of the one-factor within subjects ANOVA, the output is extensive, and not all of it is required. Three of the subtables in the left-hand pane of the SPSS Viewer can be immediately deleted by highlighting each in turn and then pressing the **Delete** key on the keyboard: **Multivariate Tests; Tests of Within-Subjects Contrasts; Tests of Between-Subjects Effects** (in this example, there are no between subjects factors).

Output 10 shows the **Title**, **Within-Subjects Factors** list and the specially requested **Descriptive Statistics** table.

Within-Subjects Factors

Measure: MEASURE_1

SHAPE	SOLIDITY	Dependent Variable
1	1	CIRCSOL
	2	CIRCLIN
2	1	SQUARSOL
	2	SQUARLIN
3	1	TRIANSOL
	2	TRIANLIN

Descriptive Statistics

	Mean	Std. Deviation	N
Solid Circle	3.60	1.84	10
Outline Circle	7.70	3.27	10
Solid Square	4.90	3.45	10
Outline Square	6.00	1.15	10
Solid Triangle	5.80	3.19	10
Outline Triangle	9.00	3.02	10

Output 10. The Within-Subjects Factors list and Descriptive Statistics table

The next table (Output 11) reports the result of the **Mauchly's Test of Sphericity** for homogeneity of covariance (see Section 9.3).

> The Chi-square values and their p-values (**Sig.**) showing that none is significant. Note that the test does not apply to factors with only two levels (e.g. SOLIDITY)

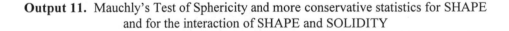

Mauchly's Test of Sphericity

Measure: MEASURE_1

Within Subjects Effect	Mauchly's W	Approx. Chi-Square	df	Sig.	Epsilon[a] Greenhouse -Geisser	Huynh- Feldt	Lower- bound
SHAPE	.67	3.25	2.00	.20	.75	.87	.500
SOLIDITY	1.00	.00	.00		1.00	1.00	1.000
SHAPE * SOLIDITY	.90	.82	2.00	.66	.91	1.00	.500

Tests the null hypothesis that the error covariance matrix of the orthonormalized transformed dependent variables is proportional to an identity matrix.

a. May be used to adjust the degrees of freedom for the averaged tests of significance. Corrected tests are displayed in the Tests of Within-Subjects Effects table.

Output 11. Mauchly's Test of Sphericity and more conservative statistics for SHAPE and for the interaction of SHAPE and SOLIDITY

The table is more extensive than that in Output 4, because there are two factors. Notice that the test is not applied when a factor has only two levels, as in the case of *solidity*. The test is not significant (i.e. there is no evidence of heterogeneity of covariance) for either *shape* or the interaction of *shape* and *solidity*, so the significance levels in the rows labelled **Sphericity Assumed** can be accepted. The edited ANOVA summary table (minus the rows with the conservative tests and the words Sphericity Assumed) for the within subjects factors *shape* and *solidity*, and their interaction is shown in Output 12.

Tests of Within-Subjects Effects

Measure: MEASURE_1

Source	Type III Sum of Squares	df	Mean Square	F	Sig.
SHAPE	46.03	2.00	23.02	2.98	.076
Error(SHAPE)	138.97	18.00	7.72		
SOLIDITY	117.60	1.00	117.60	54.56	.000
Error(SOLIDITY)	19.40	9.00	2.16		
SHAPE * SOLIDITY	23.70	2.00	11.85	1.41	.270
Error(SHAPE*SOLIDITY)	151.30	18.00	8.41		

The main effect of the factor SOLIDITY has **F** = 54.56 with a p-value (**Sig.**) less than 0.01 (i.e. significant at the 1% level)	The main effect of the factor SHAPE and the interaction SHAPE*SOLIDITY have small values of **F** with p-values greater than 0.05 and are therefore not significant

Output 12. The edited ANOVA summary table for the within subjects factors and their interaction

Output 12 shows that the factor SHAPE is not significant, since the p-value for F in the column headed **Sig.** is greater than 0.05. We can write this result as:

$$F(2,18) = 2.98; \ NS.$$

The factor SOLIDITY is significant, since its p-value is less than 0.01 (the output value 0.000 means that the p-value is less than .0005). We can write this result as:

$$F(1,9) = 54.56; \ p < 0.01.$$

Finally the interaction SHAPE*SOLIDITY is not significant, since its p-value is greater than 0.05. We can write this result as:

$$F(2,18) = 1.41; \ NS.$$

Notice that, in contrast with a two-factor between subjects ANOVA, the error terms are different for each factor and for the interaction.

Since the factor SHAPE is not significant, the **Bonferroni pairwise comparisons** table should be ignored.

The profile plot is shown in Output 13. An interaction is indicated when the profiles cross one another, diverge or converge. Obviously the slight difference in profile here is insufficient for a statistically significant interaction.

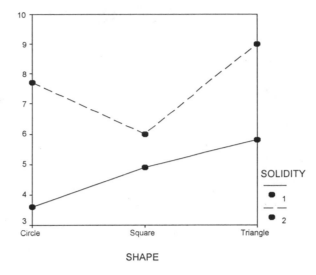

Output 13. The profile plots of the three shapes across the two levels of solidity

In conclusion, Output 12 shows that only *solidity* factor has a significant effect: the other sources, *shape* and its interaction with *solidity*, are not significant.

9.4.4 Unplanned comparisons following a factorial within subjects experiment

In the example we have just considered, the question of unplanned multiple comparisons does not arise, because
  (1)   there is no interaction and
  (2)   the sole significant main effect involves a factor with only two levels, implying that the two means must be significantly different.

Had there been a significant interaction, however, the approach already described in the context of the one-factor within subjects experiment would also have been applicable here.

The problem with the **Bonferroni test** is that even with only six cells, it is very difficult to get a difference sufficiently large to be significant. With six cells, c = 15 and each t-test has to have a p-value of 0.003 or less to be deemed significant. There is, therefore, a case to be made for testing initially for **simple main effects** of the principal experimental factor of interest at various levels of the other factor. A significant simple main effect may justify defining the comparison family more narrowly and improves the chances of finding significant differences. As in a between subjects factorial experiment, a simple main effect of a factor can be computed by carrying out a one-way ANOVA upon the data at only one level of the other factor. In the case of a within subjects factorial experiment, however, the data at different levels of either factor are not independent. It is wise, therefore, to adopt a stricter criterion for significance of a simple main effect in such cases, by applying the Bonferroni criterion and setting the significance level for each simple effect test at 0.05 divided by the number of tests that will be made.

EXERCISE 13

ONE-FACTOR WITHIN SUBJECTS (REPEATED MEASURES) ANOVA

Before you start

Before proceeding with this Exercise, we suggest that you study Chapter 9.

A comparison of the efficacy of statistical packages

Table 1 shows the results of an experiment in which the dependent variable was the time taken for ten participants to perform a statistical analysis using three statistical computer packages Pack1, Pack2 and Pack3. During the course of the experiment, each participant used every package and the order of use was counterbalanced across participants.

Table 1. Times taken by participants to carry out an analysis with different computing packages							
Case	Pack1	Pack2	Pack3	Case	Pack1	Pack2	Pack3
1	12	15	18	6	10	12	14
2	18	21	19	7	18	17	21
3	15	16	15	8	18	17	21
4	21	26	32	9	23	27	30
5	19	23	22	10	17	25	21

Opening SPSS

Open SPSS and select the **Type in data** radio button in the opening window. If **Data View** appears first, click the **Variable View** tab to open **Variable View**.

Preparing the SPSS data set

Prepare the SPSS data set as described in Section 9.2.1. Since there is just one group of participants, there is no grouping variable. Add suitable variable labels in the **Label** column such as Case Number, Package 1, Package 2, Package 3. Remember to save the data set as a data file with a suitable filename.

Exploring the data

Use the methods described in Section 9.2.3 to check for any distribution problems. Remember that outliers (which are represented by 0) are not so serious as extreme values, which are represented by *.

Procedure for the within subjects (repeated measures) ANOVA

The within subjects ANOVA (SPSS refers to it as Repeated Measures) is selected by choosing:
Analyze
    General Linear Model
        Repeated Measures...
to open the **Repeated Measures Define Factor(s)** dialog box. Follow the procedure described in Section 9.2.3. Remember to click **Plots...** and complete the **Repeated Measures: Profile Plots** dialog

box by transferring *package* to the **Horizontal Axis:** box, clicking **Add** and then **Continue** to return to the original dialog box.

Output for the within subjects (repeated measures) ANOVA

Section 9.2.4 offers some guidelines for the interpretation of the output. First, there is a **Table of Within-Subjects Factors**, which lists the levels of the *package* factor. Then there is a table of **Multivariate Tests**, which can be deleted by clicking its icon in the left-hand pane of SPSS **Viewer** and pressing the **Delete** key. Next comes **Mauchly's Test of Sphericity**. Check that the result does not show significance. If not, you need only read the row labelled **Sphericity Assumed** in the **Table of Within-Subjects Effects** below, in which case it is tidier to delete the other rows by double-clicking anywhere in the table, highlighting the material to be deleted and then pressing the **Delete** key. The remaining two tables can be ignored.

- **What is the value of the F ratio and its associated p-value (tail probability) for the *package* factor? Is *F* significant? What are the implications for the experimental hypothesis?**

Inspect the **Profile Plots** showing the means of the three packages.

- **Is the appearance of the plot consistent with the finding from the ANOVA that there is a significant main effect?**

Finally with reference to Section 9.2.4, use the Bonferroni method to ascertain which pairs of statistical packages are significantly different.

- **List which packages differ significantly.**

Finishing the session

Close down SPSS and any other windows before logging out of the computer.

EXERCISE 14

TWO-FACTOR WITHIN SUBJECTS ANOVA

Before you start

We suggest that you read Section 9.4 before proceeding. In this exercise, we consider the ANOVA of within subjects factorial experiments, that is, experiments with repeated measures on all factors.

A two-factor within subjects experiment

An experiment is carried out to investigate the effects of two factors upon the recognition of symbols briefly presented on a screen, as measured by the number of correct identifications over a fixed number of trials. The factors are Symbol (with levels Digit, Lower Case, and Upper Case) and Font (with levels Gothic, and Roman). Each of the six participants in the experiment is tested under all six combinations of the two treatment factors. The results are shown in Table 1.

	Digit		Lower Case		Upper case	
Case	Gothic	Roman	Gothic	Roman	Gothic	Roman
1	2	6	18	3	20	5
2	4	9	20	6	18	2
3	3	10	15	2	21	3
4	1	12	10	9	25	10
5	5	8	13	8	20	8
6	6	10	14	10	16	6

Table 1. Results of a two-factor within subjects experiment

Opening SPSS

Open SPSS and select the **Type in data** radio button in the opening window. If **Data View** appears first, click the **Variable View** tab to open **Variable View**.

Preparing the SPSS data set

In **Variable View**, define the variables as described in Section 9.4. Enter the data into **Data View**, under the appropriate pre-headed columns. For clarity, it is recommended that labels such as Digit-Gothic, Digit-Roman, Upper-Gothic etc. be included in the **Label** column of **Variable View**. Ensure that the values in the **Decimals** column are all 0.

Exploring the data

Obtain boxplots to check the distributions.

Running the two-factor within subjects ANOVA

To run the ANOVA, select
Analyze

General Linear Model
Repeated Measures...

and then complete the various dialog boxes following the procedure described in Section 9.4. Remember to click **Plots...** and complete the **Repeated Measures: Profile Plots** dialog box by transferring *symbol* to the **Horizontal Axis:** box and *font* to the **Separate Lines:** box, then clicking **Add** and finally **Continue**, to return to the original dialog box.

Output for the two-factor within subjects experiment

The output for the two-factor repeated measures ANOVA is explained in Section 9.4 . Remove the unnecessary tables at the beginning.

Next comes a table of **Mauchly's Test of Sphericity**. Check carefully to see whether there is evidence of non-sphericity. The main table of interest is the **Tests of Within-Subjects Effects**. For each factor and interaction, read the row **Sphericity Assumed** if the relevant Mauchly test is not significant; otherwise read the **Greenhouse-Geisser** row. If none of the Sphericity tests is significant, it is tidier to delete the conservative tests rows by double-clicking anywhere in the table, highlighting the material to be deleted and then pressing the **Delete** key. The remaining two tables can be ignored.

- **List the F ratio and p-value for each factor and the interaction. Interpret these results in terms of the aims of the study.**

Finally inspect the **Profile Plots**.

- **Describe the plot and comment on whether it confirms the various ANOVA results.**

Finishing the session

Close down SPSS and any other windows before logging out of the computer.

CHAPTER 10

EXPERIMENTS OF MIXED DESIGN

10.1 INTRODUCTION

10.2 THE TWO-FACTOR MIXED FACTORIAL ANOVA

10.3 THE THREE-FACTOR MIXED ANOVA

10.4 FURTHER ANALYSIS: SIMPLE EFFECTS AND MULTIPLE COMPARISONS

10.1   INTRODUCTION

Suppose that a researcher designs an experiment to explore the hypothesis that engineering students, because of their training in two-dimensional representation of three-dimensional structures, have a more strongly developed sense of shape and symmetry than do psychology students.

Three theoretically important shapes are presented to samples of Psychology and Engineering students under sub-optimal conditions on a monitor screen. The dependent variable is the number of shapes correctly identified. The results of the experiment are shown in Table 1.

Table 1. Results of a two-factor mixed factorial experiment with one within subjects factor and one between subjects factor				
Levels of the Student Category factor:	**Case**	**Levels of the Shape factor:**		
		Triangle	**Square**	**Rectangle**
Psychology	1	2	12	7
	2	8	10	9
	3	4	15	3
	4	6	9	7
	5	9	13	8
	6	7	14	8
Engineering	7	13	3	35
	8	21	4	30
	9	26	10	35
	10	22	8	30
	11	20	9	28
	12	19	8	27

It can be seen from Table 1 that there were two factors in this experiment:

(1) Student Category, with levels Psychology and Engineering;

(2) Shape, with levels Triangle, Square and Rectangle.

Since each participant was tested with all three shapes, Shape is a within subjects factor. Student Category, however, is a between subjects factor. It is very common for factorial designs to have within subjects (repeated measures) factors on *some* (but not *all*) of their treatment factors. Since such experiments have a mixture of between subjects and within subjects factors, they are often said to be of **mixed** design. A common alternative term is **split-plot**, which reflects the agronomic context in which this type of experiment was originally used.

10.2 THE TWO-FACTOR MIXED FACTORIAL ANOVA

Mixed factorial ANOVA with SPSS

See
Chap.
9

In Chapter 9, we saw that the ANOVA of data from within subjects experiments is obtained from the **Repeated Measures** command in the **General Linear Model** menu. The mixed ANOVA is controlled by the same command. As with between subjects ANOVA, however, it is necessary to include grouping variable(s) for the between subjects factor(s).

10.2.1 Preparing the SPSS data set

In Table 1, we chose to represent the experimental design with the levels of the within subjects factor arrayed horizontally and those of the between subjects factor stacked vertically, with Engineering under Psychology. We did so because this arrangement corresponds to the way in which the results must appear in **Data View**.

As always, the first column of **Data View** will contain the case numbers. The second column will contain a single grouping variable *category* representing the Psychologists (*1*) and the Engineers (*2*). The third, fourth and fifth columns will contain the results at the three levels of the Shape factor (i.e. Triangle, Square, and Rectangle).

See
Section
3.2

Using the techniques described in Chapter 3, Section 3.2, name five variables: *case*, *category* (the grouping variable), *triangle*, *square*, and *rectangl* (remembering that the variable names must not exceed 8 characters in length) in **Variable View**. Use the **Label** column to specify more comprehensible variable names (e.g. Case Number, Category of Student, Triangle, Square, Rectangle) and the **Values** column to specify the values and labels for the grouping variable *category* (1 = Psychology Student, 2 = Engineering Student). Ensure that the **Decimals** column has 0 for each variable.

Click the **Data View** tab and enter the data into **Data View** (Figure 1). If values rather than labels appear in the variable category, enter the **View** menu and click **Value Labels**.

	case	category	triangle	square	rectangl
1	1	Psychology Student	2	12	7
2	2	Psychology Student	8	10	9
3	3	Psychology Student	4	15	3
4	4	Psychology Student	6	9	7
5	5	Psychology Student	9	13	8
6	6	Psychology Student	7	14	8
7	7	Engineering Student	13	3	35
8	8	Engineering Student	21	4	30
9	9	Engineering Student	26	10	35
10	10	Engineering Student	22	8	30
11	11	Engineering Student	20	9	28
12	12	Engineering Student	19	8	27

Figure 1. The data from Table 1 in Data View

236

10.2.2 Exploring the results: Boxplots

As usual, the first step is to explore the data set. The boxplot was described in Section 4.3.2. Here, however, the **clustered boxplot** (which clusters the levels of the within subjects factor at different levels of the between subjects variable) is appropriate.

To obtain a clustered boxplot, proceed as follows:
- Click
  Graphs
     Boxplot...
  to open the **Boxplot** dialog box.
- Select the **Clustered** option and (within the **Data in Chart Are** section) the **Summaries of separate variables** radio button. Click **Define** to enter the **Define Clustered Boxplot: Summaries of Separate Variables** dialog box.
- Transfer the variable names *triangle square rectangl* to the **Boxes Represent:** box and the variable name Category of Student [*category*] to the **Category Axis:** box.
- Click **OK**.

The edited boxplot is shown in Output 1.

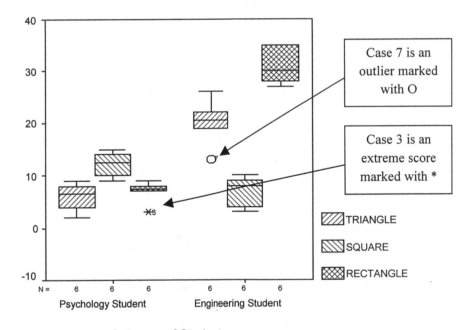

Output 1. Edited Boxplots of the three shapes for each student category

Notice the extreme score (case 3) for the number of rectangles identified by a Psychology student and the outlier (case 7) for the number of triangles identified by an Engineering student. In a real research situation, it might have been worth eliminating the two deviant scores, but here we shall work with the entire data set.

10.2.3 Running the ANOVA

- Select

  Analyze

     General Linear Model

        Repeated Measures...

  to open the **Repeated Measures Define Factor(s)** dialog box (the completed version is shown in Figure 2).

- In the **Within-Subject Factor Name** box, delete *factor1* and type a generic name (such as *shape*) for the repeated measures factor. This name must not be that of any of the three levels making up the factor and must also conform to the rules governing the assignment of variable names. In the **Number of Levels** box, type the number of levels (*3*) making up the repeated measures factor. Click **Add** and, in the lowest box in Figure 2, the entry *shape(3)* will appear.

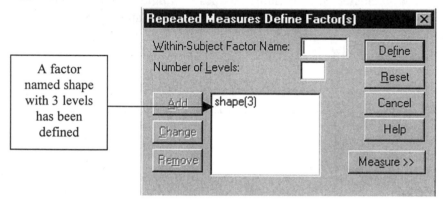

Figure 2. The Repeated Measures Define Factor(s) for three levels of *shape*

- Click **Define** to open the **Repeated Measures ANOVA** dialog box.
- Transfer the variable names *rectangl, square, triangle* to the **Within-Subjects Variables** box as shown in Figure 3.
- The new element is the presence of the between subjects factor Category of Student [*category*]. Transfer its name to the **Between-Subjects Factor(s)** box as shown in Figure 3.
- It is recommended that the user also request a number of additional options that are useful for a mixed ANOVA. A profile plot of the levels of the within subjects factor *shape* for each level of the between subjects variable *category* is requested by clicking **Plots...** and following the steps shown in Figure 15 in Chapter 9. Click **Continue** to return to the original dialog box.
- A table of descriptive statistics and a table of Bonferroni adjusted pairwise comparisons among the levels of the within subjects factor *shape* are requested by clicking **Options...** and following the steps shown in Figure 16 in Chapter 9. Click **Continue** to return to the original dialog box.
- Had there been more than two levels in the between subjects variable *category*, a Tukey post-hoc test could have been requested by clicking **Post Hoc...**, transferring the variable name category to the **Post Hoc Tests for** box, and clicking the **Tukey** check box. Click **Continue** to return to the original dialog box.
- Click **OK**.

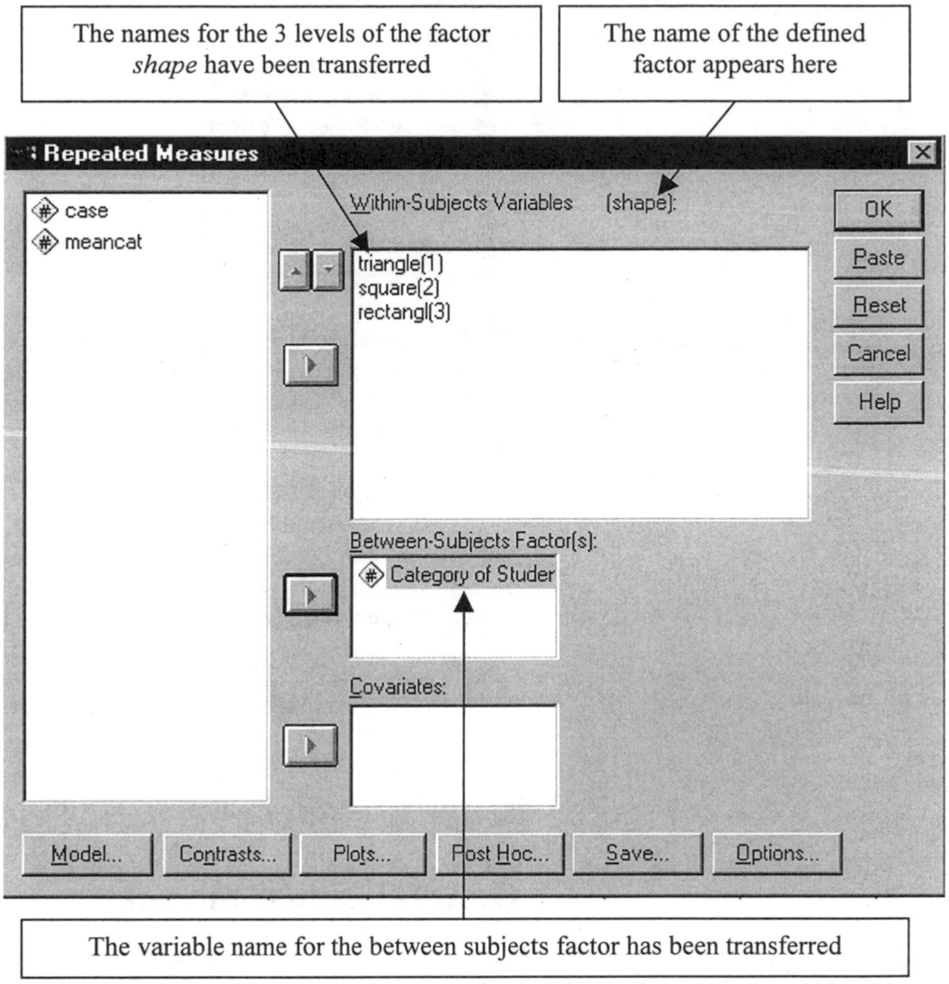

Figure 3. The Repeated Measures dialog box showing the three levels of the within subjects factor *shape* and the between subjects factor *category*

10.2.4 Output for the two-factor mixed ANOVA

Output 2 shows the left-hand pane of the SPSS Viewer listing the various items appearing in the right-hand pane.

The output is obviously very extensive, but not all of it is needed for a mixed ANOVA. Two items, **Multivariate Tests** and **Tests of Within-Subjects Contrasts**, can be deleted immediately by highlighting each in turn and pressing the **Delete** key on the keyboard. In the **Estimated Marginal Means** section, the **Multivariate Tests** table can also be deleted.

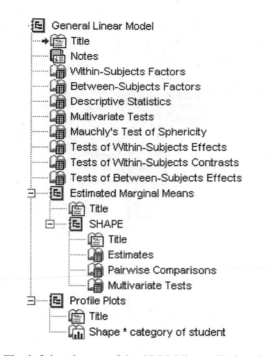

Output 2. The left-hand pane of the SPSS Viewer listing the output items for the mixed ANOVA

Output 3 shows the **Title**, **Within-Subjects Factors** list and **Between-Subjects Factors** list.

General Linear Model

Within-Subjects Factors

Measure: MEASURE_1

SHAPE	Dependent Variable
1	RECTANGL
2	SQUARE
3	TRIANGLE

Between-Subjects Factors

		Value Label	N
Category of Student	1	Psychology Student	6
	2	Engineering Student	6

Output 3. The Within-Subjects Factors and Between-Subjects Factors tables

Output 4 shows the table of descriptive statistics requested in **Options**. Inspection of the means shows different profiles across the factor *shape* for the two student categories.

Descriptive Statistics

	Category of Student	Mean	Std. Deviation	N
TRIANGLE	Psychology Student	6.00	2.61	6
	Engineering Student	20.17	4.26	6
	Total	13.08	8.13	12
SQUARE	Psychology Student	12.17	2.32	6
	Engineering Student	7.00	2.83	6
	Total	9.58	3.65	12
RECTANGL	Psychology Student	7.00	2.10	6
	Engineering Student	30.83	3.43	6
	Total	18.92	12.74	12

Output 4. The optional table of descriptive statistics

See Section 9.2.4

The next table, in Output 5, reports the result of the **Mauchly's Test of Sphericity** for homogeneity of covariance (see Section 9.2.4 which describes the correct procedure should the Mauchly statistic be significant.

In the present case, the Mauchly statistic has a p-value of 0.63, so there is no evidence of heterogeneity of covariance. The usual (Sphericity Assumed) F test can therefore be used.

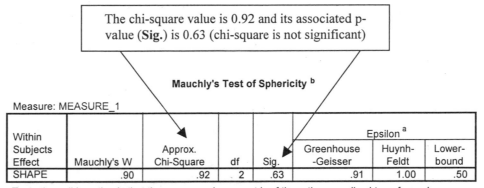

The chi-square value is 0.92 and its associated p-value (**Sig.**) is 0.63 (chi-square is not significant)

Mauchly's Test of Sphericity [b]

Measure: MEASURE_1

| Within Subjects Effect | Mauchly's W | Approx. Chi-Square | df | Sig. | Epsilon [a] | | |
					Greenhouse-Geisser	Huynh-Feldt	Lower-bound
SHAPE	.90	.92	2	.63	.91	1.00	.50

Tests the null hypothesis that the error covariance matrix of the orthonormalized transformed dependent variables is proportional to an identity matrix.

a. May be used to adjust the degrees of freedom for the averaged tests of significance. Corrected tests are displayed in the Tests of Within-Subjects Effects table.

b.

Design: Intercept+CATEGORY
Within Subjects Design: SHAPE

Output 5. Mauchly's Test of Sphericity and values of epsilon for more conservative tests

Tests for within subjects and interaction effects

Output 6 (edited to remove the more conservative tests) shows the ANOVA summary table for the within subjects factor *shape* and the *category by shape* interaction.

Tests of Within-Subjects Effects

Measure: MEASURE_1

Source	Type III Sum of Squares	df	Mean Square	F	Sig.
SHAPE	533.56	2	266.78	32.62	.00
SHAPE * CATEGORY	1308.22	2	654.11	79.99	.00
Error(SHAPE)	163.56	20	8.18		

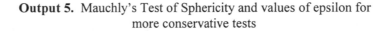

Both the factor SHAPE and the interaction SHAPE*CATEGORY have p-values (**Sig.**) less than 0.01 (significant at the 1% level)

Output 6. The edited ANOVA summary table for the within-subjects factor SHAPE and its interaction with the between-subjects factor CATEGORY

Note that the factor *shape* is significant beyond the 1 per cent level: the p-value (**Sig.**) 0.00 is less than 0.005. This result would be reported as:

$$F(2, 20) = 32.62; \ p < 0.01$$

The interaction *category* × *shape* is also significant beyond the 1% level: the p-value is less than 0.005. This result would be reported as:

$$F(2, 20) = 79.99; \ p < 0.01$$

Test for between subjects effects

Output 7 shows the ANOVA summary table for the between subjects factor *category*.

Tests of Between-Subjects Effects

Measure: MEASURE_1
Transformed Variable: Average

Source	Type III Sum of Squares	df	Mean Square	F	Sig.
Intercept	6916.69	1	6916.69	634.88	.00
CATEGORY	1078.03	1	1078.03	98.95	.00
Error	108.94	10	10.89		

The p-value (**Sig.**) for CATEGORY is less than 0.01 (significant at the 1% level)

Output 7. The ANOVA summary table for the between-subjects factor CATEGORY

Ignore the terms Intercept and Type III: these refer to the regression that was used to perform the analysis. With a p-value (**Sig.**) of less than 0.005, there is clearly a significant difference in performance between the two groups of students. This result would be reported as:

$$F(1,10) = 98.95; \ p < 0.01.$$

The ANOVA strongly confirms the patterns discernible in Table 2: the *shape* and *category* factors both have significant main effects; the interaction between the factors is also significant.

Bonferroni Pairwise Comparisons for the within subjects factor

Pairwise Comparisons

Measure: MEASURE_1

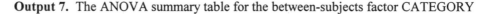

(I) SHAPE	(J) SHAPE	Mean Difference (I-J)	Std. Error	Sig.[a]	95% Confidence Interval for Difference[a] Lower Bound	Upper Bound
1	2	3.50*	.97	.01	.71	6.29
	3	-5.83*	1.22	.00	-9.34	-2.32
2	1	-3.50*	.97	.01	-6.29	-.71
	3	-9.33*	1.28	.00	-13.02	-5.65
3	1	5.83*	1.22	.00	2.32	9.34
	2	9.33*	1.28	.00	5.65	13.02

Based on estimated marginal means
*. The mean difference is significant at the .05 level.
a. Adjustment for multiple comparisons: Bonferroni.

Differences significant at the .01 level.   Difference significant at the 5% level

Output 8. The Bonferroni pairwise comparisons for the factor *shape*

Output 8 shows the pairwise comparisons requested in **Options**.

Profile plot

The requested profile plot is shown in Output 9.

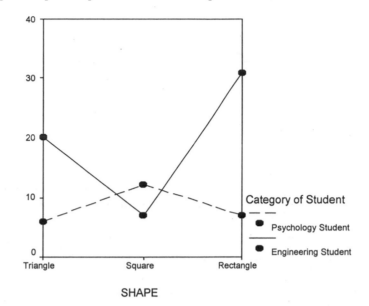

Output 9. The Shape performance profiles for each Student Category

The plot confirms the pattern of the boxplots in Output 1. With squares, the Psychology students improved, while the Engineering students slumped.

10.3 THE THREE-FACTOR MIXED ANOVA

The procedures described in Section 10.2 can readily be extended to the analysis of data from mixed factorial experiments with three treatment factors. There are two possible mixed three-factor factorial designs:

(1)   Two within subjects factors and one between subjects factor;

(2)   One within subjects factor and two between subjects factors.

10.3.1 Two within subjects factors and one between subjects factor

Suppose that to the design of the experiment described in Section 10.2, we were to add an additional within subjects factor, such as Solidity (of the shape), with two levels, Solid or Outline. The participants (either Psychology or Engineering students) now have to try to recognise both Solid and Outline Triangles, Squares, and Rectangles. Since there are six combinations of Shape and Solidity factors, we shall need to have six variables in **Data View** to contain all the scores. It is convenient to prepare these columns in **Variable View** systematically by taking the first level of one factor and combining it in turn with each of the levels of the second, and doing the same with the second level of the first factor. If we take the Shape factor first, the top part of **Data View** might appear as in Figure 4.

	case	category	trisolid	trioutln	squsolid	squoutln	recsolid	recoutln
1	1	Psychology Student	13	15	12	23	12	14

Figure 4. The variable names for a three-factor mixed factorial experiment with two within subjects factors

Care must be taken when transferring variable names within the **Repeated Measures** dialog box. The danger is that the names in **Data View** (and hence in the list in the left-hand box of the **Repeated Measures** dialog box) may not be in the required sequence. (The order of the defined factors, and hence the correct sequence of variable names, is shown in square brackets above the box.) It may be necessary to transfer the variable names one at a time to the **Within-Subjects Variables** box to ensure that the variable names are correctly placed in the slots provided. The upper part of the completed dialog box is shown in Figure 5.

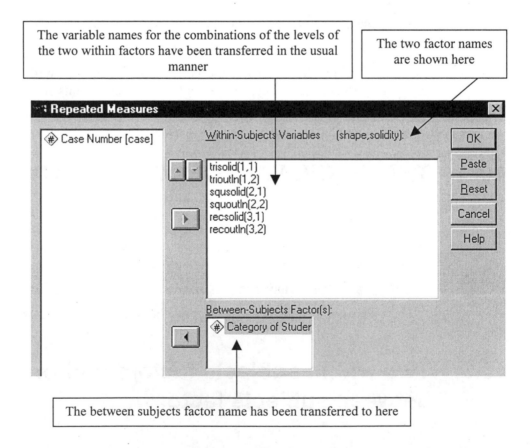

Figure 5. The upper part of the Repeated Measures dialog box for a three-factor mixed factorial experiment, with two within subjects factors and one between subjects factor

10.3.2 One within subjects factor and two between subjects factors

Suppose the experiment described in Section 10.2. were to have an additional between subjects factor, such as Sex (Male, Female). The participants (either Psychology or Engineering Students, and either Male or Female) have to try to recognise shapes (Triangles, Squares, and Rectangles).

In **Variable View**, it will now be necessary to define two grouping variables, *sex* and *category*, and the three levels (*triangle*, *square* and *rectangl*) of the within subjects factor Shape. The top of **Data View** might appear as in Figure 6.

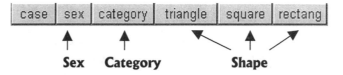

Figure 6. The variable names for a three-factor mixed factorial experiment with one within subjects factor and two between subjects factors

The completed **Repeated Measures ANOVA** dialog box would then appear as in Figure 7.

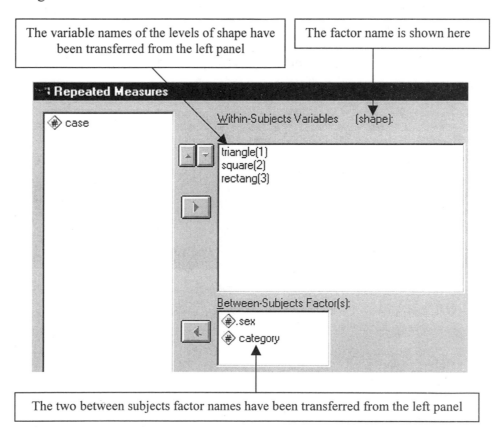

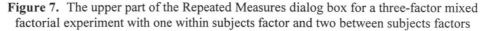

Figure 7. The upper part of the Repeated Measures dialog box for a three-factor mixed factorial experiment with one within subjects factor and two between subjects factors

10.4 FURTHER ANALYSIS: SIMPLE EFFECTS AND MULTIPLE COMPARISONS

The analysis of variance is a large topic in statistics, and there are available many more techniques than we can mention in this book. For example, following the confirmation that an interaction is significant, it is often useful to follow up the initial ANOVA with additional tests of the effects of one factor at specific levels of another. Such analysis of **simple effects** can be combined with both planned and unplanned multiple comparisons. We urge the reader who is unfamiliar with such methods to read the relevant chapters in a lucid textbook such as Howell (1997).

At this point, it may be worth reminding the reader that the dangers of committing a type I error in unplanned multiple comparisons increase enormously with the complexity of the experiment. Accordingly, the user must take precautions to control the *per family* type I error rate (the probability of at least one type 1 error). The use of simple effects tests may justify the specification of a smaller subgroup of treatment means as the 'family', increasing the power of each test.

In a three-factor experiment, for example, the significance of the three-way interaction implies that the interactions between two of the factors are not homogeneous across all levels of the third factor. Should there be a significant two-factor interaction at one particular level of the third factor (i.e., a significant **simple interaction**), one might define the comparison 'family' as the performance means <u>at that level only</u>. The user could then proceed to make pairwise multiple comparisons among this smaller set of means.

EXERCISE 15

MIXED ANOVA (BETWEEN AND WITHIN SUBJECTS FACTORS)

Before you start

Readers should study Chapter 10 carefully before proceeding with this Exercise.

Effects of ambient hue and sound on vigilance

In an experiment investigating the effect of the colour of the ambient light upon performance of a vigilance task, participants were asked to press a button when they thought they could discern a signal against a background of random noise. The experimenter expected that the ambient colour would have varying effects upon the detection of different kinds of sound. Three types of signal were used: a horn, a whistle and a bell. Each signal was presented 30 times in the course of a one-hour monitoring session, during which the participant sat in a cubicle lit by either red or blue light. The dependent variable was the number of correct presses of the button. For theoretical purposes, it was necessary to use different participants for the different colour conditions. It was considered that there would be advantages in testing each individual with all three kinds of signal. In this experiment, therefore, the factor of Colour was between subjects; whereas the other factor, Signal, was within subjects.

The results are shown in Table 1.

		Signal		
Colour	Participant	Horn	Whistle	Bell
Red	1	25	18	22
	2	22	16	21
	3	26	19	26
	4	23	21	20
	5	19	18	19
	6	27	23	27
Blue	7	19	12	23
	8	21	15	19
	9	23	14	24
	10	20	16	21
	11	17	16	20
	12	21	17	19

Table 1. The results of a two-factor mixed factorial experiment

Preparing the SPSS data set

Recast the data of Table 1 into a form suitable for entry into SPSS. In **Variable View**, after naming a variable *case*, you will need to have a grouping variable *colour* and three variables for the scores: *horn*, *whistle*, and *bell*. The last three variables will be the three levels of the within-subjects factor *signal*, which is not defined until the ANOVA command is actually being run. Follow the procedure described in Section 10.2.1. Save the data with a suitable file name.

Exploring the data set

Draw boxplots as described in Section 10.2.2.

- **Are there any markedly deviant scores as shown by * or 0?**

Running the two-factor mixed ANOVA

Run the ANOVA as described in Section 10.2.3 remembering to request **Descriptive Statistics**, a **Profile Plot** and **Bonferroni Pairwise Comparisons** for the factor *signal*.

Output for the two-factor mixed ANOVA

The main features of the output are explained in Section 10.2.4. After tables listing **the Within-Subjects Factors** and **Between-Subjects Factors**, look at the table of **Descriptive Statistics** and the **Profile Plot**.

- **Can you discern any pattern in the means for each level of signal across colours?**

The next table, **Multivariate Tests**, can be deleted by highlighting its icon in the left-hand pane of **SPSS Viewer** and pressing the **Delete** key.

Next is the **Mauchly's Test of Sphericity** table, followed by the **Tests of Within-Subjects Effects**. If the Mauchly's Test is not significant, read the rows labelled **Sphericity Assumed** and delete the conservative test rows by double-clicking anywhere in the table, highlighting the material to be deleted and then pressing the **Delete** key. Delete the **Tests of Within-Subjects Contrasts** table.

- **Write down the value of *F* and its associated p-value for the factor Signal, and for its interaction with *colour*.**

Next there is a table of **Tests of Between-Subjects Effects**.

- **Write down the value of *F* and its associated p-value for the factor *colour*.**

Finally look again at the **Profile Plot**. Does the graph show a pattern consistent with the results of the ANOVA?

- **Has the experimenter's hypothesis been confirmed?**

Finishing the session

Close down SPSS and any other windows before logging out.

EXERCISE 16

MIXED ANOVA: THREE-FACTOR EXPERIMENT

Before you start

Before proceeding with this exercise, you should study Section 10.3. From the procedural point of view, the analysis of mixed experiments with three factors is a fairly simple extension of the command for two-factor mixed experiments. In general, however, the interpretation of data from factorial experiments becomes increasingly problematic as more factors are added. In particular, where there is a complex design with repeated measures on some factors but not on others, the naming of the factors must be carried out with special care.

A three-factor mixed factorial experiment with two within subjects factors and one between subjects factor

Imagine an experiment investigating the recognition of shapes under sub-optimal conditions on a monitor screen. The experimenter is interested in whether the different shapes are more readily recognised if they are filled rather than merely outlines, and whether Engineering students are more adept at recognising shapes than Psychology students. There are three shapes (shape1, shape2, shape3), each of which can be either Open (merely an outline) or Filled. Each participant in the experiment is tested under all six combinations of these two treatment factors, which can be labelled Shape and Shade. The between subjects factor *category* is the observer group: one group consists of Psychology students, the other of Engineering students. The dependent variable is the number of correct identifications over a fixed series of trials. The results are shown in Table 1.

	Shape:- Shade:-	Shape 1		Shape 2		Shape 3	
		Open	Filled	Open	Filled	Open	Filled
Participant	Category						
1	Psychology	2	12	3	1	4	5
2	Psychology	13	22	5	9	6	8
3	Psychology	14	20	8	7	5	7
4	Engineering	12	1	3	9	6	10
5	Engineering	11	2	8	10	5	9
6	Engineering	12	7	2	4	4	10

Table 1. Three-factor mixed factorial experiment with two within subjects treatment factors

Preparing the SPSS data set

In **Variable View**, in addition to a case variable, it will be necessary to name one grouping variable *category* and six other variables (one for each combination of the Shape and Shade factors) to contain the results. We suggest that you name the variables in the systematic fashion described in Section 10.3.1.

The ANOVA

The command for running the **Repeated Measures ANOVA** is outlined in Section 10.3.1. The procedure is a straightforward extension of the routine for the two-factor mixed experiment. Name and specify the numbers of levels of two within subjects factors (Shape and Shade). Transfer the between subjects variable *category* to the **Between-Subjects Factor(s):** box. To request the profile plots, click the **Plots...** button to open the **Repeated Measures: Profile Plots** dialog box. Enter *shape* in the **Horizontal Axis:** box, *shade* in the **Separate Lines:** box and *category* in the **Separate Plots:** box. Click **Add** and then **Continue**, to return to the original dialog box. Select **Options...** to request **Descriptive Statistics** and **Bonferroni Pairwise Comparisons** for the factor Shape. Click **Continue** and **OK** to run the analysis.

The output

Check the **Within-Subjects Factors** table and **Between-Subjects Factors** table for accuracy. Inspect the table of **Descriptive Statistics** to see if you can discern a pattern of means. Delete the table of **Multivariate Tests**.

The **Mauchly** tests will appear in the table **Mauchly's Test of Sphericity**. The Mauchly test only arises with factors and interactions having repeated measures and more than two levels. In this case, there will be Mauchly tests for the Shape factor and the Shape × Shade interaction. Check that the p-values are greater than 0.05.

The within subjects tests are given in the table **Tests of Within-Subjects Effects**. If the relevant Mauchly test is not significant, you need study only the rows labelled **Sphericity Assumed** and you can delete the rows for the conservative tests by double-clicking anywhere in the table, highlighting the material to be deleted and pressing the **Delete** key. Delete the **Tests of Within-Subjects Contrasts** table. The next table is **Tests of Between-Subjects Effects** for the factor *category*.

- **Write down the F ratios (and p-values) for the three factors, their two-way interactions and the three-way interaction. Do the values of F confirm the patterns among the treatment means you have observed in the table of Descriptive Statistics and the Profile Plots?**

Look at the table of **Pairwise Comparisons**.

- **Are any of the pairs significantly different? If not, why not, considering that the factor Shape is significant in the ANOVA?**

Finally inspect the **Profile Plots** again. Compare the pattern of lines in both plots.

- **Do the graphs confirm the picture relayed by the ANOVA? Why was the triple interaction significant?**

- **Has the experimenter's hypothesis been confirmed? In your answer, cite the relevant features of the results.**

Finishing the session

Close down SPSS and any other windows before logging out.

CHAPTER 11

MEASURING STATISTICAL ASSOCIATION

11.1 INTRODUCTION

11.2 CORRELATIONAL ANALYSIS WITH SPSS

11.3 OTHER MEASURES OF ASSOCIATION

11.1   INTRODUCTION

Statistical association between quantitative variables

So far, this book has been concerned with statistical methods devised for the purpose of comparing averages between or among samples of data that might be expected to differ in general level: for example, right-handed people might be compared with left-handed people; the trained might be compared with the untrained; males might be compared with females.

Consider, however, a set of paired data of the sort that might be produced if one were to weigh each of a sample of one hundred men before and after they had taken a fitness course. Previously, our concern would have been with the **comparison** of the men's average weight before the course with their average weight afterwards. One would expect these data to show another feature, however: the person who was heaviest before the course is likely to be among the heaviest in the group afterwards; the lightest person before the course should be among the lightest afterwards; and one with an intermediate score before the course is likely to be in the middle of the group afterwards. In other words, there should be a statistical **association** or **correlation** between people's weights before and after the course.

Depicting an association: The scatterplot

See
Section
5.6

The existence of a statistical association between two variables is most apparent in the appearance of a diagram called a **scatterplot** (see Chapter 5, Section 5.6) which, in the foregoing example, would be constructed by representing each person as a point in space, using as co-ordinates that person's weights before and after taking the course. The cloud of points would take the shape of an ellipse (see bottom right scatterplot in Figure 1 on the next page), whose longer axis slopes upwards from left to right across the page. An elliptical scatterplot indicates the existence of a **linear relationship** between two variables. If the slope of the major axis is positive, the variables are said to be **positively correlated**; if it is negative, they are **negatively correlated**. The thinner the ellipse, the stronger the degree of linear relationship; the fatter the ellipse, the weaker the relationship. A circular scatterplot indicates the absence of any relationship between the two variables.

Linear association

The term **linear** means 'of the nature of a straight line'. In our current example, a straight line (known as a **regression line**) can be drawn through the points in the elliptical scatterplot so that it is as close to as many of the points as possible (though there may be one or two outliers). We can use the regression line to make quite a good **estimate** of a particular man's weight after the course from a knowledge of his weight before the course: if we have Weight Before on the horizontal axis and Weight After on the vertical axis, we need only move up to the point on the regression line vertically above his first weight, and then move across to the vertical scale to estimate his second weight. If we do that, we shall probably be in error, the difference between his true weight after the course and his estimated weight from the regression line being known as a **residual.** The value of the residual, however, is likely to be small in comparison with the man's true weight after the course.

Measuring the strength of a linear association: The Pearson correlation

A **correlation coefficient** is a statistic devised for the purpose of measuring the strength, or degree, of a supposed linear association between two variables, each of which has been measured on a scale with units. The most familiar correlation coefficient is the **Pearson correlation (r)**. The Pearson correlation is so defined that it can take values only within the range from −1 to +1, inclusive. The larger the absolute value (i.e. ignoring the sign), the narrower the ellipse, and the closer to the regression line the points in the scatterplot will fall. A perfect correlation arises when the values of one variable are exactly predictable from those of the other and the Pearson correlation takes a value of ± 1, in which case all the points in the scatterplot lie on the regression line. In other cases, the narrower the elliptical cloud of points, the stronger the association, and the greater the absolute value of the Pearson correlation. When there is no association whatever between two variables, their scatterplot should be a roughly circular cloud, in which case the Pearson correlation will be about zero (top right in Figure 1).

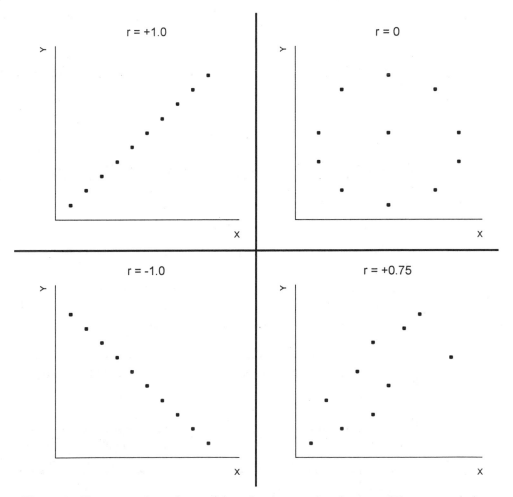

Figure 1. The scatterplots of sets of data showing varying degrees of linear association

A word of warning

It is quite possible, from inspection of a scatterplot, to do two useful things:

    (1)   see whether there is indeed a linear relationship between the variables, in which case the Pearson correlation would be a meaningful statistic to use;

    (2)   guess fairly accurately what the value of the Pearson correlation would be if calculated.

In other words, from inspection of their scatterplot alone, one can discern the most important features of the true relationship (if any) between two variables. So if we reason from the scatterplot to the statistics, we shall not go seriously wrong.

The converse, however, is not true: **given only the value of a Pearson correlation, one can say nothing whatsoever about the relationship between two variables**. In a famous paper, the statistician Anscombe (1973) presents data that illustrate how misleading the value of the Pearson correlation can be. The moral of this cautionary tale is clear: when studying the association between two variables, always construct a scatterplot, and interpret (or disregard) the Pearson correlation accordingly. In the same paper, Anscombe gives a useful rule for deciding whether there really is a robust linear relationship between two variables: should the shape of the scatterplot be unaltered by the removal of a few observations at random, there is probably a real relationship between the two variables.

To sum up, the **Pearson correlation** is a measure of a **supposed** linear relationship between two variables; but the supposition of linearity must be confirmed by inspection of the scatterplot.

11.2   CORRELATIONAL ANALYSIS WITH SPSS

The principal of a tennis coaching school considers that tennis proficiency depends partly upon general hand-eye co-ordination. To confirm this hunch, she measures the hand-eye co-ordination (Initial Co-ordination) of some pupils who are beginning the course and their proficiency in tennis at the end of the course (Final Proficiency). The data are shown in Table 1.

Table 1. Measures of Initial Co-ordination and Final Proficiency in ten pupils at a tennis school					
Pupil	**Initial Co-ordination**	**Final Proficiency**	**Pupil**	**Initial Co-ordination**	**Final Proficiency**
1	4	4	6	4	2
2	4	5	7	7	5
3	5	6	8	8	6
4	2	2	9	9	9
5	10	6	10	5	3

Preparing the SPSS data set

See Section 3.2

Using the techniques described in Chapter 3, Section 3.2, open **Variable View** and name the variables *pupil*, *coordin* and *proficy*. Use **Label** to assign more meaningful variable names such as Pupil Number, Initial Co-ordination and Final Tennis Proficiency. Switch to **Data View** and enter the data. Save the data set.

Obtaining a scatterplot

To obtain the scatterplot of Final Tennis Proficiency against Initial Co-ordination:

- Choose
  Graphs
    Scatter...
  to open the **Scatterplot** dialog box (Figure 2).

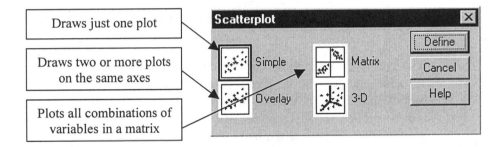

Figure 2. The Scatterplot dialog box

- Since the default scatterplot is **Simple**, click **Define** to open the **Simple Scatterplot** dialog box. The completed version is shown in Figure 3.

- Transfer the variable names *coordin* and *proficy* to the **X Axis:** box and the **Y Axis:** box, respectively, as shown in Figure 3.

- Click **OK**.

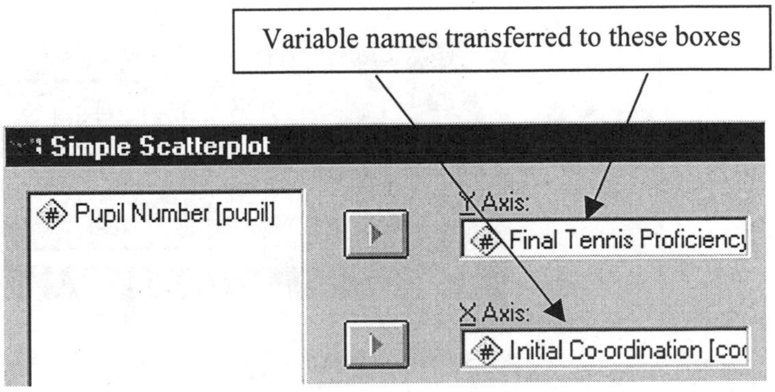

Figure 3. The upper part of the completed Simple Scatterplot dialog box

The edited version of the scatterplot is shown in Output 1. The changes included centring the axis labels and making the point markers black. The plot shows a consistent trend, with no outliers.

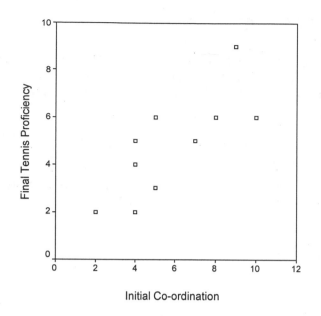

Output 1. Scatterplot of Final Tennis Proficiency against Initial Co-ordination

It is possible to categorise points on a scatterplot by the levels of a grouping variable (e.g. sex) by inserting the grouping variable name in the **Set Markers by** box in the **Simple Scatterplot** dialog box. The points for males and females will be plotted in different colours. (For black-and-white reproduction, simply use different shapes for the male and female plots.)

11.2.1 Procedure for the Pearson correlation

- Choose (Figure 4)
  Analyze
     Correlate
        Bivariate...
  to open the **Bivariate Correlations** dialog box (the completed version is shown in Figure 5).

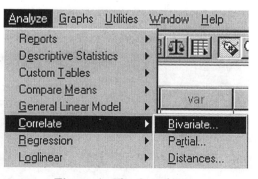

Figure 4. The Correlate menu

- Highlight both variables and click ▭ to transfer the names to the **Variables** box.

- To tabulate means and standard deviations, click the **Options** button to open the **Bivariate Correlations: Options** dialog box. Click the **Means and Standard Deviations** check box and then **Continue** to return to the **Bivariate Correlations** dialog box.
- Click **OK** to obtain the correlation coefficient and the additional statistics.

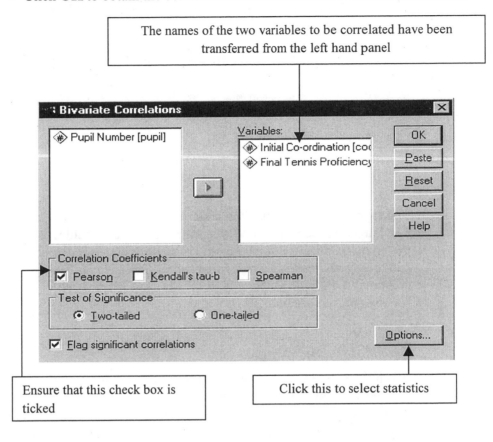

Figure 5. The Bivariate Correlations dialog box for Initial Co-ordination and Final Tennis Proficiency

11.2.2 Output for the Pearson correlation

The output begins with a tabulation of the means and standard deviations of the two variables, as requested with **Options**.

Descriptive Statistics

	Mean	Std. Deviation	N
Initial Co-ordination	5.80	2.57	10
Final Tennis Proficiency	4.80	2.15	10

Output 2 tabulates the Pearson correlation, with its p-value. With a value for r of 0.78 and a two-tailed p-value of 0.01, it can be concluded that the correlation coefficient is significant beyond the 1 per cent level. This is written as:

$$r = 0.78; n = 10; p < 0.01.$$

Correlations

		Initial Co-ordination	Final Tennis Proficiency
Initial Co-ordination	Pearson Correlation	1.00	.78**
	Sig. (2-tailed)	.	.01
	N	10.00	10.00
Final Tennis Proficiency	Pearson Correlation	.78**	1.00
	Sig. (2-tailed)	.01	.
	N	10.00	10.00

** Correlation is significant at the 0.01 level (2-tailed).

> The correlation coefficient is 0.78 and its p-value, **Sig. (2-tailed)**, is 0.01 (r is significant at the 1% level)

Output 2. The Pearson correlation

The layout of the correlations table in Output 2 may seem strange, since only one numerical cell is needed when there are two variables. The reason is that the layout is always a square matrix of correlations (see the next paragraph) and had there been more than two variables, the table would have had extra rows and columns to allow the user to read off the correlation coefficient and its p-value for any pair of variables.

Obtaining a correlation matrix

When there are more than two variables, SPSS can be commanded to construct a **correlation matrix**, a rectangular array whose entries are the correlations between each variable and every other variable. In the **Bivariate Correlations** dialog box, enter as many variable names as required into the **Variables:** box (Figure 5).

11.3   OTHER MEASURES OF ASSOCIATION

The Pearson correlation is suitable only for data in the form of measurements on quantitative variables. With ordinal or nominal data, other statistics must be used.

11.3.1 Measures of association strength for ordinal data

The term **ordinal data** includes both ranks and assignments to ordered categories. When, as in the case of the same objects ranked independently by two judges, ordinal data are paired, the question arises as to the extent to which the two sets of ranks agree. This is a question about the strength of association between two variables which, although quantitative, are measured at the ordinal level.

The Spearman rank correlation (r_S or ρ)

Suppose that the ranks assigned to the ten paintings by the two judges are as in Table 2.

Table 2. Ranks assigned by two judges to each of ten paintings									
Painting	A	B	C	D	E	F	G	H	I	J
First Judge	1	2	3	4	5	6	7	8	9	10
Second Judge	1	3	2	4	6	5	8	7	10	9

It is obvious that the judges generally agree closely in their rankings: at most, the ranks they assign to a painting differ by a single rank. One way of measuring the level of agreement between the two judges is by calculating the Pearson correlation between the two sets of ranks. This correlation is known as the **Spearman rank correlation r_S** (or as **Spearman's rho ρ**). The Spearman rank correlation is usually presented in terms of a formula which, although it looks very different from that of the Pearson correlation, is actually equivalent, provided that no ties are allowed.

The use of the Spearman rank correlation is not confined to ordinal data. Should a scatterplot show that the Pearson correlation is unsuitable as a measure of the strength of association between two measured quantitative variables, the scores on both variables can be converted to ranks and the Spearman rank correlation calculated instead.

With small samples, it is difficult to obtain an accurate p-value for a Spearman correlation, especially when there are tied ranks. When there are no tied ranks, one can obtain critical values for the Spearman rank correlation from tables in textbooks such as Neave & Worthington (1988). When ties are present, they must reduce one's confidence in the critical values given in the tables. The user can but hope that when there is only a tie or two here and there, the tables will still give serviceable p-values.

Kendall's tau (τ) statistics

Kendall's tau statistics, represented by the Greek letter τ, provide an alternative to the Spearman rank correlation as measures of agreement between rankings, or assignments to ordered categories. The basic idea is that one set of ranks can be converted into another by a succession of reversals of pairs of ranks in one set: the fewer the reversals needed (in relation to the total number of possible reversals), the larger the value of tau. The numerator of Kendall's tau is the difference between the number of pairs of objects whose ranks are concordant (i.e. they go in the same direction) and the number of discordant pairs. If the former predominate, the sign of tau is positive; if the latter predominate, tau is negative.

There are three different versions of Kendall's tau: **tau-a**, **tau-b** and **tau-c**. All three measures have the same numerator, the difference between the numbers of concordant and discordant pairs. It is in their denominators that they differ, the difference being in the way they handle tied observations. The denominator of tau-a is simply the total number of pairs. The problem with tau-a is that when there are ties, its range quickly becomes restricted, to the point where it becomes difficult to interpret. The correlation tau-b has terms in the denominator that consider, in either variable, pairs that are tied on one variable but not on the other. (When there are no ties, the values of tau-a and tau-b are identical.) The correlation tau-c was designed for situations where one wishes to measure agreement between assignments to unequal-sized sets of ordered categories. Provided the data meet certain requirements, the appropriate tau correlation can vary throughout the complete range from −1 to +1.

Kendall's tau correlations have advantages over the Spearman correlation, especially with small data sets, in which there are tied assignments, where serviceable p-values can still be obtained.

Procedures for obtaining the Spearman and Kendall rank correlations

In **Variable View**, name two variables, *judge1* and *judge2*. Click the **Data View** tab to switch to **Data View** and, from Table 2, enter the ranks assigned by the first judge into the *judge1* column and those assigned by the second judge into the *judge2* column.

- Choose
  Analyze
      Correlate
          Bivariate...
  to obtain the **Bivariate Correlations** dialog box (the completed version is shown in Figure 6).

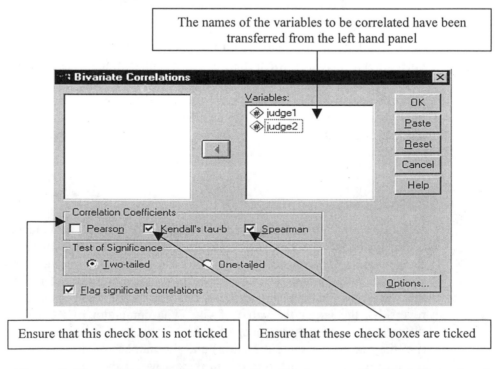

Figure 6. The completed Bivariate Correlations box for computing Kendall's tau-b and Spearman's coefficient

- By default, the **Pearson** check box will be marked. Click off the **Pearson** check box and click the **Kendall's tau-b** and the **Spearman** check boxes.
- Transfer the variable names *judge1* and *judge2* to the **Variables:** box.
- Click **OK** to obtain the correlations shown in Output 3.

Note that the calculation of Kendall's statistics with **ordinal** data, in the form of assignments of target objects to ordered categories, is best handled by the **Crosstabs** command (see next section); indeed, tau-c (which is appropriate when the two variables have different numbers of categories) can only be obtained in **Crosstabs**.

Nonparametric Correlations

Correlations

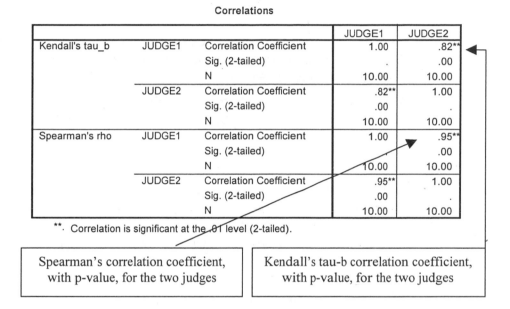

			JUDGE1	JUDGE2
Kendall's tau_b	JUDGE1	Correlation Coefficient	1.00	.82**
		Sig. (2-tailed)	.	.00
		N	10.00	10.00
	JUDGE2	Correlation Coefficient	.82**	1.00
		Sig. (2-tailed)	.00	.
		N	10.00	10.00
Spearman's rho	JUDGE1	Correlation Coefficient	1.00	.95**
		Sig. (2-tailed)	.	.00
		N	10.00	10.00
	JUDGE2	Correlation Coefficient	.95**	1.00
		Sig. (2-tailed)	.00	.
		N	10.00	10.00

**. Correlation is significant at the .01 level (2-tailed).

Spearman's correlation coefficient, with p-value, for the two judges	Kendall's tau-b correlation coefficient, with p-value, for the two judges

Output 3. Correlations between two sets of ranks

Output 3 shows that the Kendall correlation is *0.82* and the Spearman correlation is *0.95*. These values differ, but there is nothing untoward in this. The two statistics are based on quite different theoretical foundations and often take noticeably different values when calculated from the same data set. (Incidentally, the Pearson option would have given the same value as the Spearman: *0.95*.) These results would be written thus:

$$\tau = 0.82; n = 10; p < 0.01.$$

$$r_S = 0.95; n = 10; p < 0.01;$$

11.3.2 Measures of association strength for nominal data: The Crosstabs command

See Section 3.7.2

When people's membership of two sets of mutually exclusive and exhaustive categories (such as sex or blood group) is recorded, it is possible to construct a **crosstabulation**, or **contingency table** (see Chapter 3, Section 3.7.2). In the analysis of **categorical data** (that is nominal assignments or assignments to ordered categories), the crosstabulation is the equivalent of the scatterplot. Note that the categories of each variable must be mutually exclusive: no individual or case can be in more than one combination of categories.

In SPSS, crosstabulations are handled by the **Crosstabs** command, which is found in the **Analyze** drop-down menu, in **Descriptive Statistics**. In the **Crosstabs** dialog box, there is a **Statistics** subdialog box containing check boxes for several measures of association (Figure 12).

In **Crosstabs**, the correct choice from the available statistics depends upon whether the data in the table are nominal or ordinal. We have seen that for ordinal categorical data, Kendall's statistics are applicable. For nominal data, there are statistics based on the familiar **chi-square** statistic χ^2, which is used for determining the presence of an association between two qualitative variables. The rejection of H_0 by means of chi-square, however, only establishes the **existence** of a statistical association: it does not measure its **strength**. In fact, the chi-square statistic is unsuitable as a **measure** of association, because it is affected by the total frequency.

A word of warning about the misuse of chi-square should be given here. It is important to realise that the calculated statistic is only **approximately** distributed as the theoretical chi-square distribution: the greater the expected frequencies, the better the approximation, hence the rule about minimum expected frequencies, which is stated later in this Section. It is also important to note that the use of the chi-square statistic requires that **each individual studied contributes to the count in only one cell in the crosstabulation**. There are several other potential problems the user should be aware of. A lucid account of the rationale and assumptions of the chi-square test is given by Howell (1997), and a survey of the errors and misconceptions about chi-square that abound in the research literature is given by Delucchi (1983).

Several measures of strength of association for nominal data have been proposed (see Reynolds, 1984). An ideal measure should mimic the correlation coefficient by having a maximum absolute value of 1 for perfect association, and a value of 0 for no association. The choice of the appropriate statistic depends on whether the contingency table is 2×2 (each variable has two categories) or larger. Guidance can be found by clicking the **Help** box and choosing the various statistics in turn to find the most appropriate one. One such statistic, for example, is the **phi coefficient** ϕ, obtained by dividing the value of chi-square by the total frequency and taking the square root. For two-way contingency tables involving variables with more than two categories, another statistic, known as **Cramér's V**, is preferred because with more complex tables, Cramér's measure can still, as in the 2×2 case, achieve its maximum value of unity. Other measures of association, such as **Goodman & Kruskal's lambda**, measure the proportional reduction in error achieved when membership of a category on one attribute is used to predict category membership on the other.

A 2× 2 contingency table

Suppose that 50 boys and 50 girls are individually asked to select toys from a cupboard. The available toys have previously been categorised as mechanical or non-mechanical. The hypothesis is that the boys prefer mechanical toys, and the girls non-mechanical toys. There are two grouping variables here: Group (Boys or Girls); and Children's Choice (Mechanical or Non-Mechanical). The null hypothesis (H_0) is that there is no association between the variables. Table 3 shows the children's choices.

Table 3. Children's choice of toys			
Group	Children's Choice		Total
	Mechanical	Non-Mechanical	
Boys	30	20	50
Girls	15	35	50
Total	45	55	100

From inspection of this 2×2 contingency table, it would appear that there is an association between the Group and Choice variables: the majority of the Boys did, in fact, choose Mechanical toys, whereas the majority of the Girls chose Non-Mechanical toys.

Procedure for crosstabulation and associated statistics (chi-square, phi and Cramér's V)

The SPSS data set for a contingency table must include two grouping variables to identify the various cell counts, one representing the rows (*group*), the other the columns (*choice*), together with a variable for the cell counts (*count*).

- In **Variable View**, name the variables *group*, *choice*, and *count*.
- In the **Values** column, define the values and labels for the two grouping variables. For the *group* variable, assign the code numbers 1 and 2 to Boys and Girls, respectively. For the *choice* variable, assign the numbers 1 and 2 to Mechanical and Non-Mechanical toys, respectively.
- Click the **Data View** tab to switch to **Data View** and enter the data into the three columns, as shown in Figure 7.

	group	choice	count
1	Boys	Mechanical	30
2	Boys	Non-mechanical	20
3	Girls	Mechanical	15
4	Girls	Non-mechanical	35

Figure 7. Data View showing the two grouping variables and the count of the children's choices

The next step is essential. Since the data in the *count* column represent cell frequencies of a variable (not values), SPSS must be informed of this by means of the **Weight Cases** item in the **Data** menu (Figure 8).

- Choose
  Data
    Weight Cases...
  to open the **Weight Cases** dialog box, a completed version of which is shown in Figure 9.

- Click the name of the variable that contains the weightings, *count*. Now click **Weight Cases by**, cancelling the default item **Do not weight cases**. Finally click ▶ to transfer *count* to the **Frequency Variable:** box.
- Click **OK.**

Figure 8. The Data menu, showing Weight Cases

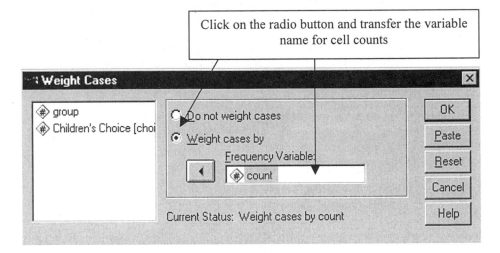

Figure 9. The Weight Cases dialog box for the variable *count*

To analyse the contingency table data, proceed as follows:
- Choose
  Analyze
    Descriptive Statistics
        Crosstabs... (Figure 10)
to open the **Crosstabs** dialog box. The completed version is shown in Figure 11.

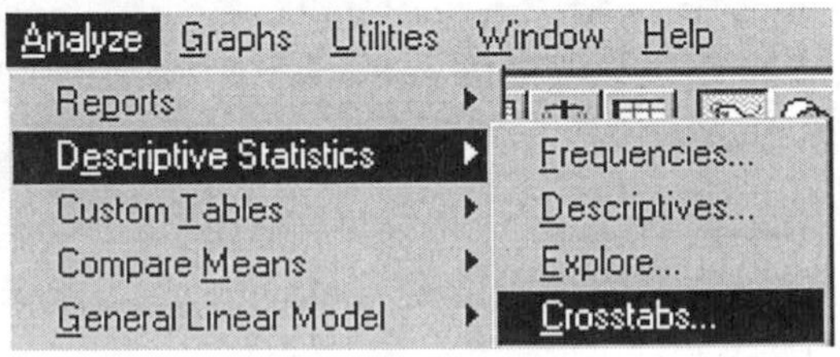

Figure 10. Finding Crosstabs in the Analyze menu

- Transfer the variable names, as shown in Figure 11.

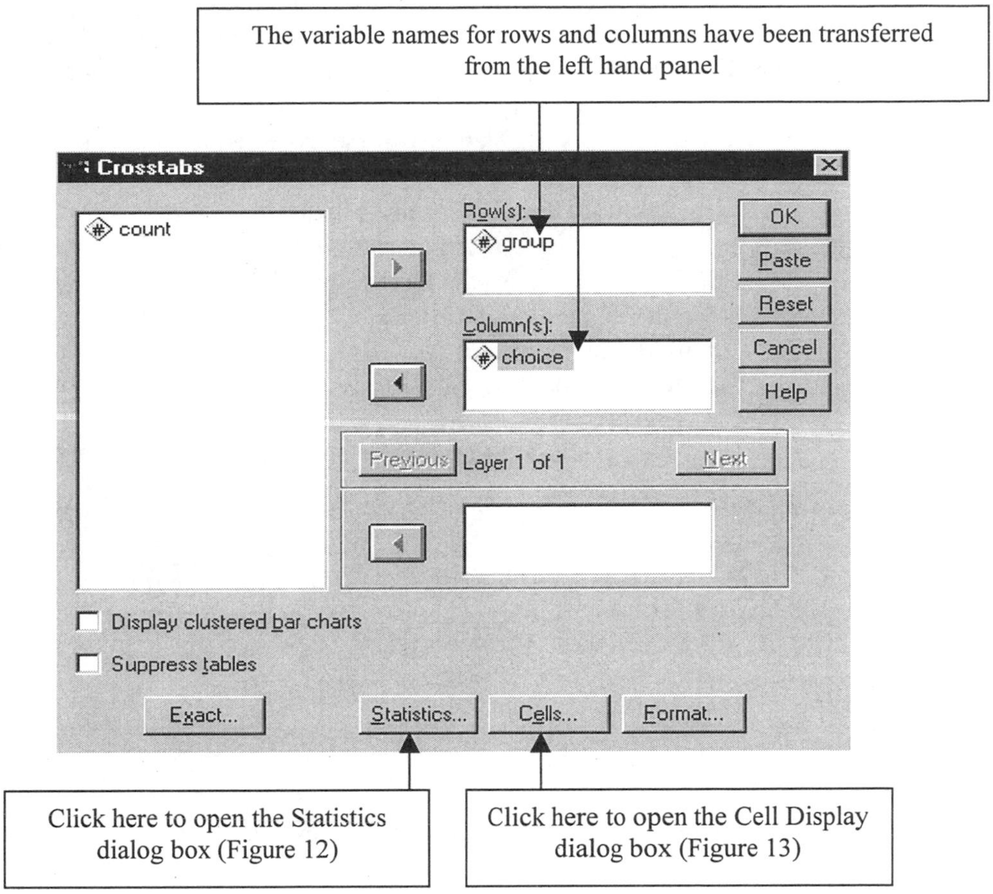

The variable names for rows and columns have been transferred from the left hand panel

Click here to open the Statistics dialog box (Figure 12)

Click here to open the Cell Display dialog box (Figure 13)

Figure 11. The Crosstabs dialog box for group in the rows and choice in the columns

- Click **Statistics...** to open the **Crosstabs: Statistics** dialog box (Figure 12) and select the statistics shown. Click **Continue**.

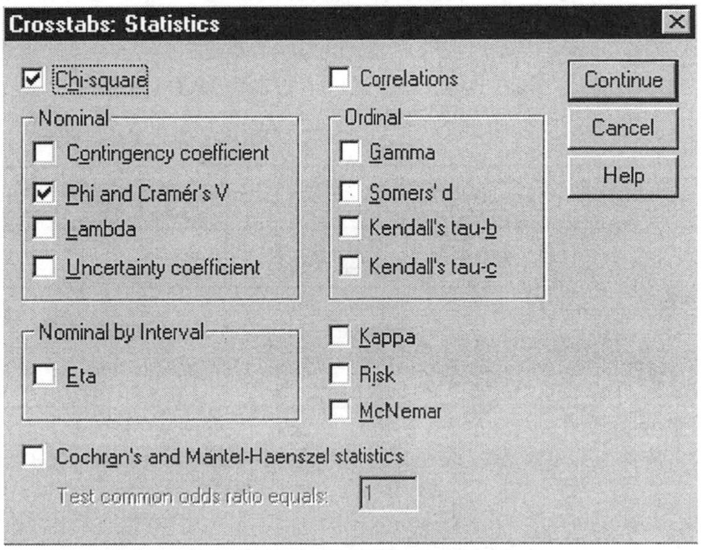

Figure 12. The Statistics dialog box with Chi-square and Phi and Cramér's V selected

We recommend an additional option for computing the expected cell frequencies. This enables the user to check that the prescribed minimum requirements for the valid use of chi-square have been fulfilled. Although there has been much debate about these, some leading authorities have proscribed the use of chi-square when:

(a)   in 2 × 2 tables, any of the expected frequencies is less than 5;

(b)   in larger tables, any of the expected frequencies is less than 1 or more than 20% are less than 5.

- Click **Cells...** to open the **Crosstabs: Cell Display** selection box (Figure 13). Select the **Expected** in **Counts** box to display the expected frequencies in the output. Click **Continue**.
- Finally click **OK**.

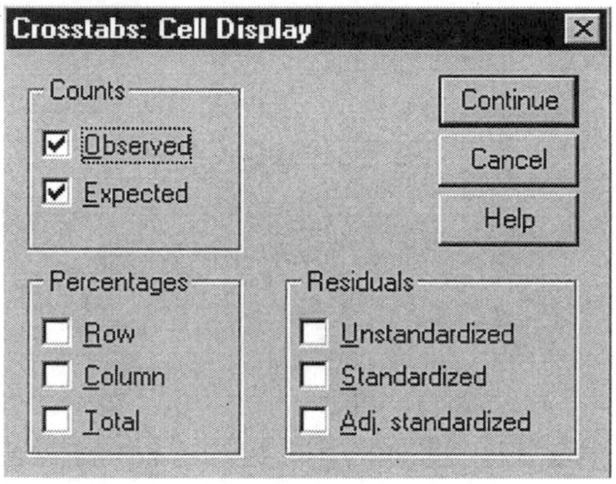

Figure 13. The Cell Display dialog box with Observed and Expected selected

Output for **Crosstabs** *and associated statistics (chi-square, phi and Cramér's V)*

In the **SPSS Viewer**, the output begins with a **Case Processing Summary** (which is not reproduced here) showing the number of valid cases used in the computation.

Output 4 displays the cross-tabulation (contingency) table, with the observed and expected frequencies, as requested in the **Crosstabs: Cell Display** dialog box. None of the expected frequencies is less than 5.

Crosstabs

GROUP * CHOICE Crosstabulation

			CHOICE		
			Mechanical	Non-mechanical	Total
GROUP	Boys	Count	30	20	50
		Expected Count	22.5	27.5	50.0
	Girls	Count	15	35	50
		Expected Count	22.5	27.5	50.0
Total		Count	45	55	100
		Expected Count	45.0	55.0	100.0

Output 4. The contingency table including the optional expected values

Output 5 shows the requested chi-square statistic, together with other statistics similar in purpose to the basic Pearson chi-square. The row labelled **Pearson Chi-Square** contains the conventional chi-square statistic, with its tail probability under H_0, **Asymp. Sig. (2 sided)**. It can be concluded from the smallness of the p-value, that there is a significant association between the variables *group* and *choice*: chi-square is significant at the .01 level. This is written as:

$$\chi^2 = 9.09; \, df = 1; \, p < 0.01.$$

Value of chi-square and its associated p-value

Chi-Square Tests

	Value	df	Asymp. Sig. (2-sided)	Exact Sig. (2-sided)	Exact Sig. (1-sided)
Pearson Chi-Square	9.09[b]	1.00	.00		
Continuity Correction [a]	7.92	1.00	.00		
Likelihood Ratio	9.24	1.00	.00		
Fisher's Exact Test				.00	.00
Linear-by-Linear Association	9.00	1.00	.00		
N of Valid Cases	100.00				

a. Computed only for a 2x2 table

b. 0 cells (.0%) have expected count less than 5. The minimum expected count is 22.50.

Output 5. Statistics of a contingency table

Note b tells the user how many cells have an expected frequency of less than 5; but in this example, there is none. In the special case of a 2×2 table, **Fisher's Exact Test** can be used instead of chi-square when the expected frequencies are small.

The last item is a table (Output 6) giving the values of the **Phi coefficient** and **Cramér's V**. These provide a measure of the strength of the association rather like that of the Pearson correlation coefficient. These are written as:

$$\phi = 0.30; \, p < 0.01$$

$$\text{Cramér's V} = 0.30; \, p < 0.01$$

Symmetric Measures

		Value	Approx. Sig.
Nominal by Nominal	Phi	.30	.00
	Cramer's V	.30	.00
N of Valid Cases		100.00	

Output 6. The Phi and Cramér's V statistics for the contingency table

11.3.3 Finding the meaning of statistics in output tables

A table such as those in Output 5 may include items that are unfamiliar to the user. SPSS supplies notes explaining such items.

Suppose you want to learn more about **Fisher's Exact Test**. Double-click anywhere in the table to open the **SPSS Output Editor**. Now follow the steps shown in Output 7.

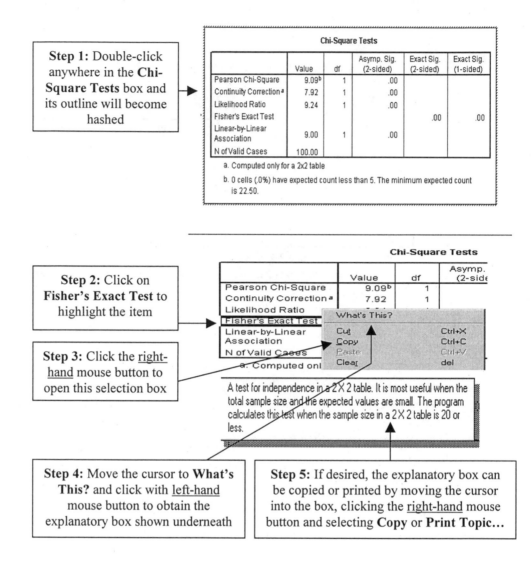

Step 1: Double-click anywhere in the **Chi-Square Tests** box and its outline will become hashed

Chi-Square Tests

	Value	df	Asymp. Sig. (2-sided)	Exact Sig. (2-sided)	Exact Sig. (1-sided)
Pearson Chi-Square	9.09[b]	1	.00		
Continuity Correction[a]	7.92	1	.00		
Likelihood Ratio	9.24	1	.00		
Fisher's Exact Test				.00	.00
Linear-by-Linear Association	9.00	1	.00		
N of Valid Cases	100.00				

a. Computed only for a 2x2 table

b. 0 cells (.0%) have expected count less than 5. The minimum expected count is 22.50.

Step 2: Click on **Fisher's Exact Test** to highlight the item

Step 3: Click the right-hand mouse button to open this selection box

Chi-Square Tests

	Value	df	Asymp. (2-side
Pearson Chi-Square	9.09[b]	1	
Continuity Correction[a]	7.92	1	
Likelihood Ratio			
Fisher's Exact Test			
Linear-by-Linear Association			
N of Valid Cases			

What's This?

Cut	Ctrl+X
Copy	Ctrl+C
Paste	Ctrl+V
Clear	del

A test for independence in a 2 X 2 table. It is most useful when the total sample size and the expected values are small. The program calculates this test when the sample size in a 2 X 2 table is 20 or less.

Step 4: Move the cursor to **What's This?** and click with left-hand mouse button to obtain the explanatory box shown underneath

Step 5: If desired, the explanatory box can be copied or printed by moving the cursor into the box, clicking the right-hand mouse button and selecting **Copy** or **Print Topic...**

Output 7. Discovering the meaning of an item in the output

EXERCISE 17

THE PEARSON CORRELATION

Before you start

Before starting to work through this practical exercise, we recommend that you read Chapter 11. The Pearson correlation *r* is one of the most widely used (and abused) of statistics. Despite its apparent simplicity and versatility, however, it is only too easy to misinterpret a correlation. The purpose of the present exercise is not only to show you how to use SPSS to obtain correlations, but also to illustrate how misleading a given value for *r* can sometimes be.

A famous data set

This exercise involves the analysis of four sets of paired data, which were contrived by Anscombe (1973). Each set yields exactly the same value for the **Pearson correlation**. The scatterplots, however, will show that in only one case are the data suitable for a Pearson correlation; in the others, the Pearson correlation gives a highly misleading impression of the relationship between the two variables. Ideally a scatterplot should indicate a **linear relationship** between the variables i.e. that all the points on the scatterplot lie along or near to a diagonal straight line as shown in the two left-hand plots in Chapter 11, Figure 1. Vertical or horizontal lines are not examples of linear relationships.

The data are presented in Table 1. The four sets we shall examine are *X1* with each of *Y1*, *Y2*, and *Y3*, and finally *X2* with *Y4*.

Participant	X1	Y1	Y2	Y3	X2	Y4
Table 1. Anscombe's four data sets						
1	10.0	8.04	9.14	7.46	8.0	6.58
2	8.0	6.95	8.14	6.77	8.0	5.76
3	13.0	7.58	8.74	12.74	8.0	7.71
4	9.0	8.81	8.77	7.11	8.0	8.84
5	11.0	8.33	9.26	7.81	8.0	8.47
6	14.0	9.96	8.10	8.84	8.0	7.04
7	6.0	7.24	6.13	6.08	8.0	5.25
8	4.0	4.26	3.10	5.39	19.0	12.50
9	12.0	10.84	9.13	8.15	8.0	5.56
10	7.0	4.82	7.26	6.42	8.0	7.91
11	5.0	5.68	4.74	5.73	8.0	6.89

Preparing the SPSS data set

After naming the first variable in **Variable View** as *case*, name the remaining variables as shown in the data table above. Ensure that the value in the **Decimals** column is 2. Switch to **Data View**, enter the data and save the set to a file called **anscombe**. (This file will be used again in Exercise 19.)

Exploring the data

Obtain scatterplots of the four data sets, as described in Section 11.2. These plots can be produced either one at a time by choosing **Simple** within the **Scatterplot** dialog box or, more dramatically, by selecting **Matrix**, which obtains a grid of scatterplots made up of all pairwise combinations of several variables. In the present exercise, however, we only want the plots of $Y1$, $Y2$ and $Y3$ against $X1$, and of $Y4$ against $X2$. Thus it is better to use **Matrix** for the plots with $X1$ and **Simple** for the plot with of $Y4$ against X2.

If the matrix scatterplot is selected and variables $X1$, $Y1$, $Y2$ and $Y3$ are transferred to the **Matrix Variables** box, only the first column of plots, (those with $X1$ on the horizontal axis), will be of interest.

- **What do you notice about the scatterplots in the first column? Which one is (in its present state) suitable for a subsequent calculation of a Pearson correlation? Describe what is wrong with each of the others**

Return to the **Graphs** menu, select **Scatter...** and **Simple**, and prepare a simple scatterplot of $Y4$ against $X2$ (see Section 4.3.3 or 11.2).

- **Is the plot suitable for a Pearson correlation?**

The plot of $Y1$ against $X1$ shows a substantial linear relationship between the variables. The thinness of the imaginary ellipse of points indicates that the **Pearson correlation** is likely to be high. This is the kind of data set for which the Pearson correlation gives an informative and accurate statement of the strength of linear relationship between two variables. The other plots, however, are very different: that of $Y2$ against $X1$ shows a perfect, but clearly non-linear, relationship; $Y3$ against $X1$ shows a basically linear relationship, which is marred by a glaring outlier; $Y4$ against $X2$ shows a column of points with a single outlier up in the top right corner.

Obtaining the Pearson correlations corresponding to the four scatterplots

Using the procedure described in Section 11.2.1, obtain the correlations between X and Y for the four sets of paired data. This is most easily done by entering the variables $X1$, $Y1$, $Y2$, $Y3$ in the first run of the command so as to get a correlation matrix, and then $X2$ and $Y4$ in the second run.

- **What do you notice about the value of r for each of the correlations?**

Anscombe's data strikingly illustrate the need to inspect the data carefully to ascertain the suitability of statistics such as the Pearson correlation.

Removing the outliers

It will be instructive to recalculate the **Pearson correlation** for the data set $(X1, Y3)$ when the values for Participant 3 have been removed. The outlier is the value *12.74* on the variable $Y3$. Use the **Select Cases...** command to select all participants except Participant 3.

Return to the **Scatterplot** and **Bivariate Correlations** dialog boxes for $X1$ and $Y3$ (ignore the other variables) to re-run these commands using the selected cases. Check that in the listing, only 10 rather than 11 cases have been used. You should find that the Pearson correlation for $X1$ and $Y3$ is now +1, which is what we would expect from the appearance of the scatterplot.

Conclusion

This exercise has demonstrated the value of exploring the data first before calculating statistics such as the **Pearson correlation**. While it is true that Anscombe's data were contrived to give his message greater force, there have been many misuses of the Pearson correlation with real data sets, where the problems created by the presence of outliers and by basically non-linear relationships are quite common.

Finishing the session

Close down SPSS and any other windows before logging out.

EXERCISE 18

OTHER MEASURES OF ASSOCIATION

Before you start

Please read Section 11.3 before proceeding with this practical exercise. The **Pearson correlation** was, devised to measure a supposed linear association between quantitative variables. There are other kinds of data (ordinal and nominal), to which the Pearson correlation is inapplicable. Moreover, even with data in the form of measurements, there may be considerations that vitiate the use of the Pearson correlation. Fortunately, other statistical measures of strength of association have been devised and in this exercise, we shall consider some statistics that are applicable to ordinal and nominal data.

ORDINAL DATA

The Spearman rank correlation

Suppose that two judges each rank ten paintings, A, B, ..., J. Their decisions are shown in Table 1.

	Best									Worst
First Judge	C	E	F	G	H	J	I	B	D	A
Second Judge	C	E	G	F	J	H	I	A	D	B

Table 1. The ranks assigned to the same ten objects by two judges

It is obvious from this table that the judges generally agree closely in their rankings: at most, the ranks they assign to a painting differ by two ranks. But how can their level of agreement be measured? The information in this table can be expressed in terms of numerical ranks by assigning the counting numbers from 1 to 10 to the paintings in their order of ranking by the first judge, and pairing each of these ranks with the rank that the same painting received from the other judge, as shown in Table 2.

Painting	C	E	F	G	H	J	I	B	D	A
Table 2. A numerical representation of the orderings by the two judges in Table 1											
First Judge	1	2	3	4	5	6	7	8	9	10
Second Judge	1	2	4	3	6	5	7	10	9	8

This is not the only way of representing the judgements numerically. It is also possible to list the objects (in any order) and pair the ranks assigned by the two judges to each object, entering two sets of ranks as before. Where the measurement of agreement is concerned, however, the two methods give exactly the same result.

Preparing the SPSS data set

In **Variable View**, name two variables, *judge1* and *judge2*, and set the value in the **Decimals** column to 0. Switch to **Data View** and enter the ranks assigned by the judges into the two columns. Save the data, because they will be used again later.

Obtaining the Spearman correlation coefficient

Select **Correlate** and then **Bivariate...** from the **Analyze** menu to open the **Bivariate Correlations** dialog box. Transfer the variables to the **Variables** box and select the **Spearman** check box (leave on the default **Pearson** check box). Click **OK** to obtain the **Pearson correlation** and the **Spearman correlation.**

- **How closely do the judges agree (state the value of the Spearman correlation coefficient)?**

- **What do you notice about the values of the two coefficients?**

Use of the Spearman rank correlation where there is a monotonic, but non-linear, relationship

Table 3 shows a set of paired interval data. On inspecting the scatterplot, we see that there is a **monotonic relationship** between the two variables: that is, as X increases, so does Y. On the other hand, the relationship between X and Y is clearly non-linear (in fact, $Y = \log_2 X$), and the use of the **Pearson correlation** is therefore inadvisable.

Table 3. A set of paired interval data showing a monotonic, but non-linear, relationship							
Y	1.00	1.58	2.00	2.32	2.58	2.81	3.00
X	2.00	3.00	4.00	5.00	6.00	7.00	8.00

Save the data from Table 2 (they will be needed later). To prepare a new data set (from Table 3) in a fresh file, enter the **File** drop-down menu, select **New** and then **Data** from the rightmost menu. Name the new variables in **Variable View** and enter the values into **Data View**. Obtain the **scatterplot** and compute the **Pearson** and **Spearman** correlation coefficients.

Describe the shape of the scatterplot and write down the values of the two correlation coefficients. Since there is a perfect (but non-linear) relationship between X and Y, the degree of association is understated by the Pearson correlation coefficient.

- **Which value of r is the truer expression of the strength of the relationship between X and Y?**

Kendall's correlation coefficients

The association between variables in paired ordinal data sets (or in paired measurements) can also be investigated by using one of **Kendall's correlation** coefficients, **tau-a**, **tau-b** or **tau-c** (see Section 11.3.1). (When there are no tied observations, **tau-a** and **tau-b** have the same value.) With large data sets, **Kendall's** and **Pearson's** coefficients give rather similar values and tail probabilities. When the data are scarce, however, Kendall's statistics are better behaved, especially when there is a substantial proportion of tied observations, and more reliance can be placed upon the Kendall tail probability. Kendall's correlations really come into their own when the data are assignments to predetermined ordered categories (rating scales and so on).

There are two ways of obtaining **Kendall's correlations** in SPSS:
- (1) In the **Bivariate Correlations** dialog box, mark the **Kendall's tau-b** checkbox.
- (2) Use the **Crosstabs** command (see Section 11.3.2).

(1)   Use the **Bivariate Correlations** command to obtain **Kendall's tau-b** (there are no ties) for the data in Table 3. Now do the same with the data set saved from Table 2.

- **Write down the values of tau-b and compare them with your previously obtained coefficient values.**

(2)   With the restored Table 2 data set, use the **Crosstabs** command to obtain Kendall's correlations. Note that in this application, there is no variable such as *count* and hence no need for **Weight Cases...**. Enter *judge1* in **Row(s):** and *judge2* in **Column(s):**. Click the **Statistics...** button to open the **Crosstabs: Statistics** dialog box and select the checkboxes for **Correlations**, **Kendall's tau-b** and **Kendall's tau-c**. Click **Continue** and **OK** to run the correlations.

- **Write down the values of all the coefficients in the output and comment on any similarities and differences**

273

EXERCISE 19

THE ANALYSIS OF NOMINAL DATA

Before you start

Before proceeding with this practical, we strongly recommend you to read Section 3.7.2 (weighting of cases) and Section 11.3.2 (measures of association strength for nominal data) in Chapter 11.

THE CHI-SQUARE TEST OF GOODNESS-OF-FIT

Some nominal data on one qualitative variable

Suppose that a researcher, interested in children's preferences, expects a spatial response bias towards the right hand side. Thirty children enter a room containing three identically-marked doors: one to the right; another to the left; and a third straight ahead. They are told they can go through any of the three doors. Their choices are shown in Table 1.

Table 1. The choices of one of three exit doors by thirty children

Door		
Left	Centre	Right
5	8	17

It looks as if there is indeed a preference for the rightmost door, at least among the children sampled. Had the children been choosing at random, we should have expected about 10 in each category: that is, the theoretical, or expected distribution (E), of the tallies is **uniform**. The observed frequencies (O), on the other hand, have a distribution which is far from uniform.

Pearson's chi-square test can be used to test the goodness-of-fit of the expected to the observed distribution. Its rationale is lucidly discussed in any good statistics textbook (e.g. Howell, 1997). Here, we shall merely describe the SPSS procedure.

Preparing the data set

In **Variable View**, name the grouping variable *position* for the three positional categories and a second variable *freq* for the numbers of children in the different categories. To the three categories, assign the values *1*, *2*, and *3* and in the **Labels** column, enter the respective labels *Left*, *Centre,* and *Right*. Check that the values in the **Decimals** column are 0. Click the **Data View** tab and enter the data.

Weight cases

To ensure that SPSS treats the entries in *freq* as frequencies rather than scores, follow the procedure described in Section 3.12.2.

Run the Chi-square test

To obtain the correct dialog box, select

Analyze

> **Nonparametric Tests**

>> **Chi-Square…**

to open the **Chi-Square Test** dialog box. Click *position* (not on *freq*) and on ▶ to transfer *position* to the **Test Variable List:** box. Click **OK** to run the command.

- **Write down the value of the chi-square statistic and its p-value. Is chi-square significant? Write down the implications for the experimenter's research hypothesis.**

Running the goodness-of-fit test on a set of raw data

When the researcher carried out the experiment, the door that each child chose was noted at the time. In terms of the code numbers, their choices might have been:

$$1\ 1\ 3\ 2\ 1\ 1\ 3\ 3\ 3\ ,\ ...,\ \text{and so on.}$$

If the user defines the variable *position*, and enters the 30 (coded) choices that the children made, the chi-square test is then run directly: there is no weighting of cases.

THE CHI-SQUARE TEST OF ASSOCIATION BETWEEN TWO QUALITATIVE VARIABLES

The reader should study Section 11.3.2 before doing this part of the exercise.

An experiment on children's choices

Suppose that a researcher, having watched a number of children enter a room and recorded each child's choice between two objects, wants to know whether there is a tendency for boys and girls to choose different objects. This question concerns two variables: *sex* and *choice*. In statistical terms, the researcher is asking whether they are associated: do more girls than boys choose one of the objects and more boys than girls choose the other object? Suppose that the children's choices are as in Table 2.

Table 2. Choices by 50 children of one of two objects		
Object	**Boys**	**Girls**
A	20	5
B	6	19

Command for the chi-square test of association between two variables

Prepare a new data set from Table 2. In **Variable View**, name the variables *object* and *sex*, assigning code numbers and explanatory labels in the usual way. Name a third variable *freq*.

The use of the **Crosstabs** command is fully described in Section 11.3.2. We recommend the inclusion of expected frequencies (using the **Cells...** option), so that you can check for the presence of cells with unacceptably low expected frequencies (see Section 11.3.2 for details).

Output for the chi-square test of association

The output is discussed in Section 11.3.2. Three tables are presented: the first is a Case Processing Summary table showing how many valid cases have been processed; the second is a Crosstabulation table with the observed and expected frequencies in each cell, along with row and column totals; and the third is a table (headed Chi-square Tests) listing various statistics, together with their associated significance levels.

- **Write down the value of the Pearson chi-square and its associated tail probability (p-value). Is it significant? In terms of the experimental hypothesis, what has this test shown?**

MEASURES OF ASSOCIATION STRENGTH
FOR NOMINAL DATA

So far we have considered the use of the **chi-square statistic** to test for the presence of an association between two qualitative variables. Recall that, provided that the data are suitable, the **Pearson correlation** measures the strength of a linear association between two interval variables. In that case, therefore, the same statistic serves both as a test for the presence of an association and as a measure of associative strength. It might be thought that, with nominal data, the chi-square statistic would serve the same dual function. The chi-square statistic, however, cannot serve as a satisfactory measure of associative strength, because its value depends partly upon the total frequency.

To illustrate the calculation of measures of association for two-way contingency tables, we shall use again the data of choice of objects by children. Run the **Crosstabs** command again but this time deselect **Chi-square** and select instead **Phi and Cramér's V** within the **Nominal** box of the **Crosstabs: Statistics** dialog box. The output consists of three tables: the first is a Case Processing Summary table, the second is a Crosstabulation table, and the third is a table called Symmetric Measures listing the values of Phi and Cramér's V together with their associated significance levels.

- **Write down the value of Phi for the strength of the association between the qualitative variables of Gender and Object.**

Finishing the session

Close down SPSS and any other windows before logging out of the computer.

CHAPTER 12

REGRESSION

12.1 INTRODUCTION

Much of Chapter 11 was devoted to the use of the **Pearson correlation** to measure the strength of the association between two measured quantitative variables.

But the associative coin has two sides. On the one hand, a single number can be calculated (a correlation coefficient) which expresses the **strength** of the association. On the other, however, there is a set of techniques, known as **regression methods**, which utilise the presence of an association between two variables to predict the values of one (the dependent variable) from those of another (the independent variable). It is with this predictive aspect that the present chapter is concerned.

12.1.1 Simple, two-variable regression

In **simple, two-variable regression**, the values of one variable (the dependent variable, y) are estimated from those of another (the independent variable, x) by a linear (straight line) **regression equation** of the general form

$$y' = b_0 + b_1(x),$$

where y' is the estimated value of y, b_1 is the slope (known as the **regression coefficient**), and b_0 is the intercept (known as the **regression constant**).

12.1.2 Multiple regression

In **multiple regression**, the values of one variable (the dependent variable y) are estimated from those of two or more other variables (the independent variables $x_1, x_2, \ldots, x_p$).

This is achieved by the construction of a linear **multiple regression equation** of the general form

$$y' = b_0 + b_1(x_1) + b_2(x_2) + \ldots + b_p(x_p),$$

where the parameters b_1, b_2, ..., b_p are the partial **regression coefficients** and the intercept b_0 is the **regression constant**. This equation is known as the **multiple linear regression equation of y upon $x_1, \ldots, x_p$**.

12.1.3 Residuals

When a regression equation is used to estimate the values of a variable y from those of one or more independent variables x, the estimates y' will usually fall short of complete accuracy. Geometrically speaking, the data points will not fall precisely upon the straight line, plane or hyperplane specified by the regression equation. The discrepancies $(y - y')$ on the predicted variable are known as **residuals**. When using regression methods, the study of the residuals is of great importance, because they form the basis for measures of the accuracy of the estimates and of the extent to which the **regression model** gives a good account of the data in question. (See Tabachnick & Fidell, 1996, for advice on **regression diagnostics**.)

12.1.4 The multiple correlation coefficient

One simple (though rather limited) measure of the efficacy of regression for the prediction of y is the Pearson correlation between the true values of the target variable y and the estimates y' obtained by substituting the corresponding values of x into the regression equation. The correlation between y and y' is known as the **multiple correlation coefficient R**. Notice that the upper case is used for the multiple correlation coefficient, to distinguish it from the correlation between the target variable and any one independent variable considered separately. It can be shown algebraically that the multiple correlation coefficient cannot have a negative value, even if there is only one independent variable correlating negatively with the dependent variable, in which case R has the absolute value of r.

12.2 SIMPLE REGRESSION

Among North American university authorities, there is much concern about the efficacy of the methods used to select students for entry. How closely are scores on the entrance tests and exam results associated? How accurately can one predict university performance from students' marks on the entrance tests?

Given data on students' final exam marks and their performance on the entrance test, a Pearson correlation can be used to measure the degree of statistical association between the two. It is also possible to use simple regression to predict exam performance at university from marks in the entrance test. It can be shown by mathematical proof, however, that when two or more independent variables are used to predict the target variable y, the predictions will, on average, be **at least as accurate** as when any one of the same independent variables is used. In other words, the multiple correlation coefficient R must be at least as great as any single Pearson correlation r. For the moment, however, we shall be considering the simple regression of university exam results upon the marks in one entrance test alone.

12.2.1 Procedure for simple regression

In Table 1, the score *fin* is a student's mark in the final university exam, and the score *ent* is the same student's mark in the entrance test. Table 1 contains the marks of 34 students: Student 1 (whose data are in the first row of the first two columns from the left) got 44 in the entrance test and 38 in the university exam. Student 34, on the other hand, (whose data are shown in the sixth row of the last two columns on the right), got 49 in the entrance test and 195 in the university exam.

Table 1. Table of the final university exam (fin) and the entrance exam (ent) scores

case	fin	ent	case	fin	ent	case	fin	ent	case	fin	ent
1	38	44	10	81	53	19	105	43	28	142	56
2	49	40	11	86	47	20	106	55	29	145	60
3	61	43	12	91	45	21	107	48	30	150	55
4	65	42	13	94	41	22	112	49	31	152	54
5	69	44	14	95	39	23	114	46	32	164	58
6	73	46	15	98	40	24	114	41	33	169	62
7	74	34	16	100	37	25	117	49	34	195	49
8	76	37	17	100	48	26	125	63			
9	78	41	18	103	48	27	140	52			

Preparing the SPSS data set

See Section 3.2

Using the techniques described in Chapter 3, Section 3.2, enter **Variable View** and name the variables *case*, *finalex* and *selectex*. In the **Label** column, add more informative names such as Case Number, University Exam and Entrance Exam. In **Data View**, enter the data in the labelled columns.

Exploring the data

Usually the user would explore the data for incorrect transcriptions and detect any outliers by examining the scatterplot. Here, for the sake of brevity, we shall proceed directly with the regression analysis and let the regression procedure itself find any problem cases.

Accessing simple regression
- Choose
    Analyze
        Regression (Figure 1)
    and click **Linear** to open the **Linear Regression** dialog box (the completed dialog box is shown in Figure 2).

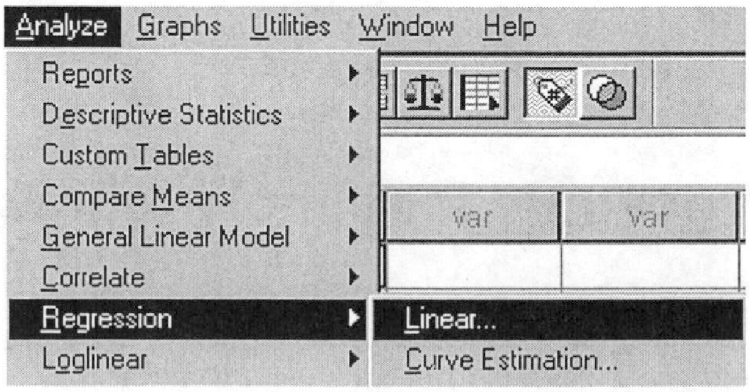

Figure 1. Finding the Linear Regression procedure

- Transfer the variable names as shown in Figure 2, taking care to select the appropriate variable names for the dependent independent variables.

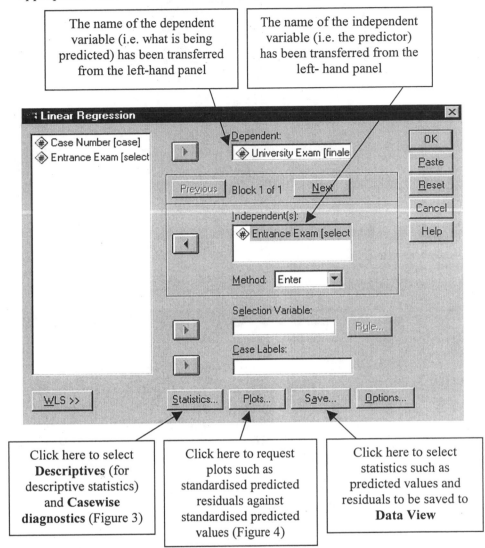

The name of the dependent variable (i.e. what is being predicted) has been transferred from the left-hand panel

The name of the independent variable (i.e. the predictor) has been transferred from the left- hand panel

Click here to select **Descriptives** (for descriptive statistics) and **Casewise diagnostics** (Figure 3)

Click here to request plots such as standardised predicted residuals against standardised predicted values (Figure 4)

Click here to select statistics such as predicted values and residuals to be saved to **Data View**

Figure 2. The Linear Regression dialog box

- It is recommended that the user request additional descriptive statistics and a residuals analysis. Click **Statistics...** to open the **Linear Regression: Statistics** dialog box (Figure 3) and click the **Descriptives** checkbox. Analysis of the residuals gives a measure of how good the prediction is and whether there are any cases that are so discrepant as to be considered outliers and dropped from the analysis. Click the **Casewise diagnostics** checkbox to obtain a listing of any exceptionally large residuals. Click **Continue** to return to the **Linear Regression** dialog box.

- Since systematic patterns between the predicted values and the residuals can indicate possible violations of the assumption of linearity, we recommend that a plot of the standardised residuals (*ZRESID*) against the standardised predicted values (*ZPRED*) also be requested. Click **Plots...** to open the **Linear Regression: Plots** dialog box (Figure 4) and transfer *ZRESID* to the **Y:** box and *ZPRED* to the **X:** box. Click **Continue** to return to the **Linear Regression** dialog box.

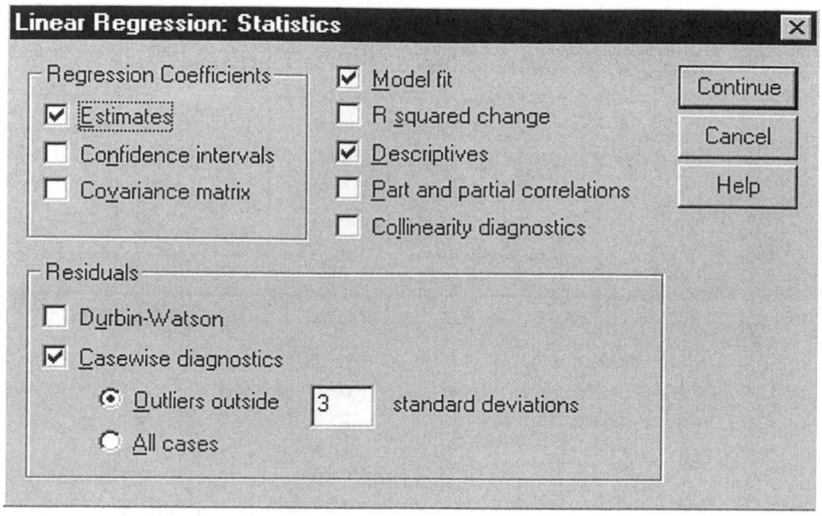

Figure 3. The Statistics dialog box with Estimates, Model fit, Descriptives and Casewise diagnostics selected

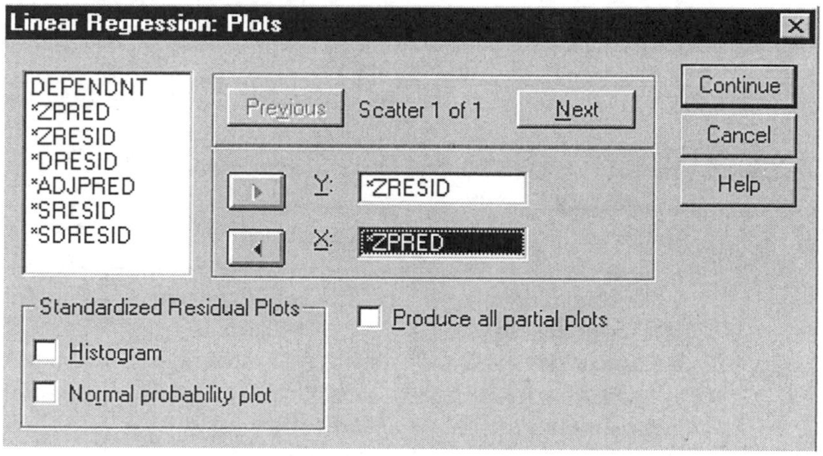

Figure 4. The Plots dialog box with *ZRESID (standardised residuals) and *ZPRED (standardised predicted scores) selected for the axes of the plot

- If desired, values of statistics such as predicted values or residuals can be saved to **Data View** by clicking **Save...** and selecting the desired statistics from the dialog box. Click **Continue** to return to the **Linear Regression** dialog box.
- Click **OK**.

12.2.2 Output for simple regression

The various tables and charts in the output are listed in the left-hand pane of **SPSS Viewer**, as shown in Output 1. The first table to scrutinise is **Casewise Diagnostics**. The information it contains may indicate that the regression analysis should be aborted and re-run after such outliers have been removed from the data set. The table can be selected directly by moving the cursor to

Casewise Diagnostics in the left-hand pane and clicking the left-hand mouse button.

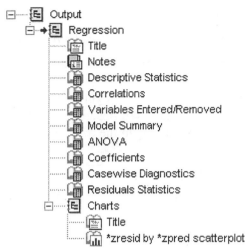

Output 1. The left-hand pane of SPSS Viewer, listing the tables and charts in the right-hand pane

Indication of residual outliers

The table of cases (**Casewise Diagnostics**) in Output 2 shows only one outlier with an absolute standardised residual greater than 3. This is Case 34, with a score of *195* for University Exam *(finalex)*. The next section describes how to eliminate this outlier and re-run the regression analysis.

Casewise Diagnostics [a]

Case Number	Std. Residual	University Exam	Predicted Value	Residual
34	3.12	195.00	110.95	84.05

[a]. Dependent Variable: University Exam

Output 2. A list of cases (Casewise Diagnostics) with residuals greater than ± 3 standard deviations

Elimination of outliers

See Section 3.7.1

A more reliable regression analysis can be obtained by eliminating outliers using the **Select Cases** procedure described in Section 3.7.1.

- Choose
  Data
    Select Cases...
  to open the **Select Cases** dialog box.
- Click the **If condition is satisfied** radio button and define the condition as *case ~=34* (the symbol ~= means 'not equal to'.)
- Click **Continue** and then **OK** to deselect this case.

If there are several outliers, it might be simpler to deselect using a cut-off value for one of the variables (e.g. defining the condition with an inequality operator such as *finalex* < 190). Sometimes, in order to see what value to use in the inequality, it is convenient to arrange scores in order of value by entering the **Data** menu and choosing **Sort Cases...** .

Output for simple regression after elimination of the outliers

When the regression analysis is re-run after deleting the original output, there will be no table of **Casewise Diagnostics**, since no cases will now have outlying residuals. We can therefore begin with the various regression tables and plots. In Output 3, are the tables of descriptive statistics and the correlation coefficient for the 33 cases remaining in the data set.

Descriptive Statistics

	Mean	Std. Deviation	N
University Exam	102.82	32.63	33
Entrance Exam	47.27	7.54	33

Correlations

		University Exam	Entrance Exam
Pearson Correlation	University Exam	1.00	.73
	Entrance Exam	.73	1.00
Sig. (1-tailed)	University Exam	.	.00
	Entrance Exam	.00	.
N	University Exam	33.00	33.00
	Entrance Exam	33.00	33.00

Output 3. The descriptive statistics and correlation coefficient for the original data set minus the outlier

Output 4 gives the value for **Multiple R** which, in the case of just one independent variable, has the same value as the correlation coefficient *r* listed in Output 3. (Had r been negative, R would have had the same value, minus the sign.)

The other statistics listed are **R Square** (a positively biased estimate of the proportion of the variance of the dependent variable accounted for by regression), **Adjusted R Square** (which corrects this bias and therefore has a lower value), and **Standard Error** (the standard deviation of the residuals).

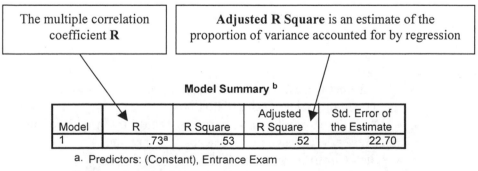

The multiple correlation coefficient **R**	**Adjusted R Square** is an estimate of the proportion of variance accounted for by regression

Model Summary [b]

Model	R	R Square	Adjusted R Square	Std. Error of the Estimate
1	.73[a]	.53	.52	22.70

a. Predictors: (Constant), Entrance Exam

b. Dependent Variable: University Exam

Output 4. The values of Multiple R and other statistics

Output 5 shows the regression ANOVA, which tests for a linear relationship between the variables. The F statistic is the ratio of the mean square for regression to the residual mean square. In this example, the value of F in the ANOVA Table is highly significant. **It should be noted, however, that only an examination of the scatterplot of the variables can confirm that the relationship between two variables is genuinely linear.**

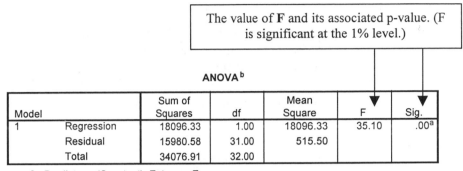

ANOVA[b]

Model		Sum of Squares	df	Mean Square	F	Sig.
1	Regression	18096.33	1.00	18096.33	35.10	.00[a]
	Residual	15980.58	31.00	515.50		
	Total	34076.91	32.00			

a. Predictors: (Constant), Entrance Exam

b. Dependent Variable: University Exam

Output 5. The ANOVA for the regression

Output 6 presents the kernel of the regression analysis, the regression equation. The values of the **regression coefficient** and **constant** are given in column **B** of the table.

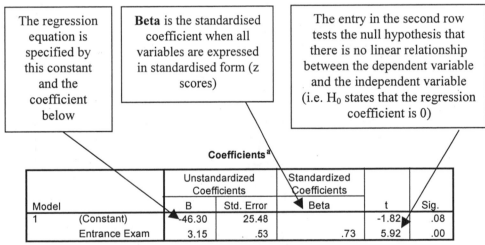

Coefficients[a]

Model		Unstandardized Coefficients		Standardized Coefficients		
		B	Std. Error	Beta	t	Sig.
1	(Constant)	-46.30	25.48		-1.82	.08
	Entrance Exam	3.15	.53	.73	5.92	.00

a. Dependent Variable: University Exam

Output 6. The regression equation and associated statistics

The equation is, therefore,

Predicted University Exam = - 46.30 + 3.15 × (Entrance Exam)

Thus a person with an Entrance Exam mark of 60 would be predicted to score

$$- 46.30 + 3.15 \times 60 = 142.7 \text{ (i.e., 143)}.$$

Notice from the data that the person who scored 60 on the entrance exam actually scored 145 on the University final exam. The residual is, therefore, 145-143 = +2.

Other statistics are also listed. The **Std. Error** is the standard error of the regression coefficient, B. **Beta** is the beta coefficient, which is the change in the dependent variable (expressed in standard deviation units) that would be produced by a positive increment of one standard deviation in the independent variable. (In multiple regression, beta coefficients are more comparable, since they are all in the same units.) The **t** statistic tests the regression coefficient for significance, and **Sig.** is the p-value of **t**. (Here .00 means <0.005, i.e. t is significant beyond the 0.01 level for the variable Entrance Exam).

Output 7 is a table of statistics relating to the residuals. The variable Predicted Value contains the unstandardised predicted values. The variable Residual contains the unstandardised residuals. The variable Std. Predicted Value (identified as *ZPRED* in the **Plots** dialog box in Figure 4) contains the standardised predicted values (i.e. Predicted Value transformed to a scale with mean 0 and SD 1). The variable Std. Residual (identified as *ZRESID* in the **Plots** dialog box in Figure 4) contains the standardised residuals (i.e. Residuals standardised to a scale with mean 0 and SD 1).

Residuals Statistics [a]

	Minimum	Maximum	Mean	Std. Deviation	N
Predicted Value	60.95	152.43	102.82	23.78	33.00
Residual	-54.49	30.97	.00	22.35	33.00
Std. Predicted Value	-1.76	2.09	.00	1.00	33.00
Std. Residual	-2.40	1.36	.00	.98	33.00

a. Dependent Variable: University Exam

Output 7. Table of statistics relating to the residuals

Output 8 is the edited scatterplot of the standardised residuals (*ZRESID*) against the standardised predicted values (*ZPRED*).

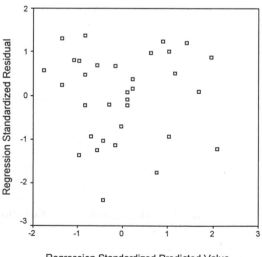

Regression Standardized Predicted Value

Output 8. Scatterplot of standardised residuals against standardised predicted scores

The plot shows no obvious pattern, thereby confirming that the assumptions of linearity and homogeneity of variance have been met. If the cloud of points were crescent-shaped or funnel-shaped, further screening of the data (or abandonment of the analysis) would be necessary.

Other diagnostic plots such as a histogram of the standardised residuals (ideally they should be distributed normally) and a cumulative normal probability plot (ideally the points should lie along or adjacent to the diagonal) could have been selected from within the **Standardized Residual Plots** box in Figure 4.

12.3 MULTIPLE REGRESSION

The process of constructing a linear equation that will predict the values of a target (dependent) variable from knowledge of specified values of a predictor (independent variable) can readily be extended to situations where we have data on two or more independent variables. The construction of a linear regression equation with two or more independent variables (or predictors) on the right hand side is known as **multiple regression**.

In Table 2, three extra variables, the subject's age, IQ, and the score obtained on a relevant academic project, have been added to the original variables in Table 1. The outlier that was detected in the preliminary regression analysis, however, has been removed.

Table 2. An extension of Table 1, with data on three additional independent variables

case	fin	ent	age	pro	iq	case	fin	ent	age	pro	iq
1	38	44	21.9	50	110	18	103	48	22.3	53	134
2	49	40	22.6	75	120	19	105	43	21.8	72	140
3	61	43	21.8	54	119	20	106	55	21.4	69	127
4	65	42	22.5	60	125	21	107	48	21.6	50	135
5	69	44	21.9	82	121	22	112	49	22.8	68	132
6	73	46	21.8	65	140	23	114	46	22.1	72	135
7	74	34	22.2	61	122	24	114	41	21.9	60	135
8	76	37	22.5	68	123	25	117	49	22.5	74	129
9	78	41	21.5	60	133	26	125	63	21.9	70	140
10	81	53	22.4	69	100	27	140	52	22.2	77	134
11	86	47	21.9	64	120	28	142	56	21.4	79	134
12	91	45	22.0	78	115	29	145	60	21.6	84	132
13	94	41	22.2	68	124	30	150	55	22.1	60	135
14	95	39	21.7	70	135	31	152	54	21.9	76	135
15	98	40	22.2	65	132	32	164	58	23.0	84	149
16	100	37	39.3	75	130	33	169	62	21.2	65	135
17	100	48	21.0	65	128						

In the following discussion, we shall be concerned with two main questions:
   (1)   Does the addition of more independent variables improve the accuracy of predictions of *finalex*?
   (2)   Of these new variables, are some more useful than others for prediction of the dependent variable?

We shall see that the answer to the first question is 'Yes'. The second question, however, is problematic, and none of the available approaches to it is entirely satisfactory.

Darlington (1968) drew attention to some widespread misunderstandings among users of multiple regression, particularly upon the thorny problem of how to say which of the independent variables in a multiple regression equation is the most 'important', or 'useful' in accounting for variability in the dependent variable. (For a non-technical treatment, see Cohen & Cohen, 1983.) There are many problems; but most of them can be summed up in a well-known aphorism: **Correlation does not imply causation**. In a situation where everything correlates with everything else, **it is quite impossible to attribute variance in the dependent variable unequivocally to any one independent variable**.

In a multiple regression equation, the coefficients of the independent variables are known as **partial regression coefficients**. A partial regression coefficient is the increase in the dependent variable that would be produced by a positive increase of one unit in the independent variable, the effects of the other independent variables, both on the independent variable and the dependent variable, being supposedly held constant. Such **statistical control**, however, is no substitute for true **experimental** control, where the independent variable, having been manipulated by the experimenter, really is independent of the dependent variable.

In this section, we shall consider two approaches to multiple regression, neither of which is entirely satisfactory. In **simultaneous** multiple regression, all the available independent variables are entered in the equation directly. In **stepwise** multiple regression, the independent variables are added to (or taken away from) the equation one at a time, the order of entry (or removal) being determined by statistical considerations. Despite the appeal of the second approach, however, there is the disconcerting fact that the addition of another 'independent' variable can completely change the apparent contributions of the other predictors to the variance of scores on the dependent variable.

Constructing the SPSS data set

Using the techniques described in Section 3.5, restore the original data set (minus the outliers) to **Data View**. In **Variable View**, name the three new variables (e.g. *age*, *project* and *iq*). Use the **Label** column to assign a variable label such as Project Mark. Now enter the scores in **Data View**. The first three cases are shown in Figure 5.

	case	finalex	selectex	age	project	iq
1	1	38	44	21.9	50	110
2	2	49	40	22.6	75	120
3	3	61	43	21.8	54	119

Figure 5. The first three cases in Data View

12.3.1 Procedure for simultaneous multiple regression

- In the **Linear Regression** dialog box, transfer the variable name University Exam [*finalex*] into the **Dependent Variable:** and Entrance Exam [*selectex*], Age [*age*], Project Mark [*project*] and IQ [*iq*] into the **Independent Variables:** box.
- Select the other optional items as in Section 12.2.1.
- Click **OK**.

Output for simultaneous multiple regression

The first table in the output is a table of the requested descriptive statistics for each variable (Output 9).

Descriptive Statistics

	Mean	Std. Deviation	N
University Exam	102.82	32.63	33
Entrance Exam	47.27	7.54	33
Age	22.518	3.046	33
Project Mark	67.94	9.14	33
IQ	129.03	9.66	33

Output 9. The descriptive statistics table

The next item is an edited table of correlations (Output 10) showing that the dependent variable University Exam correlates significantly with three of the independent variables but not with the fourth (Age).

Correlations

		University Exam
Pearson Correlation	University Exam	1.00
	Entrance Exam	.73
	Age	-.03
	Project Mark	.40
	IQ	.65
Sig. (1-tailed)	University Exam	.
	Entrance Exam	.00
	Age	.43
	Project Mark	.01
	IQ	.00

Output 10. Edited table of correlations

Output 11 lists the variables entered.

Variables Entered/Removed [b]

Model	Variables Entered	Variables Removed	Method
1	IQ, Age, Project Mark, Entrance Exam [a]	.	Enter

a. All requested variables entered.

b. Dependent Variable: University Exam

Output 11. List of variables entered, the dependent variable and the method of analysis

Output 12 shows that the multiple correlation coefficient (**R**) is 0.87 and the **Adjusted R Square** is 0.73.

Model Summary [b]

Model	R	R Square	Adjusted R Square	Std. Error of the Estimate
1	.87[a]	.76	.73	16.92

a. Predictors: (Constant), IQ, Age, Project Mark, Entrance Exam

b. Dependent Variable: University Exam

Output 12. Value of R and other statistics

Recall that when one independent variable (Entrance Exam) was used to predict University Exam (*finalex*), the value of R was 0.73 and Adjusted R Square (the estimate of the proportion of variance accounted for by regression) was 0.52 (52%). With R now at 0.87 and Adjusted R Square up from 52% to 73%, we see that the answer to the question of whether adding more independent variables improves the predictive power of the regression equation is certainly 'Yes'.

Not surprisingly, the ANOVA (Output 13) shows that the regression is still highly significant ($p < 0.01$).

ANOVA[b]

Model		Sum of Squares	df	Mean Square	F	Sig.
1	Regression	26059.63	4	6514.91	22.75	.00[a]
	Residual	8017.28	28	286.33		
	Total	34076.91	32			

a. Predictors: (Constant), IQ, Age, Project Mark, Entrance Exam

b. Dependent Variable: University Exam

Output 13. The ANOVA for regression

From column **B** in Output 14, we see that the multiple regression equation of University Exam (*finalex*) upon Entrance Exam (*selectex*), Age, Project Mark (*project*) and IQ (*iq*) is:

finalex' = **-272.13 + 2.49×(*selectex*) + 1.24×(*age*) + 0.50×(*project*) + 1.51×(*iq*)**

where *finalex'* is the predicted University Exam mark.

Thus a person aged 21.6 and scoring 60 on the Entrance Exam, 84 on the Project and having an IQ of 132 would have an estimated score of

$$-272.13 + 2.49 \times (60) + 1.24 \times (21.6) + 0.50 \times (84) + 1.51 \times (132) = 145.37$$

Notice that case 29, who meets these specifications, actually scored 145 in the University Exam. However not all cases have estimates so close to the actual values: for case 6, the estimate is 113.34, but the actual value is 73.

But what about the second question? Do all the new variables contribute substantially to the predictive power of the regression equation, or is one or more a passenger in the equation? We can learn little about the relative importance of the variables from the sizes of their regression coefficients (**B**). This is because the **values of the partial regression coefficients reflect the**

original units in which the variables were measured. For this reason, although the coefficient for *age* is larger than that for *project*, we cannot conclude that age is the more important predictor.

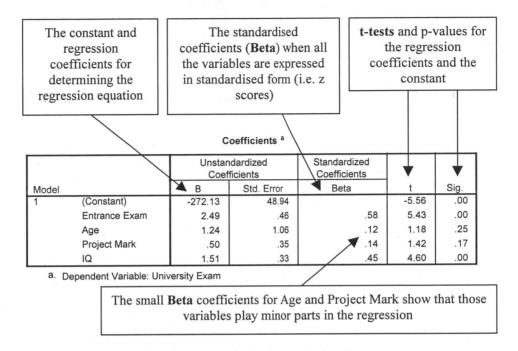

The constant and regression coefficients for determining the regression equation	The standardised coefficients (**Beta**) when all the variables are expressed in standardised form (i.e. z scores)	**t-tests** and p-values for the regression coefficients and the constant

Coefficients [a]

Model		Unstandardized Coefficients		Standardized Coefficients		
		B	Std. Error	Beta	t	Sig.
1	(Constant)	-272.13	48.94		-5.56	.00
	Entrance Exam	2.49	.46	.58	5.43	.00
	Age	1.24	1.06	.12	1.18	.25
	Project Mark	.50	.35	.14	1.42	.17
	IQ	1.51	.33	.45	4.60	.00

a. Dependent Variable: University Exam

The small **Beta** coefficients for Age and Project Mark show that those variables play minor parts in the regression

Output 14. The regression equation and associated statistics

The **beta coefficients** (in the column headed **Beta**) tell us rather more, because each gives the number of standard deviations change on the dependent variable that will be produced by a change of one standard deviation on the independent variable concerned. On this count, Entrance Exam still makes by the greatest contribution, because a change of one standard deviation on that variable produces a change of 0.58 standard deviations on University Exam. Next is IQ with a change of 0.45, but Project Mark produces a change of only 0.14 and Age a change of 0.12 of a standard deviation on University Exam. This ordering of the standardised beta coefficients is supported by consideration of the correlations between the dependent variable and each of the three predictors (Output 10). The predictor with the largest beta coefficient also has the largest correlation with the dependent variable.

The remaining items of output (the table of Residual Statistics and the scatterplot of standardised predicted values against standardised residuals) are not shown here. There were no residual outliers.

12.3.2 Procedure for stepwise multiple regression

If, in the **Linear Regression** dialog box, the choice of **Method** is changed to **Stepwise**, rather than **Enter**, a stepwise regression will be run, whereby predictors are added to (or subtracted from) the equation one at a time. In **Forward selection**, predictors are added one a time, provided they meet an entry criterion. In **Backward deletion**, the predictors are all present initially and are removed one at a time if they do not meet a retention criterion. The SPSS **Stepwise regression** routine is a combination of these two processes: a variable, having been added at an early stage, may subsequently be removed. Selected portions of the results of a **Stepwise regression** analysis are shown in Outputs 15-19.

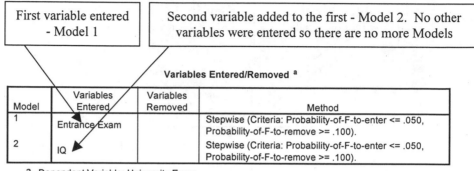

Variables Entered/Removed [a]

Model	Variables Entered	Variables Removed	Method
1	Entrance Exam		Stepwise (Criteria: Probability-of-F-to-enter <= .050, Probability-of-F-to-remove >= .100).
2	IQ		Stepwise (Criteria: Probability-of-F-to-enter <= .050, Probability-of-F-to-remove >= .100).

a. Dependent Variable: University Exam

Output 15. List of variables entered (only two achieved entry in the stepwise regression)

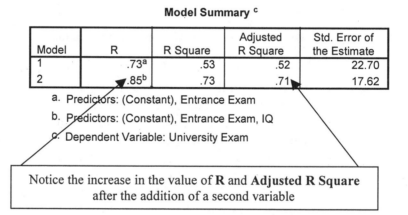

Model Summary [c]

Model	R	R Square	Adjusted R Square	Std. Error of the Estimate
1	.73[a]	.53	.52	22.70
2	.85[b]	.73	.71	17.62

a. Predictors: (Constant), Entrance Exam

b. Predictors: (Constant), Entrance Exam, IQ

c. Dependent Variable: University Exam

Notice the increase in the value of **R** and **Adjusted R Square** after the addition of a second variable

Output 16. Value of R and associated statistics for each Model

The value of R for Model 2 is smaller than the value (0.87) given for simultaneous regression of University Exam upon Entrance Exam, Project Mark, Age and IQ but only slightly so. This shows the lack of predictive value of the two excluded variables (Age and Project Mark).

The ANOVA (Output 17) for each regression Model is significant.

ANOVA[c]

Model		Sum of Squares	df	Mean Square	F	Sig.
1	Regression	18096.33	1	18096.33	35.1	.00[a]
	Residual	15980.58	31	515.50		
	Total	34076.91	32			
2	Regression	24757.87	2	12378.93	39.9	.00[b]
	Residual	9319.04	30	310.63		
	Total	34076.91	32			

a. Predictors: (Constant), Entrance Exam

b. Predictors: (Constant), Entrance Exam, IQ

c. Dependent Variable: University Exam

Output 17. The ANOVA for each regression Model

The decision of the stepwise program is that, since the increment in R with the inclusion of either of the remaining variables (Project Mark and Age) does not reach the necessary statistical criterion, these variables are excluded from the final equation (Output 18).

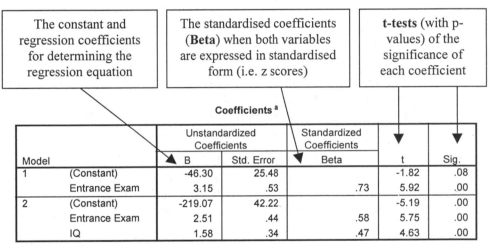

The constant and regression coefficients for determining the regression equation	The standardised coefficients (**Beta**) when both variables are expressed in standardised form (i.e. z scores)	**t-tests** (with p-values) of the significance of each coefficient

Coefficients[a]

Model		Unstandardized Coefficients		Standardized Coefficients		
		B	Std. Error	Beta	t	Sig.
1	(Constant)	-46.30	25.48		-1.82	.08
	Entrance Exam	3.15	.53	.73	5.92	.00
2	(Constant)	-219.07	42.22		-5.19	.00
	Entrance Exam	2.51	.44	.58	5.75	.00
	IQ	1.58	.34	.47	4.63	.00

a. Dependent Variable: University Exam

Output 18. The regression coefficients tables for the single variable (Model 1) and the two variables (Model 2) remaining in the stepwise regression analysis

From column **B** in Output 18, we see that the multiple regression equation of University Exam (*finalex*) upon Entrance Exam (*selectex*) and IQ (*iq*) is:

$$\textbf{\textit{finalex}}' = \textbf{-219.07} + \textbf{2.51} \times (\textit{selectex}) + \textbf{1.58} \times (\textit{iq})$$

where **_finalex_**´ is the predicted University Exam. Thus the estimated score of a person aged 21.6 scoring 60 on the Entrance Exam and having an IQ of 132 is

$$-219.07 + 2.51 \times (60) + 1.58 \times (132) = 140.09$$

Notice that case 29, who meets these specifications, scored 145 in the University Exam. In this case the simultaneous regression equation provides a better estimate than the stepwise regression equation; but there are other cases for which the opposite is true.

Output 19 lists the statistics for the excluded variables. Note the low values of t and their correspondingly high (i.e. > 0.05) p-values.

Excluded Variables[c]

Model		Beta In	t	Sig.	Partial Correlation	Collinearity Statistics Tolerance
1	Age	.18[a]	1.42	.17	.25	.93
	Project Mark	.21[a]	1.69	.10	.29	.92
	IQ	.47[a]	4.63	.00	.65	.90
2	Age	.15[b]	1.56	.13	.28	.92
	Project Mark	.17[b]	1.77	.09	.31	.91

[a]. Predictors in the Model: (Constant), Entrance Exam

[b]. Predictors in the Model: (Constant), Entrance Exam, IQ

[c]. Dependent Variable: University Exam

Output 19. The variables excluded from the stepwise regression analysis

In the table in Output 19, **Beta In** is the standardised regression coefficient that would result if the variable were entered into the equation at the next step. The **t** test is the usual test of significance of the regression coefficient. Partial correlation is the correlation that remains between two variables after removing the correlation that is due to their mutual association with the other variables. **Collinearity** is the undesirable situation where the correlations among the independent variables are high. Collinearity can be detected by the **Tolerance** statistic, which is the proportion of a variable's variance not accounted for by other independent variables in the equation. A variable with very low tolerance contributes little information to a model, and can cause computational problems.

In conclusion, the Stepwise regression confirms the conclusion from the beta coefficients in the Simultaneous regression that only the variables Entrance Exam and IQ are useful for predicting University Exam marks. The other two variables can be dropped from the analysis.

12.3.3 The need for a substantive model of causation

These results highlight an important consideration for the use of multiple regression as a research tool. The addition of new predictors can sometimes affect the relative contributions of those variables already in the equation. Therefore, when planning a multiple regression and selecting predictors, the researcher must be guided by a sound theoretical rationale. A *statistical* model alone cannot yield an unequivocal interpretation of regression results: the user also requires the guidance of a *substantive* model of causation.

12.4 SCATTERPLOTS AND REGRESSION LINES

A regression line can easily be added to a scatterplot such as Figure 4 in Chapter 11. Proceed as follows.

- After plotting the scatterplot in the usual way by completing the **Simple Scatterplot** dialog box, double-click anywhere on the scatterplot in **SPSS Viewer** to open the **Chart Editor**.
- Edit the scatterplot as desired (e.g. change the coloured points to black by clicking any of the points so that the scatterplot symbols are highlighted and then ▣ to open the **Colors** selection box. Change the colour to black, and click **Apply**. Centre the axis legends by double-clicking each in turn and changing the **Title Justification:** option to **Center**).
- To add the regression line, enter the **Chart** menu, select **Options** to open the **Scatterplot Options** dialog box and click the **Total** checkbox in the **Fit Line** section (Figure 6).
- Click **OK** to plot the linear regression line (Output 20). The colour of the regression line can be edited to make it black. Click the close button ☒ to return from the **Chart Editor** to the **Viewer**.

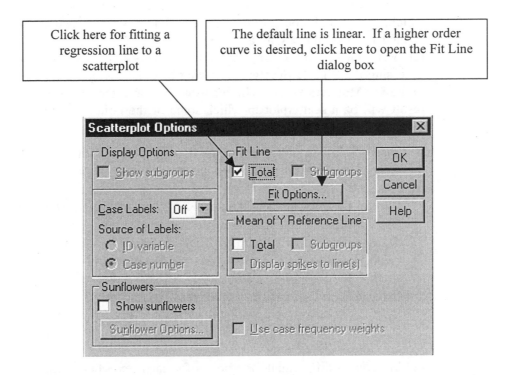

Figure 6. The Scatterplot Options dialog box with Total selected

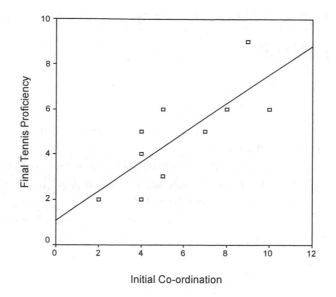

Output 20. Scatterplot with linear regression line added

Clustered scatterplots

It is possible to draw scatterplots and their regression lines for data that have been subdivided into clusters (e.g. sex). In Chapter 4, for example, a data set was introduced which consisted of observations on four variables: height, weight, sex and blood group. A scatterplot of weight against height can be refined by entering sex as a category variable. Some of the points will now represent males and others females. A clustered scatterplot is drawn by accessing the **Simple Scatterplot** dialog box and including a category variable in the **Set Markers by** box. (In this example, the category variable is *sex..*) The result will be a scatterplot in which some of the points denote one participant category and the remaining points the other.

It is also possible to plot a regression line for the points in each category. With the height/weight/gender/blood group data in the **Data Editor**, proceed as follows.

- Choose **Graphs** and select **Scatter...**, to obtain the **Scatterplot** dialog box. Click **Define**, to obtain the **Simple Scatterplot** dialog box.
- Transfer Weight in Kilograms [*weight*], Height in Centimetres [*height*] and Gender [*sex*] to the **Y Axis**, **X Axis** and **Set Markers by** boxes, respectively. Click **OK** to obtain a scatterplot in **SPSS Viewer** in which the males and females are represented by points of different colours.
- Double-click anywhere on the scatterplot to open the **Chart Editor**. Click each set of coloured symbols in turn and change the colour to black using the **Colors** dialog box.
- In order to differentiate the points for each sex, change the type of symbol for one of the sexes by highlighting the points, clicking ✳ to open the **Markers** selection box. Select a a different marker such as ×, click **Apply** and then on **Close** to close the **Markers** selection box and return to the **Chart Editor**.
- In the **Chart** menu, select **Options** to open the **Scatterplot Options** dialog box. In the area labelled **Fit Line**, mark the **Subgroups** checkbox. Click **OK** to produce a scatterplot with two regression lines, one for each group of points.

- Finally change the colours of the regression lines to black. Select appropriate line styles by clicking each line in turn to highlight it, following the procedure for changing colours that was outlined above, and finally selecting the desired line style from the **Line Styles** selection box, which is opened with the  icon.
- Click the close button ☒ to return from the **Chart Editor** to the **Viewer**.

The edited scatterplot with two regression lines is shown in Output 21.

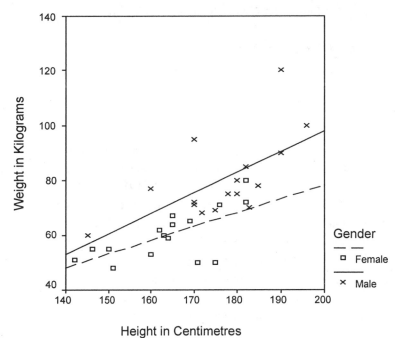

Output 21. Clustered scatterplot with two linear regression lines

EXERCISE 20

SIMPLE, TWO-VARIABLE REGRESSION

Before you start

Before proceeding with this exercise, please read Chapter 12.

Purpose of the project

In this Exercise, we shall look at some of the pitfalls that await the unwary user of regression techniques; in fact, as we shall see, all the cautions and caveats about the **Pearson correlation** apply with equal force to regression.

In Exercise 17, Anscombe's specially contrived data set (whose columns were named *X1*, *X2*, *Y1*, *Y2*, *Y3*, *Y4*) was saved in a file named **anscombe**. Scatterplots and correlation coefficients were obtained for the pairings (*X1*, *Y1*), (*X1*, *Y2*), (*X1*, *Y3*) and (*X2*, *Y4*). All sets yielded exactly the same value for the Pearson correlation. When the scatterplots were inspected, however, it was seen that the Pearson correlation was appropriate for only one data set: in the other sets, it would give the unwary user a highly misleading impression. One problem with the Pearson correlation is that it is very vulnerable to the leverage exerted by atypical data points, or **outliers** as they are termed. The Pearson correlation can also have large values with monotonic but non-linear relationships. All this is equally true of the parameters of the regression equation. In this exercise, we return to Anscombe's data to investigate the statistics of the regression lines for the four sets of paired data.

Opening SPSS

Open SPSS and select the data file *anscombe* from the opening window. This was the file saved from Exercise 17.

Running the simple regression procedure

Following the procedure described in Section 12.2.1, obtain the regression statistics of *Y1*, *Y2* and *Y3* upon *X1* and of *Y4* upon *X2*. Remember that the dependent variable is Y, and the independent variable is X. For present purposes, the plotting of the scatterplot of *ZRESID (**y-axis** box) against *ZPRED (**x-axis** box) should provide illuminating tests of the credibility of the assumption that the data are linear. Full details of preparing the **Linear Regression** dialog box are given in Section 12.2.1.

Since we want to carry out regression upon all four (*X,Y*) data sets, it will be necessary to prepare the **Regression** dialog box for the first pair to include a scatterplot of *ZRESID against *ZPRED, and then change the variable names on subsequent runs for the remaining three pairs. To return to the **Regression** dialog box after inspecting the scatterplot, click the **Analyze** drop-down menu at the top of the SPSS Viewer window and select **Regression** and **Linear** again. Change *Y1* to *Y2* in the **Dependent** box and click **OK**. Follow this procedure for each pair of variables (i.e. *Y3* upon *X1* and then *Y4* upon *X2* - here you need to change *X2* for *X1* in the **Independent(s)** box). After each run, you should record the value of **R Squared** and the regression equation, and note the appearance of the scatterplot.

Output for the simple regression analyses

The main features of the Output of a simple regression analysis are fully explained in Chapter 12.

- **Compare the regression statistics and scatterplots for all four bivariate data sets. What do you notice about the values of R Squared and the appearances of the scatterplots?**

Another example

A researcher interested in the relationship between blood alcohol level and road accidents examined the data for various levels of blood alcohol from 5 to 35 mg/100 ml. The data are shown in Table 1:

Table 1. Blood alcohol level and number of accidents							
Alcohol level	5	10	15	20	25	30	35
No of accidents (x 000)	10	17	26	30	32	38	42

Find the regression of the number of accidents upon blood alcohol level and predict the number of accidents for 40 mg/100ml. Draw the scatterplot with SPSS and fit the regression line.

Preparing the data set

Prepare the data set in the usual manner with two variables.

Running the regression and inspecting the Output

Run the regression command as described in Section 12.2.1 but omit the optional extras Descriptives, Casewise diagnostics, and the plot. Use either a calculator or SPSS to calculate the number of predicted accidents for an alcohol level of 40 mg/100 ml. To do so with SPSS, insert the value of 40 in the *blood* column of **Data View** and then complete a **Compute** command by entering the appropriate coefficients and variable name to calculate predicted values for a new variable with a name such as *predicted*.

- **Write down the regression equation.**
- **What is the predicted number of accidents for a blood alcohol level of 40 mg/100 ml?**

Drawing the regression line

Use the procedure described in Section 12.4 to draw the scatterplot and insert the regression line.

- **Does the value calculated for 40 mg/100 ml correspond with what you can see in the scatterplot with its fitted regression line?**

Finishing the session

Close down SPSS and any other windows before logging out of the computer.

EXERCISE 21

MULTIPLE REGRESSION

Before you start

The reader should study Section 12.3 before proceeding with this exercise.

A problem in reading research

Reading comprises many different component skills. A reading researcher hypothesises that certain specific kinds of pre-reading abilities and behaviour can predict later progress in reading, as measured by performance on reading tests taken some years after the child's first formal lessons. Let us, therefore, label the dependent variable (DV) in this study *progress*. While they are still very young indeed, many children evince a considerable grasp of English syntax in their speech. Our researcher devises a measure of their syntactic knowledge, *syntax*, based upon the average length of their uttered sentences. Some researchers, however, argue that an infant's prelinguistic babbling (which we shall label *vocal*) also plays a key role in their later reading performance. At the pre-reading stage, some very young children can acquire a sight vocabulary of several hundreds of words. The ability to pronounce these words on seeing them written down is known as logographic reading; but many authorities do not accept that this is true reading. Our researcher, who views the logographic strategy as important, includes a measure of this skill, *logo*, in the study.

Preparing the data set

Fifty children are studied over a period beginning in infancy and extending through their school years. Their scores on the four measures, the DV *progress* (P), and the three IVs *logo* (L), *vocal* (V) and *syntax* (S), are listed in the appendix to this exercise. Since it would be very laborious for you to type in all the data during the exercise, we must hope that your instructor has already stored them in an accessible file, with a name such as *reading*. The data are also available on the Internet as *Exer_21.sav* at:

http://www.psyc.abdn.ac.uk/teaching/spss/spssbook.htm

Exploring the data

The distributions of the variables are most easily explored by using the **Boxplot** option in the **Graphs** drop-down menu. Select **Boxplot**, click the **Summaries of separate variables** button, and then click **Define**. Transfer the variable names to the **Boxes Represent** box and click **OK**. This will plot four boxes side-by-side for easy comparison.

Regression is most effective when each IV is strongly correlated with the DV but uncorrelated with the other IVs. Although the correlation matrix can be listed from within the regression procedure, it is often more useful to scrutinise the matrix before proceeding with a regression analysis in order to make judgements about which variables might be retained and which dropped from the analysis. For example, it might be advisable to make a choice between two variables that are highly correlated with one another.

Use the **Bivariate Correlations** procedure to compute the correlation matrix. The same procedure can conveniently be used for tabulating the means and standard deviations, which are available as an option.

After transferring the variable names to the **Variables** box, click **Options** and (within the Statistics choice box) select **Means and standard deviations**. Click **Continue** and then **OK**. Notice that the DV *progress* shows substantial correlations with both *logo* and *syntax*. On the other hand, there is no appreciable correlation between *logo* and *syntax*. The remaining variable (*vocal*) shows little association with any of the other variables, although there is a hint of a negative correlation with *logo*.

Running the multiple regression analysis

Run the multiple regression of *progress* upon the three predictors, by following the procedure in Section 12.3. Remember that the **Dependent** variable is what you are predicting (*progress*) and the **Independent** variables are the predictors (*logo, vocal, syntax*). On the first run, use the **Method** *Enter* (this enters all the variables simultaneously) and on the second run the **Method** *Stepwise* (this is a forward stepwise selection procedure).

Output for the multiple regression

The main features of a multiple regression output, both for the simultaneous and stepwise methods, are explained in Section 12.3 .

- **Do the decisions of the multiple regression procedure about which variables are important agree with your informal observations during the exploratory phase of the data analysis?**

- **Write out the regression equation that you would use to predict progress from a participant's scores on logo, vocal and syntax.**

Finishing the session

Close down SPSS and any other windows before logging out of the computer.

Appendix to Exercise 21 - The data

P	L	V	S	P	L	V	S	P	L	V	S	P	L	V	S
65	75	34	48	46	55	75	32	65	50	75	68	34	32	42	27
58	29	18	67	51	31	50	66	71	65	23	64	54	64	55	32
42	40	43	38	61	69	59	46	60	56	52	44	81	82	60	69
55	55	9	48	45	19	71	59	17	10	64	20	77	66	50	79
68	81	41	54	53	48	44	45	55	41	41	55	57	30	20	54
59	28	72	68	46	45	29	45	69	51	14	62	80	82	65	58
50	39	31	42	25	28	58	28	47	49	46	59	89	51	52	48
50	26	78	56	71	70	51	54	53	14	53	77	50	34	45	60
71	84	46	50	30	55	42	25	50	40	51	31	69	49	72	72
65	71	30	52	62	53	52	57	80	45	59	90	71	69	57	60
34	30	30	20	47	20	78	69	51	18	22	61	39	25	81	49
44	71	79	22	60	46	80	67	79	58	13	82				
47	62	26	30	70	66	40	61	51	43	31	50				

CHAPTER 13

MULTIWAY FREQUENCY ANALYSIS

13.1 INTRODUCTION

13.2 AN EXAMPLE OF A LOGLINEAR ANALYSIS

13.1   INTRODUCTION

The starting point for the analysis of nominal data on two or more attributes is a **contingency table**, each cell of which is the frequency of occurrence of individuals in various combinations of categories. In an earlier chapter (Chapter 11), we described the use of the chi-square test to test for the presence of an association between qualitative variables in a two-way contingency table.

In a two-way contingency table, the presence (or absence) of an association between the attributes is often apparent from inspection alone: the formal statistical analysis merely confirms a readily discernible pattern, or the absence of one. It is quite possible, however, to have more complex contingency tables, in which individuals are classified with respect to three or more qualitative variables.

The traditional Pearson chi-square test can easily be generalised to multiway tables. Here the null hypothesis is that there is no association among any of the variables in the classification. Should the chi-square test reject the null hypothesis, the inference is that there is an association <u>somewhere</u> among the variables. In **multi-way contingency tables**, however, it is often very difficult to discern associations accurately by inspection; in fact, it is only too easy to misinterpret what one does see.

Recent years have seen great advances in the analysis of multi-way contingency tables (Everitt, 1977; Upton, 1978, 1986), and these new methods, collectively known as **loglinear analysis**, are now available in computing packages such as SPSS. These techniques allow the user to do much more than merely reject the total independence model, which is often very unlikely to be true anyway. With loglinear analysis, the precise loci of any associations can be pinpointed and incorporated into a model that accounts for the data in terms of specified associations.

13.1.1 Comparison of loglinear analysis with ANOVA

To understand how loglinear analysis works, it may be helpful to recall some aspects of the completely randomised factorial analysis of variance, because there are some striking parallels between the two sets of techniques. In the ANOVA, it is possible to test for **main effects** and for **interactions**. Suppose that, following a three-factor experiment, all systematic sources are found to be significant. That would imply that the correct model for the experimental data must contain, in addition to a random error component, a term for each and every possible systematic effect thus:

score = systematic effects* + error effects

(* 3 main effect terms + 3 two-way interaction terms + 1 three-way interaction term)

If, on the other hand, only one main effect and one of the possible two-way interactions were to prove significant, a simpler model would account for a

303

participant's score. This simplified model would contain, in addition to the error term, only one main effect term and one two-way interaction term thus:

score = systematic effects* + error effects

(* 1 main effect term + 1 two-way interaction term)

There are many parallels between ANOVA and the loglinear analysis of multi-way contingency tables. In loglinear analysis, as in ANOVA, it is meaningful to speak of 'main effects' and of 'interactions'. Loglinear analysis also offers methods of testing the various effects separately. As with ANOVA, however, the presence of an interaction often necessitates the re-interpretation of a main effect; indeed, main effects (or their absence), when considered on their own, can be deceptive. That is why the common procedure of 'collapsing' (i.e. combining the frequencies at all levels of some factors to exclude them from the classification) can produce misleading patterns in the data. The aim of a loglinear analysis is to find the model that best accounts for the data available. It contains both main effect terms and interaction terms, so that the values in the contingency table are expressed as the sum of main effects and interaction components.

There are, however, also important *differences* between loglinear and ANOVA models. In ANOVA, the target of the model is the **individual score** of a participant in the experiment. In loglinear analysis, the target is the **total frequency of observations in a cell.** The ANOVA model cannot predict the individual scores with perfect accuracy, because of the inevitable presence of errors of measurement, individual differences and experimental error. In contrast, as we shall see, it is **always** possible, by including all the possible terms in the loglinear model, to make perfect predictions of the cell frequencies in a contingency table. A model that contains all the possible effect terms is known as a **saturated model**. The purpose of a loglinear analysis is to see whether the cell frequencies can be adequately approximated by a model that contains **fewer** than the full set of possible treatment effects.

13.1.2 Why 'loglinear' analysis?

In the simple chi-square test of association in a two-by-two contingency table, the **expected frequencies** are obtained by **multiplying** marginal total frequencies and dividing the product by the total frequency. This is because the null hypothesis of independence of the variables implies that the probability of an individual occupying a cell of the classification is the **product** of the relevant main effect probabilities, the latter being estimated from the marginal totals. (Recall that the probability of the joint occurrence of independent events is the **product** of their separate probabilities.) Loglinear analysis exploits the fact that the logarithm (log) of a product is the **sum** of the logs of the terms in the product. Thus the **log** of the cell frequencies may be expressed as a **linear** (i.e., additive) function of the **logs** of the components. If one were to work directly with the cell frequencies, rather than their logs, one would require a **multiplicative** model for the data. While that is possible, the simplicity of a summative, ANOVA-type model would be lost.

13.1.3 Building a loglinear model

The purpose of a loglinear analysis is to construct a model such that the cell frequencies in a contingency table are accounted for in terms of a minimum number of terms. Several strategies can be followed in the construction of such a model, but the **backward hierarchical method** is perhaps the easiest to understand. The first step is to construct a **saturated model** for the cell frequencies, in which all the component effects are present. This model, as we have seen, will predict the cell frequencies perfectly. The next step is to remove the highest-order interaction, to determine the effect this would have upon the closeness with which the model predicts the cell frequencies. It may be that this interaction can be removed without appreciably affecting the accuracy of estimation of the target frequencies. The process continues, and each time a term is removed, a statistical test is carried out to determine whether the accuracy of prediction falls to a sufficient extent to show that the component most recently excluded should be retained as one of the components in the final model. The assessment of the goodness-of-fit at each stage of the procedure is made by means of a statistic known as the **likelihood ratio** (called **L.R. Chisq** by SPSS).

The final model is evaluated by comparing the observed and expected frequencies for each cell using the likelihood ratio. As in regression analysis, however, it is also advisable to examine the distribution of **residuals** (the differences between the observed and expected frequencies) or, more conveniently, the **standardised residuals** (residuals expressed in standardised form).

13.1.4 Small expected frequencies

Just as in the case of the chi-square test, the **expected frequency** (not the observed frequency) in each cell should exceed a minimum value. Small expected frequencies can mean a test with little power to reject the null hypothesis.

Problems with low expected cell frequencies should not arise provided:
- (1) there are not too many variables in comparison with the size of the sample;
- (2) there are no categories with very few cases.

Tabachnick and Fidell (1996) recommend examining the expected cell frequencies for all **two-way associations** to ensure that all **expected frequencies** are greater than 1 and that no more than 20% are less than 5. If there is any doubt about the assumption of adequate expected cell frequencies, they can be checked out by using the **Crosstabs** command.

13.2 AN EXAMPLE OF A LOGLINEAR ANALYSIS

In an investigation of the relationships between success on a second year university psychology statistics course and a number of possibly relevant background variables, researchers collected a body of information on a number of students, including whether or not they had taken an advanced school mathematics course and whether they had passed a data-processing examination in their first year at university. On each student's record, it was also noted whether he or she had passed the second year psychology statistics examination. The data are presented in Table 1, which is a **three-way contingency table**.

Table 1. A three-way contingency table							
Advanced Maths	Yes				No			
Data Processing	Pass		Fail		Pass		Fail	
Psychology Statistics	Pass	Fail	Pass	Fail	Pass	Fail	Pass	Fail
Cell Frequencies	47	10	4	10	58	17	10	20

It is useful to summarise the cell frequencies for the categories of the variables considered separately, as shown in Table 2. It can be seen that of the 176 students in the study, 71 had taken advanced mathematics, and 105 had not.

Table 2. Summary of cell frequencies for the categories in each variable						
Advanced Maths	Yes	71	No	105	Total	176
Data Processing	Pass	132	Fail	44	Total	176
Psych Statistics	Pass	119	Fail	57	Total	176

From Table 1, it can be seen that of those who had taken advanced mathematics, 57 passed first year data-processing and 14 did not, compared with 75 passes and 30 failures in the non-mathematical group. Relatively speaking, therefore, more of the mathematical group passed first year data-processing. Turning now to the statistics examination, it can be seen that of the mathematical group, the pass ratio was 51:20, compared with 68:37 in the non-mathematical group; and among those who had passed data-processing, the success ratio was 105:27, compared with 14:30 in the group that had failed data processing.

First, let us consider the (very unlikely) null hypothesis that there are **no links whatsoever** among the three variables studied. Suppose there is no tendency for those who have taken school mathematics to pass first year data-processing, no tendency for those who have passed data-processing to pass second year statistics and so on. It is a relatively simple matter, using a pocket calculator, to use the appropriate marginal totals to obtain the expected cell frequencies in a calculation similar to that appropriate for a two-way contingency table. Since there are three dichotomous (or pseudo-dichotomous) variables, there are 8 expected cell frequencies, the values of which are shown in Table 3. A way of computing these expected frequencies with SPSS will be described in Section 13.2.4.

Table 3. Observed (O) and expected (E) cell frequencies (Cell Freq) for Table 1								
Advanced Maths	**Yes**				**No**			
Data Processing	**Pass**		**Fail**		**Pass**		**Fail**	
Psychology Statistics	**Pass**	**Fail**	**Pass**	**Fail**	**Pass**	**Fail**	**Pass**	**Fail**
Cell Freq O	47	10	4	10	58	17	10	20
E	36.00	17.25	12.00	5.75	53.25	25.50	17.75	8.50

In several cells, the observed frequencies differ markedly from the expected values, suggesting that the complete independence model gives a poor account of the data. Clearly there are at least some associations among the three variables. But where exactly are these associations?

A loglinear analysis on SPSS can answer that question very easily. In the loglinear menu, is the **hierarchical loglinear** command. This procedure begins by constructing a fully saturated model for the cell frequencies, and works backwards in the manner described above, in order to arrive at a model with a minimum number of terms. Some of these terms are of little interest. For example, there are fewer participants in the advanced mathematics group than there are in the non-mathematical group, so we can expect a main effect term for this variable in the final model. Main effects are usually unimportant in loglinear analysis. In the terms of the ANOVA, we are seeking **interactions**, rather than **main effects**. The presence of associations among the three variables will necessitate the inclusion of interaction terms in the model.

13.2.1 Running a loglinear analysis

See Section 3.2

- In Variable View, using the procedures described in Section 3.2, name three grouping variables: *maths*, *dataproc* and *psystats*. In the Label column, add suitable expanded names such as Advanced Maths Course, Data Processing Exam and Psych Stats Exam. In the **Values** column, label the code values: for *maths*, 1 is Yes, 2 is No; for *dataproc* and *psystats*, 1 is Pass, 2 is Fail. Name a fourth variable *count* for the cell frequencies. Click the **Data View** tab and enter the data. Finally, save the data set to a file in the usual way. The complete SPSS data set is shown in Figure 1.

	maths	dataproc	psystats	count
1	Yes	Pass	Pass	47
2	Yes	Pass	Fail	10
3	Yes	Fail	Pass	4
4	Yes	Fail	Fail	10
5	No	Pass	Pass	58
6	No	Pass	Fail	17
7	No	Fail	Pass	10
8	No	Fail	Fail	20

Figure 1. Data View showing the data set

See
Section
3.7.2

- It is now necessary to inform SPSS that the variable *count* contains frequencies and not simply scores. The procedure is described in Chapter 3, Section 3.7.2. Choose
  Data
    Weight Cases...
  to open the **Weight Cases** dialog box (Chapter 3, Figure 27), and transfer the variable *count* to the **Frequency Variable:** box. Click **OK**.

See
Section
11.3.2

- The next stage is to confirm (by using the **Crosstabs** command in Chapter 11, Section 11.3.2) that the expected frequencies are sufficiently large. Choose
  Analyze
    Summarize
      Crosstabs...
  and then complete the **Crosstabs** dialog box (Figure 2) by transferring Data Processing Exam [*dataproc*] to the **Row(s):** box, Psych Stats Exam [*psystats*] to the **Column(s):** box, and Advanced Maths Course [*maths*] to the lowest box.

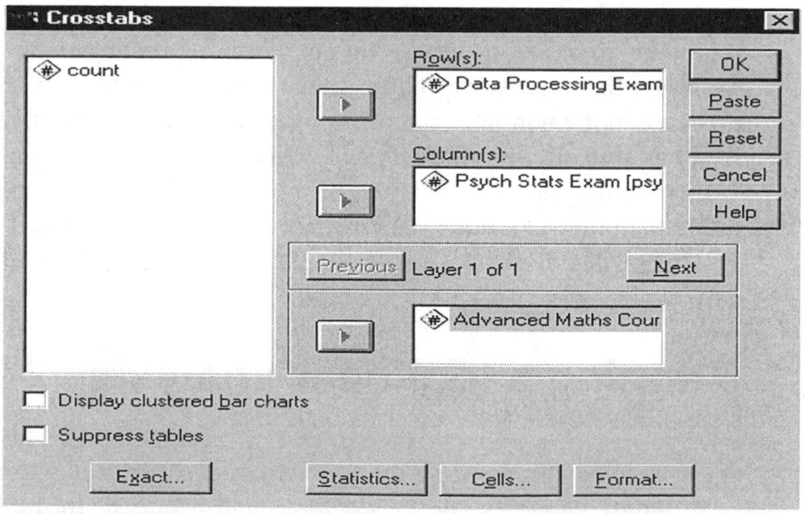

Figure 2. The completed Crosstabs dialog box

- Click **Cells...** to bring to access the **Crosstabs: Cell Display** dialog box (See Chapter 11, Figure 13). Within the **Counts** box, tick the **Expected** check box, click **Continue** and then **OK**.

The **Crosstabs** command presents two-way contingency tables for each layer of Advanced Maths Course, because that was chosen as the layering variable. The table (Output 1) shows that no cell has an expected frequency of less than 1 and only one cell has one of less than 5. There is no problem with low expected frequencies.

Data Processing Exam * Psych Stats Exam * Advanced Maths Course Crosstabulation

Advanced Maths Course				Psych Stats Exam		Total
				Pass	Fail	
Yes	Data Processing Exam	Pass	Count	47	10	57
			Expected Count	40.9	16.1	57.0
		Fail	Count	4	10	14
			Expected Count	10.1	3.9	14.0
	Total		Count	51	20	71
			Expected Count	51.0	20.0	71.0
No	Data Processing Exam	Pass	Count	58	17	75
			Expected Count	48.6	26.4	75.0
		Fail	Count	10	20	30
			Expected Count	19.4	10.6	30.0
	Total		Count	68	37	105
			Expected Count	68.0	37.0	105.0

The only expected frequency less than 5

Output 1. Observed and expected frequencies for a three-way contingency table

The hierarchical loglinear command is run as follows:
- Select
Analyze
    Loglinear
        Model Selection... (Figure 3)
to open the **Model Selection Loglinear Analysis** dialog box (the completed version is shown in Figure 4).

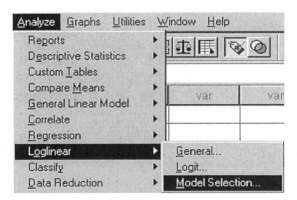

Figure 3. Finding the Model Selection Loglinear dialog box

- Transfer the three grouping variable names Advanced Maths Course [*maths*], Data Processing Exam [*dataproc*] and Psych Stats Exam [*psystats*] to the **Factor(s):** box (see Figure 4).
- Click **Define Range** and enter *1* into the **Minimum** box and *2* into the **Maximum** box. Click **Continue** and the names will appear with [1,2] after each of them. If some of the variables have different numbers of categories, it will be necessary to enter the ranges separately for each variable.
- The default model is **backward elimination**. Makes sure its radio button is on.

- Click **OK**.

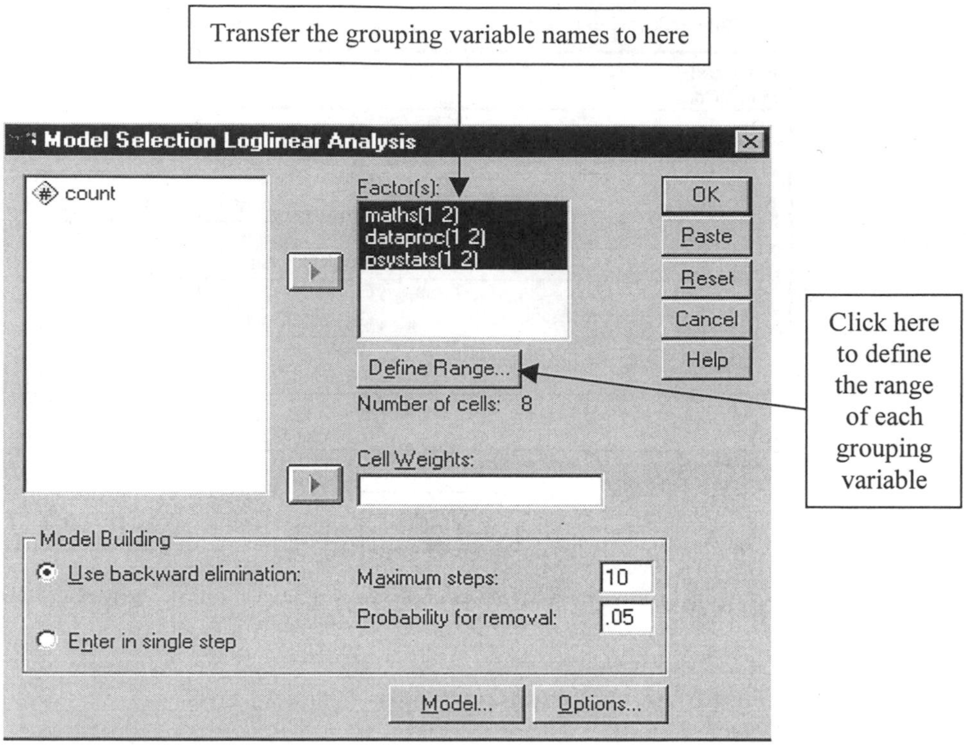

Figure 4. The Model Selection Loglinear Analysis dialog box for three factors

13.2.2 **Output for a loglinear analysis**

The output in SPSS Viewer is not in the tabulated form encountered in previous Chapters. A red triangle at the foot of the output (on the left-hand side of the right-hand pane) means that there is more output to be viewed. To view the additional material, double-click the output. The surrounding box will then become a window, which can be explored by moving the cursor or by using the **Page Up** and **Page Down** keys.

Output 2 contains information about the data and the factors.

```
* * *  H I E R A R C H I C A L   L O G   L I N E A R * * *

DATA   Information

        8 unweighted cases accepted.
        0 cases rejected because of out-of-range factor values.
        0 cases rejected because of missing data.
      176 weighted cases will be used in the analysis.

FACTOR Information

    Factor   Level   Label
    MATHS        2   Advanced Maths Course
    DATAPROC     2   Data Processing Exam
    PSYSTATS     2   Psych Stats Exam
```

Output 2. Information about the data and the factors

This is followed by a table (not shown here) listing the counts (OBS count) for the combinations of the three factors. At this stage, SPSS is fitting a **saturated model**, MATHS*DATAPROC*PSYSTATS, to the cell frequencies. The table is useful for checking the accuracy of the data transcription.

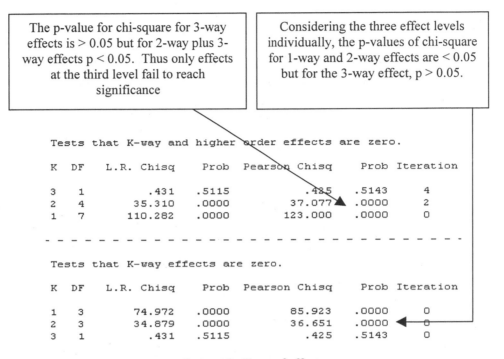

The p-value for chi-square for 3-way effects is > 0.05 but for 2-way plus 3-way effects p < 0.05. Thus only effects at the third level fail to reach significance

Considering the three effect levels individually, the p-values of chi-square for 1-way and 2-way effects are < 0.05 but for the 3-way effect, p > 0.05.

```
Tests that K-way and higher order effects are zero.

K   DF   L.R. Chisq   Prob   Pearson Chisq   Prob   Iteration

3    1         .431   .5115            .425   .5143      4
2    4       35.310   .0000          37.077   .0000      2
1    7      110.282   .0000         123.000   .0000      0


Tests that K-way effects are zero.

K   DF   L.R. Chisq   Prob   Pearson Chisq   Prob   Iteration

1    3       74.972   .0000          85.923   .0000      0
2    3       34.879   .0000          36.651   .0000      0
3    1         .431   .5115            .425   .5143      0
```

Output 3. Tests of effects

The upper table in Output 3 shows the chi-squares and p-values for effects at a specified level (K) <u>and above</u>. The lower table gives the chi-squares and p-values of effects at <u>specified levels alone</u>. That is why the chi-squares for levels 2 and 3 are smaller in the lower table. We can see that there are significant effects at levels 1 and 2, but not at level 3. (The fact that there are significant effects at level 2, however, does not imply that <u>all</u> two-way interactions are significant.)

Outputs 4-7 show the most interesting part of the output, which is headed:

'Backward Elimination (p = .050) for Design 1 with generating class . . .'

The purpose of the analysis was to find the unsaturated model that gives the best fit to the observed data. This is achieved by checking that the model currently being tested does not give a significantly worse fit than the next most complex in the hierarchy.

Recall that hierarchical backward elimination begins with the most complex model (which in the present case contains all three factors, together with all their possible interactions). Testing progresses down the hierarchy of complexity, eliminating each effect from the model in turn and determining which decrement in accuracy is less than the **least-significant change in the chi-square value.** At each step, such an effect would be eliminated, leaving the remaining effects for inclusion, as specified by the heading:

'The best model has generating class . . . '

The procedure continues until no elimination produces a decrement with a probability greater than 0.05. The model containing the remaining effects is then adopted as 'The final model'. In this example, the final model is reached after four steps.

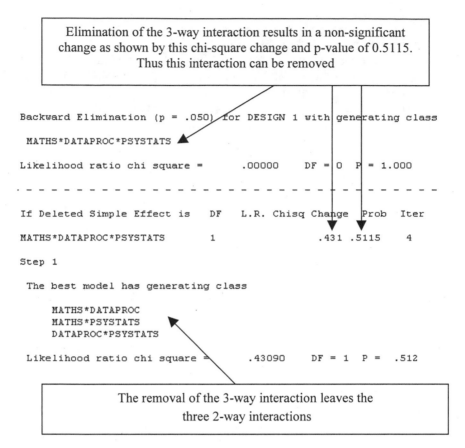

> Elimination of the 3-way interaction results in a non-significant change as shown by this chi-square change and p-value of 0.5115. Thus this interaction can be removed

```
Backward Elimination (p = .050) for DESIGN 1 with generating class

  MATHS*DATAPROC*PSYSTATS

Likelihood ratio chi square =        .00000    DF = 0  P = 1.000

- - - - - - - - - - - - - - - - - - - - - - - - - - - - - - - - - -

If Deleted Simple Effect is    DF   L.R. Chisq Change  Prob   Iter

MATHS*DATAPROC*PSYSTATS          1                 .431 .5115    4

Step 1

  The best model has generating class

       MATHS*DATAPROC
       MATHS*PSYSTATS
       DATAPROC*PSYSTATS

Likelihood ratio chi square =        .43090    DF = 1  P =  .512
```

> The removal of the 3-way interaction leaves the three 2-way interactions

Output 4. Step 1 of the loglinear analysis

At Step 2, MATHS*PSYSTATS is eliminated, because it has the largest probability (.6564).

> The 2-way interaction with the least effect (i.e. smallest chi-square change and largest p-value) is eliminated

```
If Deleted Simple Effect is    DF   L.R. Chisq Change  Prob   Iter

MATHS*DATAPROC                   1                1.029 .3104    2
MATHS*PSYSTATS                   1                 .198 .6564    2
DATAPROC*PSYSTATS                1               32.098 .0000    2

Step 2

  The best model has generating class

       MATHS*DATAPROC
       DATAPROC*PSYSTATS

Likelihood ratio chi square =        .62884    DF = 2  P =  .730
```

Output 5. Step 2 of the loglinear analysis

At Step 3, MATHS*DATAPROC is eliminated, because it has the larger probability (which is greater than the criterion level of 0.05). The remaining interaction, DATAPROC*PSYSTATS cannot be eliminated, because the p-value is less than .05. All the interactions now having been processed, it remains for any main effect that is <u>not part of the remaining 2-way interaction</u> to be tested for inclusion. In this case, only MATHS qualifies.

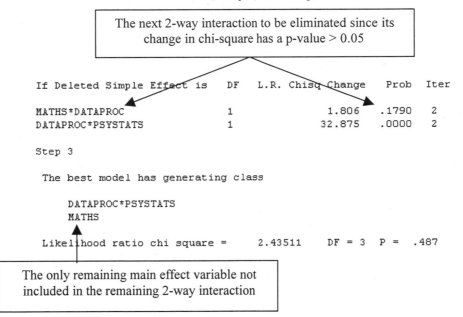

The next 2-way interaction to be eliminated since its change in chi-square has a p-value > 0.05

```
If Deleted Simple Effect is    DF    L.R. Chisq Change    Prob    Iter

MATHS*DATAPROC                  1                1.806    .1790     2
DATAPROC*PSYSTATS               1               32.875    .0000     2

Step 3

   The best model has generating class

        DATAPROC*PSYSTATS
        MATHS

   Likelihood ratio chi square =        2.43511    DF = 3  P =  .487
```

The only remaining main effect variable not included in the remaining 2-way interaction

Output 6. Step 3 of the loglinear analysis

At Step 4, neither of these effects can be eliminated, because both probabilities are less than 0.05. Both effects, therefore, must be included in the final model.

Both the one remaining 2-way interaction DATAPROC*PSYSTATS and the main effect MATHS have p-values < 0.05 and therefore remain in the model

```
If Deleted Simple Effect is    DF    L.R. Chisq Change    Prob    Iter

DATAPROC*PSYSTATS               1               32.875    .0000     2
MATHS                           1                6.610    .0101     2

Step 4

   The best model has generating class

        DATAPROC*PSYSTATS
        MATHS

   Likelihood ratio chi square =        2.43511    DF = 3  P =  .487

. - - - - - - - - - - - - - - - - - - - - - - - - - - - - - - - - - - - - .

The final model has generating class

     DATAPROC*PSYSTATS
     MATHS
```

The Step 4 model is therefore adopted as the final

Output 7. The final step of the loglinear analysis

313

The final model includes the interaction between the variables representing the Data Processing Exam and the Psychology Statistics Exam, plus a main effect of maths. Note that there are no interactions involving the maths variable. Thus the most interesting finding is the interaction between the two examinations.

Finally, the computer lists the table of observed frequencies and the expected frequencies **as estimated by the final model** (Output 8). Notice that the expected frequencies (EXP) estimated by the final model are much closer to the observed frequencies (OBS) than those for the total independence model, whose values were listed in Table 3, and are reproduced in Table 4 in the next section for the purposes of comparison.

The **Goodness-of-fit chi-square test** shows that these expected frequencies do **not** differ significantly from the observed frequencies (the p-value for chi-square is not significant since it is much greater than 0.05). Thus the final model based on the interaction of the Data Processing Exam and the Psychology Statistics Exam, together with the main effect of the Advanced Maths Course, provides an excellent fit to the data. The analysis has shown that whereas the results of the Data Processing Exam and the Psychology Statistics Exam are associated, it makes no difference whether the Advanced Maths course had been taken.

```
Observed, Expected Frequencies and Residuals.

     Factor         Code    OBS count EXP count Residual Std Resid

MATHS           Yes
  DATAPROC        Pass
    PSYSTATS        Pass       47.0      42.4      4.64      .71
    PSYSTATS        Fail       10.0      10.9      -.89     -.27
  DATAPROC        Fail
    PSYSTATS        Pass        4.0       5.6     -1.65     -.69
    PSYSTATS        Fail       10.0      12.1     -2.10     -.60

MATHS           No
  DATAPROC        Pass
    PSYSTATS        Pass       58.0      62.6     -4.64     -.59
    PSYSTATS        Fail       17.0      16.1       .89      .22
  DATAPROC        Fail
    PSYSTATS        Pass       10.0       8.4      1.65      .57
    PSYSTATS        Fail       20.0      17.9      2.10      .50
- - - - - - - - - - - - - - - - - - - - - - - - - - - - - - -
Goodness-of-fit test statistics

    Likelihood ratio chi square =  2.43511  DF = 3  P =  .487
              Pearson chi square =  2.39308  DF = 3  P =  .495
```

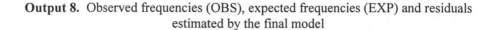

The final goodness-of-fit chi-square test. If there is a good fit, the test should not be significant (i.e. p-value should be > 0.05)

Output 8. Observed frequencies (OBS), expected frequencies (EXP) and residuals estimated by the final model

13.2.3 Comparison with the total independence model

The reader might wish to use the loglinear command to confirm the expected frequencies tabulated in Table 3 in Section 13.2.1, which are predicted by the total independence model.

- After inserting the factor names and values in the **Factor(s):** box as before, click the **Model:** box to open the **Loglinear Analysis: Model** dialog box.
- In the **Specify Model** box, select the **Custom** radio button. Enter the three factor names into the **Generating Class** box by highlighting each name and clicking on the arrow under **Build Term(s)**. Within the **Build Term(s):** box, click **Interaction** and select **All 3-way**. The completed dialog box is shown in Figure 5.
- Click **Continue** to return to the **Model Selection Loglinear Analysis** dialog box.
- Within the **Model Building** box, click the **Enter in single step** radio button.
- Click **OK**.

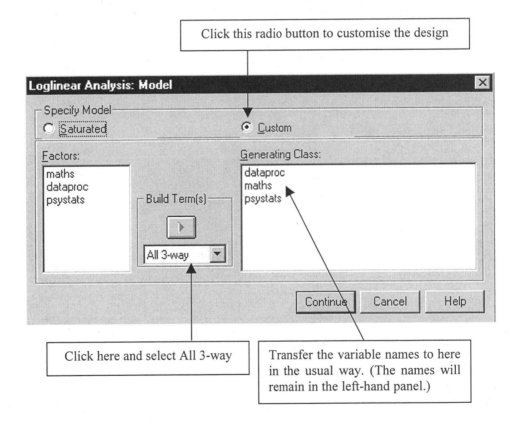

Figure 5. The completed dialog box for determining the expected frequencies from the total independence model (i.e. All 3-way)

The expected frequencies for the three-way interaction (involving all the factors) will appear in a table similar to the one in Output 8. The goodness-of-fit chi-square has a value of 37.08 and a p-value less than 0.01, showing that the correspondence between these expected frequencies and the observed frequencies is very poor.

Table 4 contrasts the observed and expected cell frequencies under the assumptions of the 'best model' generated by the hierarchical loglinear command with the corresponding discrepancies under the total independence model. Clearly, the correspondence with the loglinear model is much closer. The superiority of the loglinear analysis over the traditional Pearson chi-square approach in producing a convincing interpretation of the data has been amply demonstrated.

Table 4. Observed frequencies and expected frequencies under the final loglinear model $Exp_{(loglinear)}$ and the total independence model $Exp_{(independent)}$

Advanced Maths	Yes				No			
Data Processing	Pass		Fail		Pass		Fail	
Psychology Statistics	Pass	Fail	Pass	Fail	Pass	Fail	Pass	Fail
Cell Freq:								
Observed	47	10	4	10	58	17	10	20
Exp $_{(loglinear)}$	42.4	10.9	5.6	12.1	62.6	16.1	8.4	17.9
Exp $_{(independent)}$	36.0	17.2	12.0	5.7	53.2	25.5	17.7	8.5

EXERCISE 22

LOGLINEAR ANALYSIS

Before you start

Before you proceed with this practical, please read Chapter 13.

Helping behaviour: The opposite-sex dyadic hypothesis

In the literature on helping behaviour by (and towards) men and women, there is much interest in three questions:

(1)   Are women more likely to receive help?
(2)   Are women more likely to give help?
(3)   Are people more likely to help members of the opposite sex?
        (This is known as the opposite-sex dyadic hypothesis.)

A male or female confederate of the experimenter approached male and female students who were entering a university library and asked them to participate in a survey. Table 1 shows the incidence of helping in relation to the sex of the confederate and that of the participant.

Table 1. Results of an experiment to test the opposite-sex dyadic hypothesis			
Sex of Confederate	Sex of Participant	Help Yes	No
Male	Male	52	35
	Female	21	43
Female	Male	39	40
	Female	23	75

Preparing the SPSS data set

Prepare the data set as in Section 13.2.1 with three coding variables Confederate's Sex (*confsx*), Participant's Sex (*subjsx*), and Participant's Response (*help*), complete with appropriately defined value labels. There will be a fourth variable (*count*) for the cell frequencies. Remember to use the **Weight Cases** command for the cell frequency variable *count*.

Exploring the data

Before carrying out any formal analysis, a brief inspection of the contingency table (Table 1) may prove informative. First of all, we notice that, on the whole, help was more likely to be refused than given; moreover, the females helped less than did the males. In view of the generally lower rate of helping in the female participants, therefore, there seems to be little support for the hypothesis that females help more. Finally, turning to the third question, although the male participants did help the male confederate more often, the female participants tended to be more helpful towards the male confederate. This provides some support for the opposite-sex dyadic hypothesis.

Procedure for a loglinear analysis

To answer the three research questions, we shall use a **hierarchical loglinear analysis** (following the **backward elimination** strategy), with a view to fitting the most parsimonious **unsaturated model**. Run the loglinear command (ignoring the preliminary Crosstabs operation) as described in Section 13.2.2 by selecting
Analyze
> **Loglinear**
>> **Model Selection...**

to open the **Model Selection Loglinear Analysis** dialog box.

Enter the coding variables in the **Factor(s)** box and the **Range** values for each factor. In the **Model Building** box, select **Use backward elimination** (the default radio button). Click **OK**.

Output for the loglinear analysis

The main features of the output for a hierarchical loglinear analysis are described in Section 13.2.2.

Look at the table of **Tests that K-way and higher order effects are zero**.

- **Up to what level of complexity do you expect the effects to be significant?**

Now look for the effects retained in the **final model**.

- **List the effects in the final model. Does the highest order of complexity correspond with what you noted in the previous bullet point question?**

Finally look at the table of **Observed, Expected Frequencies and Residuals**. Compare the magnitudes of the observed (OBS) count and the expected (EXP) count assuming the final model.

- **Write down the value of chi-square for the Goodness-of-fit test and its associated p-value? Does this p-value suggest a good or a bad fit?**

Finally, test the hypothesis of total independence of all three variables, using the procedure described in Section 13.2.4.

- **Write down the value of chi-square for the Goodness-of-fit test and its associated p-value? Does this p-value suggest a good or a bad fit?**

Conclusion

It should be quite clear from the foregoing comparisons that the final loglinear model is a very considerable improvement upon the model of total independence. Loglinear models provide a powerful tool for teasing out the relationships among the variables in multi-way contingency tables.

CHAPTER 14

DISCRIMINANT ANALYSIS AND LOGISTIC REGRESSION

14.1 INTRODUCTION

14.2 DISCRIMINANT ANALYSIS WITH SPSS

14.3 LOGISTIC REGRESSION

14.1   INTRODUCTION

In Chapter 12, it was shown how the methods of regression could be used to predict scores on one target dependent (or **criterion**) variable from scores on other (independent) variables, known as **predictors** or **regressors**. In the situations we discussed, the dependent variable was always quantitative and the data were always in the form of measurements. There are circumstances, however, in which one might wish to predict, not scores on a quantitative dependent variable, but category membership.

Suppose that a pre-morbid blood condition has been discovered, which is suspected to arise in middle life partly because of smoking and drinking. A hundred people are tested for the presence of the condition and a record made of their smoking and alcohol consumption. Can people's levels of smoking and drinking be used to predict whether they have the blood condition?

Here, although the independent variables are *quantitative* variables, the dependent variable is *qualitative*, comprising the categories *Yes* and *No*. The reader may wonder why the categories cannot simply be assigned arbitrary code numbers, such as *1* for *No* and *2* for *Yes* and the regression carried out in the usual way. There are many problems with that approach, however, and it is not recommended (see, for example, Tabachnick & Fidell, 1997). The techniques that we shall describe have been specially designed to overcome these problems.

In this chapter, we shall discuss two regression techniques that have been devised for the purpose of making predictions of category membership:
   (1) Discriminant analysis;
   (2) Logistic regression.

While in some fields, the use of logistic regression has gained ground in recent years, SPSS offers this method only for dichotomous criterion variables. For variables comprising three or more categories, therefore, discriminant analysis is still the only option available in SPSS.

14.1.1 Discriminant analysis

Discriminant analysis is a technique for combining the independent variables into a single new variable, on which each participant in the study gets a score. This new variable, known as a **discriminant function**, is constructed in such a way that the participants' scores on it, to the greatest possible extent, separate, or discriminate among, those people in the different categories of the dependent variable. Ideally, if a one-way ANOVA were then to be carried out on the new scores there would be significant differences among the category means. In discriminant analysis, however, a statistic called **Wilks' lambda (Λ)** is used to test the efficacy of the discriminant function in producing significant differences among the target groups.

To express this idea a little more formally, let DV be the dependent variable, and IV_1, IV_2, ..., IV_p be p independent variables. The purpose of discriminant analysis is to find a linear function D of the independent variables, that is, a function of the type

$$D = A + B_1(IV_1) + B_2(IV_2) + \ldots + B_p(IV_p),$$

such that people's scores on D are spread out as much as possible over the categories of the dependent variable. The function D is the **discriminant function**.

If, as in the blood condition example, the dependent variable consists of just two categories, one can imagine two overlapping bell-shaped normal distributions, each being a distribution of D for one of the categories. Each distribution of D will be centred around the mean score on D for that particular group. D has been constructed in such a way (by finding just the right values for the coefficients A, B_1, ..., B_p) so that the two distributions are as far apart as possible.

As in multiple regression, techniques are available to help the researcher to identify those independent variables that make the greatest contributions to the prediction of the dependent variable. There are many other parallels between multiple regression and discriminant analysis.

14.1.2 Types of discriminant analysis

There are three types of discriminant analysis (DA): **direct**, **hierarchical**, and **stepwise**. In **direct** DA, all the variables enter the equations at once; in **hierarchical** DA, they enter according to a schedule set by the researcher; and in **stepwise** DA, statistical criteria alone determine the order of entry. Since in most analyses, the researcher has no reason for giving some predictors higher priority than others, the third (**stepwise**) method is the most generally applicable and is the only one discussed in this chapter.

14.1.3 Stepwise discriminant analysis

The statistical procedure for stepwise discriminant analysis is similar to that for multiple regression, in that the effect of the addition or removal of an IV is monitored by a statistical test and the result used as a basis for the inclusion of that IV in the final analysis. When there are only two groups, there is just one discriminant function. With more than two groups, however, there can be several functions (one fewer than the number of groups); though it is unusual for more than the first three discriminant functions to be useful.

Various statistics are available for weighing up the addition or removal of variables from the analysis, but the most commonly used is **Wilks' Lambda (Λ).** The significance of the change in Λ when a variable is entered or removed is obtained from an **F test**. At each step of adding a variable to the analysis, the variable with the largest F (**F TO ENTER**) is included. This process is repeated until there are no further variables with an F value greater than the critical minimum threshold value. Sometimes a variable, having been included at one point, is removed later when its F value (**F TO REMOVE**) falls below a critical level. (This can happen with the stepwise regression procedure as well - see Section 12.2.3.)

Eventually, the process of adding and subtracting variables is completed, and a summary table is shown indicating which variables were added or subtracted at each step. The variables remaining in the analysis are those used in the discriminant function(s). The next table shows which functions are statistically reliable. The first function provides the best means of predicting group membership. Later functions may or may not contribute reliably to the prediction process. Additional tables displaying the functions and their success rates for correct prediction can be requested. Plots can also be specified.

14.1.4 Restrictive assumptions of discriminant analysis

While it is assumed that the independent variables will usually be quantitative, it is also possible to include some qualitative independent variables (e.g. sex, marital status) just as it is in multiple regression.

The use of discriminant analysis, however, carries several restrictive assumptions. It is assumed, for example, that the data are **multivariate normal** (i.e. that the sampling distribution of any linear combination of predictors is normally distributed). The procedure is sufficiently robust to cope with some skewness, provided the samples are not too small. The problem of outliers, however, is more serious. It is important to search for extreme values and eliminate them. In addition, there is the usual assumption of **homogeneity of variance-covariance matrices**. It is also important to avoid **multicollinearity** (high correlations among the independent variables). In particular, no variable must be an exact linear function of any of the others, a condition known as **singularity**.

14.2 DISCRIMINANT ANALYSIS WITH SPSS

A school's vocational guidance officer would like to be able to help senior pupils to choose which subjects to study at university. Fortunately, some data are available from a project on the background interests and school-leaving examination results of samples of architectural, engineering and psychology students. The students also filled in a questionnaire about their extra-curricular interests, including outdoor pursuits, drawing, painting, computing, and kit construction. The problem is this: can knowledge of the pupils' scores on a number of variables be used to predict their subject category at university? In this study, then, subject category at university (psychologists, architects or engineers) is the dependent variable, and all the others are independent variables.

14.2.1 Preparing the data set

Since the data for this example are the scores of 118 participants on ten variables, it would be extremely tedious for readers to type the data into **Data View**. The data are available on WWW at:

(http://www.psyc.abdn.ac.uk/teaching/spss/spssbook.htm).

Select **Chap14_1.sav** and save it to the hard disk (or a floppy) for easier access.

A section of the data set in **Data View** is shown in Figure 1.

case	studsubj	sex	conkit	model	draw	paint	outdoor	comput	vismod	quals
32	Architect	Male	4	2	7	4	2	2	4	9
33	Architect	Female	4	10	7	3	5	1	6	7
34	Psychologist	Male	2	2	0	0	1	1	2	9
35	Psychologist	Female	2	4	3	1	1	1	6	9

Figure 1. Some cases in the SPSS data set

14.2.2 Exploring the data

Before embarking on the discriminant analysis, the user should probe the data for possible violations of the underlying assumptions. A full treatment of this topic is beyond the scope of this book, but the interested reader should consult a statistical text such as Tabachnick & Fidell (1997) for more details.

See Section 4.3.2

Here we recommend the user to check for extreme scores and outliers by using the **Explore** command (see Chapter 4, Section 4.3.2) to examine the distributions of the independent variables within the different categories of the dependent variable (*studsubj*).

- In the **Explore** dialog box, click the **Plots** radio button in the **Display** options, and transfer the variable names of all the predictors except *sex* into the **Dependent List** box. Transfer the variable name Study Subject [*studsubj*] into the **Factor List** box, and the variable name Case Number [*case*] into the **Label Cases by** box.
- Click **OK** to plot all the boxplots and stem-and-leaf displays.

Most of the **boxplots** are satisfactory except for Interest in Painting [*paint*] (see Output 1). Here one box is much larger than the others. There are also some extreme values, which are represented by *. The corresponding **stem-and-leaf** displays also show discrepancies among the distributions. It might be advisable to omit Interest in Painting, should the first run indicate that there are problems with the data.

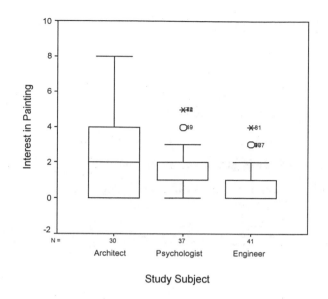

Output 1. The boxplots of Interest in Painting for the three subject categories

14.2.3 Running discriminant analysis

Discriminant analysis is run as follows:

- Choose
  Analyze
  Classify (see Figure 2)
  Discriminant...
  to open the **Discriminant Analysis** dialog box, the completed version of which is shown in Figure 3.

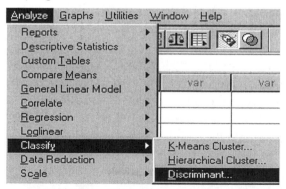

Figure 2. Finding the Discriminant Analysis command

- Transfer the dependent variable name (here it is *studsubj*, the subject of study) to the **Grouping Variable** box. Click **Define Range** and type *1* into the **Minimum** box and *3* into the **Maximum** box.
- Drag the cursor down the names of the independent variables to highlight them and transfer them all to the **Independents** box.
- Since a stepwise analysis is going to be used, click the radio button for **Use stepwise method**.

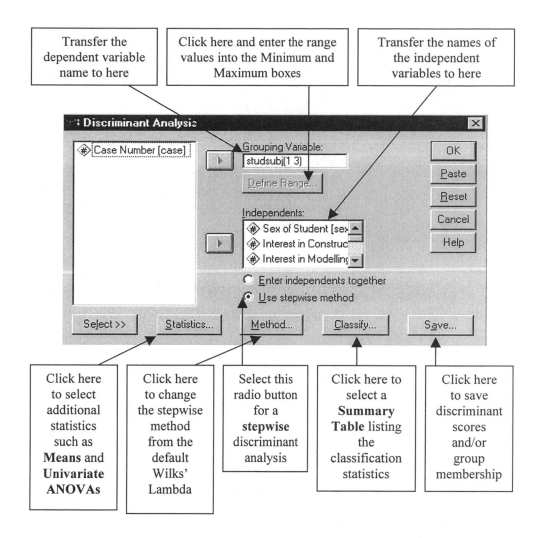

Figure 3. The Discriminant Analysis dialog box for the grouping variable studsubj (with three levels) and several independent variables, using the stepwise method

- Recommended options include the means and one-way ANOVAs for each of the variables across the three levels of the independent variable. To obtain these options, click **Statistics...** and select **Means** and **Univariate ANOVAs**. Click **Continue** to return to the original dialog box.
- Another recommended option is a final summary table showing the success or failure of the analysis. Click **Classify...** and select **Summary table**. Click **Continue** to return to the original dialog box.
- Click **OK** to run the **Discriminant Analysis**.

14.2.4 Output for discriminant analysis

The output, as listed in the left-hand pane of the **SPSS Viewer** (Output 2), is rather daunting. Fortunately, as with the regression output, not all of it is required.

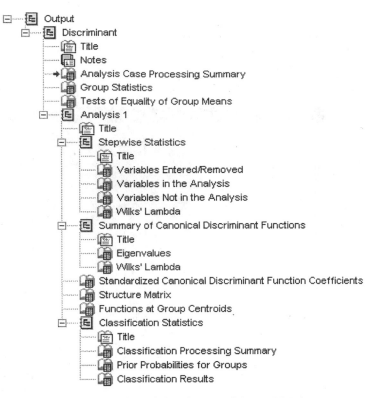

Output 2. The left-hand pane of the SPSS Viewer

Information about the data and the number of cases in each category of the grouping variable

Output 3 shows how many valid cases were used in the analysis. Ten cases, which were missing a score on one or more of the independent variables, have been excluded.

Analysis Case Processing Summary

Unweighted Cases		N	Percent
Valid		108	91.5
Excluded	Missing or out-of-range group codes	0	.0
	At least one missing discriminating variable	10	8.5
	Both missing or out-of-range group codes and at least one missing discriminating variable	0	.0
	Total	10	8.5
Total		118	100.0

Output 3. Information about the number of valid cases

Statistics

The next table (Output 4) is **Group Statistics**, which shows the optional statistics and the number of cases for each independent variable at each level of the grouping variable. The **Univariate ANOVAs** (Output 5) show whether there is a statistically significant difference among the grouping variable means (*studsubj*) for each independent variable. All these differences are significant (as shown in the column **Sig.**), except Interest in Computing and Interest in Modelling Kits.

Group Statistics

Study Subject		Mean	Std. Deviation	Valid N
Architect	Sex of Student	1.27	.45	30
	Interest in Construction Kits	3.33	1.58	30
	Interest in Modelling Kits	3.97	2.68	30
	Interest in Drawing	5.10	2.29	30
	Interest in Painting	2.50	2.18	30
	Interest in Outdoor Pursuits	2.30	2.07	30
	Interest in Computing	1.77	1.45	30
	Ability to Visualise Model	5.53	1.25	30
	School Qualifications	6.63	2.86	30
Psychologist	Sex of Student	1.59	.50	37
	Interest in Construction Kits	2.35	1.46	37
	Interest in Modelling Kits	3.32	2.04	37
	Interest in Drawing	3.57	2.13	37
	Interest in Painting	1.54	1.37	37
	Interest in Outdoor Pursuits	3.43	2.29	37
	Interest in Computing	1.78	1.51	37
	Ability to Visualise Model	4.08	1.44	37
	School Qualifications	9.32	3.32	37
Engineer	Sex of Student	1.07	.26	41
	Interest in Construction Kits	3.93	1.69	41
	Interest in Modelling Kits	2.90	1.80	41
	Interest in Drawing	3.24	2.47	41
	Interest in Painting	.80	1.08	41
	Interest in Outdoor Pursuits	2.37	2.00	41
	Interest in Computing	1.78	1.29	41
	Ability to Visualise Model	4.56	1.34	41
	School Qualifications	9.73	4.15	41
Total	Sex of Student	1.31	.46	108
	Interest in Construction Kits	3.22	1.71	108
	Interest in Modelling Kits	3.34	2.18	108
	Interest in Drawing	3.87	2.42	108
	Interest in Painting	1.53	1.68	108
	Interest in Outdoor Pursuits	2.71	2.17	108
	Interest in Computing	1.78	1.40	108
	Ability to Visualise Model	4.67	1.46	108
	School Qualifications	8.73	3.76	108

Output 4. An edited table showing the optional statistics and the number of cases for each independent variable at each level of the grouping variable Study Subject

Tests of Equality of Group Means

	Wilks' Lambda	F	df1	df2	Sig.
Sex of Student	.77	15.99	2	105	.00
Interest in Construction Kits	.84	9.71	2	105	.00
Interest in Modelling Kits	.96	2.11	2	105	.13
Interest in Drawing	.90	6.09	2	105	.00
Interest in Painting	.83	10.41	2	105	.00
Interest in Outdoor Pursuits	.94	3.24	2	105	.04
Interest in Computing	1.00	.00	2	105	1.00
Ability to Visualise Model	.84	9.74	2	105	.00
School Qualifications	.88	7.38	2	105	.00

All ANOVAs are significant except those with p-value > 0.05

Output 5. Univariate ANOVAs

The summary table

The Stepwise Statistics section begins with a summary table (Output 6) showing which variables were entered and removed (though in this analysis none was removed), along with values of Wilks' Lambda and the associated probability levels. Notice the values of **F to Enter** and **F to remove** in footnotes b and c. These are the default criteria, which can be changed in the Stepwise Method dialog box.

Stepwise Statistics

Variables Entered/Removed [a,b,c,d]

		Wilks' Lambda							
						Exact F			
Step	Entered	Stat-istic	df1	df2	df3	Stat-istic	df1	df2	Sig.
1	Sex of Student	.77	1	2	105	16.0	2	105	.00
2	Interest in Painting	.64	2	2	105	16.0	4	208	.00
3	School Qualifications	.54	3	2	105	12.4	6	206	.00
4	Ability to Visualise Model	.48	4	2	105	11.3	8	204	.00
5	Interest in Outdoor Pursuits	.44	5	2	105	10.3	10	202	.00
6	Interest in Construction Kits	.40	6	2	105	9.59	12	200	.00
7	Interest in Computing	.37	7	2	105	8.99	14	198	.00

At each step, the variable that minimizes the overall Wilks' Lambda is entered.

a. Maximum number of steps is 18.

b. Minimum partial F to enter is 3.84.

c. Maximum partial F to remove is 2.71.

d. F level, tolerance, or VIN insufficient for further computation.

Output 6. Summary table of variables entered and removed

Entering and removing variables step by step

The next table, **Variables in the Analysis**, lists the variables in the analysis at each step. Output 7 shows only Steps 1-3 and the final stage, Step 7.

Variables in the Analysis

Step		Toler-ance	F to Remove	Wilks' Lambda
1	Sex of Student	1.00	15.99	
2	Sex of Student	.88	15.71	.83
	Interest in Painting	.88	10.19	.77
3	Sex of Student	.88	15.26	.70
	Interest in Painting	.85	12.34	.67
	School Qualifications	.95	9.78	.64
7	Sex of Student	.59	7.47	.43
	Interest in Painting	.73	10.92	.46
	School Qualifications	.91	10.83	.46
	Ability to Visualise Model	.90	7.96	.43
	Interest in Outdoor Pursuits	.84	3.96	.40
	Interest in Construction Kits	.80	4.33	.41
	Interest in Computing	.70	3.85	.40

Output 7. Variables in the analysis at Steps 1 to 3, and finally at Step 7

In Output 7, the column labelled **Tolerance** lists the tolerance for a variable not yet selected and is one minus the square of the multiple correlation coefficient between that variable and all the other variables already entered. Very small values suggest that a variable can contribute little to the analysis. The column **F to remove** tests the significance of the decrease in discrimination should that variable be removed. But since no F-ratio is less than the criterion of 2.71, none of the variables entered has been removed subsequently.

The table, **Variables not in the Analysis**, tabulates the variables not in the analysis at the start and at each step thereafter until the final step (Output 8 shows only Steps 1 & 2, then Step 7). It can be seen that Sex of Student has the highest **F to Enter** value initially (and the lowest Wilks' Lambda) and is, therefore, selected as the first variable to enter at Step 1 (Output 7).

At Step 1, the variable with the next highest **F to Enter** value is Interest in Painting which is then entered as shown in Output 7. Finally at Step 7, the variables Interest in Modelling Kits and Interest in Drawing are never entered because their **F to Enter** values are smaller than the criterion of 3.84.

Variables Not in the Analysis

Step		Tolerance	Min. Tolerance	F to Enter	Wilks' Lambda
0	Sex of Student	1.00	1.00	15.99	.77
	Interest in Construction Kits	1.00	1.00	9.71	.84
	Interest in Modelling Kits	1.00	1.00	2.11	.96
	Interest in Drawing	1.00	1.00	6.09	.90
	Interest in Painting	1.00	1.00	10.41	.83
	Interest in Outdoor Pursuits	1.00	1.00	3.24	.94
	Interest in Computing	1.00	1.00	.00	1.00
	Ability to Visualise Model	1.00	1.00	9.74	.84
	School Qualifications	1.00	1.00	7.38	.88
1	Interest in Construction Kits	.93	.93	3.43	.72
	Interest in Modelling Kits	.94	.94	2.20	.74
	Interest in Drawing	1.00	1.00	6.04	.69
	Interest in Painting	.88	.88	10.19	.64
	Interest in Outdoor Pursuits	.98	.98	1.49	.75
	Interest in Computing	.75	.75	4.20	.71
	Ability to Visualise Model	1.00	1.00	8.83	.66
	School Qualifications	.98	.98	7.69	.67
7	Interest in Modelling Kits	.72	.57	.36	.37
	Interest in Drawing	.63	.52	.91	.37

This variable is entered at Step 1 (Output 7) with the largest F to Enter value

This variable is entered at Step 2 (Output 7) with the largest F to Enter value

These variables at Step 7 are excluded because their F to Enter values are < 3.84

Output 8. Part of the table of variables not in the analysis at Steps 0, 1 and 7

The next table in the output, Wilks' Lambda, is a repeat of the table given in Output 5 and is not reproduced.

Statistics of the discriminant functions

Output 9 shows the percentage (**% of Variance**) of the variance accounted for by each discriminant function and how many of them (if any) are significant (see the **Sig** column in the **Wilks' Lambda** table). Here we see that both functions are highly significant.

Summary of Canonical Discriminant Functions

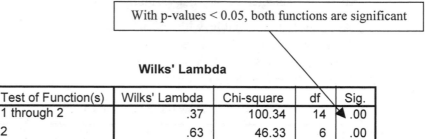

Percentage of variance accounted for by each function and cumulatively

Eigenvalues

Function	Eigenvalue	% of Variance	Cumulative %	Canonical Correlation
1	.70[a]	54.83	54.83	.64
2	.58[a]	45.17	100.00	.60

a. First 2 canonical discriminant functions were used in the analysis.

With p-values < 0.05, both functions are significant

Wilks' Lambda

Test of Function(s)	Wilks' Lambda	Chi-square	df	Sig.
1 through 2	.37	100.34	14	.00
2	.63	46.33	6	.00

Output 9. Statistics of the discriminant functions

Standardised coefficients and within groups correlations with discriminants

Two tables follow in the listing, the first (not reproduced here) being the **Standardized Canonical Discriminant Function Coefficients**, and the second (Output 10) the **Structure Matrix**, which is a table of pooled within groups correlations between the independent variables and the discriminant functions.

Structure Matrix

	Function	
	1	2
Ability to Visualise Model	-.51*	-.10
School Qualifications	.43*	-.16
Interest in Painting	-.42*	.36
Interest in Drawing [a]	-.22*	.12
Interest in Modelling Kits [a]	-.12*	.07
Interest in Computing	.01*	.00
Sex of Student	.19	.70*
Interest in Construction Kits	-.15	-.54*
Interest in Outdoor Pursuits	.19	.25*

Pooled within-groups correlations between discriminating variables and standardized canonical discriminant functions
Variables ordered by absolute size of correlation within function.

*. Largest absolute correlation between each variable and any discriminant function

a. This variable not used in the analysis.

Output 10. The structure matrix

It is clear from the information in Output 10 that the first function is contributed to positively by participants' school qualifications and their interest in painting, and negatively by their ability to visualise models. The second function is contributed to positively by sex and negatively by interest in construction kits, and in outdoor pursuits. The asterisks mark the correlations with the higher value for each variable.

The next table in the output (not reproduced), **Functions at Group Centroids**, lists the within-group means for each canonical variable by group (i.e. Architect, Psychologist, Engineer).

Success of predictions of group membership

The optional selection of **Summary table** from the **Classify** options in the **Discriminant Analysis** dialog box provides an indication of the success rate for predictions of membership of the criterion grouping variable's categories using the discriminant functions developed in the analysis (see Output 11). The table indicates that the overall success rate is 72.2%.

Classification Results^a

		Predicted Group Membership			
	Study Subject	Architect	Psychologist	Engineer	Total
Count	Architect	22	2	6	30
	Psychologist	4	25	8	37
	Engineer	5	5	31	41
%	Architect	73.3	6.7	20.0	100.0
	Psychologist	10.8	67.6	21.6	100.0
	Engineer	12.2	12.2	75.6	100.0

a. 72.2% of original grouped cases correctly classified.

Output 11. Classification results

Output 11 also shows that Engineers are the most accurately classified, with 75.6% of the cases correct. Architects are next with 73.3%, and Psychologists are last with 67.6%. Notice that incorrectly classified Architects are more likely to be classified as Engineers than as Psychologists, and that incorrectly classified Psychologists are more likely to be classified as Engineers than as Architects!

14.2.5 Predicting group membership

Section 14.2 posed the problem of whether knowledge of pupils' scores on a number of variables could be used to predict their subjects of study at university. The analysis has demonstrated that two discriminant functions can be generated using all the variables except Interest in Modelling Kits, Interest in Drawing and Interest in Computing, and that these functions can predict 68.5% of the cases correctly. But what about future students, for whom only the data on the predicting variables are known? Can the program be used to predict which subject they should study? The answer is yes.

Proceed as follows:
- Enter the data for the new students at the end of the data in **Data View**. Leave the grouping variable blank or enter an out-of-range number so that the

analysis does not include these cases when it is computing the discriminant functions.

- Complete the **Discriminant Analysis** dialog box as before but, in addition, click **Save...** and then click the radio button for **Predicted group membership**. Click **Continue** and **OK**.

- The predicted group membership will appear in a new column labelled **Dis_1** in **Data View**, along with the predictions for all the other cases.

14.3   LOGISTIC REGRESSION

There is another approach to category prediction that entails fewer assumptions than does discriminant analysis. This is known as **logistic regression**. Returning to the example of the blood condition, suppose that of the hundred people studied, forty-four people have it and fifty-six do not. Let us assign code numbers to the two categories: to those who have the condition, we assign 1; and to those who do not, we assign 0. In this section, we shall outline the use of logistic regression to predict category membership.

Since the probability that a person selected at random having the condition is .44, our best prediction of category membership for everyone is to assign them all to the 'condition absent' category. On that basis, we should be right in 100% of the cases in which the condition was absent, but wrong in the 44% cases in which the condition was present, giving us a net success rate of 56%. The purpose of logistic regression is to improve upon this success rate by exploiting association between the dependent and independent variables to predict category membership (the dependent variable) with the greatest possible accuracy.

It is not an unreasonable assumption that, although an individual may or may not have the blood condition, certain variables such as number of cigarettes smoked and amount of drink consumed actually increase the probability of developing the condition <u>continuously</u> throughout the range of consumption. This probability, however, cannot be expected to be a linear function of the independent variables. In fact, the probability of the condition is likely to rise more rapidly as scores on the independent variable begin to increase and less rapidly at a later stage, so that the probability graph would be rather like a flattened S. An estimate of this curve is called the **logistic regression function**.

Once the logistic regression function has been estimated, the probability estimates can be used to assign individuals to the two categories of the dependent variable. When the value of the probability estimate exceeds .5, the participant is assigned to the group with the blood condition; if the probability is less than .5, the participant is assigned to the other category.

Recall that in **multiple regression**, the dependent variable Y is predicted from the p independent variables $X_1, X_2, ..., X_p$ by means of the regression equation

$$Y' = B_0 + B_1X_1 + B_2X_2 + ... + B_pX_p$$

where B_0 is the constant and $B_1, B_2, ...$ are the regression coefficients. The logistic regression function, although itself nonlinear, also involves a linear function Z of the independent variables, where

$$Z = B_0 + B_1X_1 + B_2X_2 + ... + B_pX_p \quad ----- \quad (1)$$

We shall say more about the meaning of Z in the next section.

In logistic regression, as in ordinary multiple regression, the values of the parameters B_0, B_1, ..., B_p are chosen so that the logistic regression equation predicts the independent variable (in this case category membership) as accurately as possible. In multiple regression, formulae can be derived from which the B values can be calculated. In logistic regression, however, a brute-force algorithm must be used, whereby, after so-many cycles or **iterations**, the estimates of the B-values appear to be converging to fixed values.

14.3.1 Interpretation of logistic regression coefficients

In the simplest case of logistic regression, there is just one independent variable and (1) simplifies to:

$$Z = B_0 + B(\text{independent variable}).$$

In the present example, if we take *smoking* as the independent variable,

$$Z = B_0 + B(smoking).$$

The odds and the logit function

Returning to our example of the blood condition, in which 44 of the hundred people studied have the condition, we can express this by saying that the **odds** in favour of having the condition are 44 to 56 (i.e. 11 to 14). We shall write the odds as a fraction, 11/14.

Unfortunately, there is a difficulty with the odds as a measure of the likelihood of an event. When an event is very likely to occur, the odds can be a huge number; whereas, when the event is very unlikely, the odds can only be a fraction between zero and one. This asymmetry of range can be rectified by taking the natural logarithm (i.e. the log to the base e) of the odds, giving the **log odds**, or **logit**, function, where

$$\text{logit} = \log_e(\text{odds}) \quad \text{- - - -} \quad (2)$$

In the present example, logit $= \log_e(11/14) = -0.24$. (The reader can confirm this either with a calculator or by using the **LN(numexpr)** function in SPSS's **Compute...** command). Notice that here the logit has a <u>negative</u> value, meaning that the odds are <u>against</u> the occurrence of the event. When the odds are in favour of an event, that is, greater than 1/1, the logit has a positive value. When the chances of an event are even (that is, the odds are 1/1), the logit is zero.

The logit and the logistic regression equation

The probability of an event and the odds in favour of the event are, by definition, measures of likelihood related according to

$$p = \frac{\text{odds}}{1 + \text{odds}} \quad \text{- - - -} \quad (3)$$

From the definition of the logit given above, therefore, the **logistic regression equation** is

$$p = \frac{e^{\text{logit}}}{1 + e^{\text{logit}}} \quad \text{- - - -} \quad (4)$$

Although the probability cannot be a linear function of the independent variables, it is assumed (because of the scaling properties of the log odds mentioned in the introduction) that the logit is such a linear function. In fact, the term **Z** in equation (1) is the **logit**, and we can write the **logit equation** as

$$Z = B_0 + B_1 X_1 + B_2 X_2 + \ldots + B_p X_p \quad \text{- - - -} \quad (5)$$

The logistic regression coefficient and the logit (or log odds)

Recall that in simple bivariate regression, the slope of the regression line is the average change in the criterion variable that will result from a change of a unit in the independent variable. From the foregoing, it is seen that in logistic regression, the regression coefficient is the increase in the logit in favour of an individual being in the target category produced by an increment of one unit in the independent variable.

For example, suppose that $B = 1.1$, that is, an increase of one smoking unit (say ten cigarettes) increases the logit in favour of the blood condition by an increment of 1.1. This means that in terms of the odds (rather than the log odds), the original odds are <u>multiplied</u> by the <u>antilog</u> of B, that is e^B, or **exp(B)**. Recall that when logs are added, the original numbers are <u>multiplied</u>. So

$$\exp(1.1) = 3.0$$

(The reader can confirm this value either by using a calculator or the **EXP**(numexpr) function in SPSS's **Compute...** command). Thus by **exponentiating** B (i.e., raising e to the power of B), we find that an increase of one Smoking unit results in the odds being <u>multiplied</u> by 3, that is, that the event is <u>three times</u> as likely to happen.

In summary:

(1) The logistic regression coefficient B is the change in the **logit** (log odds) in favour of target category membership produced by an increase of one unit in the dependent variable.

(2) The quantity **exp(B)** is the factor by which the original odds must be <u>multiplied</u> when the IV increases by one unit.

14.3.2 An example with two independent variables (covariates)

Table 1 shows the first eight cases from some data on the incidence of a pre-morbid blood condition in 100 people, together with their average daily smoking levels and alcohol consumption. (The complete data set is given at the end of this chapter.) The units have been selected to cover the entire range of consumption for each variable: one smoking unit is ten cigarettes; one drinking unit is the equivalent of a glass of wine or a half-pint of beer.

Table 1. The first eight cases showing the presence or absence of a blood condition along with their smoking and drinking habits

Case	Blood	Smoke	Alcohol	Case	Blood	Smoke	Alcohol
1	Yes	7	18	5	Yes	5	11
2	Yes	6	15	6	Yes	2	18
3	Yes	1	10	7	No	0	0
4	Yes	7	16	8	Yes	6	12

14.3.3 Preparing the data set

The data set for this example is large, and it would be extremely tedious for readers to type it into **Data View**. The set is available on WWW at:

(http://www.psyc.abdn.ac.uk/teaching/spss/spssbook.htm).

Select *Chap14_2.sav* and save it to your hard disk (or a floppy for easier access).

14.3.4 Running logistic regression

In its logistic regression dialog box, SPSS uses the term **covariate** instead of independent variable.

- Choose
  Analyze
     Regression
        Binary Logistic ...
  to obtain the **Logistic Regression dialog box** (Figure 4).
- Transfer the dependent variable name Blood Condition [*blood*] to the **Dependent:** box, and the covariate (i.e., independent variable) names Smoking [*smoking*] and Alcohol [*alcohol*] to the **Covariate:** box.
  Notice the button labelled >a*b> underneath the transfer arrow outside the **Covariates** box. This is the **interaction button**. Had we wished to include an interaction term in the regression, both the independent variables would have been selected together in the left-hand panel and transferred by clicking the interaction button, resulting in the appearance, in the Covariates box, of an additional term, smoking*alcohol. In the present example, since we have no theoretical basis for expecting an interaction, we shall include main effect terms only.
- It is advisable to supplement the default output with some useful additional statistics and displays. Click **Options...** to obtain the **Options** dialog box (Figure 5) and select **Hosmer-Lemeshow goodness-of-fit** and **Iteration history**. Click **Continue** to return to the **Logistic Regression** dialog box.
- Click **OK**.

Note that the default **Method** setting is **Enter**. As in multiple regression, this inputs all the independent variables (covariates) into the model at once and achieves the equivalent of a simultaneous multiple regression. This is the strategy we shall follow in our example.

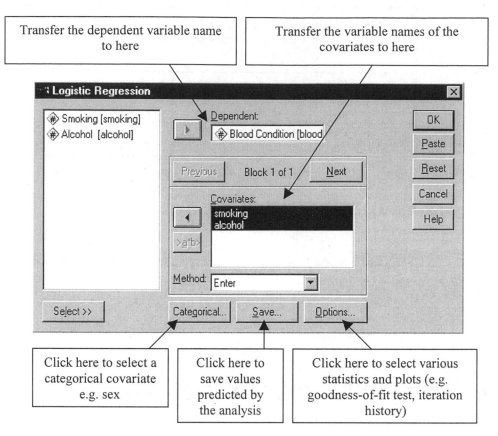

Figure 4. The logistic regression dialog box

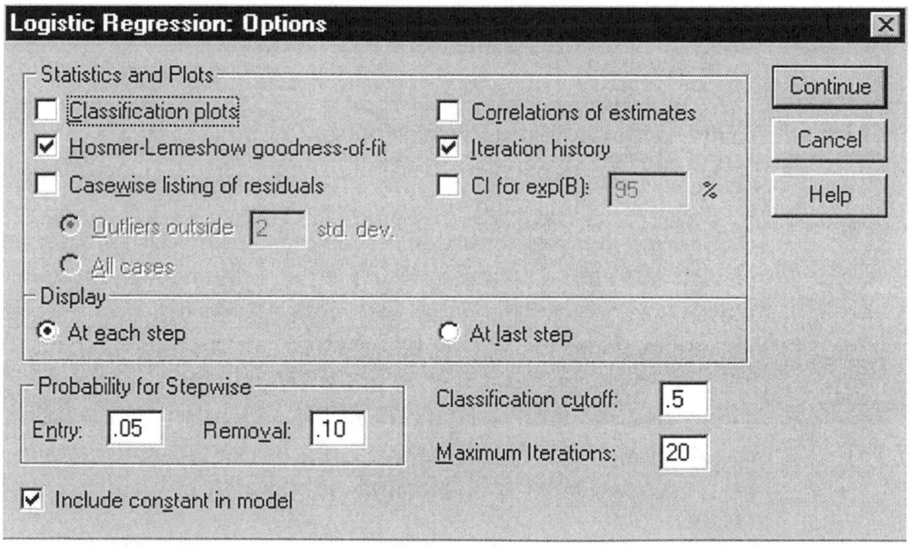

Figure 5. The Options dialog box with various options selected

In the **Logistic Regression** dialog box, there is another button labelled **Save...** which accesses the **Save New Variables** dialog box (not shown). Selecting items from this box will add several new variables to those already in **Data View**, including predicted probabilities, predicted group membership, and standardized and studentized residuals. Also available are measures of the leverage that highly deviant scores can exert on the regression parameters, namely, Cook distances, standardized Cook distances and leverage values, all of which are useful tools for regression diagnostics. We suggest that, for the present, the reader should focus on the basic regression and explore the **Save...** button later.

14.3.5 Output for logistic regression

The output for logistic regression is extensive, even if no options are selected. In this section, we shall describe some of the most useful items. First, however, some preliminary points are in order.

In logistic regression, pivotal use is made of a statistic which is written variously as **-2 log(likelihood)**, **-2LL**, or **–2LogL**. This **log likelihood statistic** behaves as chi-square, and has a large value when a model fits poorly, and a small value when the it fits the data well. The log likelihood statistic is analogous to the error sum of squares in multiple regression: the larger its value, the more the variance that remains to be accounted for.

In the introduction, we saw that the best bet of a person's category membership was the more frequently occurring category. Logistic regression begins by finding a log likelihood for a model with neither of the dependent variables present. The **log likelihood chi-square** should be large and significant, since 'guessing' category membership on the basis of membership frequency alone leaves much variance unexplained. This 'guessing' stage is called **Step 0** by SPSS. In our example, the success rate at Step 0 will simply be the proportion of cases that did not have the blood condition, since that was the more frequent category.

The next step (**Step 1**) is to add <u>both</u> independent variables. (We are following the simultaneous strategy. In stepwise methods, the independent variables are added or subtracted one at a time, or in blocks.) We should now find that the **log likelihood chi-square** is substantially smaller, meaning that there is now substantially less residual variance. Obversely, we should find that the success rate has now increased substantially. Clearly the logistic regression model is doing some useful work.

When it comes to assessing the relative importance of the independent variables, matters are not so simple. The **Wald** statistic is available to test the regression coefficients individually for significance. There are circumstances, however, in which the Wald statistic may lead the user astray. Better is the **Hosmer-Lemeshow** statistic, which measures the relative improvement achieved by addition of the independent variables. The Hosmer-Lemeshow statistic is based on the log likelihood ratios with and without the independent variables in the model.

After a summary of the number of cases read and SPSS's internal coding of the categories of the criterion variable, the output is divided into two sections, headed **Block 0: Beginning Block** and **Block 1: Method = Enter**.

Block 0 reports the results of an 'intercept only' analysis, in which all cases are assigned the same probability of belonging to the target criterion category. Since only 44 of the hundred participants in the study had the blood condition, the program assigned a probability of 0.44 to each case and therefore estimated that none was in the target category. (Had more than fifty of the participants tested positive on the blood condition, the program would have assigned them all to the target category.) The initial success rate for this analysis before the covariates are included is presented in the **Classification Table** (Output 12) showing that 100% of the observed cases without the blood condition (NO) are correctly predicted whereas none of the cases with the blood condition (YES) is correctly predicted. The net success rate is 56%, in agreement with the reasoning in the second paragraph of the introduction to this section.

Classification Table [a,b]

			Predicted		
			Blood Condition		Percentage
	Observed		No	Yes	Correct
Step 0	Blood Condition	No	56	0	100.0
		Yes	44	0	.0
	Overall Percentage				56.0

a. Constant is included in the model.

b. The cut value is .500

Output 12. The Classification Table before including any of the covariates in the analysis

Step 1 presents the results of a regression analysis after both covariates (independent variables) have been included. Here, the **Classification Table** (Output 13) tells quite a different story: the participants have been correctly assigned in 85% of cases, a very considerable improvement.

Classification Table [a]

			Predicted		
			Blood Condition		Percentage
	Observed		No	Yes	Correct
Step 1	Blood Condition	No	51	5	91.1
		Yes	10	34	77.3
	Overall Percentage				85.0

a. The cut value is .500

Output 13. The Classification Table after including the covariates in the analysis

The iteration history table

Output 14 displays the iteration history, the success at each stage being measured by the chi-square statistic **–2 Log likelihood**. With each run, the value of chi-square decreases, but after a few iterations, it tends to converge to a fixed level. The iteration process is terminated when the change in chi-square falls below 0.01 percent.

Notice that the log likelihood given in Output 14 for Step 0 ('Initial –2 Log Likelihood') is 137.19. The final log likelihood (also shown in Output 14) is 78, showing that the addition of the independent variables to the model accounts for much of the residual variance.

Iteration History [a,b,c,d]

	Iteration	-2 Log likelihood	Coefficients Constant	SMOKING	ALCOHOL
Step 1	1	98.52	-.91	.47	.00
	2	88.27	-1.03	.88	-.03
	3	80.47	-1.20	1.53	-.06
	4	78.11	-1.36	2.11	-.08
	5	78.00	-1.39	2.26	-.08
	6	78.00	-1.39	2.26	-.08

a. Method: Enter

b. Constant is included in the model.

c. Initial -2 Log Likelihood: 137.19

d. Estimation terminated at iteration number 6 because log-likelihood decreased by less than .010 percent.

-2 Log likelihood is a statistic like chi-square which decreases with each iteration. The process is stopped when the change in the statistic from the previous iteration is less than 0.01%

Output 14. The iteration history showing the improvement in goodness-of-fit with each iteration

Several of the tables in the output tabulate statistics showing a model's goodness-of-fit. The **Model Summary** table (Output 15) includes two such statistics similar to the coefficient of determination (R^2) in ordinary least-squares regression. The **Cox & Snell R-square** is based on the log likelihood for the model compared with the log likelihood for a baseline model. The **Nagelkerke R-square** is an adjusted version of the Cox & Snell R-square. It adjusts the scale of the statistic to cover the full range from 0 to 1.

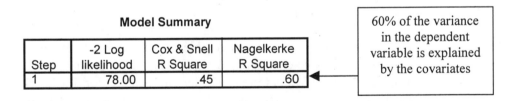

Model Summary

Step	-2 Log likelihood	Cox & Snell R Square	Nagelkerke R Square
1	78.00	.45	.60

60% of the variance in the dependent variable is explained by the covariates

Output 15. Tests of how well the model fits the observed data

The optional **Hosmer and Lesmeshow Test** table (Output 16) is a chi-square test showing the goodness-of-fit between the observed and predicted number of cases for the two categories of the blood condition. (A good fit is indicated by a <u>high</u> p-value.)

Hosmer and Lemeshow Test

Step	Chi-square	df	Sig.
1	6.16	7	.52

A high p-value showing a good fit (i.e. no difference between the predicted and observed number of cases)

Output 16. Test of goodness-of-fit of the predicted and observed number of cases for the two categories of the blood condition

The next table **Variables in the Equation** (Output 17) lists the coefficients for the **logit equation**. From the first column of entries, it can be seen that the intercept (constant) and the coefficients of the Smoking and Alcohol covariates, A, B_1 and B_2, are -1.39, 2.26 and -0.08, respectively. The logit equation is thus:

(estimated logit) = 2.26(Smoking) - 0.08(Alcohol) - 1.39

The constant and coefficients for the logit equation	Wald test of the significance of the constant and coefficients, and associated p-values. The coefficient for Alcohol is not significant

Variables in the Equation

		B	S.E.	Wald	df	Sig.	Exp(B)
Step 1ᵃ	SMOKING	2.26	.51	19.49	1	.00	9.62
	ALCOHOL	-.08	.08	.85	1	.36	.92
	Constant	-1.39	.37	13.98	1	.00	.25

a. Variable(s) entered on step 1: SMOKING, ALCOHOL.

Output 17. The coefficients for the logistic regression equation

The coefficient of 2.26 for Smoking means that, on average, smoking ten more cigarettes (one smoking unit) adds 2.26 to the log odds in favour of having the blood condition: that is the odds in favour of having the condition are multiplied by $e^{2.26}$ = 9.62. This multiplier is shown in the rightmost column, headed **Exp(B)**, which is the predicted change in odds for a unit increase in the covariate.

The negative value of the regression coefficient for Alcohol (first entry in the second row) is of no account, since the p-value from the **Wald** test, in the column labelled **Sig.**, is 0.36. (The null hypothesis is that the coefficient is zero.) Since alcohol has a negligible effect, the analysis can be re-run with Smoking as the sole covariate. When this is done, the number of cases correctly classified is still 85% but the coefficient in the equation for Smoking is reduced slightly to 2.20 for Smoking and the value of the constant changes to -1.56.

As an example, let us use the **logistic regression equation** to calculate the predicted probability for Case 6 (see Table 1) who had a score of 2 for smoking and 18 for alcohol. The logit value is

logit = 2.26(2) - 0.08(18) - 1.39 = 1.69

The predicted probability from the logistic regression equation is

$$\frac{\exp(logit)}{1 + \exp(logit)} = 0.84$$

With a classification cut-off set at 0.5, then a probability of 0.84 represents a positive example (i.e., Case 6 is correctly predicted to have the blood condition). If the value had been less than 0.5, then the prediction would have been that Case 6 did not have the blood condition.

In conclusion, it is clear that smoking has a strong effect upon the likelihood of having the blood condition whereas alcohol consumption has a negligible effect. Eighty-five per cent of the cases were correctly classified.

14.3.6 Different approaches to logistic regression

As with multiple regression, there are three different kinds of logistic regression: direct (or simultaneous); sequential; and stepwise. These terms have exactly the same meanings as they do in multiple regression.

The testing of models in logistic regression

As with any other regression method, it is often highly desirable to account for a set of data in terms of a minimum number of independent variables. Perhaps, for example, we can account for the incidence of the blood condition using smoking rate alone, without considering the intake of alcohol.

In the example we considered, this proved to be possible using the simultaneous entry of both independent variables into the regression model. In our example the properties of the data made life easy for us. Multiple regression is always least problematic when

(1) some independent variables correlate substantially with the dependent variables and

(2) the independent variables correlate with one another only to a very small extent.

It is when there are substantial correlations among the independent variables that problems arise. These problems, which are serious for any kind of regression, intensify when one is following a stepwise regression strategy. One obvious solution to the problem of a high correlation between two independent variables is to remove one of them. But which one should be removed? There may be no clear-cut statistical answer to this question.

The need for a substantive, as well as a statistical, model

When independent variables are correlated, there is always dubiety about which (if any) variable is causally prior. Earlier, in the context of multiple regression, we made the point that decisions about such matters require a sound theoretical rationale. They cannot be made on the basis of any automatic statistical testing procedure.

The point is trivial with the sequential approach, which obviously requires a strong rationale for imposing a specific *a priori* order on the independent variables. However, essentially the same basic consideration applies to the other approaches also. Even the direct or simultaneous method is not without its risks, even where there is no multicollinearity. It is true that each independent variable is treated as if it had been entered into the equation last. But there is no guarantee that if a new variable were to be added, the picture would remain the same. The safe use of any multiple regression method requires not only a sound statistical model, but also a cogent **causal model**.

Appendix

The data for logistic regression

Blood	Smoke	Alcohol	Blood	Smoke	Alcohol	Blood	Smoke	Alcohol
Yes	7	18	Yes	2	15	Yes	1	0
Yes	6	15	Yes	7	12	No	1	0
Yes	1	10	Yes	4	6	Yes	8	0
Yes	7	16	Yes	3	4	Yes	1	0
Yes	5	11	Yes	2	14	Yes	8	0
Yes	2	18	Yes	2	10	Yes	1	0
No	0	0	Yes	6	16	Yes	8	0
Yes	6	12	Yes	2	0	Yes	8	0
Yes	7	13	No	2	0	No	1	0
Yes	2	14	No	0	0	Yes	1	0
Yes	3	2	Yes	1	0	Yes	1	0
Yes	8	18	Yes	8	0	No	1	0
Yes	1	0	No	0	4	Yes	0	4
Yes	1	0	No	0	6	No	0	4
No	0	6	No	0	2	No	0	4
No	0	6	No	0	6	No	0	4
No	0	6	No	0	6	No	0	4
No	0	6	No	0	6	Yes	0	1
No	0	6	No	0	3	No	0	4
No	0	6	No	0	6	No	0	4
No	0	6	No	0	4	No	0	4
No	0	6	No	0	4	No	0	2
Yes	0	1	No	0	1	No	0	1
No	0	4	Yes	0	1	No	0	1
No	0	4	No	0	1	No	1	0
Yes	0	1	No	0	1	No	0	0
No	0	1	Yes	0	1	Yes	0	1
No	0	1	No	0	1	No	0	0
No	0	1	No	0	1	Yes	1	0
No	0	1	No	0	1	Yes	0	0
No	0	1	No	0	1	No	0	2
No	0	1	No	0	1	Yes	0	0
Yes	0	1	No	0	1	Yes	1	0
No	0	0						

EXERCISE 23

PREDICTING CATEGORY MEMBERSHIP: DISCRIMINANT ANALYSIS AND LOGISTIC REGRESSION

Before you start

Before proceeding with this practical, please read Chapter 14.

Prediction of reading success at the school-leaving stage

Just before they leave school, students in the most senior class of a school are regularly tested on their comprehension of a difficult reading passage. Typically, only 50% of students can perform the task. We shall also suppose that, for a substantial number of past pupils, we have available data not only on their performance on the comprehension passage but also on the very same variables that were investigated in the exercise on multiple regression, namely, the reading-related measures that we have referred to as *logo*, *syntax* and *vocal*, all of which were taken in the very earliest stages of the children's education.

The full data set is given in the appendix of this exercise. As with the multiple regression example, we hope that the data have already been stored for you in a file with a name such as **discrim**, the contents of which you can access by using the **Open** procedure. The data (***Exer_23.sav***) are also available for saving to the hard disk on WWW (http://www.psyc.abdn.ac.uk/teaching/spss/spssbook.htm). Table 1 shows the first and the last two lines of the data set.

Table 1. Part of the data set			
Logo	**Syntax**	**Vocal**	**Comprehension**
10	20	64	1
28	28	58	1
...	...	...	...
82	69	60	2
51	48	52	2

The rightmost variable is a coding variable whose values, *1* and *2*, denote, respectively, *failure* and *success* on the comprehension task.

Exploring the data set

Before moving on to the main analysis, a preliminary exploration of the data will bring out at least some of their important features. For example, if a particular variable is going to be useful in assigning individuals to categories, one might expect that, if its scores are subdivided by category membership, there should be a substantial difference between the group means. If there is no difference, the variable will probably play a minimal role in the final discriminant function. To investigate these differences, **one-way ANOVAs** can be used to compare the group means on the various independent variables.

These tests, however, are requested by options in the **Discriminant** procedure. We shall therefore return to the descriptive statistics when we come to prepare the dialog box.

Since discriminant analysis assumes that the distribution of the independent variables is multivariate normal, we shall also need to look at their distributions.

In the **Graphs** drop-down menu choose **Boxplot...** (see Section 14.2.2). Choose the **Summaries of Separate Variables** option and define the variables as *logo syntax* and *vocal*.

- **Study the output and note whether the boxplots reveal any outliers. Do the side-by-side boxplots show anything of interest?**

DISCRIMINANT ANALYSIS

Procedure for discriminant analysis

Run the discriminant analysis as described in Section 14.2.3. There, however, we recommended the **Stepwise** method of minimisation of **Wilks' Lambda**. In the present example, because of its simplicity, it is better to use the default method known as **Enter**, in which all the variables are entered simultaneously. Since **Enter** is the default method, there is no need to specify it. In the **Discriminant Analysis** dialog box, click **Statistics** to open the **Discriminant Analysis: Statistics** dialog box. Select **Univariate ANOVAs** and click **Continue**. In the **Discriminant Analysis** dialog box, click **Classify** to open the **Discriminant Analysis: Classification** dialog box and (in **Display**) select **Summary table**. Click **Continue**, then **OK**.

Output for discriminant analysis

The main features of the output for a discriminant analysis are explained in Section 14.2.4, which you should review. In the present example, the table labelled Group Statistics shows the number of cases in each of the categories of the variable *comp*. The next table, headed Tests of Equality of Group Means lists **Wilks' Lambda** and **F-ratios** (with their associated p-values in the column **Sig.**) for the comparisons between the groups on each of the three independent variables.

- **Which variables have significant F ratios and which do not?**

There now follows the first of the tables labelled Eigenvalues, which show the output of the discriminant analysis proper. Because there are only two groups, there is only one function. The next table, **Wilks' Lambda**, tabulates the statistic **lambda**, its **chi-square value** and the associated p-value (**Sig.**). You will notice immediately that the value of lambda is smaller than the value for any of the three IVs considered separately. That is well and good: the discriminant function *D*, which uses the information in all the IVs should do a better job than any one IV alone. Here there is an obvious parallel with multiple regression, in which the predictive ability of the multiple regression equation cannot be less than the simple regressions of the target variable on any one predictor alone. Just as, in multiple regression, predictions can only improve when more predictors are added, the addition of another variable to the discriminant function can only improve its efficacy (although, in the case of the variable *vocal*, the improvement is negligible). Since, however, two of the IVs can each discriminate reliably between the groups, the result of the chi-square test of lambda in the discriminant analysis table is a foregone conclusion. As expected, the p-value is very small. The discriminant function *D* can indeed discriminate reliably between the two groups on the basis of performance on the independent variables.

Ignore the table labelled Standardized Canonical Discriminant Function Coefficients. A more useful table is the next one, labelled **Structure Matrix**, which lists the pooled-within-groups correlations between discriminating variables and the standardized canonical discriminant function.

- **Are the correlations as you expected?**

Ignore the table Functions at Group Centroids.

The next set of tables relate to the classification of cases. We have shown that the discriminant function D discriminates between the two groups; but how effectively does it do this? This is shown under the heading: 'Classification Results'.

- **Write down the percentage of grouped cases correctly classified, the percentage of correct group 1 (failure) predictions and the percentage of correct group 2 (success) predictions.**

Now try out the discriminant function on some fresh data by adding them at the end of the data file (e.g. enter in the columns for *logo*, *syntax*, *vocal*, the values 50, 50, 50; 10, 10, 10; 80, 80, 80 and any others you wish). Leave the column blank for *compreh*. Then re-run the analysis after selecting **Save** in the **Discriminant Analysis** dialog box, clicking the radio button for **Predicted group membership**, and then clicking **Continue** and **OK**. The predicted memberships will appear in the variable called **dis_1**.

- **Would someone with logo, syntax and vocal scores of 50, 50, 50 respectively be expected to pass or fail the comprehension test?**

Conclusion

This exercise is intended to be an introduction to the use of a complex and sophisticated statistical technique. Accordingly, we chose an example of the simplest possible application, in which the dependent variable comprises only two categories. The simplicity of our interpretation of a number of statistics such as **Wilks' lambda** breaks down when there are more than two categories in the dependent variable. For a treatment of such cases, see Tabachnick & Fidell (1996).

LOGISTIC REGRESSION

Procedure for logistic regression

We shall use the same data set for the logistic regression analysis. Use the procedure described in Section 14.3.4.

Output for logistic regression

The main features of the output for logistic regression are explained in Section 14.3.5, which you should review.

Examine the tables in Block 1.

- **What is the value of R^2 as calculated by the Nagelkerke formula? What is the meaning of this value?**

- **What is the value of chi-square for the Hosmer and Lemeshow test and is it significant? What do you conclude about the fit of the model?**

- **What is the overall percentage of correct predictions? How does this compare with the success rate of the discriminant analysis?**

- **Write down the logit equation.**

Conclusion

In this example, the results of the discriminant analysis and logistic regression are similar but where there are several binary predictors, logistic regression would be the preferred analysis. Currently, SPSS can only handle two categories in the dependent variable for logistic regression.

Appendix to Exercise 23 - The Data

L	S	V	C	L	S	V	C	L	S	V	C	L	S	V	C	L	S	V	C
10	20	64	1	45	45	29	1	43	50	31	1	56	44	52	2	84	50	46	2
28	28	58	1	62	30	26	1	48	45	44	1	69	46	59	2	70	54	51	2
55	25	42	1	20	69	78	1	14	77	53	1	53	57	52	2	65	64	23	2
30	20	30	1	49	59	46	1	64	32	55	1	75	48	34	2	69	60	57	2
32	27	42	1	39	42	31	1	55	48	9	1	71	52	30	2	66	79	50	2
25	49	81	1	26	56	78	1	41	55	41	2	50	68	75	2	58	82	13	2
40	38	43	1	40	31	51	1	30	54	20	2	81	54	41	2	45	90	59	2
71	22	79	1	34	60	45	1	29	67	18	2	51	62	14	2	82	58	65	2
19	59	71	1	31	66	50	1	28	68	72	2	49	72	72	2	82	69	60	2
55	32	75	1	18	61	22	1	46	67	80	2	66	61	40	2	51	48	52	2

CHAPTER 15

FACTOR ANALYSIS

15.1   INTRODUCTION

15.2   A FACTOR ANALYSIS OF DATA ON SIX VARIABLES

15.3   USING SPSS COMMAND LANGUAGE

15.1   INTRODUCTION

15.1.1 The nature of factors

Suppose that the participants in a sample are each tested on several variables, perhaps an assortment of tests of intellectual ability, such as vocabulary, short term memory, reaction speed and so on. The correlations of performance on each test with every other test in the battery can be arranged in a rectangular array known as a **correlation matrix**, or **R-matrix**. Each row (or column) of R would contain all the correlations involving one particular test in the battery. The cells along the **principal diagonal** (running from the top left to the bottom right of the matrix) would remain empty (or contain the entry *1*), since each cell on that diagonal represents the combination of a particular test with itself; but each off-diagonal cell would be occupied by the correlation between the tests whose row and column intersect at that particular cell. The R-matrix can be the starting point for several statistical procedures, but in this chapter we shall consider just one: **factor analysis.**

The presence in the R-matrix of clusters of sizeable correlations among subsets of the tests in the battery would suggest that the tests in a subset may be tapping the same underlying psychological dimension, or ability. If the traditional British theories of the psychology of intelligence are correct, there should be fewer (far fewer) dimensions than there are tests in the battery. The purpose of factor analysis is to identify and to quantify the dimensions supposed to underlie performance on a variety of tasks. The **factors** produced by factor analysis are mathematical entities, which can be thought of as classificatory axes, with respect to which the tests in a battery can be 'plotted'. The greater the value of a test's co-ordinate, or **loading**, on a factor, the more important that factor is in accounting for the correlations between that test and the others in the battery.

A factor, then, has a geometric interpretation as a classificatory axis in an axial reference system with respect to which the tests in the battery are represented as points in space.

But the term **factor** also has an equivalent algebraic, or arithmetical interpretation as a linear function of the observed scores that people achieve on the tests in a battery. For example, if a battery comprises 8 tests, and each testee were also to be assigned a ninth score consisting of the sum of the 8 test scores, that ninth, artificial, score would be a **factor score**, and it would make sense to speak of correlations between the factor and the real test scores. We have seen that the loading of a test on a factor is, geometrically speaking, the co-ordinate of the test point on the factor axis. But that axis represents a 'factor' in the second, algebraic sense, and the loading is the correlation between the test scores and those on the factor.

In factor analysis, a major assumption is that the mathematical factors represent **latent variables** (i.e. psychological dimensions), the nature of which can only be guessed at by examining the nature of tests that have sizeable co-ordinates on any particular axis. It should perhaps be said at the outset that this claim is controversial, and there are those who insist that the factors of factor analysis are statistical realities, but psychological fictions.

The topic of factor analysis is not elementary, and the SPSS output bristles with highly technical terms. If you are unfamiliar with factor analysis, we suggest you read the lucid texts by Kim and Mueller (1978a, 1978b) and by Tabachnick and Fidell (1996), which contain relatively painless introductions to the technical jargon.

15.1.2 Stages in a factor analysis

A factor analysis usually takes place in three stages:

(1)   A **matrix of correlation coefficients** is generated for all possible pairings of the variables (i.e., the tests).

(2)   From the correlation matrix, **factors** are extracted. The most common method is called **principal factors** (often wrongly referred to as **principal components** extraction, hence the abbreviation **PC**).

(3)   The factors (axes) are **rotated** to maximise the relationships between the variables and some of the factors and minimise association with others. The most common method is **varimax**, a rotation method which maintains independence among the mathematical factors. Geometrically, this means that during rotation, the axes remain **orthogonal** (i.e. they are kept at right angles).

A fourth stage can be added at which the scores of each participant on each of the factors emerging from the analysis are calculated. It should be stressed that these **factor scores** are not the results of any actual test taken by the participants: they are estimates of the participants' standing on the **supposed** latent variables that have emerged as mathematical axes from the factor analysis of the data set. Factor scores can be very useful, however, because they can subsequently be used as input for further statistical analysis.

It is advisable to carry out only Stage 1 initially, in order to be able to inspect the correlation coefficients in the correlation matrix R. Since the purpose of the analysis is to link variables together into factors, those variables must be related to one another and therefore have correlation coefficients larger than about 0.3. Should any variables show no substantial correlation with any of the others, they would be removed from R in subsequent analysis. It is also advisable to check that the correlation matrix does not possess the highly undesirable properties of **multicollinearity** and **singularity**. The former is the condition where the variables are very highly (though imperfectly) correlated which can arise, for example, from the use of two psychometric tests essentially measuring the same aptitude. The latter, an extreme case of the former, would obtain in the unlikely event of some of the variables being exact linear functions of others in the battery. Should the matrix show multicollinearity, some the variables must be omitted from the analysis.

15.1.3 The extraction of factors

The factors (or axes) in a factor analysis are **extracted** (or, pursuing the geometric analogy, **constructed**) one at a time. The process is repeated until it is possible, from the loadings of the tests on the factors so far extracted, to generate good approximations to the correlations in the original **R matrix**. Factor analysis tells us how many factors (or axes) are necessary to achieve a reconstruction of R that is sufficiently good to account satisfactorily for the correlations that R contains.

15.1.4 The rationale of rotation

If we think of the tests in the battery and the origin of the axis (factor) set as stationary points and rotate the axes around the origin, the values of all the loadings will change. Nevertheless, the new set of loadings on the axes, *whatever their new position*, can still be used to produce exactly the same estimates of the correlations in the R-matrix. In this sense, the position of the axes is quite arbitrary: the factor matrix (or **F-matrix**) only tells us *how many* axes are necessary to classify the data adequately; but it does not thereby establish that the initial position of the axes is the appropriate one.

In **rotation**, the factor axes are rotated around the fixed origin until the loadings meet certain criteria. The set of loadings that satisfies the criteria is known as the **rotated factor matrix**. The purpose of any rotation is to achieve a configuration of loadings having the qualities collectively known as **simple structure** which, loosely conceived, is the set of loadings that shows the maximum number of tests loading on the minimum number of factors.

The idea is that the fewer the factors that are involved in accounting for the correlations among a group of tests, the easier it is to invest those factors with meaning. In fact, simple structure is an ideal never achieved in practice, partly because the concept, in its original form, is actually rather vague and embodies contradictory properties. Modern computing packages such as SPSS offer a selection of rotation methods, each based upon a different (but reasonable) interpretation of simple structure.

15.1.5 Confirmatory factor analysis and structural equation modelling

So far, we have considered the use of factor analysis to ascertain the minimum number of classificatory variables (or axes) we need to account for the shared variance among a set of tests. While the researcher will almost certainly have expectations about how many factors are likely to emerge, the process of factor extraction proceeds automatically until the criterion is reached, after which the process terminates. In several fields, such as human abilities and intelligence, 'factor invariance' has been found with those factors accounting for the greatest amounts of variance, such as the general intelligence (g) factor and the major group factors.

There are, nevertheless, several problems and issues associated with factor analytic methodology. Even when the same battery of tests is used, the precise number of factors extracted has been found to vary from study to study. Moreover, the pattern shown by the loadings in the final rotated factor matrix depends upon the method of rotation used: some methods (such as varimax) keep the factor axes at right angles; but others (such as quartimax) allow **oblique** (correlated) factors. There has been much argument about which method of rotation is best, and the preferred method tends to reflect the theoretical views of the user. In the circumstances, traditional factor analytic methods seem ill-suited to the testing of specific hypotheses, and many hold the view that they are appropriate only in the early stages of investigation in a research area.

In view of such considerations, the methods we have been describing have been termed **exploratory factor analysis** (Maxwell, 1977, p.60), and over the past three decades, there has been much interest in developing techniques for testing specific hypotheses about the factorial composition of specific test batteries (or other variables). In **confirmatory factor analysis**, the user decides in advance that there will be a specific number of factors; indeed, assumptions may also be made about the pattern of zero and non-zero loadings of the tests on the factors and the correlations among them. On the other hand, such formulations, like other **models**, can arguably be put to the empirical test and are more suited to the evaluation of precise hypotheses than the traditional exploratory factor analysis.

Recent years have seen dramatic developments in what is known as **structural equation modelling** (for example, see Tabachnick & Fidell, 1996, Chapter 14) of which confirmatory factor analysis is just one aspect. There are also, for example, **causal modelling** (or **path analysis**), **regression models** with constrained weightings of the regressors, and **covariance structure models**, which test assumptions about a variance-covariance matrix, such as equality of the variances of all the tests in the battery. Several computing packages have been designed to test such models (see Bentler, 1993, on EQS; Joreskog & Sorbom, 1989, on LISREL). At present SPSS for Windows does not include a module for confirmatory factor analysis.

15.2　A FACTOR ANALYSIS OF DATA ON SIX VARIABLES

Suppose a researcher has available the marks of 10 children in six tests: **French, German, Latin, Music, Mathematics** and **Mapwork** as shown in Table 1.

In order to identify the psychological dimensions tapped by these six variables, it is decided to carry out a factor analysis.

Table 1. Scores of 10 children on six variables						
Case	**French**	**German**	**Latin**	**Music**	**Maths**	**Mapwork**
1	72	69	81	45	53	51
2	41	32	40	78	91	81
3	47	54	46	50	47	49
4	33	34	40	56	65	63
5	75	76	91	46	54	47
6	41	46	48	92	88	90
7	67	72	68	56	45	47
8	32	41	35	32	36	37
9	84	76	92	44	51	43
10	45	36	45	72	67	79

15.2.1 Entering the data for a factor analysis

Enter the data using the procedures described in Section 3.2. In **Variable View**, name the six variables for the factor analysis. Include an extra variable for the case number. Ensure that there are no decimals by changing the **Decimals** column value to 0. Click the **Data View** tab at the foot of **Variable View** and enter the data in **Data View**.

Note that there are no grouping variables in this data set. This is a purely correlational (as opposed to experimental) study. Inasmuch as there can be said to be an 'independent' variable, it is one whose existence must be inferred from whatever patterns may exist in the correlation matrix. It is the *raison d'être* of factor analysis to make such an inference credible. The first five cases in **Data View** are shown in Figure 1.

case	french	german	latin	music	maths	mapwork
1	72	69	81	45	53	51
2	41	32	40	78	91	81
3	47	54	46	50	47	49
4	33	34	40	56	65	63
5	75	76	91	46	54	47

Figure 1. Data View, showing the scores of the first five children on six variables

15.2.2 The factor analysis command

To run the factor analysis command:
- Choose
  Analyze
    Data Reduction
        Factor... (Figure 2)
  to open the **Factor Analysis** dialog box (Figure 3).

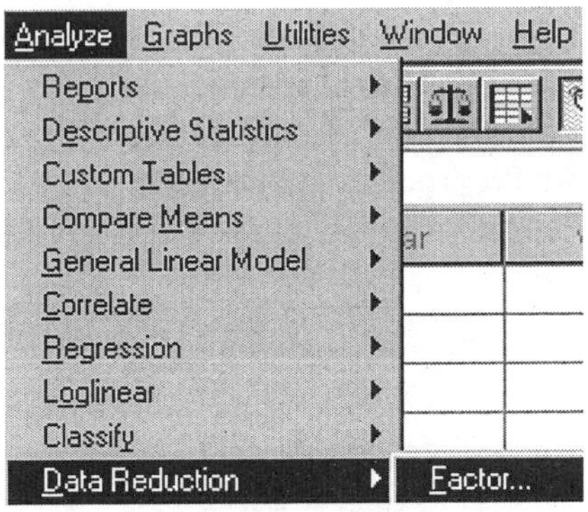

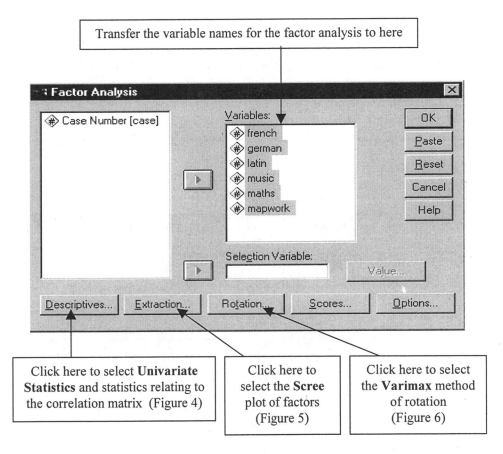

Figure 2. Finding the factor analysis dialog box

- Transfer all the variable names except Case Number [*case*] to the **Variables** box.

Figure 3. The Factor Analysis dialog box

Before running the analysis, it is necessary to select some options that regulate the manner in which the analysis takes place and add some useful extra items to the output. This is done by clicking some of the buttons at the bottom of the main **Factor Analysis** dialog box.

- Click **Descriptives...** to open the **Descriptives** dialog box (Figure 4). Click the following check boxes: **Univariate descriptives**, to tabulate descriptive statistics; **Initial solution**, to display the original communalities, eigenvalues and the percentage of variance explained; **Coefficients**, to tabulate the R-matrix; and **Reproduced**, to obtain an approximation of the R-matrix from the loadings of the factors extracted by the analysis. The **Reproduced** option will also obtain communalities and the residual differences between the observed and reproduced correlations.

- Click **Continue** to return to the **Factor Analysis** dialog box.

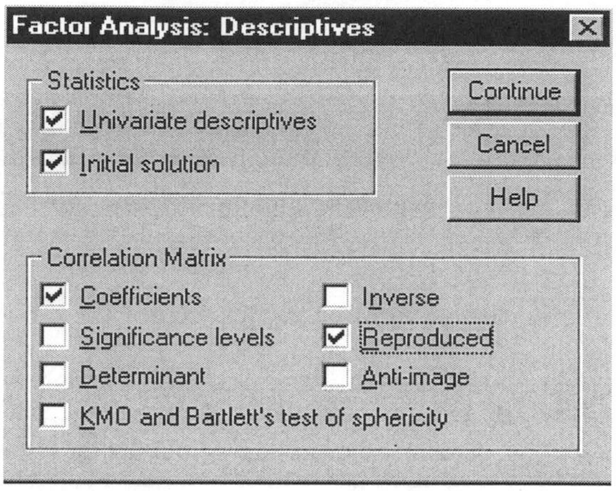

Figure 4. The Descriptives dialog box with Univariate descriptives, Initial solution, Coefficients and Reproduced selected

- Click **Extraction...** to open the **Extraction** dialog box (Figure 5). Click the **Scree plot** check box. The scree plot is a useful display showing the relative importance of the factors extracted.
- Click **Continue** to return to the **Factor Analysis** dialog box.

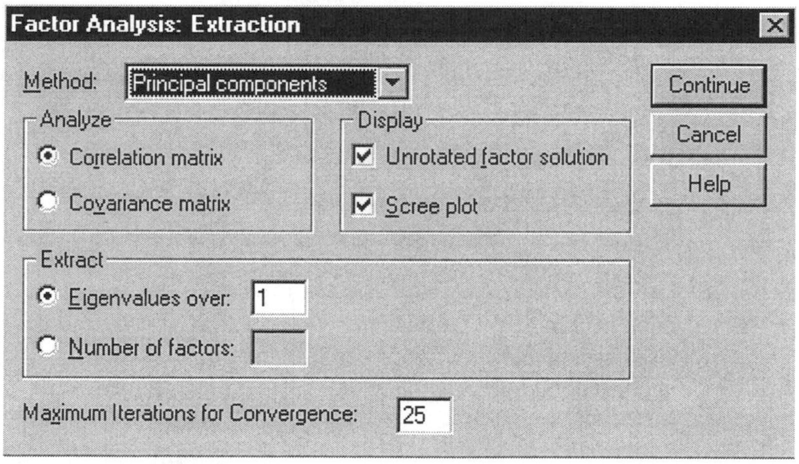

Figure 5. The Factor Analysis: Extraction dialog box with Scree plot selected

- To obtain the rotated F-matrix, click **Rotation...** to obtain the **Rotation** dialog box (Figure 6). In the **Method** box, click the **Varimax** radio button.
- Click **Continue** and then **OK**.

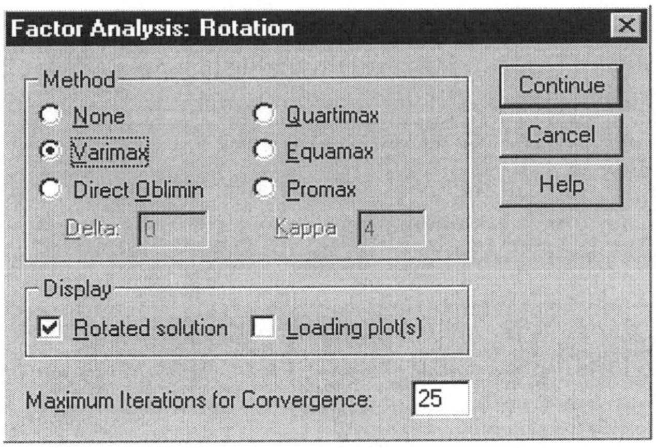

Figure 6. The Factor Analysis: Rotation dialog box with Varimax selected

15.2.3 Output for factor analysis

Descriptive statistics

Output 1 shows the specially requested descriptive statistics for the variables.

Descriptive Statistics

	Mean	Std. Deviation	Analysis N
FRENCH	53.70	18.93	10
GERMAN	53.60	18.12	10
LATIN	58.60	22.26	10
MUSIC	57.10	18.26	10
MATHS	59.70	18.12	10
MAPWORK	58.70	18.42	10

Output 1. Descriptive statistics for the variables

Correlation matrix (R-matrix)

The correlation matrix is shown in Output 2.

Correlation Matrix

	FRENCH	GERMAN	LATIN	MUSIC	MATHS	MAPWORK
FRENCH	1.00	.93	.98	-.35	-.33	-.46
GERMAN	.93	1.00	.93	-.47	-.52	-.61
LATIN	.98	.93	1.00	-.37	-.31	-.45
MUSIC	-.35	-.47	-.37	1.00	.91	.96
MATHS	-.33	-.52	-.31	.91	1.00	.94
MAPWORK	-.46	-.61	-.45	.96	.94	1.00

Output 2. The correlation matrix (R-matrix)

In its basic form, a correlation matrix is *square*, that is, there are as many rows as there are columns. The diagonal of cells running from top left to bottom right is known as the **principal diagonal** of the matrix. Since the variables are labelled in the same order in the rows and columns of **R,** each of the cells along the principal diagonal contains the correlation of one of the variables with itself (i.e. *1*). The correlations in the off-diagonal cells are the same above and below the principal diagonal. (The correlation of FRENCH with GERMAN is the same as that of GERMAN with FRENCH.)

Inspection of the correlation matrix in Output 2 reveals that there are two clusters of high correlations among the tests: one among FRENCH, GERMAN and LATIN, the other among MUSIC, MATHEMATICS and MAPWORK. Another interesting feature is that in either cluster, each test, while correlating highly with the others in the same cluster, does not correlate substantially with the tests in the other cluster. This pattern is what we should expect if the two groups of tests are tapping different abilities.

From inspection of the R-matrix, therefore, it would appear that we can account for the pattern of correlations in terms of two independent dimensions of ability. Presently, we shall see whether such an interpretation is confirmed by the results of a formal factor analysis. Are two factors sufficient to account for the correlations among the tests?

Communalities

Output 3 is a table of communalities assigned to the variables by the factor analysis. The **communality** of a variable (the column labelled **Extraction**) is the squared multiple correlation (R^2) between the variable and the factors emerging from the factor analysis. The communality, therefore, is the proportion of the variance of the test that is accounted for by the factors. For example, we see that 98% of the variance of the scores on FRENCH is accounted for by the factors.

Communalities

	Initial	Extraction
FRENCH	1.00	.98
GERMAN	1.00	.96
LATIN	1.00	.98
MUSIC	1.00	.95
MATHS	1.00	.95
MAPWORK	1.00	.98

Extraction Method: Principal Component Analysis.

Output 3. Table of variable communalities

The next table (Output 4) displays information about the factors (components) that have been extracted. An **eigenvalue** is a measure of the total test variance that is accounted for by a particular factor, the total variance for each test being unity. The first block of three columns, labelled **Initial Eigenvalues**, comprises the eigenvalues and the contributions they make to the total variance. The eigenvalues determine which factors (components) remain in the analysis: following Kaiser's criterion, factors with an eigenvalue of less than 1 (i.e. factors 3-6) are excluded. From the eigenvalues, the proportions of the total test variance accounted for by the factors are readily obtained. For example, the eigenvalue of the first factor is 4.18. Since the total test variance that could possibly be accounted for by a factor is 6, the proportion of the total test variance accounted for by the first factor is 4.18 ÷ 6 = 69.65 %, the figure given in the **% of Variance** column. In this analysis, the two factors that meet the Kaiser criterion account for nearly 97% of the variance (see column labelled **Cumulative %**).

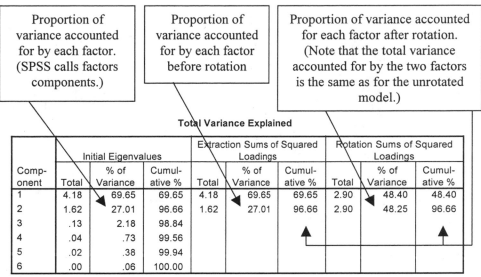

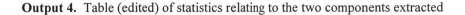

Total Variance Explained

Comp-onent	Initial Eigenvalues			Extraction Sums of Squared Loadings			Rotation Sums of Squared Loadings		
	Total	% of Variance	Cumul-ative %	Total	% of Variance	Cumul-ative %	Total	% of Variance	Cumul-ative %
1	4.18	69.65	69.65	4.18	69.65	69.65	2.90	48.40	48.40
2	1.62	27.01	96.66	1.62	27.01	96.66	2.90	48.25	96.66
3	.13	2.18	98.84						
4	.04	.73	99.56						
5	.02	.38	99.94						
6	.00	.06	100.00						

Extraction Method: Principal Component Analysis.

Output 4. Table (edited) of statistics relating to the two components extracted

The second block of three columns (**Extraction Sums of Squared Loadings**) repeats the output of the first block for the two factors that have met Kaiser's criterion.

The third block (**Rotation Sums of Squared Loadings**) tabulates the output for the rotated factor solution. Notice that the proportions of variance explained by the two factors are similar in the rotated solution, in contrast with the unrotated solution, in which the first factor accounts for a much greater percentage of the variance. Notice also that the accumulated proportion of variance from the two components is the same for the unrotated and unrotated solutions.

The communalities for each test, i.e., the total proportion of the variance of each test accounted for by the factor analysis, are also unchanged by the rotation process.

Scree plot

Figure 7 shows the **scree plot**, which was specially requested in the **Factor Analysis: Extraction** dialog box. The plot provides a graphic image of the eigenvalue for each component extracted. The amount of variance accounted for (the eigenvalue) by successive components plunges sharply as successive factors (components) are extracted.

The point of interest is where the curve connecting the points begins to flatten out, a region which has been fancifully likened to the rubble or scree on a mountain-side. It can be seen that the 'scree' begins to appear between the second and third factors. Notice also that Component 3 has an eigenvalue of less than 1, so only the first two components have been retained.

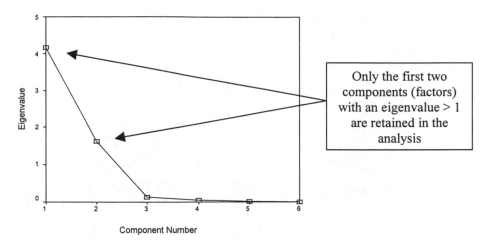

Figure 7. The component scree plot

The component matrix (unrotated factor matrix)

Output 5 shows the component (factor) matrix containing the loadings (partial correlations) of the six tests on the two factors extracted.

Component Matrix a

	Component	
	1	2
FRENCH	.81	.57
GERMAN	.89	.40
LATIN	.81	.57
MUSIC	-.81	.54
MATHS	-.80	.55
MAPWORK	-.88	.45

Extraction Method: Principal Component Analysis.

a. 2 components extracted.

Output 5. The component matrix (correlations between the variables and
the unrotated components)

When the factors (or 'components') are **orthogonal** (i.e. uncorrelated with each other), the factor loadings are the partial correlation coefficients between the variables and the factors. Thus the higher the absolute value of the loading (which can never exceed a maximum of 1), the more the factor accounts for the total variance of scores on the variable concerned.

It can be seen that the factor analysis has extracted two factors, in agreement with the impression given by the correlation matrix. On the other hand, it is not particularly easy to interpret the unrotated factor matrix. Both groups of tests show substantial loadings on both factors, which is not in accord with the obvious psychological interpretation of the original R-matrix.

Reproduced correlation matrix and residuals

Output 6 shows the **reproduced correlation matrix** of coefficients, computed from the extracted factors (components).

| | | If the factor analysis is correct, these correlations should match the original ones in Output 2. | | The loadings labelled b are the communalities listed in Output 3 (i.e. the proportion of the variance of the test that is accounted for by the two factors extracted in the analysis) | | |

Reproduced Correlations

		FRENCH	GERMAN	LATIN	MUSIC	MATHS	MAPWORK
Reproduced Correlation	FRENCH	.98b	.95	.98	-.35	-.33	-.46
	GERMAN	.95	.96b	.95	-.50	-.49	-.61
	LATIN	.98	.95	.98b	-.34	-.33	-.45
	MUSIC	-.35	-.50	-.34	.95b	.95	.96
	MATHS	-.33	-.49	-.33	.95	.95b	.96
	MAPWORK	-.46	-.61	-.45	.96	.96	.98b
Residual a	FRENCH		-.02	.00	-.01	.00	.00
	GERMAN	-.02		-.02	.04	-.02	.00
	LATIN	.00	-.02		-.03	.02	.00
	MUSIC	-.01	.04	-.03		-.04	.00
	MATHS	.00	-.02	.02	-.04		-.02
	MAPWORK	.00	.00	.00	.00	-.02	

Extraction Method: Principal Component Analysis.

a. Residuals are computed between observed and reproduced correlations. There are 0 (.0%) nonredundant residuals with absolute values > 0.05.

b. Reproduced communalities

The residuals show the differences between the reproduced correlations and the original correlations: the smaller the residuals, the better the fit

Output 6. The reproduced correlation matrix and residuals

Each reproduced correlation between two tests is the sum of the products of their loadings on the factors emerging from the analysis. For example, the sum of the products of the loadings of FRENCH and GERMAN on the two factors extracted is, from the loadings in the unrotated F-matrix in Output 6, [(0.81 × 0.89) + (0.57 × (0.40)] = 0.95, which is the value given for the reproduced correlation between FRENCH and GERMAN in Output 6. The diagonal values labelled b are the reproduced communalities listed in Output 3.

The residuals are the differences between the actual and reproduced correlations. For example, the original correlation between FRENCH and GERMAN was 0.93 (Output 2) and the reproduced correlation is 0.95 so the difference is -0.02 which is the residual shown in the lower half of Output 6. Footnote *a* states the number and proportion of residuals (i.e. the differences) that are greater than 0.05. There is none. Thus in the present case, all the residuals are very small, showing that the two-component model accounts for the covariance among the six tests very well indeed. Had the residuals been large, there would have been reason to doubt the two-component interpretation of the correlation matrix.

The values in Output 6 labelled with the superscript *b* are the communalities, previously shown in Output 3. Notice that they are all large - at least 90%.

The rotated factor (component) matrix

Output 7 shows the rotated factor (component) matrix, which should be compared with the unrotated matrix in Output 5.

Rotated Component Matrix [a]

	Component	
	1	2
FRENCH	-.17	.98
GERMAN	-.35	.91
LATIN	-.17	.98
MUSIC	.96	-.19
MATHS	.96	-.17
MAPWORK	.94	-.30

Extraction Method: Principal Component Analysis.
Rotation Method: Varimax with Kaiser Normalization.

[a] Rotation converged in 3 iterations.

Output 7. The rotated component matrix

The purpose of rotation is not to change the number of components extracted, but to try to arrive at a new position for the axes (components) which is easier to interpret in psychological terms. In fact, the rotated component matrix is much easier to interpret than the unrotated matrix in Output 5. The three language tests now have high loadings on one factor alone (Component 2); whereas *Mapwork*, *Mathematics* and *Music* have high loadings on the other (Component 1). These factors are uncorrelated. This is quite consistent with what we gleaned from our inspection of the original R-matrix, namely, that the correlations among the six tests in our battery could be accounted for in terms of two independent psychological dimensions of ability.

15.3   USING SPSS COMMAND LANGUAGE

Throughout this book so far, the statistics provided by SPSS have been accessed by exploiting the advantages of the graphics environment that the Windows operating system provides. Although this is by far the most painless way of familiarising oneself with SPSS, there is an alternative approach which, for some purposes, has considerable advantages.

It is also possible to run SPSS procedures and analyses by writing instructions in SPSS **command language**. This is done in a special **syntax window**, either by typing in commands from the keyboard or by pasting them in. Commands are then given by selecting (emboldening) them and pressing the **Run** button (see below).

For many users, SPSS syntax is daunting, to say the least. It is possible to appeal to **SPSS Help** and obtain what is known as a **syntax map**, but at first sight a syntax map seems even more opaque than the written commands themselves. There are, nevertheless, great advantages in learning how to use

SPSS syntax, because for some analyses there are more options available than those accessible via dialog boxes. Moreover, the syntax for a particular analysis (even one set up initially from dialog boxes) can be saved as a syntax file and re-used later. If an analysis has been set up from dialog boxes, pressing **Paste** in the final dialog box will paste the hitherto hidden syntax into the **syntax window** from which it can be saved to a file in the usual way.

We believe that the most efficient way of learning SPSS syntax is by working from the dialog boxes in this way, rather than ploughing through the available texts on SPSS syntax, which are better left until one has already acquired a working knowledge of the language.

15.3.1 The power of SPSS syntax: An example

With the children's scores in **Data View**, access the **Factor Analysis** dialog box in the usual way. Make the selections as before, remembering to select the buttons at the bottom of the dialog box to specify the rotation, order a scree test, request a correlation matrix and so on. Now click **Paste**. When this is done, a window with the title **!untitled syntax 1** will appear on the screen. This is the **syntax window**, which will contain the commands written in SPSS command language, that have just been specified by your choices from the dialog boxes, (see Figure 8).

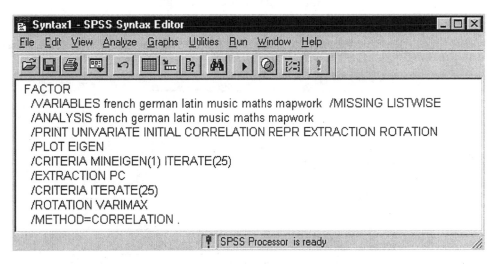

Figure 8. The syntax window and the FACTOR command

Some **commands** (the **data commands**) control the entry of data into SPSS. Others select and direct the statistical analysis. *In SPSS syntax, a command always ends in a full stop.* In the statement in the syntax window, there is only one full stop at the very end. This is because there is only a single command: the FACTOR command. The statement, nevertheless, is not a short one. Notice the terms /PLOT EIGEN, /ROTATION VARIMAX and so on. A phrase that begins with / is a **subcommand**. Subcommands are requests for optional extras. They are the written equivalent of pressing those special buttons at the bottom of the original dialog box.

Now select the whole of the written FACTOR command by emboldening the entire contents of the syntax window. Click the **Run** button ▣ in the toolbar above the syntax window. This has the effect of re-running the entire factor analysis. Inspect the contents of the output window to confirm that the output is the same as before.

Saving the contents of a syntax window

To save this syntax file, select
File
     Save

and select a suitable disk drive and/or folder where the file is to be saved. Type in a file name in the **File name** box with an **.sps** extension to show that it is a syntax file.

Running SPSS from a syntax file

After opening a saved data file or entering new data into **Data View**, it is a very simple matter to run a routine from a saved syntax file.

- Select
  File
     Open
        Syntax...
  to open the **Open File** dialog box (Figure 9).

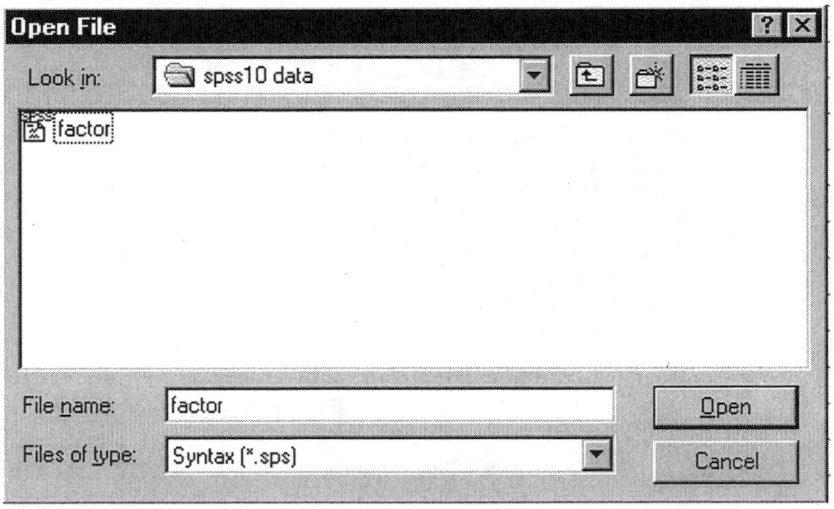

Figure 9. The Open File dialog box with Files of Type: changed to Syntax (*.sps) and file factor selected

- It may be necessary to change the setting of **Look in:** so that the source file appears in the slot.
- Select the appropriate file name (here it is factor).
- Click **Open** to open the syntax file factor in the **SPSS Syntax Editor** window.
- Now, one need only embolden the command in the window and click the **Run** button ▣ in the toolbar above the syntax window to re-run the complete factor analysis.

It is easy to see that with another data set comprising scores on a different battery of tests, it would be easy to edit the FACTOR command by changing the variable names and other specifications to match the new data in **Data View**. Inevitably, the experienced user of SPSS builds up a library of written commands, because it is quicker to carry out the analysis by editing the display in the **SPSS Syntax Editor** than to complete all the dialog and subdialog boxes again.

15.3.2 Using a correlation matrix as input for factor analysis

The graphical interface is a comparatively recent development. Historically, SPSS (like several other major statistical packages) was designed to respond to the user's written commands. The translation, moreover, is as yet incomplete: there are some routines that are available on older mainframe versions of SPSS, but cannot yet be accessed in the graphical interface. Ultimately, to harness the full power of SPSS, one sometimes needs to use the command language (SPSS syntax).

Factor analysis from a correlation matrix

So far we have been considering the statistical analysis of *raw scores*, that is, data sets comprising original measurements or observations, upon which no statistical manipulations have yet been carried out. In the present, factor analytic context, for example, our starting point has been a data set comprising the participants' scores on a set of tests.

Sometimes, however, it may be more convenient to use correlations (rather than raw scores) as the input for a factor analysis. The user may already have an R-matrix and wish to start at that point, rather than going back to the raw data. Unfortunately, since this cannot be done with dialog boxes, the user must turn to SPSS syntax. The procedure has two stages:
  (1)   preparing the correlation matrix in a suitable format;
  (2)   commanding SPSS to read in the matrix and run the factor analysis.

Preparation of the correlation matrix
- Choose
  File
    New
        Syntax (Figure 10)
  to open the **SPSS Syntax Editor** window.

Figure 10. Finding the Syntax Editor

The commands have to be of a specific form, but help with the matrix data command syntax is available by entering *matrix data* in the **Syntax Editor** and clicking [icon] in the toolbar to open a window showing the structure of the syntax. Figure 11 shows the correct syntax of the commands needed for the entry of a correlation matrix into SPSS. Note that it is immaterial whether upper or lower case text is used.

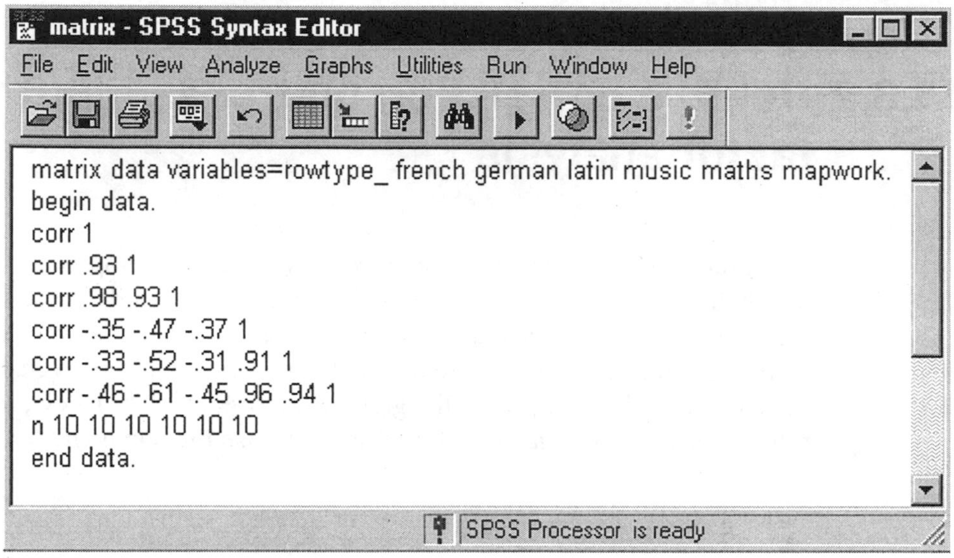

Figure 11. The commands for entering a correlation matrix in Data View

The first command is **matrix data**, whose purpose is to tell SPSS to prepare to receive data in the form of a matrix whose dimensions are specified by the number of variables in the list. Like all commands, it must end in a full stop. Note the term **rowtype_,** which is a special string variable used to identify the type of data for each record (row).

Next comes the data command: first there is **begin data**; then come the data themselves; and finally the command ends with **end data.**. *Note the full stop at the end of the command: this is absolutely essential.*

The first six rows of the data begin with the word **corr**, which tells SPSS that the data are in the form of correlation coefficients. The final (7th) row begins with **n**, which is a count of the number of data points in each column. The terms **corr** and **n** are instances of the generic term **rowtype_** which appeared in the matrix data command.

The default structure of a correlation matrix is a lower triangular matrix. (This is a square matrix with all entries above the principal diagonal omitted.) If an upper triangular or rectangular matrix were to be input, an additional */format* subcommand would be required. The value of *n* is not needed for a basic factor analysis, but it is required for tests of significance and for assessing the sampling adequacy of the data. The correlation matrix and value of *n* are then entered (preceded in each row with *corr* or *n*, as appropriate) between the usual *begin data* and *end data* commands.

- Give the **Matrix Data** command by dragging the cursor over all the syntax in Figure 10 to highlight the entire command, and clicking the **Run** button [icon]

in the toolbar above the syntax window to obtain the correlation matrix in **Data View** (Figure 12). If there are any errors in the syntax, they will be flagged in the **SPSS Viewer**.

rowtype_	varname_	french	german	latin	music	maths	mapwork
N		10.00	10.00	10.00	10.00	10.00	10.00
CORR	FRENCH	1.00	.93	.98	-.35	-.33	-.46
CORR	GERMAN	.93	1.00	.93	-.47	-.52	-.61
CORR	LATIN	.98	.93	1.00	-.37	-.31	-.45
CORR	MUSIC	-.35	-.47	-.37	1.00	.91	.96
CORR	MATHS	-.33	-.52	-.31	.91	1.00	.94
CORR	MAPWORK	-.46	-.61	-.45	.96	.94	1.00

Figure 12. The data set after running the Matrix Data commands

Preparation of the factor command

Return to the syntax window and type the *factor* command below the previous syntax as shown in Figure 13.

Notice that the identification of the source of the matrix in the */matrix =in* subcommand is given as (*corr=**). This shows that it is a correlation matrix (and not, say, a factor matrix), and that it is in the current data file (represented by *), as shown in **Data View** window. The */print* options are those selected in the **Descriptives** dialog box and the */plot* option is that selected in the **Extraction** dialog box. It is not necessary to enter */rotation varimax* because this is the default choice if none is specified. Again note the full stop at the end of the command: it is absolutely essential.

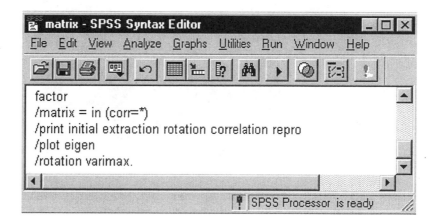

Figure 13. The factor command for running a factor analysis from a correlation matrix in Data View with various options as chosen in Section 15.2.2

- Give the **Factor** command by highlighting the whole command with the cursor and then clicking the ▶ icon in the toolbar at the top of the syntax window. The Output for the factor analysis will be identical with that previously described in Section 15.2.3.

15.3.3 Progressing with SPSS syntax

We recommend that the best way of learning SPSS syntax is by pasting the minimal basic commands into the **syntax window** from the appropriate dialog boxes in the manner described, and observing how these become more elaborate when extra options are chosen from the subdialog boxes.

The more experienced user will find it helpful, when writing a command in SPSS command language, to access the **Syntax Help** window by writing the command in the syntax window and clicking in the toolbar to open a window showing the structure of the syntax, as mentioned in the previous Section. Optional subcommands are shown in square brackets. Relevant parts can either be typed in the syntax window. Alternatively, the whole block of syntax can be copied over for editing from the **Syntax Help** window to the **Syntax** window by using **Copy** and **Paste** in the usual way. (These are in the **Options** menu of the **Syntax Help** window.) We do not recommend that you follow this procedure until you have already acquired some experience with SPSS syntax in the way we have described.

EXERCISE 24

FACTOR ANALYSIS

Before you start

Before proceeding with this practical, please read Chapter 15.

A personality study

Ten participants are given a battery of personality tests, comprising the following items: Anxiety; Agoraphobia; Arachnophobia; Extraversion; Adventure; Sociability. The purpose of this project is to ascertain whether the correlations among the six variables can be accounted for in terms of comparatively few latent variables, or factors (see Chapter 15).

Preparing the data set

The data are shown in Table 1. Name the variables in **Variable View** and assign longer names in the **Label** column. Ensure that the values in the **Decimals** column are 0. Click the **Data View** tab to open **Data View** and enter the data.

Table 1. The questionnaire data						
Participant	**Anxiety**	**Agora**	**Arachno**	**Advent**	**Extrav**	**Sociab**
1	71	68	80	44	54	52
2	39	30	41	77	90	80
3	46	55	45	50	46	48
4	33	33	39	57	64	62
5	74	75	90	45	55	48
6	39	47	48	91	87	91
7	66	70	69	54	44	48
8	33	40	36	31	37	36
9	85	75	93	45	50	42
10	45	35	44	70	66	78

Procedure for the factor analysis of the raw data

Follow the procedure described in Section 15.2.2, requesting the **Univariate descriptives**, **Initial solution**, **Coefficients**, **Reproduced**, **Scree plot**, and **Varimax** options.

Interpretation of the results

After a table of descriptive statistics, there is a table labelled Correlation Matrix. Is there any evident pattern that would suggest that the R-matrix might be accounted for in terms of relatively few factors (components)? Examine the remainder of the Output in the manner outlined in Section 15.2.3, considering the scree plot, the table labelled Component (factor) Matrix listing the unrotated loadings for each factor, the residuals and the final rotated matrix in the table labelled Rotated Component Matrix.

- **How might the patterns among the correlations in the R-matrix be explained psychologically? Look at the table Rotated Component Matrix and make a list of the loadings that are greater than about 0.5 on each factor (component).**

Procedure for the factor analysis of the correlation matrix

Sometimes (e.g., after a large psychometric study) it is convenient to run a factor analysis from a table of correlation coefficients rather than from raw scores. Following the procedure described in Section 15.3.2, type the appropriate commands and the lower triangular version of the R-matrix (the correlation matrix in the SPSS Viewer) into the syntax window. Include the following items.

- The *matrix data variables* command with the appropriate variable names (including *rowtype_*)
- A *begin data* command
- Rows of correlation coefficients (each preceded by *corr*)
- A row indicating the size of n (preceded by *n* and then the size of n repeated for as many variables as you have)
- An *end data* command concluding with a period (.)

When the data syntax is complete, run the factor analysis by dragging the cursor over all the syntax and clicking ▣. **Data View** should now appear similar to that shown in Chapter 15, Figure 12.

If all is well, proceed to prepare the *factor* command by studying the model shown in Chapter 15, Figure 13. Run the factor analysis by selecting the command and clicking the **Run** button, as described above. Confirm that the results of the analysis are the same as those obtained when you began with the raw scores.

REVISION EXERCISES

The revision exercises are designed to challenge the reader as to what is the most appropriate exploratory data analysis (EDA) and/or statistical test to employ given the experimental situation presented and, where appropriate, the experimental hypothesis specified. For this reason, no help is given.

It is strongly recommended that an EDA is conducted initially in case any extreme values need to be deselected or the distribution of values makes certain statistical tests unsuitable. If necessary, deselect extreme values before conducting the appropriate statistical test.

The bullet points after each exercise are provided in case your tutor wants to know what you have done.

REVISION EXERCISE 1

In order to test the hypothesis that, when presented with lists of words, younger children process more information than do older children, a psychologist asked groups of older and younger children to inspect and commit to memory the same list of words and then recall the words in the list. The results were as follows:

Number of words recalled by younger and older children							
Case	Younger	Case	Younger	Case	Older	Case	Older
1	16	6	16	11	12	16	4
2	223	7	21	12	20	17	16
3	20	8	20	13	10	18	9
4	23	9	18	14	13	19	11
5	17	10	20	15	15	20	9

- **Do the data confirm the hypothesis?**
- **Describe how you reached your conclusion.**
- **Name the statistical test and express the result in the usual manner.**

REVISION EXERCISE 2

To test the hypothesis that, in families with two female children, the second-born child is more sociable than the first-born, a researcher selected twenty two-child families. In order to ensure, in each family, the comparability of the social backgrounds of the children, only families with children of Primary School age were selected. The children were tested for sociability, each child receiving a score in the range from 0 (very unsociable) to 10 (very sociable). The scores the children obtained are shown in the table below.

Sociability scores of the first- and second-born children from twenty families					
Family	First-born	Second-born	Family	First-born	Second-born
1	4	7	11	1	5
2	1	5	12	5	8
3	8	6	13	8	9
4	2	4	14	9	9
5	0	2	15	1	4
6	8	8	16	5	7
7	9	8	17	3	4
8	2	7	18	3	6
9	4	6	19	4	5
10	6	8	20	6	7

- **Do the data confirm the hypothesis?**
- **Describe how you reached your conclusion.**
- **Name the statistical test and express the result in the usual manner.**

REVISION EXERCISE 3

A clinician has carried out a study on the efficacy of a type of cognitive therapy, in which the aim is to reduce the number of negative, self-destructive thoughts, as recorded by the patient in a special diary. The Table shows the numbers of negative thoughts recorded by 9 patients over five days, the first two days before therapy and the remaining three days after therapy. The therapy did not begin until the third day, because the therapist wanted to establish a baseline rate with which subsequent frequencies during therapy could be compared.

Numbers of negative thoughts recorded during a course in cognitive therapy					
Patient	First day	Second day	Third day	Fourth day	Fifth day
1	22	22	9	7	6
2	20	20	10	4	4
3	18	15	6	4	5
4	25	30	13	12	16
5	31	26	13	8	6
6	19	27	8	7	4
7	25	16	5	2	5
8	17	18	8	1	5
9	25	24	14	8	10

- **Was the cognitive therapy effective?**
- **Describe how you reached your conclusion.**
- **Name the statistical test and express the result in the usual manner.**

REVISION EXERCISE 4

For some years there was, in social psychology in the US, much emphasis upon the advantages of a 'democratic', as opposed to an 'authoritarian' leadership style in enhancing group performance. It was suspected by some, however, that the efficacy of leadership style might depend upon the nature of the task. Perhaps, for some tasks, an authoritarian (i.e. instructional) style might actually be more effective than a democratic one (i.e. one encouraging questions and discussion)? This is the hypothesis under test.

In a project designed to test the efficacy of leadership style on group performance, groups of soldiers were trained under democratic or authoritarian leadership styles. Later, groups who had been trained under each regime were tested on one of two tasks:

(1) a Structured Task, namely, the assembly of a field gun;
(2) a Group Problem, in which, given equipment such as barrels and ropes, the group was required to construct a bridge across a fast-flowing river.

On the basis of their performance, each group was awarded a mark on the scale from 1 (low efficacy) to 20 (high efficacy). The results are shown in the Table:

Scores achieved on a criterion group task by twenty groups of soldiers trained under democratic or authoritarian leadership styles		
CriterionTask	**Leadership Style**	
	Authoritarian	**Democratic**
Structured Task (Gun Assembly)	13	5
	13	5
	17	8
	15	11
	18	10
Group Problem (Bridge Construction)	9	19
	2	15
	5	18
	12	13
	7	14

- **Is the hypothesis supported?**
- **Describe how you reached your conclusion.**
- **Name the statistical test and express the result in the usual manner.**

REVISION EXERCISE 5

There is a widespread belief (supported by actuarial evidence) that, in tests of decision-making in driving, those between the ages of fifty-five and sixty-five should outperform those in their twenties, despite the inevitable slowing of reaction speed that occurs as a person gets older. To investigate this claim, ten volunteers, five in their twenties and five in their late fifties and early sixties, were recruited to take part in a driving-simulation study.

Driving was assessed under simulated conditions of light and heavy road traffic in both daytime and in night-time illumination. Each driver received a score between 1 (poor) and 100 (excellent) for their performance in each of the four conditions.

The results are shown below:

Performance of drivers in two age groups, driving under simulated conditions of light and heavy traffic, and of daytime and night-time illumination				
	Light Traffic		**Heavy Traffic**	
Group	**Day**	**Night**	**Day**	**Night**
Older	74	55	75	15
	72	70	70	10
	70	60	60	10
	68	50	50	10
	66	65	45	5
Younger	40	15	30	30
	25	20	20	20
	30	30	10	10
	25	40	15	15
	10	45	25	25

- **Is the hypothesis supported?**
- **Describe how you reached your conclusion.**
- **Name the statistical test and express the result in the usual manner.**

REVISION EXERCISE 6

A researcher investigated people's ratings of their state of happiness and whether they considered life to be exciting or dull in relation to whether they were white or non-white and whether they were male or female. Is there any evidence of differences among the races and sexes for their ratings of happiness and lifestyle?   Is there a relationship between happiness and lifestyle?

The data were as follows:

Number of white and non-white males and females rating themselves for happiness and lifestyle							
Race	Sex	Very Happy		Fairly Happy		Not very Happy	
		Exciting	Dull	Exciting	Dull	Exciting	Dull
White	Male	84	33	92	129	5	20
White	Female	88	52	96	162	6	44
Non-White	Male	8	4	10	14	7	2
Non-White	Female	10	8	14	36	2	15
	TOTAL	190	97	212	341	20	81

- Describe how you reached your conclusions about the researcher's questions.
- Name the statistical tests and express the results in the usual manner.

REFERENCES

Anscombe, F. J. (1973). Graphs in statistical analysis. *American Statistician, 27,* 17-21.

Bentler, P. M. (1993). *EQS structural equations program manual.* Los Angeles, CA: BMDP Statistical Sofware.

Cohen, J., & Cohen, P. (1983). *Applied multiple regression/correlation analysis for the behavioral sciences.* (2nd ed.). Hillsdale, N. J.: Lawrence Erlbaum.

Darlington, R. B. (1968). Multiple regression in psychological research and practice. *Psychological Bulletin, 69,* 161-182.

Delucchi, K. L. (1983). The use and misuse of chi-square: Lewis and Burke revisited. *Psychological Bulletin, 94,* 166-176.

Everitt, B. S. (1977). *The analysis of contingency tables.* London: Chapman and Hall.

Gravetter, F. J., & Wallnau, L. B. (2000). *Statistics for the behavioral sciences: A first course for students of psychology and education.* (5th ed.). St. Paul: West.

Howell, D. C. (1997). *Statistical methods for psychology.* (4th ed.). Belmont, CA: Duxbury.

Jöreskog, K. G., & Sörbom, D. (1989). *LISREL 7: A guide to the program and applications.* Chicago: SPSS Inc.

Keppel, G. (1973). *Design and analysis: A researcher's handbook.* Englewood Cliffs, NJ: Prentice-Hall, Inc.

Kim, J., & Mueller, C. W. (1978a). *Introduction to factor analysis: What it is and how to do it.* Sage University paper series on quantitative applications in the social sciences, 07-013. Newbury Park, CA: Sage.

Kim, J., & Mueller, C. W. (1978b). *Factor analysis: Statistical methods and practical issues.* Sage University paper series on quantitative applications in the social sciences, 07-014. Newbury Park, CA: Sage.

Kirk, R. E. (1982). *Experimental design: Procedures for the behavioral sciences.* (2nd ed.). Belmont: Brooks/Cole.

Maxwell, A. E. W. (1977). *Multivariate analysis in behavioural research.* London: Chapman & Hall.

Neave, H. R. & Worthington, P. L. (1988). *Distribution-free tests.* London: Unwin Hyman.

Reynolds, H. T. (1984). *The analysis of nominal data.* (2nd ed.). Sage University paper series on quantitative applications in the social sciences, 07-007. Newbury Park, CA: Sage.

Siegel, S., & Castellan, N. J. (1988). *Nonparametric statistics for the behavioral sciences.* (2nd ed.). New York: McGraw-Hill.

Tabachnick, B. G., & Fidell, L. S. (1996). *Using multivariate statistics.* (3rd ed.). New York: Harper and Row.

Upton, G. J. G. (1978). *The analysis of cross-tabulated data.* Chichester: John Wiley.

Upton, G. J. G. (1986). Cross-classified data. In A. D. Lovie (Ed.), *New developments in statistics for psychology and the social sciences.* London and New York: The British Psychological Society and Methuen.

Winer, B. J., Brown, D. R., & Michels, K. M. (1991). *Statistical principles in experimental design.* (3rd ed.). New York: McGraw-Hill.

INDEX